The Pakistan Anti-Hero

HISTORY OF PAKISTANI NATIONALISM THROUGH THE LIVES OF ICONOCLASTS

The Pakistan Anti-Hero

HISTORY OF PAKISTANI NATIONALISM THROUGH THE LIVES OF ICONOCLASTS

By
Nadeem Farooq Paracha

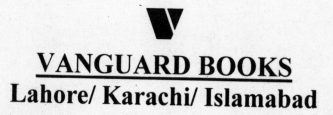

VANGUARD BOOKS
Lahore/ Karachi/ Islamabad

ISBN: 978-969-402-605-3

Plot # 52-53, Gulberg-II,
Main Guru Mangat Road, Lahore.
Ph: # 92+42+35754275-76
email: sales@vanguardbooks.com
www.vanguardbooks.com

Printed at:
Maktaba Jadeed Press
14-Empress Road, Lahore
Phone No. 92-42-36307639-40

Dedicated to
Khalida, Roohi and Amber
Mother, Sister and Soulmate

CONTENTS

CHAPTER 1

RE-IMAGINING HEROES AND VILLAINS: THE PROTO-NATIONALIST IMPULSE IN CONTEMPORARY PAKISTANI NATIONALISM

In South Asia, when the Muslim imperial power began to erode from the 19th century onward, various Muslim thinkers and activists responded by rejecting the decaying memories of a glorious imperial past. They adopted certain notions of nationalism to find their peoples' place in the rapidly changing paradigms of international order. Rejecting the past, one major branch of Muslim nationalism in India advocated the embracement of 'modern education' and the sciences so that an 'enlightened' Muslim nation could emerge in India to face the challenges of British colonialism and 'Hindu majoritarianism.'

This nationalism was intellectually driven by an emerging Muslim bourgeoisie, and largely bankrolled by the Muslim landed elite. It saw the Muslims of India as a separate cultural entity, united by memories of a once glorious past, and by an urge to revitalize its shared faith through a more rational, modern, and flexible reading. A major dimension of Indian Muslim nationalism also largely bypassed pan-Islamism because it believed that Muslim culture in the region had bearings which were separate from how Islam had evolved elsewhere. Pakistan nationalism, which was an off-shoot of Muslim nationalism in the region, was, in essence, integrally pluralistic but politically exclusivist. And, even though, due to the dynamics of the Cold War and Pakistan's relations with India, the country was unable to construct a steady democratic system; the government and state institutions continued to toe and popularize Pakistani nationalism as a modernistic expression of social and political Islam.

However, from the mid-1970s, certain drastic internal as well as external events, especially a calamitous war with India in 1971, severely polarized the Pakistani society. With the absence of an established form of democracy, a rather assertive aspect of this polarization began to be expressed through certain radical pan-Islamist alternatives. The pan-Islamic alternative in Pakistan managed to elicit a popular response from a new generation of urban bourgeoisie and petty-bourgeoisie. Its proliferation was also bankrolled by oil-rich Arab monarchies which had always considered modern Muslim nationalism as a peril – especially in the context of how it had evolved in the Middle East, generating secular concepts such as Arab nationalism and Ba'ath Socialism.

As a response to the growing popularity of this alternative, the Pakistani state changed tact and tried to realign the wavering ideological status quo by rapidly co-opting various aspects of pan-Islamism; even to the extent of sacrificing many of the state's original notions of Pakistani nationalism. The gradual erosion of the original nationalist narrative created wide open spaces. These spaces were largely occupied and then dominated by ideas which had been initially sidelined by the Pakistani state and nationalist intelligentsia. The alternative narrative was opposed to the original nationalist narrative, criticizing it for going against the grain of Islamic universalism and for creating a separatist mindset based on indigenous cultures and languages in Muslim-majority regions. The alternative nationalist ideas were mostly based on a contemporary understanding of pan-Islamism.

But some three decades after these ideas managed to engrain themselves in the state and polity of Pakistan, the country was left facing a rather drastic existentialist crisis. For example, the generation of young Pakistanis today is now completely disconnected from the original notions of their country's nationalism because in the past few decades, Pakistani students in educational institutions were more exposed to ideas of a hybrid pan-Islamic version of Pakistani nationalism.

In Pakistan, a young millennial is not quite sure what being a Pakistani now means. Does it mean being a citizen of a Muslim-majority nation in South Asia which evolved on the banks of River Indus and is part of the region's 5000-year-old history; or does it mean being a native of some approaching global Islamic set-up or someone who should just see Pakistan as a temporary abode to mark time in till that universal set-up emerges? Is he or she first a Pakistani and then a Muslim, or vice versa? And exactly what is the status of the non-Muslim citizens of Pakistan?

This confusion was prompted by the gradual erosion of the initial idea of Pakistani nationalism, and the rise of a rather ambitious notion of politico-religious universalism in a world which is still defined by geo-nationalistic boundaries. This has also made a whole generation vulnerable to the ways of those who are now promising the same widespread utopia, but through unprecedented violence against the state, and a number of imagined 'enemies'.

Pakistan today is facing a serious predicament. Even though the Pakistani state and society now seems to have finally understood that much of the sectarian, ethnic and religious violence of the past decades (especially ever since the 1980s), has been cultivated by a rather convoluted nationalist ideology and narrative which the state has been peddling ever since the 1970s, there is still confusion about exactly what should such an ingrained narrative be replaced with.

I believe the solution is present in the increasingly elapsed elements of early Pakistani nationalism. A reinvigorated version of the original notions of nationalism in Pakistan just might help future generations of young Pakistanis feel more comfortable and confident of being entities defined by their shared cultural heritage of a region that was encapsulated and bordered by coherent nationalist notions of state and society — and not as some epic launching pad to jump-start a theological utopia from.

****

The gates of divergence

Ever since the early 1970s, one of the oldest religious parties in Pakistan, the Jamaat-i-Islami (JI), has been organizing 'Yaum-i-Babul Islam' — an event in which the party celebrates the conquest of Sindh by Arab commander Mohammad Bin Qasim (in the 8th century CE). JI explains the event as the 'advent of Islam in South Asia'.[1] Speakers at this event often describe Qasim as the 'first Pakistani'[2] and then trace and place the creation of Pakistan to the arrival of the Arab commander 1300 years ago. Curiously, the JI was originally opposed to the man who actually did create Pakistan (in 1947): Mohammad Ali Jinnah.

---

[1] Asif Haroon: *Muhammad Bin Qasim To Gen. Parvez Musharraf* (Sang-e-Meel Publications, 2004) p.377
[2] Newsline, Vol: 16, 2004. p.63

JI's founder, Abul Ala Maududi, had regarded Jinnah as a man steeped in the 'Western notion of nationalism' and too westernized to deliver and head an exclusive Muslim state.[3] So one can suppose that the whole idea of an ancient Arab commander being posthumously raised to become the main architect of what hundreds of years later would become Pakistan, was more in tune with JI's concept of Pakistani nationhood.

But it wasn't really the JI which had first initiated the idea of dressing up an 8th century Arab as the founder of Pakistan. This impression, which, from the late 1970s onward, has found ample space in the country's school text books, was first alluded to in a 1953 book, *Five Years of Pakistan*. In a recent essay on the subject[4], Manan Ahmed Asif , a professor of history at Columbia University), informs that the whole notion of Qasim's invasion of Sindh being the genesis of a separate Muslim state in South Asia was initially imagined by a handful of Pakistani archaeologists writing in 1953's Five Years of Pakistan. The book was published by the government to commemorate the fifth anniversary of the country. A chapter authored by archaeologists associated with a state-funded archaeology project in Pakistan's Sindh province, described Sindh 'as the first Islamic province in South Asia'.

This proclamation then found its way into the nationalist narrative of various religious parties such as the JI, before being weaved into school text books by the populist Z.A. Bhutto regime after the country faced a severe existential crunch after its eastern wing (former East Pakistan) broke away in December 1971 to become Bangladesh. The notion was then aggressively promoted by the intransigent Ziaul Haq dictatorship in the 1980s

---

[3] R. Kalia: Pakistan: *From the Rhetoric of Democracy to the Rise of Militancy* (Routledge, 2012) p.39
[4] *The Advent of Islam in South Asia* (Oxford University Press, 2015)

to explain Pakistan as a nation that had deeper ideological, and, in some cases, even genealogical roots in the ancient deserts of Arabia and Central Asia than in the expanses of South Asia.

However, the fact is that as far as the region's history is concerned, or even that of the Arabs, Qasim's foray into Sindh was not quite the significant event it is made out to be in Pakistan. Professor Manan speaks of a silence that usually greets historians when they go looking for ancient sources about the event. There are almost none. This gives rise to the question, if Qasim's invasion of Sindh was such a grand undertaking, why is it only scarcely mentioned in the available literary sources from that period?

The earliest available source to mention the invasion is the 9th century book, *Kitab Futuh al-Buldan*, by Arab historian al-Baladhuri. It was written more than a hundred years after Qasim's invasion. Then there is also the Persian text called *Chachnama* which mentions the invasion but this tome was authored almost 400 years after Qasim's forces arrived on the shores of Sindh.[5]

When historians such as Manan piece together whatever little early sources there are about the event, it transpires that the Arabs had first begun to exhibit interest in Sindh in 634 AD. The Umayyad - the first major Arab Muslim Empire, based out of Syria - sent troops to conquer Sindh on numerous occasions between 644 CE and 710 CE. Most of these raids were repulsed by local tribes, even though at times Arab armies did manage to hold parts of Makran (in the present-day Pakistani province of Balochistan).

The reasons for the Umayyad to enter the region were many. The Umayyad were a rapidly expanding empire and wanted to

---

[5] Ibid.

get a toehold in South Asia. It wanted to gain control of the region's lucrative port trade. It also sent troops to crush renegades and rebels who used to escape to Makran from the Umayyad mainland, sometimes to hide and sometimes to organize attacks against the empire from here. Such rebels mainly comprised the radical Muslim Kharajites who had established a small and elusive clandestine traction in Balochistan.[6]

The popular account found in most post-9th-century Muslim history records about Qasim's invasion sees him being sent here by an Umayyad governor in Baghdad to avenge the plundering of Arab ships by Sindh's pirates, and the refusal of Sindh's Hindu ruler, Raja Dahir, to do anything about it. Historians such as Prof. Manan who have tried to search for more sound sources that can substantiate this account have found only sketchy evidence. Manan concludes: 'Qasim's expedition was merely the latest in a 60-year-long campaign by the Arabs to gain a foothold over the port trades and to extract riches from these port communities (in Sindh and Makran) ...'

Qasim's supposedly genesis-like maneuvers in Sindh in which he supposedly managed to convert a large number of Sindh's inhabitants to Islam, are also largely a myth. In 731 CE when al-Hakim al-Kalbi was appointed governor of Sindh (some 20 years after Qasim's demise), he found a land where even those who had converted to Islam during Qasim's stay there, had reverted back to becoming either Hindu or Buddhist[7]. So much for Qasim's Sindh heralding the genesis of Pakistan.

The question now is, if Qasim's invasion was comparatively a minor historical event, how did it become so inflated in

---

[6] S Badal Khan: *Baloch History and Folklore* (University of Napoli, 2013) p.37
[7] Ibid.

Pakistan? Truth is, it remained largely overlooked for hundreds of years, even during much of the Muslim rule in India between the 13th and 19th centuries. Interest in Qasim was ironically reignited by British colonialists in the 19th century. In 1817, British author, James Mill, in his book, The History of British India, mentioned Qasim as an invader who created a rupture in the region.

Hill offers only wooly evidence; but his lead was followed by other British authors of the era who all saw Qasim as the man who opened the gates for hoards of Muslim invaders to pour in and destroy the Indian civilization. This narrative of a bloodletting Qasim was then picked up by early Hindu nationalists, some of whom had otherwise largely forgotten about this 8th century Arab.

19th century Muslim historians, Syed Suleman Nadvi, and Mohammad Hanif, responded by offering a more deliberate look at Qasim's invasion, describing it as nothing like the one that was being peddled by the British authors and early Hindu nationalists. They portrayed Qasim as a just, tolerant and gallant man. Both these versions of the man emerged from the highly polemical debates on Qasim's invasion between the British, Hindu and Muslim historians.

Fact is, to non-aligned history, Qasim remains to be an enigmatic figure about which ancient sources say very little. But ever since the 19th century, he has become a glorified myth to some, and an equally mythical force of destruction to others. Yet, the elusive memory of this man complemented by a largely imagined history of his conquest, has produced a character who became much more than just a debate between navel-gazing historians. His 20th century construction as the 'first Pakistani' can actually be seen as an event which sits at the point from where the trajectory of Pakistan nationalism begins to diverge and heads towards a place where, probably, it was never supposed to go?

The construction of Muhammad Bin Qasim as the 'first Pakistani' is an important point of entry for a nationalist narrative which departs from the one which was devised by the early founders of Muslim nationalism in South Asia, and, subsequently, of nationalism in Pakistan. Advocates of the divergent narrative insist that the context of Pakistan's nationalism must be understood from a point in history which begins with the 8th century invasion of Sindh by Muhammad Bin Qasim. Consequently, one should thus expect the advocates of the divergent narrative to also declare Muslim invaders who entered India from Central Asia (from the 13th century onward) and then ruled here for five hindered years, as proto-Pakistanis as well?

Indeed, but such is not the case. For example, in this context, two of the most prominent Muslim rulers who reigned India are treated quite differently from each other. Mughal king, Akbar, who was king of a vast Indian empire from 1556 till 1605 CE, is largely treated with disdain by the divergent narrative. Yet, the same narrative sees another great Mughal king, Aurangzeb (1658-1707 CE), as an exemplary proto-type Pakistani sovereign.

Akbar is scorned at for bringing Islam into disrepute by adopting an overtly pluralistic disposition and overriding the concerns of the *ulema*. Some of his detractors also go as far as accusing him of being a heretic who wanted to create his own religion. However, Aurangzeb, the last major Mughal monarch of India, is praised for dismantling the 'deviances' introduced by his great-grandfather, Akbar. Aurangzeb's long rule is seen as the first genuine example of a regime in South Asia based on *sharia* laws, and, thus, an example of how Pakistan should be ruled as well. But was Akbar really a heretic; or Aurangzeb, a radiant symbol of piety?

One of Pakistan's most accomplished historians and authors, Dr. Mubarak Ali, answered the question in this manner:

Akbar as emperor, realized that to rule the country exclusively with the help of Muslims of foreign origin posed a problem as there would not be enough administrators for the entire state. He realized that the administration had to be indianised. Therefore, he broadened the Muslim aristocracy by including Rajputs in the administration. He eliminated all signs and symbols which differentiated Muslims and Hindus, and made attempts to integrate them as one.[8]

On Aurangzeb he wrote:

Even Aurangzeb, in spite of his dislike of Hindus, had to keep them in his administration. He tried to create a semblance of homogeneity in the Muslim community by introducing religious reforms. But all his attempts to create a consciousness of Muslim identity came to nothing.[9]

Mubarak Ali believes that Muslim monarchs in India who were ruling over a region which had a Hindu majority were always more pragmatic than pious. But, again, if to the supporters of the divergent narrative, Qasim was the first Pakistani, then how were other Muslim rulers in the region not? Suggesting that those who served Islam, were, and those who didn't, weren't, is highly problematic, even embarrassing. One of the earliest advocates of the divergent narrative was the prolific historian, IH Qureshi (1903-1981). When faced with the above query, he went to great lengths to explain why (in the context of Pakistan) Akbar could never be praised in the same breath as Aurangzeb.

---

[8] Mubarak Ali: *Pakistan in Search of Identity* (Aakar Books, 2011) pp. 15-16
[9] Ibid.

In a 1962 book of his,[10] Qureshi wrote that Akbar's inclusive policies were detrimental to the process of early Muslim nationalism which was being organically constructed in India ever since the rise of Muslim rule here in the 13th century CE. Qureshi suggested that despite the fact Aurungzeb somewhat corrected the course of the evolution of early Muslim nationalism, it was too late, and the empire collapsed after the arrival of the British and due to the gradual strengthening of the Hindus - a process which Qureshi believes began during Akbar's reign.

No concrete evidence has ever surfaced which can substantiate that, indeed, an idea of Muslim nationalism was evolving in India between the 13th and 18th centuries. On the contrary, Muslim invaders explained themselves according to their ethnic and regional lineages and languages and also recruited men from among their own ethnic and cultural communities. One group of invaders was distrustful of the other on the basis of differing ethnic and regional backgrounds and origins; and dynasties were established when one set of Muslim conquers overwhelmed and overthrew another group of imperial Muslims.[11]

Also, there is ample evidence to suggest that 'local Muslims', or India's Hindus who had converted to Islam, were largely kept away from important posts in the government. In fact, even during Akbar's reign, Persian-speaking Muslim migrants and high-bred Hindu Rajputs were preferred over local Muslim converts.[12] 14th century Muslim thinker, Ziauddin Brani, wrote that Muslim rulers in India should continue to hire 'Muslims of racially pure families' in

---

[10] *The Muslim Community of Indo-Pakistan Sub-Continent*
[11] Mubarak Ali: *Pakistan in Search of Identity* (Aakar Books, 2011) p. 15
[12] WC Smith: *Modern Islam in India* (1943)

the government and discourage extending educational opportunities to local Muslim converts because education would make them arrogant.[13]

Claiming that some prototype version of Muslim nationalism was developing during the height of Muslim rule in India is quite clearly a concoction. IH Qureshi tried to give this claim some scholarly weight[14] but his argument was devoid of any concrete clues, and was, thus, nothing more than a historical aberration. Such claims continue to come up in debates, but their frequency has appreciably lessened. So much so, that in 1999, a member of the JI tackled the problem of such claims by (partially) cleaning the slate clean. He wrote that after Qasim, no other Muslim conquer who invaded and stayed in India was interested in waging 'holy war', and almost all of them were simply attracted by the prospects of plundering and looting.[15]

This was not coming from so-called 'liberal' and 'secular' historians of India and Pakistan. It was being stated by a member of a political party which had championed the divergent narrative. His swipe was partial because the myth of Qasim being the 'first Pakistani' was left untouched, despite the fact that there is precious little evidence to back the claim of him arriving in Sindh for entirely holy purposes, as opposed to probably invading the region for political and economic motives. It is also a fact that the religious demography of Sindh remained largely intact after Qasim's brief command here.

There was little or no concept of a united Muslim nationhood in India before the 19th century. Muslims were a diverse lot, divided by race, class, languages and ethnicity. And,

---

[13] *Tariqa-e-Firuz Shahi*
[14] IH Qureshi: *Miuslm History of The Ind0-Pakistan Sun-Continent* (1962)
[15] *And the fall became a destiny*: Zahid Ali Wasti. Awaz (October, 1999).

in fact, these divisions were actively encouraged by the Muslim rulers for various racial and political reasons. Islam only appeared as a battle cry during the Muslim invasions; but after the invaders had settled down to rule this region, they did so through sheer pragmatism. In fact, they even subdued the *ulema* who desired the imposition of the *sharia* because such an imposition would have politically empowered the *ulema* at the expense of the powers enjoyed by the monarchs.[16]

Even during Aurangzeb's rule, it was the monarch himself who made it his prerogative to interpret and impose Islamic laws.[17] And his regime was also depended on hundreds of Hindus which remained employed by his vast administration. Aurangzeb's active proclivity towards Islam was more of a reaction. In his bid to come to power and replace his ailing father, Shah Jehan, Aurangzeb's chief opponent in this regard was his elder brother, Dara Shikho. Dara was deeply impressed by the policies and spiritual disposition of his great-grandfather, Akbar. More of a scholar than a warrior, Dara studied Muslim and Hindu scriptures and was also an ardent follower of Sufi Islam which had been the prominent religious conviction of the Mughal court. Sufism was also the main folk-religion of the common Muslims of India. Dara had managed to gather support and popularity from the common Muslims and Hindus in and around the seat of power in Delhi. So when he was defeated by Aurangzeb, and then captured, he was immediately executed. A group of clerics and *ulema* who had risen in prominence by siding with Aurangzeb, declared Dara to be an apostate.[18]

---

[16] Mubarak Ali: *Pakistan in Search of Identity* (Aakar Books, 2011) p. 13

[17] *Fatwa-e-Alamgiri* – a book of Islamic laws complied by Aurangzeb and authored by *ulema* approved by the monarch.

[18] Waldemar Hansen: *The Peacock Throne* (Orient Books, 1986) p.375

An interesting later-day aspect of the whole conflict between Aurangzeb and Dara has been the manner in which it has become part of the on-going debate on what constitutes Pakistani nationalism. For example, till this day, Dara is championed by those who see Pakistani nationalism as something whose original intent was pluralistic and very much rooted in the history of the sub-continent. A 2014 play authored by a leading Pakistani playwright, Shahid Nadeem, tried to figure out what the fate of Muslim rule in India would have been had Dara managed to defeat Aurangzeb and become king.

Nadeem believes that the theological conflict between the two brothers bore the hallmarks of the same sectarian and sub-sectarian conflicts found in Pakistan today, such as those between the followers of Sufism and the 'Salafis'; and between the inclusive pluralists and the conservative exclusivists.[19] Aurangzeb, on the other end, is hailed as a hero by those who claim that Pakistani nationalism is a by-product of the Muslim nationalism which began to develop in South Asia after the 8th century invasion of Muhammad Bin Qasim, and then rapidly evolved during the 500-year-rule of the Muslims here.

They believe that this nationalism's roots are more prominent in the cultures of the Muslims who galloped in from Arabia and Central Asia.[20] And despite the fact that many enthusiasts of this theory agree that not all Muslim rulers of India were driven by faith, they claim that Aurangzeb tried to correct the theological failings of his predecessors by putting the evolution of Muslim nationalism in India on a course it should have taken after Qasim's demise. They suggest that for Aurangzeb this was only possible by imposing Islamic laws

---

[19] Dara – the Pakistani play set to make waves in London's National Theatre (DAWN, December 22, 2014).
[20] Ahmad Hassan Dani: *Pakistan Through Ages* (Sang-e-Meel, 2007) p.395

and discouraging the contamination which Islam in India suffered due to the inclusive policies of the Muslims who ruled before him.

Though Aurangzeb ruled for almost fifty years, after his death in 1707 CE, the once powerful Mughal Empire began to crumble, suffering from the social and political inertia which had begun to develop during his regime. In 1857, the last remnants of the empire completely collapsed. It is actually from this point in time that one can credibly trace the start and evolution of Muslim nationalism in India, and, subsequently, that of Pakistan.

****

The lost Mughal

Today in Pakistan, the divergent narrative seems to be floundering. We will try to investigate just how and why this is happening across the length of this book, but let me share with you a curious anecdote which, I believe, is a brief but telling evidence of this. During the fourth year of General Ziaul Haq's dictatorship in 1981, I was a 9th grade student at an elitist school in Karachi.[21] The divergent narrative was starting to peak during this period, fully sanctioned by the dictatorship, and proliferated through the state-owned media and school text books. One of the annual plays at the school that year was to be about Mughal rule in India. Though none of my more talented classmates had managed to bag roles of Mughal kings up to Aurangzeb, the producers of the play were

---

[21] The Karachi Grammar School which was established by the British in the 19th century and is one of the most prestigious (and expensive) in Pakistan.

still struggling to find boys for the roles of Aurangzeb, Dara Shikho, and for another one of Shah Jehan's sons, Murad. Almost all the interested boys from my class auditioned for Aurangzeb's role. No one was interested in playing Dara. Incidentally, a boy from the same class (but different section) did manage to win the audition and a chance to play Aurangzeb. He was the proudest fellow on that day, and so were his parents.

33 years later, in 2014, the same guy, who had retained his interest in acting, appeared in front of the producers of Shahid Nadeem's play, *Dara*. No, not to play Aurangzeb, but Dara Shikho. When he failed to win the role, he was advised to try for some other role in the play, maybe even that of Aurangzeb. He refused. He told the producers: 'I am best suited to play Dara, because I personally identify with him ...'[22]

---

[22] Told to the author by a mutual acquaintance of the actor in 2014.

CHAPTER 2

THE MAKINGS OF A COMMUNITY: EMERGENCE OF MUSLIM NATIONALISM IN INDIA

I have already tried to establish that Muslim nationalism in South Asia did not exist till the end of Muslim rule here. Decline of the Mughal Empire, rise of British Colonialism, and the political reassertion of Hindus, provided the materials with which Muslim nationalism would first begin to shape itself in India.

Dr. Mubarak Ali has insightfully noted an often ignored factor which helped create an early sense of nationhood among the Muslims in India: i.e. the manner in which Urdu began to replace Persian as the preferred language of Muslims in the region.[1] As Muslim rule receded, immigrants from Persia and Central Asia stopped travelling and settling in India[2] because now there were little or no opportunities left for them to bag important posts in the courts of Muslim regimes here. The importance and frequency of Persian ebbed, gradually replaced by Urdu – a language which began to form in India from the 14th century CE. Although around 99 percent of Urdu verbs have roots in ancient South Asian languages such as Sanskrit and

---

[1] Mubarak Ali: *Pakistan in Search of Identity* (Aakar Books, 2011) p.17
[2] Ibid.

Prakrit,[3] Persian and Arabic too have contributed significantly to Urdu's vocabulary.[4] [5]

Urdu was mostly spoken by local Muslims (most of whom were converts). But by the early 19th century, Urdu had also begun to make its way into the homes of the elite Muslims as well. This helped the local Muslims to climb their way up the social ladder[6] and begin to fill posts and positions which were once the exclusive domain of Persian and Central Asian immigrants. This initiated the early formation of a new Muslim community, mostly made-up of local Muslims who were now enjoying social mobility. This community also included some members of the old Muslim elite, who began adapting to the change.

But all this was happening when the Muslim empire was rapidly receding and the British were enhancing their presence in India. This facilitated a process through which the Hindus reasserted themselves socially and politically after remaining subdued for hundreds of years. With no powerful Muslim monarch or elite now shielding the interests of the Muslims in the region, the emerging community of local Muslims became fearful that its new-found status (or at least the perception of it) might be swept aside by the expansion of British rule and Hindu reassertion.

Some historians have suggested that the early movements which triggered the formation of Muslim nationalism in India were squarely a reaction (within the old Muslim elite) to the decline of Muslim imperial rule. But this was not the only

---

[3] Not a camp language: Urdu's origins (DAWN, July 5, 2015).

[4] Hans Dua: *Pluricentric Languages* (Walter de Gruyter, 1992)

[5] See also Prof. Tariq Rehman's *From Hindi to Urdu* (Oxford University Press, 2013) for a detailed study of the evolution of Urdu.

[6] Mubarak Ali: *Pakistan in Search of Identity* (Aakar Books, 2011) p.17

reason. Another prominent motive was to sustain the rise of the community of local Muslims. This community felt vulnerable and many of its members began accusing the later-day Mughals of squandering an empire due to decadence. Even some famous Muslim rulers of yore were criticized for putting too much faith in pragmatic politics and in inclusive policies, and not doing enough to use their powers to prompt wide-scale conversions.

During much of the Muslim rule in India, the ulema had only been allowed to play a nominal role in the workings of the state. But as Muslim rule retreated, the ulema took upon themselves the right to air the ambitions and fears of the community of local Muslims. The ulema insisted on explaining the decline of the Mughal Empire as a symptom of the deterioration of 'true Islam' due to the inclusive policies of the Mughals which, according to the ulema, strengthened the Hindus and also extended patronage to Sufi saints and orders. This, in turn, encouraged 'alien ideas' to seep into the beliefs and rituals of the region's Muslims.

Such a disposition saw a number of *ulema* and clerics from the emerging community of local Muslims in India become drawn towards a radical puritan movement which had mushroomed 2000 miles away in Arabia (present-day Saudi Arabia) in the 18th century. It was led by one Muhammad Al-Wahhab, a celebrant in the Nejd area of central Arabia who preached the expulsion and rejection of various practices and rituals from Islam which he claimed were distortions and heretical.[7] His movement had gained momentum when it was patronized by influential Arab tribes in the area.

---

[7] Simon Ross Valentine: *Force and Fanaticism* (Oxford University Press, 2014) p.82

A Muslim scholar from the Bengal in India, Haji Shariatullah, who was the son of an impoverished farmer, became smitten by Wahhab's movement when he travelled to and stayed in Arabia in 1799.[8] On his return to India, he was extremely dismissive of the conduct of the last remnants of the Mughal Empire, and conjectured that the social, political and economic condition of the Muslims of India had been deteriorating mainly due to the Muslims practicing an inaccurate strain of Islam which was 'adulterated by rituals borrowed from Hinduism'.[9] Shariatullah was equally harsh towards the centuries-old fusion of Sufism and Hinduism in the sub-continent.[10]

Another figure in this regard was Syed Ahmad Bareilly who, though, an ardent follower of Sufism, believed that Sufism in India too was in need of reform, and that this could only be achieved by reintroducing the importance of following *sharia* laws, something which was rare within the historically heterogeneous Sufi orders of India. Sufism in the region had, in fact, largely opposed Islamic orthodoxy and was comfortable with the rituals and beliefs which had grown around it, especially among the local Muslims. Bareilly theorized that the Muslim condition was in decline because the beliefs of the common Muslims of India repulsed the idea of gaining political power through force. He suggested that this can only be achieved through the practice of the Islamic concept of *jihad* (holy war)[11] which was missing in the make-up of Islam in the subcontinent. Bareilly gathered a following from among common Muslims and

---

[8] Razia Aktar Banu: *Islam in Bangladesh* (BRILL, 1992) p.35
[9] Entry on Shariatullah by Moinuddin Ahmad in *National Encyclopedia of Bangladesh* (2012).
[10] Ibid.
[11] Edward Mortimer: *Faith and Power* (Random House, 1982) p.68

set up a movement in the present-day Pakistan province of Khyber Pakhtunkhwa (KP). The area at the time was under the rule of the Sikhs who had risen in power at the end of Aurangzeb's regime.

Bareilly gathered over one thousand followers[12]. He implored them to shun their tribal customs and strive to fight a *jihad* against the 'infidels' and help him set up a state run on *sharia* laws. After offering stiff resistance to the Sikhs and the British, Bareilly managed to establish a strong base in the region. He began to impose laws grounded in his idea of the *sharia*. The move backfired when leaders of Pashtun tribes accused him of undermining their established customs. Many of these tribes rose up against him and pushed his movement deep into the hills near Charsaada.[13] In the town of Balakot, Bareilly was surrounded by the Sikh army and killed (1831).

The idea of 'purifying' Islam and Muslims in India (through vigorous preaching and holy war) formulated by Shariatullah and Bareilly were expressions of the fears haunting the local Muslims. They had risen in status after the immigration of 'high-bred' Persians and Central Asians to India decreased. But the rise in status was taking place at a time when Muslim political power was weakening and the Hindus and the Sikhs were reaffirming themselves.

The fears were also prompted by the mushrooming of rigorous Hindu reformist movements and also by the arrival of Christian missionaries from Britain.[14] The missionaries enjoyed a good response from lower-caste Hindus and from some local Muslims as well. Men such as Shariatullah and Bareilly believed

---

[12] Qeyamuddin Ahmad: *The Wahhabi Movement in India* (South Asia Books, 1994) p.50

[13] Ibid. p.55

[14] Mubarak Ali: *Pakistan in Search of Identity* (Aakar Books, 2011) p.18

that the nature of Muslim beliefs in India (especially among common Muslims) was such, that it could be easily molded and then eroded by the missionaries and the Hindu reformers. To them, only a strict adherence to Islamic laws and rituals could save the Muslim community from being completely absorbed by the changing political and social currents.

It is this dimension of Muslim history of India which found an important place in the post-1970s' divergent narrative of Pakistani nationalism. This narrative uses examples of Bareilly and Shariatullah to suggest that Muslim nationhood in the subcontinent was largely concerned about adopting 'true Islam' as a social and political inspiration, and that Pakistan was a natural culmination of what was begun by men such as Qasim, Aurangzeb and then Shariatullah and Bareilly.

This indeed is a prominent dimension of the formation of Muslim nationalism in South Asia, but the divergent narrative tends to largely skim over another dimension which was actually more influential in building Muslim nationalism in India, and, in fact, one which emerged as a reaction to the course taken by the likes of Shariatullah and Bareilly. The movements formed by Shariatullah and Bareilly made mosques and madrassas the cornerstones to formulate the idea of community among the local Muslims.[15] The movements elicited a surge of passion among many Indian Muslims. But these passions put the community on a course leading to further alienation and confusion, especially after the 1857 Sepoys Mutiny against the British was crushed.

****

---

[15] Ibid.

The Unflappable Scholar

The Mutiny[16] involved an uprising within sections of Hindus and Muslims in the British Army; but most of its leaders were Muslims from the local Muslim community, and remnants of the old Muslim elite.[17] After the bloody commotion was brought under control, the last vestiges of Mughal rule in the shape of an immobilized and nominal Muslim emperor, were eradicated. According to the British, it were the Muslims who had played the more active role in the rebellion. Consequently, influential British authors such as Sir William Muir began fostering the myth of the Muslim as someone with a sword in one hand and the Quran in the other.[18]

Two factors influenced the creation of this image. The first was, of course, the puritanical and radical nature of the movements led by Shariatullah and Bareilly decades before the Mutiny; and second was the lingering imagery in the West of Muslims that was concocted by European Christian perseveres during the Crusades (1095-1291). It is interesting to note that in their writings on India before the 1857 upheaval, the British had largely conceived India to be a racial whole.[19] Not that they were ignorant of the fact that the region was populated by multiple religions - mainly Hinduism and Islam - the British, however, saw most reformist activities of both as ways to regenerate their respective faiths which had fallen by the wayside. They did not predict that some of these movements may actually go on to inspire rebellions.

---

[16] Remembered as a War of Liberation in India and Pakistan.
[17] Thomas R. Metcalf: *The Aftermath of Revolt* (Princeton, 1965) p.298
[18] H. Hardy: *Muslims of British India* (Cambridge University Press) p.62
[19] Ibid.

But things in this respect began to change drastically when the British (after 1857) started to investigate the political and cultural dynamics of the religious differences between the Muslims and the Hindus, and then utilize their findings to exert more control over both the communities. Here emerges the second phase and dimension of what eventually emerged as Muslim nationalism in India.

The British attempted to dissect the Muslim belief system for political purposes. One of the earliest exhibitions of this emerged in the shape of a book, *Life of Mohammad.* Published in 1861 and authored by an Englishman, the book was squarely criticized by Muslim scholars in India for looking at Islamic history from a Christian point of view and presenting the legacy of Islam as something which was destructive and retrogressive.[20] One of the first Muslim scholars to offer a detailed rebuttal did not come from the *ulema* circles and neither was he a cleric. He belonged to a family which had roots in the old Muslim nobility and elite. His name was Syed Ahmad Khan. During the 1857 Mutiny, Khan had already established himself as a member of the scholarly Muslim gentry who had studied Sufism, mathematics, astronomy and the works of traditional Islamic scholars.

When literature which casted a critical eye on Muslim history began to emerge, Khan put forward a detailed proposal which he hoped would not only contest the perceptions of Islam and Muslims being formulated by the British, but also help the region's Muslims to reassess their beliefs, character and status according to the changes taking shape around them.[21]

Khan reminded the British that Islam was inherently a modern religion which had inspired the creation of some of the world's biggest empires and encouraged the study of philosophy

---

[20] Edward Said: *Orientalism* (Penguin Books, 2006) p.151
[21] Wilferd Smith: *Modern Islam in India* (1943) p.15

and the sciences during a period in which Europe was lurking aimlessly in the 'Dark Ages.' Khan also asserted that the modernity of the West was originally inspired and informed by the scholarly endeavors of mediaeval Muslim scientists and philosophers, and that the Muslims had been left behind because this aspect of Islam stopped being exercised by them. Khan then turned his attention towards his own community. He was vehemently opposed to the militancy of men like Shariatullah and Bareilly, and he was also critical of the 1857 uprising,[22] suggesting that such endeavors did more harm to Islam and the Muslims. However, he refused to agree with the assessment of the British that it were the Muslims alone who instigated the 1857 Mutiny. He wrote that the Mutiny had been triggered by reckless British actions based on their ill-informed concepts of Indian society.[23]

According to historian, Ayesha Jalal, the emergence of both Muslim and Hindu nationalism were also largely the result of British social engineering which they began as a project after the 1857 Mutiny.[24] The project began when the British introduced the idea of conducting a consensus. A lot of emphasis was put on an individual's faith; and the results of the consensus were then segmented more on the bases of religion than on a person's economic and ethnic status.[25]

The outcome of this was the rather nonconcrete formation of communities based on faith and constructed through an overwhelmingly suggestive consensus, undertaken, not only to comprehend the complex edifice and nature of Indian society,

---

[22] Sir Syed Ahmad Khan: *Asbab-e-Baghawat-e-Hind* (First published in 1859)
[23] Ibid.
[24] Ayesha Jalal: *Self and Sovereignty* (Sang-e-Meel Publications, 2001) p.45
[25] Ibid. p.44

but to also devise a more structural method to better control it in accordance to colonial interests in the region. Khan was quick to grasp this, and also the fact that the Hindu majority was in a better position to shape itself into becoming a holistic community because of its size and better relations with the British after the 1857 Mutiny.

Khan's thesis inferred that the Muslims needed to express themselves as a holistic community too, especially one which was positively responsive to the changes the British were implementing. This constituted a break from the early dimension of Muslim nationhood imagined by the likes of Shariatullah and Bareilly who had tried to express the idea of forming a Muslim community in India as a purely religious endeavor. They wanted to construct a homogenous Muslim whole in India which followed a standardized pattern of Muslim rituals and beliefs. This scheme was largely a failure because within the Muslim community of the region were stark sectarian, sub-sectarian, class, ethnic and cultural dissections. And as was seen during Bareilly's uprising in KP, once he began to implement his idea of the *sharia*, he faced a fateful rebellion by his erstwhile supporters who accused him of trying to usurp their tribal influence and eradicate their centuries-old customs.

However, this dimension did not fade away entirely. In 1867, *ulema* inspired by the 18th century Islamic scholar, Shah Waliullah, founded a madrassa in Deaoband, a town in the Indian region of Uttar Pradesh. From here emerged scholars and clerics who were fervently opposed to the changes being introduced by the British. They saw these changes as a way of 'corrupting Islam' [26] because certain Muslim reformers were advising the Muslim community to embrace these vicissitudes.

---

[26] Tahir Abbas: *Islamic Radicalism and Multicultural Politics* (Taylor & Francis, 2011)

Another hardline movement to emerge during the same period was the Ahal-e-Hadith which was closer to the puritan impulses of Abdul Wahab's movement in Arabia. Both these movements remained largely evangelical in nature, even though the Deobandi strain in 1919 would go on to sprout an exclusive political expression as well (the Jamiat Ulemea-i-Islam Hind).

Khan was conscious of these divisions. He decided to address the dilemma by localizing the European concept of nationalism – an idea which emerged in Europe in the early 18th century. So when the British began to club together economically, ethnically and culturally diverse groups into abstract Muslim, Hindu and Sikh communities, reformers from within these communities leveraged the European idea of nationalism and localized it to address the contradictions inherent in the whole idea of consensual community formation in India by the British.

But this was easier said than done. Nationalism was a modern European idea which required a particular way of understanding history, society and politics for a people to come together as a nation. This idea was absent in India before the arrival of the British. As Muslim rule began to ebb, men such as Shariatullah and Bareilly attempted to club together the Muslims of India as a community which shared theological commonalities with Muslim communities elsewhere in the world. During the last days of Muslim rule in India, clerics in mosques had begun to replace the names of Mughal kings in their sermons *(khutba)* with those of the rulers of the Ottoman Empire,[27] as if to suggest that the interests of the Muslims of India now lay outside the country.

---

[27] Mubarak Ali: *Pakistan in Search of Identity* (Aakar Books, 2011) p.18

Indeed, men such as Shariatullah, Bareilly and the scholars of Deoband had begun to conceive the Muslims of India as a unified whole, but this whole was not explained as a nation in the modern context, but as part of a larger Muslim *ummah*.[28] Khan saw a problem in this approach. Even though he overtly referenced scholarly and scientific achievements of the 'Golden Age of Islam'[29] in Arabia and Persia (to substantiate his assertion that Islam was inherently a progressive faith with a rich scholastic tradition), he lamented the absence of this tradition among the Muslim community of India; and also decried the approach taken by the *ulema* as something which went against the tide of this tradition.

Khan was perturbed by three main attitudinal negatives which he believed had crept inside the psyche of the Muslims, and were stemming their intellectual growth, and, consequently, causing their economic and political decline. They were: decadence; worship of the past; and theological dogma. Khan wrote that after reaching the heights of imperial power, Muslims had become decadent and lazy.[30] When this led to them losing political power, they became overtly nostalgic about past glories, which, in turn, solidified their inferiority complex. This caused a hardening of views against modernity and the emergence of a dogmatic attitude in matters of faith.

To Khan, the Muslims of India stood still, and, in fact, refused to move because they believed a great conspiracy had

---

[28] An Arabic term meaning a global supra-national community with a common religion.
[29] A period in the history of Islam, traditionally dated from the 8th century to the 13th century, during which much of the Islamic world was ruled by various caliphates, and science, economic development and cultural works flourished.
[30] Shafique Ali Khan: *Sir Sayyed Ahmad Khan & His Movement* (Ilm-o-Agahi, 1987) p.23

been hatched against them. He suggested that the Muslims had lost political power because 'they had lost their ability to rule.'[31] He castigated the *ulema* for forcing the Muslims to reject science (because it was 'Western'). He warned that such a view towards the sciences will keep Muslims buried under the weight of superstition and religious dogmatism.[32]

When the *ulema* responded by accusing him of creating divisions in a community which they were trying to unite, he wrote that since he was a reformer, his job was not to unite but to jolt members of his community by questioning established but corrosive social, intellectual and political norms.[33] He asked the *ulema*: The Greeks learned from the Egyptians; the Muslims from the Greeks; the Europeans from the Muslims ... so what calamity will befall the Muslims if they learned from the British?

But he was using a modern method of history to understand how knowledge flowed between civilizations; whereas to most of his orthodox *ulema* critics, history was a set of traditions passed on by one Muslim scholar to another and disseminated among the masses by the *ulema* and the clerics. Khan's initial work was largely analytical and pedagogic. He did not have the kind of a platform which his detractors had to address a large number of Muslims (i.e. the mosques and the madrassas). But this did not seem to worry him. He believed that the changes taking shape (under the British) will impact the Muslims in such a manner that many of them would eventually come to understand his point of view.[34] He wanted them to overcome

---

[31] Altaf H. Hali: *Hayat-e-Javed* (Ishrat Publishing House, 1971) p.558.
[32] Dr. Amna Afreen: *The Reformers of Islam* (University of Karachi, 2013) p.76
[33] Sir Sayyed Ahmad Khan: *Madamin-e-Tahdhib-al-Aklaq*
[34] Ibid.

their cultural and theological inertias and embrace what was on offer, especially contemporary education.

There was to be no meeting point between the *ulema* and him, simply because both where viewing the Muslim condition in India from different lenses. However, Khan did try to meet the *ulema* by dissecting their theological critiques of modernity. He wrote that a man's spiritual and moral life cannot improve without the flourishing of his material life.[35] Writing in a (Urdu) journal[36] which he launched in 1870, he reminded his critics that not only were Muslims once enthusiastic patrons of science, but the Quran too urged its readers to 'research the universe' which was one of God's greatest creations. To further his argument that Islam was inherently an enlightened religion, and, in essence, timeless (in the sense that it was easily adaptable to the ever-changing social trends), Khan authored a meticulously researched and detailed commentary on the Quran.

Tafslr Qur'an was published in 1880 and for its time was a rather original and even bold interpretation of Islam's holiest book because it tried to construe the book's contents in the light of the 19th century.[37] Khan insisted that decrees passed by ancient *ulema* were time-bound and could not be imposed in a much-changed scenario of what was taking place here and now. He wrote that the Muslims were in need of a new theology of Islam[38] which was rational and which rejected all doctrinal notions that were in disagreement with common sense, nature and with the essence of the Quran.[39]

---

[35] M. Ismail: *Maqalat-e-Sir Sayyid* (Majlis-e-Taraqi-Adab, 1990)
[36] *Tahdhib-al-Aklaq*
[37] JMS Baljon: *Modern Muslim Koran Interpretation* pp-19-20
[38] Dr. Amna Afreen: *The Reformers of Islam* (University of Karachi, 2013) p.88
[39] SW Cantwell: *Modern Islam in India* (Minerva Books, 1943) p.15

He wrote that the codes of belief and spirituality were the main concerns of Islam and that cultural habits (pertaining to eating, dressing, etc.) are mundane matters for which Islam provides only moral guidance because they change with time and place.[40] He believed that if faith is not practiced through reason, it can never be followed with any real conviction. He wrote that ancient scholars of Islam were not infallible and were as vulnerable to making mistakes as the Muslims of the 19th century. He insisted that the *ulema* were conceiving their world view and that of Islam by uncritically borrowing from the thoughts of ancient *ulema*. This, to him, had made them dogmatic in their thinking and hostile towards even the most positive aspects of the changes taking place around them.

Another ideological tendency which was introduced to the Muslims of India in the 19th century was pan-Islamism. One of its earliest advocates was Jamal Al-Din Al-Afghani – a bright young Afghan ideologist who arrived in India in 1855. Afghani passionately supported the 1857 Mutiny and was exasperated when it failed. Unlike the orthodox *ulema*, Afghani did not see any good in turning inwards and radically rejecting the modernity associated with British rule. He acknowledged the supremacy of western education and emphasized that Muslims should embrace it to improve their lot but then turn the tables against Western imperialism by overthrowing it and establishing a global Islamic caliphate.

Afghani, and, subsequently, pan-Islamism, viewed western modernity (especially in the field of education), as an elixir to regenerate the Muslims, not as a way to help them excel and find a place within colonial settings, but to fully understand and

---

[40] Dr. Amna Afreen: *The Reformers of Islam* (University of Karachi, 2013) p.90

then eradicate colonialism, and, consequently, set up a reinvigorated and enlightened global Islamic set-up. Like Khan, Afghani too was an early Muslim modernist. But Khan's Muslim modernism was largely interested in the intellectual, economic and social fate of the Muslim community of India alone. He thought that Afghani's idea of radically confronting the British would produce the same demoralizing results as did the failure of the 1857 Mutiny.

Interestingly, Afghani was one of the first people to notice the notion of Muslim nationalism in Khan's writings, despite the fact that Khan never explained himself as a nationalist. This happened when Afghani censured Khan for harming the global Muslim cause by speaking only about India's Muslims and/or treating them as a community which was separate from the Muslim communities elsewhere. Afghani was vocal in his denunciation of the orthodox ulema who were rejecting modern education, but quite like the ulema, Afghani too saw the Muslims as a global community (ummah). Pan-Islamism was thus inherently anti-nationalism.

Dissimilar to later-day pan-Islamists, Afghani was rather progressive and modernistic in his thinking. More than seeing Islam as a theistic route to a political revolution, he, instead, saw it as a slogan to rally Muslims around the world[41] against European imperialism. The pan-Islamist thought which he pioneered valued the importance of reforming the Muslim mindset through modern intellectual means, and then using the reformed as weapons against the imperial supremacy of western colonialism. But in the next century, only the shell of what he first conceived would remain in the idea of pan-Islamism.

---

[41] Ervand Abrahamian: *Iran between Two Revolutions* (Princeton University, 1982). p.62

For example, the pan-Islamist notions in the post-1970s divergent narrative of Pakistani nationalism are not so much inspired by Afghani as they are by how the Islamic orthodoxy began to perceive pan-Islamism i.e. as an ideology which attempts to erect a global caliphate, not through a faith strengthened by progressive reform, but by a largely mythical understanding of the faith's bygone militaristic splendor. Perhaps Khan opposed the idea of pan-Islamism because he understood that it was bound to evolve in this manner?

In 1879 one of Khan's staunchest supporters, the poet and intellectual, Altaf Hussain Hali, wrote a long poem[42] which passionately advanced Khan's ideas of reform and modernity. But the most protuberant feature of the poém was Hali's declaration that the Muslims of India were a separate cultural entity, distinct from other communities of India, especially the Hindu majority. But Hali explained that this distinction was not based on any hostility towards the non-Muslims of the region; but on the notion (which Hali believed was a fact) that the Muslims of India were descendants of foreigners[43] who came and settled here during Muslim rule.

By the late 1800s many local Muslims had begun to claim foreign ancestry (mainly Persian, Central Asian and Arabian). With the erosion of Muslim rule in India, some Muslim empires still existed elsewhere. So the claims of having foreign ancestry was also a way of expressing the separateness of India's Muslims. Another aspect in this context was the rise of the Urdu language among the Muslims. Though having (or claiming to have) Persian, Central Asian and Arabic ancestry was a proud feature to flaunt (and concoct), Urdu, which had been the language of 'lower Muslims' of (North) India, ascended and

---

[42] *Musadas-i-Hali*

[43] Ayesha Jalal: *Self and Sovereignty* (Sang-e-Meel Publications, 2001) p.65

began to rapidly develop into a complex literary language, now also preferred by the newly emerging Muslim elite.

The British didn't have a problem with this. Because since Persian had been the language of the court during Muslim rule, its rollback symbolized the retreat of the memory of Muslim rule in India. In 1837, the British replaced Persian with Urdu (in the northern regions) as one of the officially recognized vernacular languages of India. But in the 1860s Urdu became a symbol of Muslim cultural distinctiveness not through the efforts of the Muslims, but, ironically, due to the way some Hindu nationalists reacted to Urdu becoming an official language. They argued that Hindi alone should be the majority language of India. Linguistically, Hindi and Urdu are two registers of the same language. Hindi is written in the Devanagari script and uses more Sanskrit words,[44] whereas Urdu is written in the Perso-Arabic script and uses more Arabic and Persian words.[45] The resultant controversy triggered by Hindu reservations helped establish Urdu as the language of the Muslims and supplemented an additional perception of separation between the Muslims and the Hindus.

By the late 1800s, Khan had managed to attract the support and admiration of a growing number of young intellectuals, authors and poets. But whereas the list of his supporters would continue to grow, he was the target of some vicious polemical attacks. The Deobandi *ulema*[46] were extremely harsh in their criticism, and one of them even went on to accuse Khan of being an apostate.[47] They censured him for trying to tear away the Muslims from the unchangeable

---

[44] Online article: Death of Urdu greatly exaggerated in India: Shoaib Danyal (Scroll.in, June, 2016).
[45] Ibid.
[46] A latter-day label for those following the decrees of the scholars associated with the madrassa in Deoband.
[47] Ayesha Jalal: *Self & Sovereignty* (Sang-e-Meel Publications, 2001) p.72

tenants of their religion, and for promoting *'Angraziat'* (western ethics and customs) among the believers. The Ahl-e-Hadith was equally harsh. It asked Muslims to 'keep unbelievers (such as Khan) at an arm's length.'[48]

Khan also received criticism from the supporters of Afghani's pan-Islamism. Afghani himself admonished Khan for not only undermining the idea of global Muslim unity (by alluding to Muslim unity in the context of India's Muslims only); but he also censured him for creating divisions between the region's Muslims and Hindus. Afghani was of the view that Hindu-Muslim unity was vital in India to challenge British rule.[49]

Despite the attacks, it would be Khan's ideas which would manage to dominate the most prominent dimensions of Muslim nationalism in India. According to Ayesha Jalal[50], his strategic and pragmatic alignment with the British helped his ideas to make vital in-roads in a more organized and freer manner because they were about the formation of a separate Muslim identity (in India) which was not antagonistic to British rule, but, rather, was being formed to assist the Muslims to compete effectively within the new colonial system. One of the major schools founded by Khan in Aligarh (which soon evolved into becoming a college and then a university) went on to produce a particular Muslim elite and Muslim urban bourgeoisie who would go on to govern Muslim nationalist thought in India and decide what course it was to take.

****

---

[48] Ibid. p.68
[49] N R. Keddie: *An Islamic Response to Imperialism* (Berkeley University Press, 1968) p.453
[50] Ibid. p.76

The Flippant

Traditionalist religious passions (in the context of India) erupted during the 1857 Mutiny. They then began to rapidly mutate (among both the Hindu and Muslim populations) and plunged into a flux after the Mutiny was crushed. The mid and late 19th century was a highly charged period in India. The centuries-old Muslim Empire in the region had collapsed and the British were consolidating their rule over a vast expanse teeming with millions of people belonging to a number of faiths. A wave of reformist religious movements emerged in India just after the complete downfall of the Mughal Empire in 1857.

These movements largely arose from within the Hindu majority and from among the significant Muslim and Sikh minorities of India. One of the triggers in this respect was the intensifying of Christian missionary activity that was initially encouraged by the British.[51] The reformist movements also tried to tackle ideas introduced by the British culled from the zeitgeists of the Age of Reason and the Age of Enlightenment which had appeared in the West (in the 17th and 18th centuries).

In 1875 the Hindu reformist movement, the Arya Samaj, emerged. It attempted to reconfigure Hinduism as a unified and 'enlightened' faith. To counter Christian and rationalist criticism of it being outmoded and even exploitative, the Samaj introduced a Hinduism that was centred entirely on the Vedas[52] and devoid of idol worship.[53] It accepted women's rights and the belief in a

---

[51] A Johnston: *The British Empire, Colonialism and Missionary Activity* (Cambridge University Press, 2003) p.13-37
[52] Any of the four collections forming the earliest body of Indian scripture, consisting of the Rig Veda, Sama Veda, Yajur Veda, and Atharva Veda.
[53] N Nair: *Hindu Politics and Partition of India* (Permanent Black, 2011) p.53

single supreme deity, the *Om*. It also claimed to be superior to Christianity and Islam. On the other hand, various strands of reformers appeared from among multiple strands of Muslims, already discussed in this chapter.

As frantic polemical treatises flew thick and fast between these strands; and between the Hindus and Christians; and then between Hindus, Christians and Muslims, a battle of propaganda too erupted in which reformist religious groups proudly paraded the number of converts they had managed to bag. One of the most intriguing cases in this context was of Ghazi Mehmood that became all the rage in the early 1900s but has faded from history books.

In 2011, a Pakistani historian and researcher, Dr Ali Usman Qasmi, brought it back to life in his brilliant study of the enigmatic 'Ahl-i-Quran' Movement[54] in the Punjab (that appeared in the late 19th and early 20th centuries). Some historians also believe that the Ahe-i-Quran Movement was inspired by Syed Ahmad Khan's writings which advocated the rational interpretation of the Quran. Others also add that Ghazi's topsy-turvy disposition (as we shall see) was mainly due to how Khan's iconoclastic work had impacted sections of young Muslim youth.

Ghazi Mehmood was born into a middle-class Sunni Muslim family and exhibited a great interest in the study of Islam. As a teenager, however, he was put off by a sermon which he had heard in a mosque. He increasingly became skeptical about his faith. In 1899, he moved close to a small Hindu reformist outfit,

---

[54] The movement described any form of Islam that accepts the Quran as revelation, but rejects the religious authority, and/or authenticity of the reported sayings of Islam's revered figures. Quranists followed the Quran alone. They believed that its message was clear and complete, and that it could therefore be fully understood without referencing the Hadith. It was often termed heretical by the orthodox ulema.

the Dev Samaj. Though he did not convert to Hinduism, he did change his surname to Dharampal and became Ghazi Dharampal. Unable to reconcile to some beliefs of the Dev Samaj, Ghazi broke away from the group. But soon he was successfully engaged by the Arya Samaj. In 1903, at the age of 21, he finally embraced Hinduism and began working for the Arya Samaj.

The Samaj extensively publicized this conversion through pamphlets and Hindi newspapers and then financed Ghazi's first book, *Tark-i-Islam*, in which he explained why he renounced his original faith. He continued to publish treatises for the Samaj. He was challenged by counter-treatises which attempted to blunt his criticism. Most of these were authored by Sanaullah Amritsari, an aggressive Ahl-i-Hadith polemicist, and Hakim Nuruddin, a member of the Ahamadiyya community.[55]

Ghazi also began publishing a Hindi monthly dedicated to promoting Arya Samaj beliefs. In 1913, he fell in love with a Brahmin widow and married her. This is when he had a falling out with the Samaj whose leadership did not approve of the marriage. Distressed by the way his friends in the Samaj had responded to his marriage to a Brahmin widow, Ghazi authored an appeal to scholars of all faiths (in India) asking which religion could guarantee the rights of his wife and children without discrimination.

He received dozens of replies. But it was the response from a judge and scholar from the Ahl-i-Hadith, Sulayman Mansurpuri, which was most alluring to Ghazi.[56] The judge wrote that he (Ghazi) was lawfully married and that his children had equal rights even if their mother chose to remain

[55] A U. Qasmi: *Questioning the Authority of the Past* (Oxford University Press, 2012)
[56] Ibid.

a Hindu. This response saw Ghazi visit the judge and agree to re-enter the fold of Islam. Ghazi now spent his scholastic energies in writing treatises against the Arya Samaj[57] (denouncing their 'hypocrisies').

But he was soon at loggerheads with the Ahle-i-Hadith, founding their ideas to be too cumbersome and retrogressive. It was at this point that he was adopted by the Ahl-i-Quran Movement.[58] The movement insisted that the Quran alone should be the focus of all law-making in Islam and rejected all other Muslim sacred texts as being largely 'man-made'. So, from being a curious young Sunni Muslim, Ghazi became a poster-boy of Hindu reformists, to becoming a scholar of the conservative Ahl-i-Hadith, to finally being adopted by the rationalist Ahl-i-Quran Movement.

His conversion to Hinduism and re-conversion to Islam were both highly publicized events. Interestingly, though the memory and mention of his many conversions eventually faded away, historians who dragged it out again referred to him as Ghazi Mehmood Dharampal. This is because, though, after his re-conversion to Islam he restored his Muslim surname, Mehmood, he did not discard the Hindu surname that he had adopted in 1899. He died in 1960 at the age of 78 and was given a proper Muslim burial. Little is known what became of his beliefs after the withering away of the Ahl-i-Quran Movement in the early 1940s.

---

[57] Ibid.
[58] P. Ghosh: *Civil Disobedience in Bihar – 1930-34* (Manak Publications, 2008) p.209

CHAPTER 3
THE MUSLIM ÜBERMENSCH

In 1886, Syed Ahmad Khan founded the All Indian Muhammadan Educational Conference (AIMEC). It was launched as an education advocacy body which would also undertake social engagement to promote the seeking of western education and science among the Muslims of India. Its main base of operations was the Mohammadan Anglo-Oriental College (MAO), a college founded by Khan in the city of Aligarh. Khan insisted that AIMEC's work remained social and educational, and he debarred its members from indulging in politics.[1] The organization and the college started to shape a new elite of educated Muslims.

The aftermath of the failure of the 1857 Mutiny had galvanized Khan to valiantly challenge not only the perceptions which the British held of Muslims, but also the perceptions that the *ulema* were fostering against the British and modern education. Even though Khan was largely successful in somewhat making the British to gradually come around his point of view (as long as it was not political), his polemical tussles with the *ulema* had greatly intensified.

---

[1] John Keay: *India: A History* (Grove Press, 2001) p.468

In 1885, the Indian National Congress (INC) was founded. Khan saw its formation as a folly which would only give token membership to the Muslims.[2] INC's idea of Indian nationalism did not sit well with him. He feared that educated Muslims who were emerging from his 'Aligarh Movement' will be tempted to join INC, and that his idea of forming an influential Muslim civil society imbedded in the grid of British rule, will get submerged underneath the weight of the INC.

His fears were well-founded because many members and supporters of his social and educational movement, after disagreeing with his advice of staying clear of politics, joined the INC. Khan had managed to infuse a sense of community (albeit a largely cultural one) in some prominent sections of India's Muslims. But he never saw the community as a political whole, as such. He was more interested in using the broad cultural aspects of the concept of nationalism to define (and distinguish) the Muslims of India.

The *ulema* and spiritual leaders (*pirs*), though taken to task by him in his complex treatises, still enjoyed influence over common Muslims. What's more, by the late 1800s, stark sectarian and sub-sectarian divisions became prominent among the Muslims. The Deobandis sparred with the Ahle-Hadith; and then both indulged in vicious polemical battles with what would become to be known as the 'Barelvis' – another Sunni Muslim sub-sect which rose in the late 1800s [3] as a reaction to the stands of the Deobandis and the Ahle Hadidh against the centuries-old practice of worshipping at the shrines of Sufi saints. All three then questioned the status of the Shia sect (and vice versa).

---

[2] SM Akram: *Mauj-e-Kausar* pp.85-86
[3] Simon Valentine: *History, Belief & Practice* (Columbia University Press, 2008) p.xv

Khan's thesis and activism also drew criticism from a section of non-theological Muslim intelligentsia who disagreed with his negation of politics. They (the critics) insisted that the views of the 'English-speaking Muslims' (a reference to Khan and his supporters), were not the united voice of the Muslims.[4] Finally, in 1901, three years after Khan's demise, members of the AIMEC began discussing the need of a Muslim political outfit to counter the impact of the INC. When an influential Urdu newspaper, *Sada-e-Hind* lambasted AIMEC members for being '*babus*'[5] and being 'under the thumb of the British', a Bombay-based English daily, *Tribune*, hailed the criticism as a 'revolt against Aligarh.'[6]

Khan's reaction to the failure of the 1857 Mutiny, and, more so, his ideas about the regeneration of the Muslim community and culture in India through the seeking of modern education, British patronage, and theological reform, had flung open a Pandora's Box out of which emerged various distinct political, social and theological tendencies. These tendencies laid bare ideological and theological divisions in the Muslim community, and then went on to politicize these dissections. Khan was correct to fear that such a scenario was bound to overtake his largely educational movement. In 1906, members of AIMEC lifted the ban (on indulging in political activities) that Khan had imposed in the organization.[7]

The members then announced the formation of a political party, the All India Muslim League (AIML). It was to be a party which would 'look after the interests of India's Muslims'[8] and

---

[4] Sada-e-Hind (12 November 1901)
[5] Term used to explain locals (in India) behaving like westerners.
[6] Tribune (26 November, 1901)
[7] Shahid J. Burki: *Pakistan: Fifty Years of Nationhood* (Westview Press, 1999)
[8] Ibid.

further evolve Khan's ideas – but this time through politics. The evolution of AIMEC into becoming the AIML, saw the students of Khan's MAO College become increasingly political as well. Their discourses mostly revolved around ways to give Khan's ideas a political dimension; and what it meant to be a separate cultural entity in a political whole ruled by the British and having a Hindu majority. Yet, much of the college's focus remained on producing Muslims which were apt to be accepted into the workings of the British Raj. The League's growth was slow, but Khan's MAO Collage became the intellectual epicenter of Muslim politics in India. It was given the status of a university in 1920 (Aligarh University).

Muslim League's political disposition became a lot more pronounced when Muhammad Ali Jinnah joined the party in 1913. Jinnah, a sharp lawyer but with an aloof and dispassionate demeanor, was also a member of the INC. He was a fervent advocate of Hindu-Muslim unity and of Indian nationalism. In 1916 he led the League to strike a pact with INC in Lucknow. Both the parties agreed to work together to pressurize the British to grant India self-governance. However, in 1919, when the already depleted Ottoman regime in Turkey was defeated by a British-led alliance during the First World War, the *ulema* of India, who till then had largely remained stationed in their mosques and madrassas, poured out to agitate against the possible dismantling of the Ottoman Empire.

The leadership of the League wasn't quite sure how to respond because being a party built on the scholastic and social groundwork undertaken by Syed Ahmad Khan, it was only logical that the party would oppose an emerging movement being led by religionists. However, as the specter of the complete fall of the last surviving major Muslim empire became ever so ominous, the emerging modern Muslim

middleclass in India began to feel uncomfortable about the
League's silence on the issue.[9]

The resultant movement, dubbed the Khilafat Movement,
which began to ferment during the last years of the First World
War, finally managed to capture the attention and interest of a
large number of Indian Muslims when it was decided that the
land considered holy by the Muslims and once held by the
Ottomans, was to be put under the control of British and French
forces. The movement demanded that the defeated Ottoman
regime must not be dismantled and the sacred lands which it had
lost in the War handed back to the Muslims. The Khilafat
Movement was the window through which the *ulema* groups
entered mainstream politics of India.

But why did the imminent fall and disintegration of a depleted
Muslim empire quartered thousands of miles away generate such
resentment and concern among the Muslims of India? We have
already investigated in preceding chapters how the decline of the
centuries-old Muslim empire in India made many Muslims feel
vulnerable as a minority in a land which was not being ruled by a
Muslim dynasty anymore; and how this had made them look for a
theological and political connection outside India and towards the
surviving Muslim empires elsewhere.

Indeed, this was a reason. But wasn't this effectively tackled
and addressed by the likes of Syed Ahmad Khan who were
advocating a new way of finding social and economic relevance
with the help of an alignment with India's new overlords, the
British? To a certain extent, yes, but the *ulema* and the pan-
Islamists never agreed with the course purposed by Khan; in fact
they scoffed at it. They had continued to describe India's Muslim
population as part of the larger global Muslim community. The

---

[9] Dr. Mubarak Ali: *The Khilafat Movement*

ulema had thus conceived the Ottoman Empire to be the last major bastion of Muslim military and political might.

But, ironically, just as one project of social engineering by the British had given birth to the concept of modern nationalism in India (the consensus)[10], another such tactic by them helped make the Ottoman Empire become an integral concern of the Muslims of India. Here's how it happened. Some 60 years before the Ottoman regime in Turkey allied itself with the Germans against the British-led alliance in the First World War, it was cultivating amicable relations with the British. The regime had begun to lose territory and influence over the Muslim world and wanted to retain its status as the only legitimate caliphate. During the 1857 Mutiny, the British managed to extract a *fatwa*[11] from the Ottoman caliph urging the Muslims not to fight against the British.[12] Due to tensions between the British and the Russian kingdom at the time, Britain promoted a pro-Ottoman line. They encouraged loyalty to the Ottoman Caliph among the Indian Muslims.[13]

According to Dr. Mubarak Ali:

This is how the Indian Muslims slowly started to regard the Ottoman Caliph as the head of Muslim world. In the wake of Pan-Islamic movement of Jamaluddin Afghani, the Ottoman Caliph Sultan Abdul Hamid I (1876-1909) tried to use it to establish his political position in the Muslim world. Sir Sayyid, realizing the danger of this extra territorial loyalty, warned the Indian Muslims not to look to the Caliph as their protector or defender ... the Muslims of India became more

---

[10] See chapter 2.
[11] A ruling on a point of Islamic law given by a recognized authority.
[12] Dr. Mubarak Ali: The Khilafat Movement.
[13] TW Arnold: *The Caliphate* (Oxford University Press, 1966) p.137

conscious about the existence of Turkey. They started to relate Islam with Turkey and that any danger to Turkey became the danger to Islam. [14]

The League which had remained to be a largely liberal outfit changed tact under the pressure exerted by the growing resentment among the emerging Muslim middle-classes against the defeat of the Ottoman forces at the hands of the British. Pan-Islamists (many of whom were also operating from within the secular-nationalist INC), and ulema groups were in the forefront of the Khilafat Movement. The League's pre-War position was being undermined by its inaction in this regard and by its adherence to the rules of engagement laid down by Syed Ahmad Khan.

Feeling sidelined and overwhelmed by the religious passions of the movement which also became apparent within the party's main Muslim urban middle-class constituency, a leading Muslim League member, Dr. Ansari, headed a special party convention in Delhi in 1918, and invited a group of *ulema* to the session. [15] However, another core League member, Chaudhry Khaliquzzaman, worried that Muslim politics in India were being mixed with religious passions and that this would dwarf the 'more real issues' facing the Muslims. [16]

Jinnah too decried Dr. Ansari's move to make the League enter the fray prompted by the Khilafat Movement. Jinnah's fervent opposition in this regard created a rift within the League. He opposed the Khilafat Movement [17] because he believed that it was destined to be a failure and end in a disaster for the Indians. [18] Jinnah was also

---

[14] Dr. Mubarak Ali: The Khilafat Movement
[15] Ibid.
[16] Ibid.
[17] Akbar Ahmad: *The Search for Saladin* (Routledge, 2005)
[18] Ibid.

not amused when pan-Islamists such as Mohammad Ali Johar and his brother Shaukat Ali formed the All India Khilafat Committee with a group of *ulema* and some members of the Muslim League. In 1920, the Committee managed to attract the interest of the INC which was being guided by the much revered Hindu leader and activist, Mahatma Gandhi. Gandhi was already planning to launch a countrywide movement against the British and he saw the Khilafat Movement as an opportunity to mobilize and bring in a large number of Muslims on the side of his anti-British cause.

Jinnah warned that the movement would be detrimental to the Hindus and Muslims of India and roll back whatever the two communities had managed to extract from the British. Jinnah was also concerned about how the League was being undermined and overwhelmed by the Khilafat Committee which, he believed, had become a tool in the hands of the INC and the pan-Islamists. Jinnah confessed that he was unable to curtail the rapid flow of the movement [19] but continued to advise the Muslims to not be swept away by its populist currents because they were ill-conceived and unfeasible.

As riots and violence broke out and hundreds of Muslims and Hindus were arrested, Jinnah's group within the League stayed aloof from the movement. Then, when the intensity of the violence between the protesters and the police developed even further, a radical Islamic preacher and scholar, Maulana Abdul Bari, asked the Muslims to leave India because it had become a *darul harab*.[20] Thousands of young Muslims decided to move to Afghanistan (because it was being ruled by a Muslim *amir*). Many of the migrants, however, were robbed and looted by mountain and highway bandits and then turned away by the

---

[19] Ibid.
[20] Arab term meaning 'home of war' (opposite of *dar-ul-Islam*, meaning home of Islam).

Afghan regime.[21] And those who returned to India found their homes occupied by their neighbors.[22]

The Muslim-Hindu unity being celebrated by the Khilafat Committee began to erode as well when the violent currents of the movement also created opportunities for certain other tense tendencies to emerge within the anarchic scenario that the movement had generated. At the start of the movement, British troops massacred hundreds of Indians (mostly Sikhs) in Amritsar. Then, at the height of the commotion in 1921, Muslim peasants in India's Malabar area rose up against their Hindu landlords[23] triggering clashes between the two communities there. Hundreds of Hindus were forcibly converted,[24] before the authorities brutally crushed the uprising, killing and arresting dozens of Muslim peasants.

Then, in 1922, a violent mob burned alive 21 policemen in Chairi Chaura.[25] This gruesome incident forced Gandhi to pull the INC out of the movement and also halt his own 'non-corporation movement' against the colonial regime. In a 1919 letter to Gandhi, Jinnah had raised fears that the movement had the potential to whip up untapped religious passions of the masses which would be disastrous for the Indians and lead to chaos. This is exactly what happened, even though Gandhi finally abandoned the movement and was criticized for doing so by the Khilafat Committee and also by some members of the INC who quit the party and formed their own Swaraj Party.

[21] Khursheed Kamal Aziz: *The Indian Khilafat Movement* (Pak Publishers, 1972) p.272

[22] Akbar Ahmad: *The Search for Saladin* (Routledge, 2005)

[23] Prabhu Bapu: *Hindu Mahasaba in Colonial North India* (Routledge, 2013) p.49

[24] Khallid bin Sayeed: *Pakistan's Formative Years* (Oxford University Press) p.196

[25] J. Chandra: *Gandhiji and Haryana* (Usha Publications, 1977) p.13

The movement was particularly damaging to the Muslims. Hundreds perished and many Muslim youth (who were encouraged by pan-Islamists such as Maulana Abdul Kalam Azad and Muhammad Ali, to quit their schools and colleges[26]) became part of a disoriented and rudderless generation. The movement eventually collapsed when a Turlish nationalist and general, Mustafa Kamal, drove out foreign forces from parts of Turkey, abolished the caliphate, and formed a secular republic based on Turkish nationalism.

The INC was weakened and most of its top leadership was in jail; the Muslim League was left severely disjointed; and groups of radical Muslim activists and *ulema* who had risen to prominence during the commotion, fragmented. The Ali brothers departed from their radical pan-Islamist leanings; whereas other pan-Islamists, such Maulana Abdul Kalam Azad and former Muslim League member, Dr. Ansari, became firm supporters of the INC. Another set of radicals from the Khilafat Committee formed the Majlis-e-Ahrar-e-Islami, a radical Sunni Muslim outfit.

A number of deep-seated Hindu organizations also sprouted, mainly as a reaction to the INC's initial reluctance to condemn the forced conversions of Hindus by the rebelling Muslims in Malabar. These outfits were almost entirely anti-Muslim and saw the British as liberators of Hindus from 'Muslim atrocities'.[27]

****

---

[26] Khallid bin Sayeed: *Pakistan's Formative Years* (Oxford University Press) p.214
[27] Ibid.

Furnishing a Revolution

The Khilafat Committee's rise and fall were rapid. The Committee was largely a spontaneous pan-Islamist and religious initiative feeding on the stew of information coming from the War front about the defeat and possible fall of the Ottoman Empire. Ironically, the emerging Muslim middleclasses that had been largely shaped by the groundwork done by the likes of Syed Ahmad Khan, and which, in turn, had placed many Muslims inside the economic grid of colonial rule in India, became ardent supporters of the movement.

The Muslim League was originally unable to gauge the intensity of the sympathy brewing within the Muslim middleclass which was one of its main bases of support. This was largely the result of the intensifying of the politics of Muslim students who had been charmed by the pan-Islamist rhetoric. A faction from the Muslim League hastily decided to hang from the coat-tails of the Khilafat Committee once it realized that the party was losing ground to the *ulema* and the pan-Islamists, especially among Muslim students and the Muslim middle-classes.

Another group in the League (led by Jinnah) was repulsed by the populist and radical nature of the Committee and advised the party to stay away from it. Gandhi's INC, on the other hand, adopted the Khilafat Movement because Gandhi believed it would bolster his 'non-cooperation movement' against the British. The Committee was mostly run on donations. Some of its leading donors were Muslim *Seths* [28] stationed in Bombay who had become rich from the business opportunities provided by the colonial economic system. This would have pleased Syed

---

[28] Urdu/Hindi word meaning rich businessmen.

Ahmad Khan, but not the fact that some of the money being made by a class of rising Muslim businessmen was going to a cause he would likely to have found to be imprudent.

Other sections of the Muslim bourgeoisies too regularly contributed, especially students who then urged their families to dish out money for a 'holy cause.'[29] Fiery leaders of the Committee would tour towns and cities, making passionate speeches and pleads for donations. Young Muslims and businessmen would donate whatever they could and women would go to the extent of donating their jewelry.[30] But most aspects of the movement were rather chaotic and frenzied. Euphoria and violence would emerge side-by-side and one was not sure which was which. And when the violence intensified, cracks began to emerge within the movement. Someone asked on what was the donated money being spent and how much. Then someone else demanded an audit should be done of the funds. The result of the audit validated that much of the money had been embezzled.[31]

This greatly discredited the Committee. My late paternal grandfather who was just a minor in 1923 often spoke about how his father (my great-grandfather) - who had done well as a trader in our ancestral town of Makhad in the northern most area of Punjab - was approached by a group of young members of the movement. He had gone to Lahore to meet a fellow trader when he came across a group of passionate young men asking for donations from Muslim shopkeepers. They were requesting contributions for a holy war to save the Ottoman Caliphate and to also drive out the British. My grandfather used to say that his

---

[29] MH Zubairi: *Voyage Through History* (Hamdard Foundation, 1987) p.60
[30] Ibid.
[31] Ibid. pp-59-60

father had no interest whatsoever in politics, but being a pious man, he donated Rs.100 (a rather big amount in 1923) to the young men.

A year later, he returned to Lahore, and found a business acquaintance of his who was an owner of a large furniture shop, in a very good mood. When my great-grandfather asked him why he was so chirpy, he told him that he was just pleased to see that young Muslims now had the power to buy expensive and tasteful furniture. Apparently a young man had visited the furniture store the day before and bought an expensive bed and sofa.

My great-grandfather smiled along, until told by the shop-owner: 'only months ago, this young man was making political speeches against the British.' My great-grandfather asked, 'did he belong to that Khilafat Committee?' 'Yes,' the shop-keeper replied. 'How much were the bed and the sofa for?' my great-grandfather asked.

'Rs.100' came the answer. 'Young Muslims are prospering.'

****

The New Muslim Man

The INC and the League gradually began to pick up the pieces scattered during the commotion and collapse of the Khilafat Movement. Jinnah had rejected the idea of joining the Khilafat Movement and felt disillusioned by the state of Indian politics in the immediate aftermath of its collapse. He flew out to the UK where he decided to stay. Much had changed and was changing in the spheres of Muslim politics in India. The Muslim community was stricken by a sense of disorientation. The agitation witnessed during the Khilafat Movement had hurled the community out of the paradigm designed for it by Syed Ahmad Khan and deeply politicized it.

But Muslim political leadership was weak and fragmented, scattered between a debilitated and fractured Muslim League, and religious groups who had been radicalized by the movement. From this tense scenario emerged a man who would become the second major figure in the evolution of Muslim nationalism in India after Syed Ahmad Khan, and, consequently, that of Pakistani nationalism.

Muhammad Iqbal was a poet and a philosopher of considerable intellectual prowess. Though he had initially supported and then joined the Khilafat Committee, his stay in it was brief. He resigned from the Committee after accusing its leaders of being 'overtly sentimental.'[32] He then went on to deride the Ottomans for 'being a shame to the Muslims'.[33] In fact he believed that the fall of the Ottoman caliphate in Turkey could be catalytic to the emergence of a renaissance in Islam. He also applauded the take-over of Turkey by Mustafa Kamal, a secular-nationalist who abolished the caliphate and declared Turkey to be a modern republic. On Kamal's reforms, Iqbal wrote:

The truth is that among the Muslim nations today, Turkey alone has shaken off its dogmatic slumber and attained self-consciousness ...'[34]

Even though, later on in life Iqbal would begin to alter his views about Kamal's reforms,[35] for a while he did see the new

---

[32] Alama Iqbal aur Thereek-e-Khilafat: Amir Riaz (Daily Dunya, August 7, 2013).

[33] Khurram A. Shafique: *Iqbal: His Life and Our Times* (Libredux Publishing, 2014)

[34] Muhammad Iqbal: *The Reconstruction of Religious Thought* (first published 1930).

[35] F. Vahadat: *Islamic Ethos and the Specter of Modernity* (Anthem Books, 2015) p.50

Turkish republic as a dynamic political and social model of Muslim evolution, the sort which should be emulated by the Muslims of India.[36] Iqbal was born in Sialkot. His ancestors were from a Hindu clan in Kashmir who had converted to Islam during the reign of 16th century Mughal king, Shah Jahan.[37] Iqbal got his initial education from a madrasah before moving on to a school and then to a college in Sialkot. In 1897, he received his Bachelor's degree from a college in Lahore and then a Master's degree from the Punjab University.

In 1905, encouraged by a British teacher of his, Sir Thomas Arnold, Iqbal travelled to the UK to study law. He then moved to Munich, Germany, where he earned a Doctor of Philosophy degree from the Ludwig Maximillian University. Iqbal became increasingly aware of the nature of changes which had swept across India's Muslim community during and after the eruption and collapse of the Khilafat Movement. For example, by the late 1920s, a Muslim business class had emerged. Historians such as WC Smith[38] suggest that this class began to find many of its avenues (of growth) 'blocked by the Hindus and the British' and its members 'could not develop large-scale capital.'

This was one overriding reason why the Muslim business class had supported the Khilafat Movement. A Muslim middle-class too had emerged, largely from within the paradigm and rules of engagement drawn by Syed Ahmad Khan. In the early 20th century the educational progress of the Muslims was quite rapid.[39] Many teachers, lawyers, professors, military officers and

---

[36] Ibid.
[37] JN Sharma: *Encyclopedia of Eminent Thinkers* (Concept Publishing, 2008) p.14
[38] *Modern Islam in India* (1946)
[39] Wayne A. Wilcox: The Wellsprings of Pakistan in *Pakistan: The long View* ed. L. Ziring (Duke University Press, 1977). p.30

bureaucrats were recruited from this class. Most of them were aligned with the politics of the Muslim League.

In the aftermath of the Khilafat Movement, these two classes were feeling susceptible. As a consequence, some sections of these classes hurried out to support the radical Islamic groups which had emerged from the movement; whereas the rest tried to figure out what course Muslim politics would take after the League had been weakened by infighting, and when the hopes of communal harmony and anti-British politics raised by the Khilafat Movement had crashed.

Iqbal became the intellectual consequence and expression of this turmoil whirling within the Muslim community after the Khilafat Movement had buckled. More than just an expression, he became a possible answer. Till 1905, Iqbal had been a passionate Indian autonomist[40]. He was a strong proponent of *wataniyat*[41] or love of the territorial homeland. He often wrote about his despondency over the rising strife between the Hindus and Muslims of India. By the time the Khilafat Movement had begun to implode, Iqbal was convinced that the Muslims of India required a new expression; one which should emerge from 'individual autonomy' and was not chained to the worldview of the religious guardians of Islam.[42] Many *ulema* were not amused by this. In response to their criticism, he wrote:

Zhud taang nazar ne mujhe kafir jana,
Aur kafir samajhta hai Mussalman hoon mein[43]

(The religious bigot considers me an infidel; and the infidel deems me a Muslim).

---

[40] Ayesha Jalal: *Self and Sovereignty* (Sang-e-Meel, 2001) p.168
[41] Ibid.
[42] Ibid. p.167
[43] Hakim: *Fiqr-i-Iqbal* p.121

Iqbal was conscious of the fact that the post-1857 Muslim community in India was evolving with two competing sets of ideas: one was encouraging the community to embrace western education to regenerate itself; and the other was explaining this community as being a part of a global Muslim *ummah* striving to cleanse itself and move towards the formation of a pious caliphate.

Iqbal uniquely merged the two tendencies to come up with a complex synthesis which would go a long way in adding a weighty ideological dimension to the Muslim League, and, eventually, become an important building block in the construction of what would become Pakistani nationalism.

Iqbal thought highly of Syed Ahmad Khan. He praised Syed for being the first Muslim (in India) 'to glimpse the positive character of the age which was coming.'[44] Iqbal wrote:

(Sir Syed) was the first Indian Muslim who felt the need of a fresh orientation of Islam and worked for it. We may differ from his religious views, but there can be no denying the fact that his sensitive soul was the first to react to the modern age. The extreme conservatism of Indian Muslims which had lost its hold on the realities of life failed to see the real meaning of the religious attitude of Syed Ahmad Khan. [45]

But in his attempt to create the aforementioned synthesis, Iqbal was somewhat critical of an excessive use of rationalism (in matters of faith) which Syed had championed. Iqbal explained that this did not mean he (Iqbal) was advocating irrationalism but that too much rationalism in this context could create cleavages within a larger (but varied) community of people with a shared religious history. To him, excessive rationalism impedes members of a community from enriching

---

[44] LA Sherwani: *Writings, Speeches and Lectures of Iqbal* (Iqbal Academy, 2005)
[45] Ibid.

themselves through the exchange of differing cultural behaviors (within the community).

Though Iqbal was highly appreciative of the fact that Syed's endeavors had put so many Muslims in schools, colleges and universities, he lamented that these Muslims had submerged themselves too much in European values which contradicted those present in their (Indian) culture and religion (Islam). Iqbal believed that this had uprooted them from the collective history of their own land and community. In a way, Iqbal was lauding Khan's reformist spirit and modernist outlook; but at the same time lamenting that those Muslims who had been rescued from religious obscurantism and social stagnation by Khan's deeds, had thoughtlessly hurled themselves to the other side of the divide which was populated by western ideas, which, to Iqbal, were 'alien' to the cultural make-up of the Muslims.

Iqbal then turned his attention towards the ideas that had opposed Khan's reformist, rationalist and modernist propensity. He agreed that the Muslims of India were part of a larger global Muslim community, but believed that this idea was being upheld by men who wanted to retain a stagnant and dogmatic status quo. Iqbal maintained that the only way Muslim distinctiveness in India can be realized was through a jolting rejuvenation of Islam and the 'ethical education of the Muslim masses.'[46] He wrote that this duty was in the hands of 'half-educated religionists' and regressive clerics (*mullahs*)[47]. He wanted this obligation to be snatched away from them and put in the hands of the new Muslim man[48] which he was out to create.

---

[46] M Abbas (ed.): *The Muslim Community – A Sociological Study* (Maktab-e-Aliya, 1983) p.28
[47] Ibid. p.29
[48] The author's own interpretation of Iqbal's idea of *Khudi* which is discussed in the following pages.

Cobwebs of religious dogma and obscurantism on the one side, and a blind adherence to European ideas and values on the other, had to be done away with. Doing this would be the new Muslim man – a kind of a Muslim *Übermensch*[49] who was morally and politically strengthened by a self-affirmation that can inspire collective action. The self-affirmation was to be gained from self-realization and/or a firm and clear realization of one's inherent ethical and spiritual strengthens buried underneath the weight of ignorance and materialistic distractions. Iqbal called it *khudi* – or informed individualism. *Khudi* was clearly inspired by the study of the ego by German philosophers such as Nietzsche and Hegel; but Iqbal presented it as an attribute which did not lead to selfishness and conceit, but to the spiritual and intellectual blossoming of a human being, and, consequently, of the community he was a part of.

The idea first appeared in its matured form in Iqbal's 1915 book, *Asrar-i-Khudi* (The Secrets of the Self). In it he asserted that God had created man and blessed him with *khudi* so that he is fit for the role of being His vicegerent on earth. The new Muslim man was thus unable to agree to or create a sense of nationhood which did not include his community's cultural distinctiveness. And for a Muslim, this also meant the inclusion of Islam as a political impulse, and not just a label. The new Muslim man's purpose was to discover his *khudi* by demolishing the torpors of obscurantism, dogmatism and inertia. He was then to inspire *khudi* in his community, which, in order, would inspire the community to turn itself into a polity driven by a dynamic, ever-advancing Islam. This process will lead to the creation of a powerful nation of forward-looking and motivated Muslims who would be able to convincingly and effectively challenge

---

[49] German for 'Overman', Superman, Superhuman, Hyperman, Hyperhuman - a concept in the philosophy of Friedrich Nietzsche.

European colonialism, economic exploitation, and western ideas, which, to Iqbal, had become 'morally bankrupt.'[50]

Iqbal, though, never shied away from confessing the impact certain European philosophers had on him. What's more, in dealing with the western idea of parliamentary democracy, Iqbal suggested that it (democracy) was 'a political ideal in Islam.'[51] Nevertheless, he lambasted the way the West had been practicing it, making it depend more on weight and numbers at the expense of individualism and talent.

So what was the new Muslim man to do, since he was supposed to also reject the ideas and institutions of kingship, monarchy and clergy? Iqbal wrote that the self-realized and rejuvenated Muslim polity should elect a national assembly made up of members who were well-versed in both Islamic as well as modern (secular) sciences, laws and philosophies. Such an assembly will make sure that the spiritual as well as political and economic interests and issues of the polity are advanced and resolved according to the progressive and dynamic spirit of its faith, and a consensus (*ijma*) is reached which is representative of the whole community.

Iqbal was a thorough idealist; a glorious romantic in the guise of an ideologue and a reformist. His new Muslim man was to be an unprecedented presence in the Muslim universe. This new man was to offer a bold challenge – to the 'morally bankrupt' but ubiquitous ideas of the modern western man; to the dogmas and intransigent attitude of the old Islamic man; and even to the ascetic disposition of the Muslim spiritual man (Sufi). Yet, much of Iqbal's own thinking revolves around abstract concepts and ideas of the human psyche. But he insisted

---

[50] JL Esposito's entry Contemporary Islam in *Oxford History of Islam* (Oxford University Press) pp.649-650.
[51] Ibid.

that they were sprouting from physical historical events and currents, especially those related to Muslim history. And even though his new Muslim man was to be a thoughtful being who had overcome religious dogma and the indoctrination of 'alien ideas' to realize his full intellectual and spiritual potential, he was to be an entirely social entity, capable and willing to positively interact with society.

Yet, the process one had to go through to spark his *khudi* and become the new Muslim man, in essence, is a metaphysical pursuit. Thus, the new Muslim man is a mystical being, but one who rejects the more established and traditional routes of mysticism. It replaces it with one which expresses itself as a more extroverted and even political countenance. The new Muslim man realizes his potential through intellectual introspection but wasn't introverted or cut off from society. To Iqbal the whole idea of the annihilation of the ego in Sufism (*fana*) was detrimental to the pursuit of discovering *khudi*. The ego was vital to the new Muslim man because he had transformed it into becoming a vivacious and constructive force of life, instead of a one-dimensional urge which led to conceit.

Iqbal was a staunch individualist. After had suddenly dropped out of the Khilafat Movement, he was visited by a leader of the movement who found Iqbal relaxing on a sofa and smoking a hookah. The leader complained: 'We read your poems and go to jail. But here you are, enjoying a smoke?' Iqbal casually replied: 'I am the nation's *qawaal*.[52] If the *qawaal* begins to sway with the crowd and gets lost in a trance, then the *qawaali* is over.'[53]

---

[52] A person who sings the Sufi devotional music, the qawaali.
[53] Zafar Anjum: *Iqbal: Life of a poet, philosopher and politician* (Random House, 2014)

So the question is, would the new Muslim man, who too had to be a radical individualist, change course once he had sparked the creation of a whole community of people driven by *khudi*? He has to continue to stand out; to not become part of the crowd, even after he had left them swaying. This paradox does not seem to bother Iqbal because to him the realization of the *khudi* was an incessant process which one had to continue adding to and evolve. This is also why he was critical of ancient Islamic scholars such as Al-Ghazali (1058-111 CE), and Ibn-e-Taymiyah (1268-1328 CE)[54], who had cautioned against the dangers of philosophy because too much of it might lead one to start indulging in heretical, even, irreligious thoughts. Iqbal wrote that Islam was not opposed to Philosophy because the Quran urged believers to reflect upon God's creations and to peruse knowledge for the sake of it.[55] Iqbal did not see Islam as a 'block universe'; instead he saw it as a process of continual actualization.[56]

Iqbal and his new Muslim man was to reconcile faith with the realities of the now and the here. Like Syed Ahmad Khan, Iqbal too was a steadfast advocate of interpreting the scriptures according to the realities of the day. To him, the Quran was a dynamic work which was not fixed in any particular period of time, but, instead, could be 'reconciled to the environment which humanity finds itself in.'[57] He lamented that the quality of Islamic scholarship in the Muslim world was unable to dynamically and imaginatively interpret the scriptures according to the realities of modern times.[58] Iqbal's ideas were highly

---

[54] Majid Faruky: Philosophy and Theology in *Oxford History of Islam* p.297
[55] Ibid.
[56] Ibid.
[57] M. Iqbal: *The Recreation of Religious Thought in Islam* (ed. M. Saeed Shiekh) p.2
[58] SA Wahid Mu'ni: *Maqala-e-Iqbal* (Lahore, 1963) p.54-55

complex and iconoclastic. And even though these ideas did ruffle feathers in various sections of the conservative *ulema* community, their (the *ulema's*) anger towards him was not as pronounced as it had been against Syed Ahmad Khan.

Dr. M Khalid Masud in his essay, *Iqbal's Reconstruction of Ijtihad*[59], noted that Syed Ahmad Khan had used the word 'reformation' to explain his ideas which had made the conservatives believe that he was somewhat changing the doctrines of Islam. Iqbal, on the other hand, consciously used the term 'reconstruction'[60] which did not carry the same negative perception (in the minds of the *ulema*). Both Khan and Iqbal were urging the Muslim community to modernize and evolve Islamic theology. But whereas Khan was trying to mold and shape the Muslim community as an enlightened cultural and economic entity, Iqbal was doing the same but also attempting to further transform it into becoming a distinct political polity.

Iqbal's passion to rejuvenate all aspects of Islam remained a constant. But he wasn't immune to often change his mind and ideas. He fell in and out with pan-Islamism; with the secular Turkish republic of Mustafa Kamal; and with modernism as well as orthodoxy. At one point he was fascinated by communist ideologue and scholar, Karl Marx, and at the same time admired Italy's fascist leader, Mussolini. Then he ended up denouncing both.

Throughout his career as a prolific poet, philosopher and author, Iqbal kept broadcasting the need to demolish all which he believed was keeping Islam and Muslims pressed down inside the nadirs of dogma, superstition and myopia; yet he could not reconcile to the fact that the open-minded thinking he was professing in matters of faith also meant that India's patriarchal

---

[59] p.5
[60] Ibid.

society should have no qualms about letting women go to schools and colleges. But Iqbal believed women should only be trained to become 'good mothers.'[61]

Dr. Masud wrote that 'while the conservative Muslim critics find Iqbal departing radically from tradition; Western scholars criticize him for his conservatism.[62] Iqbal tried to reconcile and then merge intellectual rationalism with religious emotionalism.[63] Looking to transform the Muslim community into a distinct polity, Iqbal, unlike Khan, was not repulsed by politics. He was a prominent member of the Muslim League who often contested elections. In December 1930, while speaking at a Muslim League convention in Allahabad, Iqbal finally announced what he expected the Indian Muslim polity to do. He urged the creation of a separate Muslim state within the Indian British Empire. But even more interesting is how he explained this state's ideologically:

(This state) for India means security and peace resulting from an internal balance of power; (and) for Islam, an opportunity to rid itself of the stamp that Arabian Imperialism was forced to give it, to mobilize its law, its education, its culture, and to bring them into closer contact with its own spirit and with the spirit of modern times.[64]

This is a remarkable statement which was increasingly downplayed during the rise of the divergent narrative of Pakistani nationalism. The statement clearly suggests that Iqbal saw the Indian Muslim polity to lead the way in rejuvenating

---

[61] I S. Sevea: *The Political Philosophy of Muhammad Iqbal* (Cambridge University Press, 2012) p.180

[62] Ibid. p.181

[63] Dr. Amna Afreen: *The Reformers of Islam* (University of Karachi, 2013) p.206

[64] AIML Allahbad session, 1930.

Islam according to modern times, and, in the process, neutralize the impact of 'Arab imperialism' on it.

Genius provides lucidity and a brilliant clarity, but at the same time it plagues a person with some startling contradictions. This is what genius is about and most geniuses in history actually went on to celebrate this dilemma by describing it as a testament to their dynamic and ever-evolving thinking. So did Iqbal. Bestowed with a powerful mind, an equally powerful style of writing and a rich imagination, Iqbal was not a recluse. His physical make-up was robust and his disposition, restless. This saw him marry thrice but end up lamenting that most of his spouses were mediocre and forced upon him by circumstances. He would often visit Lahore's red light districts[65] and was extremely fond of music.[66] When some clerics pointed out some of his contradictions and asked where he stood, he wrote:

Iqbal bhi Iqbal sey aga nahi hai ...[67]

(Even Iqbal does not know who Iqbal is)

****

The Map Man

Iqbal was one of the first prominent Muslim figures to envision a separate homeland for the Muslims of the region. But it was one Chaudhry Rehmat Ali who coined the word, Pakistan. Not much else is mentioned in Pakistani text books about Rehmat Ali. He is presented as a one-hit wonder, someone who came up with the name, Pakistan. He then just simply vanishes from the pages of official Pakistani text books.

---

[65] Ayesha Jalal: *Self and Sovereignty* (Sang-e-Meel, 2002) p.166
[66] Ibid.
[67] Ibid.

In June 2015, while going through a pile of books at a second-hand bookstore in Karachi's Boat Basin area, I came across a grubby thin publication called The Fatherland of Pak Nation. This book which I ended up buying was a 1956 reprint of a 1934 pamphlet authored by Rehmat Ali. It is a fascinating read. More so because it can actually help one understand the intellectual (and maybe even psychological) disposition of a vital character in the history of the making of Pakistan; but someone who never managed to get more than a paragraph or two in most Pakistani text books. The mentioned book reproduced a 1934 pamphlet that Rehmat Ali wrote when he was a student in England.

In it, Ali outlines a theory which recommends that Muslims of India should be working towards carving out their own sovereign homeland not only because a Hindu-majority India was detrimental to the political, cultural and economic interests of the Muslims, but also because such a homeland already existed across various periods of history. After the creation of Pakistan in 1947, many religious parties picked up Rehmat Ali's idea and began to claim that the seeds of Pakistan's creation were first sowed by the invading forces of Arab commander, Mohammad Bin Qasim in the early 8th century CE.[68] But Rehmat Ali's imagined history actually went back even further.

To him, the separate homeland in the region that he was musing about first emerged during a period of time which he calls 'The Dawn of History.' Though he doesn't attach any date or year to this, but with the help of a self-drawn map, he explains how the civilizations which first emerged on the banks of the Indus River (in present-day Pakistan) and those which sprang

---

[68] S. Akbar Zaidi: *Continuity and Change: Socio-Political and Institutional Dynamics in Pakistan* (City Press, 2003) p.55

around the banks of River Ganges (in present-day India) were somewhat culturally different.

But to Rehmat the 'dawn' fully appears in the 8th century when the Arab Umayyad Empire extended its reach into Sindh, a largely arid region situated on both sides of the Indus. This he also explains with the help of a map. The Sindh part on the map is labelled as 'Pakistan.' Then follow 12 more maps in the book covering various periods from the 8th to early 20th centuries. The area that Rehmat Ali called Pakistan, expands and shrinks, enlarges and then contracts again across the Delhi Sultanate, the Mughal era, and the early British period, all the way up to 1942 (which was still some 8 years away from the year the pamphlet was first published).

The last of these maps in the book is titled 'The Pak Millat, 1942'. The Pak Millat constitutes all of what is Pakistan and Bangladesh today; and pieces of Muslim-majority areas in central and north India which Ali calls 'Usmanistan', 'Farooqistan', 'Siddiqistan' and Haideristan.' Rehmat Ali's style of writing is almost frantic, impulsive, and that of an alarmist, informing the Muslims of India that a Pakistan or 'Pak Millat' that he was purposing is already out there and needed to be reclaimed. So, in a way, instead of actually propagating a new Muslim homeland, Rehmat Ali was asking the Muslims to reclaim areas that had always been their domain for centuries.

When Rehmat Ali first published his pamphlet, he was largely ignored by Muslim political leaders and intellectuals in India. Some even saw him as being an overexcited youth lost in the haze of political fantasies, if not being an outright crank.[69] Muhammad Ali Jinnah, when he saw Ali's maps, described them

---

[69] Raja Afsar Khan: The Concept, Vol: 26, Issue 1-6 (2005). P.27

as 'ravings of a student.'[70] Jinnah was still very much interested in maintaining a united India.[71]

Though the word which Rehmat Ali had coined eventually managed to stir the imagination of thousands of young Muslims, its inventor was soon at loggerheads with most Muslim leaders. Jinnah saw the name as a throwaway anomaly, and an impulsive invention of certain students.[72] In a 1943 speech, Jinnah told a crowd in Delhi that before 1940 the word Pakistan had been used more by the Hindu and British press than by the Muslims; and that it was actually imposed upon the Muslims by these two communities.[73] However, in the same speech, Jinnah announced that he will embrace the word because now it had become synonymous with Muslim struggle in India.[74] Rehmat Ali had met Jinnah in 1934, only days after he had authored the pamphlet. But Jinnah, after noticing the restive and impulsive nature of the young ideologue, told him: 'My dear boy, don't be in a hurry; let the waters flow and they will find their own level.'[75]

Jinnah's unruffled disposition ran against Rehmat Ali's impulsive and volatile personality. Ali remained in England during most of what became to be known as the 'Pakistan Movement;' and even after the creation of a Pakistan which he had first theorized in his explosive pamphlet in 1934, Rehmat Ali arrived in the new country almost a year after its formation in 1947. He vehemently criticized Jinnah and his party (the Muslim League) for

[70] Alyssa Ayres: *Speaking Like A State: Language & Nationalism in Pakistan* (Cambridge University Press, 2009).p.124
[71] Safdar Mahmood: *Pakistan: Political Roots & Development* (Oxford University Press, 2000). pp.27-28
[72] KK Aziz: *Rehmat Ali: A Biography* (University of Michigan, 1987).
[73] Alyssa Ayres: *Speaking Like A State: Language & Nationalism in Pakistan* (Cambridge University Press, 2009).p.124
[74] Ibid
[75] Dalip Hiro: *The Longest August: The Unflinching Rivalry Between India & Pakistan* (Nation Books, 2015) p.57

compromising the 'full idea of Pakistan' and getting only a portion of what he had envisioned[76] (in his pamphlet). Though Jinnah too was not satisfied with what he got, he had decided to make the best of whatever he had managed to acquire. But Rehmat Ali continued to deliver his scathing criticism. After Jinnah's demise in 1948, Prime Minister Liaquat Ali Khan, lambasted Ali and ordered him to leave the country. Rehmat returned to England, feeling bitter. He was living a life of a recluse in Cambridge when in 1951 he fell sick and was shifted to a nursing home.[77]

Here he passed away in his sleep. He was 55. He was buried in a cemetery in Cambridge in an unmarked grave. The grave was finally marked 26 years later in 1975.[78] Rehmat Ali ended up becoming nothing more than a footnote in the history of Pakistan — a country that he claimed had existed since the 'dawn of history.'

[76] KK Aziz: *Rehmat Ali: A Biography* (University of Michigan, 1987).
[77] Ghazi Mujahid: Last Days of Rehmat Ali (DAWN, 23 March, 1981).
[78] Ibid

CHAPTER 4

THE HAPPENING: SYNTHESIZING THE MATTER AND SOUL OF MUSLIM NATIONALISM IN INDIA

The All India Muslim League was a moderate Muslim party which was largely pro-British and also an advocate of Hindu-Muslim unity, as long as the region's Muslim community was treated as a separate polity requiring certain special legislative concessions, and maybe even a distinct state of its own within the larger Indian federation.

Jinnah's reentry into politics in 1936 and his elevation as the League's leading man saw him pulling the party staunchly towards a more centrist position. From here he gradually and more strongly began to define India's Muslim community as a distinct cultural and political entity. At the end of the Second World War, Britain's hold over its colonial territories was weakening and it was finally decided by the colonial regime that an election should be held so that a government of Indian political parties be formed which could then work with the British towards providing India self-governance.

The federal and provincial elections of 1945-46 became vital for the League. Its stature and membership had grown after

Jinnah's reentry, but it was still not sure whether it was being taken as the only major political mouthpiece of India's Muslims. Apart from the Indian National Congress (INC), which refused to accept the League as a major Muslim party, various radical Muslim outfits and mainstream Islamic parties too disputed the League's claim of being the only serious representative of the Muslims of India. The League had also to convince the British if it had to make them accept the League's central urge and demand of creating a new homeland for Muslims (within or without the Indian federation).

But exactly what was the League now asking for? Years later, Pakistan's original nationalist narrative explained the League's demand as a call to build a separate homeland for the Muslims of India because of their cultural differences with the Hindu majority. This was, of course, derived from the League's open call for Pakistan during the 1945-46 election. However, what gets entirely missed today is the fact that the League was envisioning a separate country which, though, having a Muslim majority, would also become home to India's other minorities (such as Sikhs, Christians, Zoroastrians, Buddhists, etc.) and certain 'oppressed groups' (such as lower-caste Hindus).

A number of lower-caste Hindus (especially in the Bengal) had joined the League.[1] It was in Bengal (during the 1946 election) where the League's leaders talked the most about forming a separate country in which there will be no discrepancies made on the bases of caste and creed and where those communities which were in a minority in India and those Hindu groups who were being 'exploited and oppressed by the higher-caste Hindus' would be treated fairly and granted every

[1] PS Ghosh: *Migrants, Refugees and the Stateless in South Asia* (SAGE, 2016) p.71

opportunity to follow their cultural and economic aspirations without any discrimination.

The League in this respect was responding to INC's accusations of it (the League) being a Muslim communal party. The INC had positioned itself as a secular-nationalist outfit. Though it was largely popular among the Hindus of the region, it also had in its fold many prominent Muslim leaders. Many of these INC Muslims were Indian nationalists who had been active as pan-Islamists during the Khilafat Movement. The INC also had the backing of mainstream Islamic parties such as the Jamiat Al Ulema-i-Islam Hind (JUIH) and the more radical Islamic groups such as the Majlis-i-Ahrar-i-Islam (Ahrar). These groups dismissed the League's claim of being the sole representative of India's Muslims and also its call for a separate Muslim-majority state because they (the Islamic groups) considered the League to be made up of 'fake Muslims' (even 'apostates')[2] hell-bent on trying to disperse the unity of the Muslims of India.

As mentioned earlier, even till the early 1940s, the leadership of the League wasn't quite sure exactly what its status was among the sizeable Muslim minority of India. In 1944, Jinnah, while talking to reporters in Bombay, was lamenting that even though his opponents in INC were doing much to undermine the League's influence among the region's Muslims, more damage in this context was being done by certain Muslim politicians and outfits.

Confessional religious parties such as the JUIH and radical outfits such as the Ahrar were staunchly opposed to the creation of a separate Muslim homeland. These groups believed that every Indian's first goal should be independence from the

---

[2] M Asghar Khan: *Islam, Politics and the State* (Zed Books, 1985) p.172

British. They believed that the Muslims of India were a significant minority (approximately 30 per cent at the time) and (thus) would be in a position (after independence from the British) to carve out a more powerful political, economic and cultural role for themselves in India. They also claimed that the League's Muslim Nationalism was a construct based on the European idea of the nation-state and that Islam cannot be confined within the boundaries of geo-political nationalism.

The League had performed poorly in most elections held in India's Muslim-majority provinces. Bengal and Punjab had the largest Muslim populations. Though by the 1940s the League had managed to make important inroads in Bengal, the party had been routed in Punjab in the elections held there in the 1930s. During the 1945-46 election, the INC's aim was to win a majority in most provinces so it could press its claim to form a government at the centre. The League's goal was to win the polls in Muslim majority provinces so it could not only claim to be the largest Muslim party, but also assert its demand of carving out a separate state from areas where the Muslims were in a majority.

The situation in the Punjab was tricky. Even though 57 percent of Punjab's population was Muslim, the League had badly lost the previous elections in this province. Another defeat in Punjab was guaranteed to deal a decisive blow to Jinnah and his party's claims and demands. The Congress understood this well and went all out to defeat it in the Punjab. The province was under the electoral dominance of the Unionist Party — a large outfit mostly headed by Muslims belonging to the landed gentry and influential *pirs* (Muslim spiritual leaders). The party also had some wealthy Hindu leaders in its fold. The Unionist Party was an entirely secular outfit, but was overtly elitist with much of its financial muscle being provided by powerful Muslim landlords[3] in concert with the interests of the equally powerful *pirs*.

In the last major election in the province (in 1937), the Unionists had won 95 seats (out of a total of 175). Congress had bagged 18 whereas the League had managed to win just one seat. To guarantee another thrashing of the League in the Punjab, INC's ace strategist, Sardar Patel, and the party's foremost Muslim leader, Maulana Abdul Kalam Azad, immediately went about constructing an airtight anti-League arrangement.[4]

The INC, apart from contesting the election from its own platform (of Indian Nationalism), was also backing the Unionists in areas where the latter was expecting a tough fight from the League. Patel dispatched a check of Rs 50,000[5] (a hefty sum in those days) to Azad whose job it was to fund and co-ordinate with anti-League groups such as the JUIH and the Ahrar. The Ahrar enjoyed support among Punjab's Muslim petty-bourgeoisies. It along with JUIH provided the INC with fiery clerics who went around denouncing the League as a party of 'British agents,' and 'fake Muslims'. The Unionist Party on the other hand claimed that it alone was the true representative of Punjab's Muslim majority. Jinnah, who had till then been repulsed by populist political tactics, met with the Punjab League's President, Khan of Mamdot, to chalk out a strategy to

---

[3] S Toor: *Cultural nationalism and moral regulation in Pakistan, 1947-1971* (Cornell University, 2005) p.102

[4] KS Hassan *The Punjab Muslim League and the Unionists* (Ushba Publishing, 2005) pp.156-157

[5] Azad to Patel, 21 Oct. 1945, Durga Das (ed.), Sardar Patel's Correspondence (Ahmedabad: Navajivan Publishing House, 1972), II: 24-25. The funds allocated by Patel were only for the Muslim candidates and Muslim constituencies; "For the non-Muslim candidates, the province must make its own arrangements", he told the local leaders.

counter the ruckus being raised by the INC with the help of the Unionists, the Ahrar and the JUIH.

Mamdot's men first brought in hundreds of members of the League's student-wing, the All India Muslim Students Federation (AIMSF) from various parts of India. These also included members of the AIMSF's women's wing.[6] College and university students (both male and female) belonging to the AIMSF were dispatched across the Punjab in groups and asked to hold small rallies in the cities, villages and towns of the province.

They were to explain the League's manifesto as a fight against economic exploitation and a struggle to create a separate Muslim nation-state where there will be economic benefits for all and religious harmony. To counter the fiery denouncements being issued by members of the Ahrar and the JUIH, the League managed to win the support of a breakaway group of JUIH leaders who had disagreed with their party's policy of siding with the INC. [7] Led by Islamic scholar, Alama Shabir Ahmad Usmani[8], this batch of JUIH renegades successfully began to counter the theological arguments (against a separate Muslim nation-state) being leveled by the anti-League clerics and *ulema*. The pro-INC clerics and *ulema* had accused the League of 'misguiding the Muslims of India' and working to keep the Muslims under the influence of the forces of exploitation. The pro-League clerics retaliated by accusing the Ahrar and other such outfits of being INC agents [9] who were working to keep the Muslims 'under the thumb of India's Hindu majority.'

---

[6] S Mujahid: Elections in Pakistan: Punjab's Pivotal Role in *Pakistan Vision* Vol.2 p.4
[7] Ibid.
[8] Ibid.
[9] Ibid. p.5

The League was also armed with a rather radical manifesto. Another (last minute) attainment that Jinnah and his party managed to achieve was the support of the influential *pirs* of the province. Punjab's *pirs* had been associated with the Unionist Party, but just as the elections drew near, many of them were convinced by the League's leadership to switch sides. The *pirs* in turn convinced some Unionist leader to join the League as well.[10]

The voter turnout was high on the day of the polls. The Unionists were expected to win the bulk of the seats, followed by the INC. But the results shocked the INC and the Unionists. The League managed to win 73 seats (out of 175). The Unionists could only bag 20. The INC won 51 and the Sikh Akali Dal, 22.[11] The Ahrar failed to win even a single seat. The League bagged the largest share of the total Muslim vote (65pc). Just 19pc of the Muslim votes went to the Islamic parties.[12] However, INC, the Unionists and the Akali Dal managed to form a wobbly coalition government in the Punjab, the League finally managed to augment itself as India's largest Muslim party. The League also did well in two other Muslim-majority provinces. It won 113 (out of 230) seats in the Bengal, and 27 (out of 60) in Sindh. The results fast-tracked the party's demand for a separate state. And after winning the provincial election in another Muslim-majority region, the NWFP (in early/mid-1947), the party finally managed to carve out Pakistan from the rest of India (August 1947).

****

---

[10] S Mujahid: Elections in Pakistan: Punjab's Pivotal Role in *Pakistan Vision* Vol.2 p.5
[11] Ibid. p.6
[12] Ibid.

The Diminutive Ideologue on Jinnah's Left

The League had performed dismally in the two elections that were held in the Punjab in the 1930s. Desperate to bag widespread support for the League in the province, Jinnah agreed to a suggestion made to him by Mumtaz Daultana — a leading member of the party in the province. Daultana recommended that certain sympathetic Muslim ideologues belonging to the Communist Party of India (CPI) be drawn into the League's fold. The CPI had exhibited support for the League and saw the party as being revolutionary (as opposed to communal); and that it was more in a position to carry out radical reforms and policies compared to the INC.[13] CPI termed the INC as being 'counter-revolutionary.'

As policy, the CPI politburo had decided to encourage the party's Muslim members to join the Muslim League as a way to navigate its ideological orientation. It was an unambiguous infiltration ploy by the communists[14] who were vehemently opposed to the INC and British colonialists. Nevertheless, to Daultana, the CPI men had the experience and the skill to organize the League in the Punjab and successfully disseminate its message and appeal. Jinnah agreed.[15]

In 1944, after getting the go-ahead from Jinnah, Daultana brought in a few CPI ideologues who immediately joined the League in the Punjab. One of them was a slightly-built but high-strung lawyer called Danial Latifi. Latifi was born in Lahore and had travelled to Oxford University in England to

---

[13] Markus Daechsel: *Politics of Self-Expression: The Urdu Middleclass Milieu in the mid-20th Century India & Pakistan* (Routledge, 2006) p.44

[14] Ibid

[15] Ibid

study law. After returning to India, he joined the CPI. He was one of the most vocal members in the CPI to advocate that the party supports the League. In 1944 he joined the Punjab chapter of the League.

A committed Marxist, Latifi urged the League to draft a strong message that could immediately get the attention of the Muslims in Punjab. As a result, Daultana asked him to author the party's manifesto.[16] Latifi did that. The manifesto was approved by Jinnah in 1944. It's a remarkable piece of writing in which Latifi tries to undermine claims made by the INC and the Islamic parties which were opposing the League. In this pursuit, Latifi wedded ideas of Muslim economic advancement (through meritocracy) to Mohammad Iqbal's idea of 'spiritual democracy.' According to the manifesto, the League would promote policies that would benefit and encourage the enterprising economic spirit of the Muslim middle-classes, and at the same time protect the Muslim masses from the oppression of the Hindu, Muslim and British Colonial elites. Latifi also expressed the League's idea of a Muslim state as an organ that would eventually transcend and resolve religious differences in the region[17] because (according to the manifesto) a Muslim-majority state (or a state constructed by a minority community in India) was inherently more equipped to appreciate religious plurality, harmony and diversity than a state dominated by a large Hindu majority. Furthermore, Latifi envisaged the League's idea of the state as something that had a soul. According to him, the state in the suggested Muslim-majority country 'will be the alter-ego of the national being,

---

[16] Shalini Sharma: *Radical Politics in the Punjab* (Routledge, 2009) p.108

[17] Sharif Mujahid: 1945-46 Election and Pakistan: Punjab's Pivotal Role (University of Punjab).

and in good time the two would merge to form an ordered and conflict-free society.'[18]

Latifi's manifesto was put at the frontlines of the League's campaign during the 1946 provincial election in the Punjab. Latifi used CPI's contacts in the province's student and peasant communities and this helped the League to successfully organize its own organs within these communities. Consequently, on the eve of the 1946 election, the League had been dramatically turned into a robust and populist party that went on to win the election.

Ironically, Latifi, who was a passionate supporter of Pakistan's creation, and whose manifesto was an instrumental document behind the League's victory in Punjab, did not migrate to the new country. He stayed back in India. Later he was constantly asked why, but he always refused to answer this question.

Latifi was a good friend of famous Indian writer, Khushwat Singh. In fact, one of the main characters in Singh's celebrated novel about India's partition (1956's *Train to Pakistan)* is largely based on Latifi. Singh described Latifi to be a man who ate very little but who was always absorbed in his own thoughts and just could not stop talking about Marxism.[19] Latifi married a Syrian Christian woman and after Pakistan's creation he remained in India and began to study Islamic law. He quit politics and became a prominent lawyer representing trade unionists, leftist activists and working-class Muslims.

After his first wife passed away, he married Pakeezah Begum — a descendant of the last Moghul emperor.[20] Latifi

---

[18] Markus Daechsel: *Politics of Self-Expression: The Urdu Middleclass Milieu in the mid-20th Century India & Pakistan* (Routledge, 2006) p.80
[19] Kushwat Singh: *Truth, Love & A Little Malice* (Penguin Books, 2003) p.99
[20] Ibid

passed away in 2000 at the age of 83. Some believe he visited Pakistan on a couple of occasions, but kept his visits private. There are also those who claim that he never visited Pakistan. But none of them seem to know why he stayed back when he had been such a fervent advocate of the creation of a separate Muslim-majority state.

Even more curious is how the man who almost single-handedly authored the League's manifesto which won it an election that became the catalyst for the creation of Pakistan, went missing from almost all history books in the new country. There is little or no mention of him in Pakistani text books. Maybe this is due to the fact that he was a communist and that almost immediately after coming into being, Pakistan had become an ally of the US-led anti-communist pacts? The fact that Latifi had decided to stay back in India may also have contributed to his absence in Pakistani text books.

****

The Outsiders, Inside

Over the decades so much has been written and discussed about exactly what sort of a country the founder of Pakistan, Muhammad Ali Jinnah, envisioned. One of the reasons why this debate is still raging is because Jinnah passed away just a year after the country's inception in 1947. In the decades which followed Jinnah's demise, numerous theories and claims have been aired by historians, intellectuals and politicians about what Jinnah wanted Pakistan to evolve into.

One side has insisted that he wanted a progressive Muslim-majority state where the state would devise and then infuse into the society a modern, democratic spirit of Muslim nationalism, but where matters of faith and the state would be kept separate from each other.[21] The other side suggests that though the founder was largely 'Westernized' in his habits, he eventually grew into becoming a leader who strived for a separate Muslim country which could then be evolved (through legislation) into becoming an 'Islamic state'.

Both sides liberally dig out and air assorted quotes attributed to Jinnah in this regard. And the truth is, apart from certain sayings of the man which have been clearly concocted, many quotes do strengthen the arguments of both the sides! This is the other reason why this debate has continued to mushroom without reaching any consensual conclusion. Nevertheless, the response to the question, 'what kind of a Pakistan Jinnah was envisioning', may more convincingly be found well outside of complex intellectual debates, and, certainly, away from the awkward agitprop battles which continue to rage between the two views.

An answer can be extracted by simply studying the make-up and mindset of the country's first ever federal cabinet. In her book, *The Federal Cabinet of Pakistan*, professor of history, Naumana Kiran Imran, provides the names of the men who constituted Pakistan's first federal cabinet. More interestingly, she uses the archived minutes of the meetings of this cabinet to explain what these men were discussing during the initial days of the country.

She informs that Section 17 of Pakistan's interim Constitution which was framed and adopted by the country's first Constituent Assembly, gave the powers of appointing the cabinet to Pakistan's governor-general, Muhammad Ali Jinnah. Thus, the country's first cabinet (headed by Prime Minister Liaquat Ali Khan) was entirely picked and constituted by Jinnah.

---

[21] Jinnah's address to the country's first Constituent Assembly in August 1947 in which he insisted that in Pakistan, religion and faith would be kept apart.

Formed on Aug 15, 1947, the cabinet initially had eight ministers. Names of two of these ministers stand out in the much polarized Pakistan of today: Zafarullah Khan (Minister of Foreign Affairs & Commonwealth Relations), and Jogendra Nath Mandal (Minister of Law). Khan was a member of the Ahmadiyya community, which, 27 years later in 1974, and on the demands of the religious parties, was outlawed as a Muslim sect by the populist regime of Z.A. Bhutto. A highly respected diplomat, Khan has been an often-discussed man by Pakistani historians because he was from the Ahmadiyya community and yet one of Jinnah's closest colleagues.

In the early 1940s, when Jinnah was trying to form a broad-based coalition to bolster the fortunes of the Muslim League, he was asked by some of his potential non-League allies to declare the Ahmadis as non-Muslim.[22] In May 1944, during a press conference in Kashmir, Jinnah said to the gathered pressmen: 'who am I to call a person non-Muslim who calls himself a Muslim.'[23] It is now a well-documented fact that Jinnah insisted on Khan becoming the country's first foreign minister.

The case of the other stand-out minister in the first cabinet has, however, largely been forgotten. Mandal was a Hindu from Bengal. He belonged to a scheduled caste of Hindus in India and had joined the League believing that in Pakistan his caste would be able to flourish more than it would in an India dominated by higher caste Hindus. Mandal became a member of the League in 1943 and mustered the support for the party among Bengal's scheduled caste Hindus in the important 1945 general and then the 1946 provincial elections in India.[24]

---

[22] Y L. Hamidi: *Jinnah: Myth and Reality* (Vanguard Books, 2012)
[23] Usman Ahmad article (DAWN, June 18, 2016).
[24] Faisal Devji: *Muslim Zion: Pakistan as a Political Idea* (Hurst, 2013) p.176

On Aug 11, 1947, when Pakistan's first Constituent Assembly chose Jinnah as Governor-General, Jinnah asked Mandal to chair the assembly's inaugural session.[25] Ayesha Jalal has maintained that Jinnah did this to physically manifest a portion of the speech which he (Jinnah) delivered in that session, and in which he declared: 'You will find that in course of time [in Pakistan] Hindus would cease to be Hindus and Muslims would cease to be Muslims; not in the religious sense, because that is the personal faith of each individual, but in the political sense as citizens of the State.'[26]

Mandal was gradually isolated after Jinnah's demise in 1948. In 1950 he wrote a long letter of resignation to Prime Minister Liaquat Ali Khan. In it he bemoaned that Jinnah's vision was being undermined by the politicians and bureaucrats, and that the scheduled caste Hindus who had followed his (Mandal's) lead to become Pakistanis were not being treated any better than they were in India.[27] Mandal migrated to India in 1950 and died there in 1968.

****

The Action Man

On July 26, 1943, a young man managed to sneak into the Bombay residence of Jinnah. He was carrying a knife in his front pocket. He calmly asked to see Mr. Jinnah because he claimed he was an admirer of his. Jinnah was reading a newspaper in his bedroom when he was told (by a house help) about the young

---

[25] N Khan: *The Federal Cabinet of Pakistan* (Oxford University Press, 2016)
[26] August 11, 1947, Karachi.
[27] R Chattarjee article in *The Modern Review* Vol.88, 1950 p.347

man's visit. Jinnah put down the newspaper and went out to meet him, cigarette in hand. Watching Jinnah come out, the young man began to rapidly approach him. He also started to curse and abuse Jinnah, as he whipped out the concealed knife and swiftly fell upon him.

According to the July 27, 1943 edition of Bombay daily, *The Tribune*, the house helpers nearby managed to overpower the man and take the knife away from him. The newspaper went on to report that Jinnah got cut a bit on the chin and across his right hand with which he had tried to stop the man from stabbing him in the stomach. The young man was Rafiq Sabir, a member of the radical Khaksar party. Even though the party, led by Inayatullah Khan Mashriqi, insisted that Sabir was not a member of the Khaksar, the League rejected the refutation.

Sabir's connections to the Khaksar were never convincingly proven; but a large number of people believed the League's claims. The main reason for this was the reputation that the chief of the Khaksar party, Mashriqi, had gained over the years. In a 1941 essay, conservative Islamic scholar, Abul Ala Maududi, had described Mashriqi as 'an anarchist'[28]. Maududi had even gone to the extent of describing Mashriqi's thoughts 'like that of a car being driven by a drunk'.[29] Yet, at one point, the Khaksar was passionately being followed by thousands of young Indian Muslims, who had hailed Mashriqi as a 'genius'. By 1940, the Khaksar had become a major thorn in the side of the British colonial government, which threw him in jail.

As a child, Mashriqi was considered a prodigy who excelled in mathematics. He was just 19 when he received a Master's degree from the Punjab University. He then won a scholarship at

---

[28] R Jackson: *Mawdudi and Political Islam* (Routledge, 2010)
[29] Ian Talbot: *Region and Partition* (Oxford University Press, 1999) p.55

Cambridge University in the UK. On his return to India, he was immediately appointed as the principal of Peshawar's Islamia College. He was just 25 at the time. A few years later, he became a civil servant, one of the youngest Muslims to be accepted in the colonial bureaucracy. In 1924, Mashriqi authored his first major book, *Tazkira*. The book is a detailed commentary on the Quran in the light of science; and in which Mashriqi tried to prove that Islam was a 'modern and scientific faith'. The book was nominated for a Nobel Prize, but it failed to win it when Mashriqi refused to translate it into English or in any other European language.[30]

Mashriqi had become vehemently anti-British and began to dabble in Indian nationalism. But he was disappointed by Mahatma Gandhi's passive approach. Mashriqi suggested that the INC and Muslim outfits in India must use more aggressive methods to dislodge the British. In an article, he denounced Gandhi as an 'effeminate leader',[31] and insisted that only through conflict and violence could the Hindus and Muslims remove the British from India. It was for this purpose he formed the Khaksar in 1930. The party was organized on fascist lines, in which the members were given special khaki-coloured uniforms and spades. Regular marches were held in which Khaksar members paraded through the streets with their spades and indulged in voluntary social work.

Mashriqi was an enthusiastic student of the concept of revolutionary conflict. He closely studied the writings of revolutionary ideologue, Karl Marx, and controversial German philosopher, Friedrich Nietzsche. He was also impressed by the rise of fascism in Italy. Soon, Mashriqi became notorious for

---

[30] Nasim Yousuf: *Pakistan's Birth and Alama Mashraqi* (AMZ Publications, 2005) p.323
[31] M A Malik: *Alama Inayatullah Masriqi: A Political Biography* (Oxford University Press, 2000) p.56

actively seeking out violence and conflict. Though influenced by fascism and Marxism (rather, Stalinism), Mashriqi eventually immersed himself in the study of sacred Islamic texts. He concluded that divisions in Islam and the conflict between various faiths were the work of self-serving preachers and politicians, and that all religions carried a singular message: 'civilized unity of mankind.'

To him this message was best served by Islam and for this the Khaksar would attempt to create (through a violent revolution) an 'Islamic government on earth'.[32] Unlike Islamic outfits such as the JI, the Ahrar and the JUIH, the Khaksar supported Jinnah's League when it called for the creation of a separate Muslim-majority state within India. However, in the early 1940s, Mashriqi had had a falling out with Jinnah as well when Jinnah refused to explain the Muslim-majority country which he was demanding as an Islamic state. Jinnah denounced Mashriqi as being 'dogmatic.'

Ironically, Mashriqi was also criticized by the anti-League Islamic parties such as JI and the Ahrar. Both accused him of confusing Islam with communism,[33] and for ignoring the promotion of Islamic rituals. The Khaksar was banned in 1940 by the British after the party got into a violent confrontation with the Punjab government (headed by the Unionist Party and the INC). Mashriqi was jailed. As a response, he offered the British 50,000 Khaksar volunteers to fight for them in the Second World War[34]. The British politely declined the offer.

In 1945 Mashriqi again made peace with Jinnah. After the creation of Pakistan in 1947, Khaksar members helped the Pakistan

---

[32] Ibid.

[33] Nasim Yousuf: *Pakistan's Birth and Alama Mashraqi* (AMZ Publications, 2005) p.117

[34] M A Malik: *Alama Inayatullah Masriqi: A Political Biography* (Oxford University Press, 2000) p.99

government in transporting refugees from Indian Punjab to the newly created country. Mashriqi disbanded the Khaksar in 1949 and formed the Islam League (IL) in Pakistan. With IL he became a vehement opponent of communism. He welcomed Pakistan's 1954 military pact with the US (against the Soviet Union).

But his conflict with the JI and the Ahrar continued. The IL did not take part in the anti-Ahmadiyya movement initiated by the two parties in 1953. In 1955, he offered to merge his party with the Muslim League. The merger could not take place and Mashriqi once again turned against the League. He accused it of not supporting Egypt's Arab nationalist government in its 1956 war against Israel and Britain. In 1958, Mashriqi was in trouble again. Along with another IL leader, Ata Muhammad, Mashriqi was arrested for assassinating the chief minister of West Pakistan, Dr Khan Sahib.[35] Mashriqi was released by a court, but his party was banned. Ata Muhammad, however, remained in jail and was hanged in 1961.

After his release, Mashriqi welcomed the 1958 martial law of Field Marshal Ayub Khan. He was left alone by the Ayub regime as long as he stayed away from doing politics. Mashriqi agreed. In August 1963, he quietly passed away, aged 75. Thousands of people turned up to attend his funeral in Lahore. In a twist of irony, though Mashriqi's party remained banned during the Ayub regime, the Field Marshal issued a glorious tribute of him on the day of his funeral. Many believe that among the heroes of the Pakistan Movement, Mashriqi was an 'anti-hero.' A man unafraid (or unable) to conceal his emotional vulnerabilities and some rather reckless political passions.

---

[35] Ibid. p.vii

CHAPTER 5

BIRTH PANGS: EARLY MODERNIST MUSLIM DISCOURSE IN THE NEW REPUBLIC

How was Muslim nationalism which, in India, had given birth to the creation of a separate country, was to be transformed into a much concerted idea encompassing this country's ideological identity? As we saw in the preceding chapters, Muslim nationalism in India had become a multi-dimensional entity. The one emerging from the writings and activism of Syed Ahmad Khan had explained the Muslims of the region as a separate cultural segment which had been shaped by the 500-year-old Muslim political supremacy in India but at the same time was part of a shared historical evolution of the Muslims elsewhere. To him, the Indian Muslims were to become an enlightened community, regenerated through modern education and a rational reinterpretation of their faith.

Though Khan himself never described himself as a nationalist, yet, while trying to explain and even mold the Muslims of India as a separate cultural community, he did inspire the latter efforts of men who turned this community into becoming a distinct political polity. Khan's scholastic endeavors in this context played a prominent role in the development of Muslim modernism in India which energized the formation and evolution of All India Muslim League (AIML). This modernism was further evolved by the likes of Muhammad Iqbal who tried to fuse it with the other dimension of Muslim nationalism in the region.

The other dimension was one which understood the Muslims of India as being a part of the larger global Muslim community (*ummah*). According to this version, the Muslims (which were India's largest minority group), would be able to thrive more as a separate cultural group and political polity in an independent and democratic India as opposed to the desires of the version which was looking to create a separate Muslim-majority state. The opponents of such a state warned that not only would the creation of this state disperse the Muslims of the region, but also dilute the religious impulse of the Muslims because it (the state) was being demanded by devious secularists.

Proponents of this dimension of Muslim nationalism also had pan-Islamist tendencies and were also more radical in their understanding of Islam. So, rather ironically, the more intransigent and 'fundamentalist' components of India's Muslim nationalism were propagating a united and pluralistic India, whereas as this nationalism's more modernist and 'liberal' version was demanding a separate Muslim-majority country.

Iqbal had rather creatively attempted to resolve this by reconciling the theological, political and cultural modernity of one dimension with the radical and traditionalist conservatisms of the other. But since he had then gone on to string this reconciliation with the demand for a separate Muslim region, he became the go-to-man for the 'fundamentalists' as well after some of them decided to migrate to Pakistan.

Here lies an important component within the tense tussle between the original narrative of Pakistani nationalism and its divergent version (which began to emerge in the 1970s). Iqbal's merger of the two opposing strands of Muslim nationalism was first worked into a political narrative by the League, especially when the party had started to become more populist in tone and action. The party banked heavily on Syed Ahmad Khan and Iqbal's pleas to modernize faith (through a rational reading of the scriptures). Then, especially during the all-important election in the Punjab in 1946 and in the NWFP in 1947, when the League had to attract the votes of the masses in the more rural areas, the League drew inspiration from the other aspect of Iqbal's reconciliation.

For example, in Punjab's urban areas, the League promoted the creation of Pakistan as the formation of a modern Muslim-majority country where the Muslims will be able to rapidly advance culturally, politically and economically and so would other minorities of India, and those Hindu segments who were being repressed by the dominant castes. In the rural and semi-rural areas of the same province, however, the League turned towards the clergy and religious leadership closely associated with the powerful *pirs* of Punjab. These were largely 'Barelvi Muslims'[1] representing the 'folk-Islam' of a majority of India's Muslims. They were theologically opposed to the anti-League *ulema* and clerics who belonged to the Deobandi Sunni Muslim sub-sect. Nevertheless, some prominent Deobandi *ulema* too joined the League[2], thus giving the party the firepower it needed to counter the damning rhetoric of the anti-League firebrands in Punjab's villages and towns.

Most pro-League *ulema* took the rightward route of Iqbal's reconciliation and explained Pakistan as an Islamic entity. They countered the anti-League clergy by simply declaring that voting

---

[1] Ibid.
[2] Ibid.

against the League meant voting against Islam.[3] The modernist and the radical conservative currents in the two versions of Muslim nationalism in India which were reconciled to become a merged entity by Iqbal, had emerged with force during the League's election campaigns in the Punjab and the NWFP. However, soon after the creation of Pakistan in 1947, this fusion did not survive as a whole. Instead it split in the middle and became a matter of contention between the modernists and the conservatives with both claiming to be expressing Iqbal's vision.

In 1946, while talking to British journalist, Doon Campbell, Jinnah was stating that Pakistan was not to be a theocracy but a modern, democratic state.[4] At the same time, a slogan '*Pakistan ka matlab kya, laillaha illalah*' (What does Pakistan mean? It means, there is no God but Allah) was ringing in some towns of the Punjab. The slogan was coined in 1945 by a minor poet, Malik Ghulam Nabi, in Sialkot.[5] Malik was an admirer of Iqbal's writings and ideas; but then so was Jinnah. But whereas Jinnah and most of the League's leadership had admired Iqbal's attempt to reconcile political and social modernity with the traditionalist theological interpretations of Islam, men such as Malik Ghulam Nabi and the pro-League *ulema* responded more to Iqbal's writings in which he had celebrated Islam as a rallying impulse that needed to be expressed passionately. Furthermore, even those clerics and *ulema* who were against the League's idea of creating a separate country but who eventually migrated to this country, began to point at Iqbal's Islamic impulse when they began to demand the 'Islamization' of Pakistan.

---

[3] Haroon K. Ullah: *Vying for Allah's Vote* (Georgetown University Press, 2013) p.60
[4] *Pakistan Journal of History and Culture* Vol.27, 2006. P.164
[5] T Wasti: *The Application of Islamic Criminal Law in Pakistan* (BRILL, 2009)

Jinnah was not an ideologue. He was a sharp politician and an articulate lawyer. Though there is now enough evidence to suggest that he was envisioning Pakistan as a modern Muslim-majority country where the culture would be Muslim but the state was to remain detached from the matters of the faith; he was also conscious of the thin line which separated the idea of a modern Muslim-majority state from that of an emerging theocracy – especially in a region where a Muslim minority had suddenly become a ruling majority.

During a meeting of the League in Karachi in 1947, a man in the audience suddenly got up and interrupted Jinnah's address, shouting, 'we have been telling the people, *Pakistan ka matlab kya, laillaha ilallah.*'[6] Jinnah shot back: 'Sit down. Neither I, nor my working committee, nor the council of the Muslim League has ever passed such a resolution wherein I committed to the people of Pakistan (this slogan). You might have done so to catch a few votes.'[7]

Jinnah passed away in 1948, just a year after the birth of Pakistan. Since he was not an ideologue, he did not leave behind a systematically conceived ideological model of what Pakistan was to be. There were just his speeches and interviews, but which he had delivered and given as a politician and a rather pragmatic one to boot. His political disposition was that of a level-headed and dispassionate parliamentarian and constitutionalist who had begun to appreciate Muslim nationalism as a progressive idea to mobilize and carry the Indian Muslim community into the modern age and towards political sovereignty. Admired by the new country's citizens and intelligentsia, Jinnah's speeches, however, did not seem to figure

---

[6] Ibid.
[7] Islam, Shariat and the Holy Ghost: Ahmad Bashir (Frontier Post, May 9, 1991)

much when the state of Pakistan first began to formulate the whole idea of Pakistani nationalism. Between the creation of Pakistan in 1947 and the late 1950s, not a lot was written on him.

The 1950s were a highly fluctuating period in Pakistan. The country's founding party was constantly ravaged by infighting and unable to address the many economic, ethnic and religious challenges that had sprung up when a minority of India became a majority in Pakistan. Problems in this context were hardly ever tackled by evoking Jinnah's sayings. Instead, the government and the state depended more on the works of Iqbal. This was not only due to the fact that Jinnah was not an ideologue, but also because a narrative which would in the next 30 years replace the original nationalist narrative, had also began to form on the fringes. It too was turning towards Iqbal.

Three intellectuals would come into play in this context, all highly impressed by Iqbal. Two would try to elaborate and evolve Iqbal's aforementioned merger of Muslim modernity with Islamic traditionalism and express it in the context of Pakistani nationalism, and one would go to great lengths to incorporate the pan-Islamist impulse and religious fervour in Iqbal's writings to insist that a Muslim-majority state is inherently inclined to evolve into becoming a theocracy.

****

The Spiritual Scientist

Two prominent religious scholars hailed the contents of the country's first constitution which was authored and passed by Pakistan's Constituent Assembly in 1956. Not only did the constitution declare Pakistan to be a republic, but an 'Islamic Republic.' Yet, the two scholars were at loggerheads with each other. One was Ghulam Ahmad Parvez and the other was Abul Ala Maududi.

As a young man, Ghulam Ahmed Parvez would frequently wondered: why is the unvarying practice of Islamic rituals by Muslims not creating more upright Muslims? He would repeatedly ask why all this ritualism wasn't creating the kind of a society that Islam's holy book talks about. He would often be advised by his elders to keep his inquires to himself. But Parvez continued to study the Quran and other Islamic literature under various religious scholars to look for the answers. He then went on to bag a Master's degree from the Punjab University in 1934.

Parvez was now on his way to becoming one of the most well-informed and prolific Islamic scholars in South Asia. When he migrated to Pakistan in 1947, he rapidly rose to become a prominent figure on the rationalist sides of the Islamic discourse in the country. Consequently, he also became a controversial thinker who would often clash with the traditionalists.

In the 1930s, after mastering the works of some of Islam's leading scholars and texts, Parvez moved towards studying the faith's esoteric strains, such as Sufism.[8] He also managed to strike a friendship with famous poet and philosopher, Muhammad Iqbal, and took him as his mentor. His relationship with Iqbal facilitated the young Parvez to come into contact with Muhammad Ali Jinnah. Impressed by the young man's intellectual energy and prowess, Jinnah asked Parvez to edit an Urdu weekly, *Tulu-i-Islam* — a magazine Jinnah's All India Muslim League had begun to patronize and use to fend off the attacks Jinnah and his comrades were facing from orthodox clerics and anti-Jinnah Islamic parties who had accused him of being a 'fake Muslim'.[9]

---

[8] Khalid Ahmad: *Pakistan Behind The Ideological Mask* (Vanguard Books, 2001) p.129

[9] Akbar S. Ahmed: *Jinnah, Pakistan and the Islamic Identity* (Psychology Press, 1997) p.199

In one of his editorials for the magazine, Parvez claimed that Islam (unlike other monolithic faiths) was not supposed to be an organized religion.[10] He maintained that Islam's holy book is a philosophy that goes beyond rituals and that anything practiced or believed by Muslims that was outside of the holy book was a fabrication.[11] According to Parvez, a majority of Muslim traditions were concocted by those who wanted to portray the faith as being amoral and violent. Parvez had become a prominent 'Quranist'[12] — someone who rejects any Muslim text that is not part of the Quran. Understandably the orthodox clergy and scholarship were not amused.

One of the first cover features to appear in the magazine (under Parvez) was titled, 'Mullahs have hijacked Islam.' In it Parvez lambasted conservative Islamic parties and the clergy as being 'agents of rich men' and enemies of the well-being and enlightenment of common Muslims. He held a sympathetic view of socialism and suggested that that Islam was inherently socialist in nature.

After the creation of Pakistan in 1947, Parvez became part of the Muslim League government but retired in 1956 to concentrate on his scholarly work. In 1961, some orthodox Islamic *ulema* created an uproar of sorts when they accused him of trying to popularize the saying of the Muslim prayers (*namaz*) in Urdu, a language that most Pakistanis understood (unlike Arabic). Parvez denied the accusation, calling it an attempt to confuse his followers. In the 1930s, modern Turkey's founder, Kamal Ataturk, had attempted to introduce prayers and the call for prayer

[10] Sheila McDonough: *The Authority of the Past: A study of three Muslim Modernists* (American Academy of Religion, 1970) p.2
[11] Khalid Ahmad: *Pakistan Behind The Ideological Mask* (Vanguard Books, 2001) p.129
[12] The Voice of Islam Vol: 13, 1965. p.406

(*aazan/baang*) in Turkish.[13] Critics of Parvez claimed that he (Parvez) wanted to repeat the experiment in Pakistan with Urdu.

By the early 1960s, Parvez had also become a close advisor of Field Marshal Ayub Khan[14] and helped Khan's military regime (1958-69) to contextualize its largely secular outlook and idea of Muslim nationalism with the genre of Islamic modernism first ventured by the likes of Sayed Ahmad Khan and then by Muhammad Iqbal. Undeterred by the criticism that was being continuously hurled towards him by religious parties and conservative Islamic scholars, Parvez kept emphasizing and propagating his views through books and lectures.

Throughout his career, Parvez not only managed to invite the wrath of the conservatives from within Pakistan, but in various other Muslim countries as well. For example, in the mid-1970s, his books were banned in several Arab states — especially the UAE and Saudi Arabia, countries that were (and still are) ruled by monarchies which follow the more rigid strands of Islam. Parvez responded to the bans by accusing the Arab monarchies for behaving like ancient Muslim kings who had used 'fabricated religious traditions' to justify their rule and subjugate the people.[15]

Parvez had begun to upset some of his supporters as well. Though the conservative Islamic scholars had continued to lambast him for undermining Islamic traditions,' a few progressive Islamic scholars started to complain that his writing style was coarse and that he was too much in favour of using his interpretations of Islamic scriptures to create a political ideology

---

[13] Shelomo Dov Goitein: *Studies in Islamic History & Institutions* (BRILL, 2010) p.7
[14] Farahnaz Isphahani: *Purifying the Land of the Pure* (Harper Collins, 2015)
[15] *Faith and Philosophy of Islam* (Gyan Publishing House, 2009) p.154

of the left.[16] Parvez's 'leftist' stage lasted till about the late 1970s in which he continued to insist that religious rituals and laws based on 'non-Quranic traditions' were contrary to the revolutionary as well as the rational spirit of Islam's holy book.

From the late 1970s onward his views had begun to move away from his Islamic interpretations of leftist ideologies. This may be due to the fact that with the gradual withering away of popular secular ideas such as Arab Nationalism and Ba'ath Socialism (from the late 1960s onward), a radical Islamic conservatism had begun to make in-roads in the Muslim world. A detailed 1979 essay that I managed to glance through a few years ago (that did not carry a by-line), accused Parvez of being 'pro-West' because he had suggested that modern-day (Western) scientists were closer to the Quran's emphasis on intellectual enquiry than the *ulema* and the clerics. This means that by the late 1970s, Parvez had moved away from contextualizing leftist ideas through Islamic concepts, but he was sticking to Islamic modernism.

Parvez was attacked with shoes in 1978 during a lecture that he was delivering at a function organized by the Mughalpura Railway Workers Union. Some of his supporters believed that his move towards becoming 'pro-West' and 'pro-capitalism' provoked the attack, but a report in Urdu daily, *Nawa-i-Waqt*, quoted some of the participants claiming that the attack was engineered by his conservative opponents. By now, the Machiavellian military man, General Ziaul Haq had become the new ruler of Pakistan (after toppling Z.A. Bhutto's regime in July 1977). But the General resisted the demands of Parvez's opponents to declare him and his followers as heretics. Maybe Zia had already sensed that Parvez was getting old and posed no threat to his (conservative) regime.

---

[16] Ghulam Ahmad Parvez Ki Fikar: Lecture by Ghulam A. Ghamidi, Aug. 10, 1989, Karachi.

In the early 1980s, when Parvez entered the 80th year of his life, he began to rediscover the Sufism that he had first studied in the 1930s. In 1983, he dropped out from the mainstream and decided to visit Makkah to perform the Hajj.[17] He did this by refusing to wear any footwear whatsoever throughout the trip. He is believed to have roamed the streets of Medina barefoot. In spite of the fact that the Zia regime discouraged book-stores from selling his books and Parvez was now too old to give lectures, his previous lectures began appearing on audio-cassettes. But Parvez was slipping into disillusionment. Not only due to the political triumph of the obscurantists that he had battled for over four decades, but perhaps also due to the ultimate failure of his own hectic intellectual project which desired the creation of a progressive Muslim society based on the egalitarian concepts of the holy book and having a scientific temperament. In 1985, suffering from intellectual exhaustion, Parvez quietly died at the age of 83. The news of his death was only briefly reported in the press.

****

A Report on Islamic Modernity

Much has been written and debated about the 1954 'Munir-Kayani Report'. The hefty report was based on an exhaustive inquiry conducted by the Chief Justice of Pakistan, Mohammad Munir, and a Punjab High Court judge, Rustam Kayani. The inquiry was first demanded by Shaukat Hayat Khan, a veteran politician and colleague of Pakistan's founder, Mohammad Ali Jinnah. Hayat had had a falling out with his former associate and Chief Minister of Punjab, Mian Mumtaz Daultana, when, in

---

[17] Hajj is the annual Islamic pilgrimage to Makkah.

1953, violent riots erupted in the Punjab against the Ahmadiyya community. The riots were largely perpetrated by a group of religious parties demanding the excommunication of the Ahmadiyya from the fold of mainstream Islam.

Martial Law was proclaimed in the province and the riots were ultimately crushed by the army. The commotion badly shook the centrist Muslim League government. Hayat accused the Punjab CM, Mumtaz Daultana, of 'engineering' the turmoil in the Punjab to dethrone the then sitting prime minister, Khwaja Nazimuddin.[18] He claimed that Daultana had given the rioters his 'tacit support.' Two government ordinances were issued a few months later, ordering a full inquiry into the causes of the disturbances.

Over the decades, the Munir-Kayani Inquiry Report has often been quoted in the many debates between the country's 'modernist Muslims' and conservatives. The modernists specifically mention the section of the report which suggests that no two Muslim scholars agree upon even a single aspect of the faith. Each had their own interpretations which they believed were the correct ones. This finding was penned by the judges after they had interviewed 117 Islamic scholars from all Muslim sects and sub-sects in the country.[19] The conservatives, however, are critical of the report, claiming that it was biased against them and that both the judges had preconceived notions about the ulema and the clergy.

In his book, *Religious Exclusion in Pakistan*, professor of history and author, Ali Usman Qasmi, writes that more than being just an inquiry into the 1953 disturbances, the extensive

---

[18] AU Qasmi: *The Ahmadis and the Politics of Religious Exclusion in Pakistan* (Anthem Press, 2015) p.72
[19] Anas Malik: *Political Survival in Pakistan: Beyond Ideology* (Routledge, 2010) p.41

report actually took the shape of becoming an elaborate mediation on the evolution of Muslim nationalism and Islamic Modernism in South Asia. The report remarked that Muslim nationalism upon which Jinnah's Pakistan came into being was a moderate and modern entity which was being challenged by those trying to raise a 'religious Leviathan' (totalitarian state) based on an intransigent and rigid understanding of the faith.

Opponents of the report claim that, in 1953, the judges were influenced by the government to 'implicate the ulema' by already 'painting them in a bad light' before the inquiry.[20] By this the critics of the report mean an incident which Ali Usman also details in his book. Right after the military crushed the rioting, famous Islamic scholar, Khalifa Abdul Hakim, penned a pamphlet titled, *Iqbal & Mullahism.* An authority on Islamic texts and also on the writings of Mohammad Iqbal, Khalifa used verses from some of Iqbal's poems and quoted Iqbal's scholarly opinions on the clergy to suggest that the views of the Muslim clerics and many of the *ulema* were contrary to the understanding of the faith of Pakistan's founders. The government published 5,000 copies of the pamphlet and then another 4,500, including an Urdu translation of the text. The government then distributed them free of cost across the Punjab.

Justice Munir was born into an affluent family in Hoshiarpur. After bagging a degree in Economics from college, he passed the bar exam and became a successful lawyer. In 1943, he became a judge of the Lahore High Court. He was well liked by Jinnah. In 1954 he was elevated to the position of chief justice of Pakistan. Munir was a sophisticated, well-read and calm man. In 1958 he went on to back the military coup of Ayub

---

[20] AU Qasmi: *The Ahmadis and the Politics of Religious Exclusion in Pakistan* (Anthem Press, 2015)

Khan and partially influenced Ayub's public disposition as a 'moderate and modernist Muslim'.

Justice Kayani on the other hand was born in a village near Kohat. After his initial schooling at a village school, he was sent to Lahore by his father to further his studies at a college. He did well there and got accepted into the civil service. He then won a scholarship to study at the prestigious Cambridge University in the UK. On his return, he joined law and became part of the judiciary. Kayani was well-versed in English, Persian, Pashto, Punjabi and Urdu, and was a practicing Muslim. Ali Usman informs that though Kayani was regular in his prayers and read the holy book every morning before going to court, he was vehemently against the mixing of religion and politics. In the 1960s, Kayani and Munir drifted apart when, unlike Munir, Kayani opposed the Ayub dictatorship.

Their report's relevance went beyond Pakistan. For example, in an era when Muslim nationalists in most Muslim-majority countries were aggressively trying to merge the concept of their respective nationalisms with modernity, the Munir-Kayani Report was requested to be studied in Iran (during the Shah regime), in Turkey, and in Egypt (during the Arab nationalist government of Gamal Abdel Nasser).

****

The Man who kept Faith in Politics

Abul Ala Maududi is considered to be one of the most influential Islamic scholars of the 20th century. He is praised for being a highly prolific and insightful intellectual and author who creatively contextualized the political role of Islam in the 20th century, and consequently gave birth to what became to be known as 'Political Islam.'[21] Concurrently, his large body of work was also severely critiqued as being contradictory and for inspiring those bent on committing violence in the name of faith.

Interestingly, Maududi's theories and commentaries received negative criticism not only from those on the left and liberal sides of the divide, but from some of his immediate religious contemporaries as well. Nevertheless, his thesis on state, politics and Islam managed to influence a number of movements within and outside of Pakistan. For example, the original ideologues of the Egyptian Muslim Brotherhood organization (that eventually spread across the Arab world), were directly influenced by Maududi's writings.[22] These writings also influenced the rise of 'Islamic' regimes in Sudan in the 1980s, and, more importantly, some of the same writings were recycled by the Ziaul Haq dictatorship in Pakistan (1977-88)[23] to indoctrinate the initial batches of Afghan insurgents (the 'mujahedeen'), fighting against Soviet troops stationed in Afghanistan.

In Pakistan, Maududi is mostly remembered as an Islamic scholar who founded the Jamaat-i-Islami (JI), a right-wing religious party. But he also remains to be a controversial figure here. To the left and liberal segments, he is remembered as the man who was 'used by the United States' (during the Cold War)[24] to undermine leftist and progressive politics in Pakistan; whereas many Islamic parties opposed to the JI once declared him to be a theoretical innovator who attempted to create a

---

[21] Dr. Zakirullah Firdausi: *Political Ideology of Abul Ala Maududi* (Lulu Publications, 2014) p.9

[22] Phillip Jenkins: *God's Continent: Christianity, Islam and Europe's Religious Crisis* (Oxford University Press, 2007) p.129

[23] Husain Haqani: *Pakistan: Between Mosque & Military* (University of Michigan, 2005) p.139

[24] Sarwat Sualat: *Maulana Maududi* (International Islamic Publishers, 1979) p.57

whole new sect in Islam. They coined the word '*Mauduiat*' as a derogatory term[25] to sum Maududi's ideas.

Maududi arrived in Pakistan from India as a migrant and scholar with the ambition to transform what to him was a nationalistic abomination. He wanted to help turn it into becoming a 'true Islamic state' run· on the laws of the *sariah*. Maududi had formed his party in 1941 like a Leninist outfit in which a vanguard of a select group of learned and 'pious Muslims' would work to bring an 'Islamic revolution' and do away with the forces of what Maududi called the modern-day *jahiliya* [26] [27]. To him such forces included socialism, communism, liberal democracy, secularism, and strands of Islam which had emerged after the faith was 'distorted' by some 'modernizers'.[28]

He began to lay down the foundations of what came to be known as 'Islamism' — a theory that advocated the formation of an Islamic state by first 'Islamizing' various sections of the economy and society so that a fully Islamized polity could be built to launch the final Islamic revolution. This was largely a utopian impulse. In the 20th century, the modern-day Islamic Utopia that Maududi was conceptualizing had become the main motivation behind several political and ideological experiments in various Muslim countries. Yet, unlike most of today's Islamic scholars and leaders, Maududi did not emerge from an entirely conservative background.

He did not come raging out of a madrasah swinging a fist at the vulgarities of the modern world. On the contrary, he was

---

[25] Barbara Daly Metcalf: *India's Muslims* (Oxford University Press, 2007) p.203

[26] Barbra Zollner: *The Muslim Brotherhood: Hasan Al-Hudaybi and Ideology* (Routledge, 2009) p.79

[27] *Jahiliya* is an Arabic word used to describe the decadent state of the society in Makkah just before the arrival of Islam in the 7th century CE.

[28] By this he meant the folk Islam that had evolved in South Asia and was popular among the majority of the region's Muslims.

born into a family in the town of Auranganad in colonial India that had relations with the modern Muslim scholar and reformist, Syed Ahmed Khan. Khan had formed the MAO College (later known as Aligarh University) to impart western education to the Muslims of India. This is the college Maududi's father attended.[29] Khan had convinced Maududi's father, Ahmed Hassan, to join the college against the wishes of Maududi's conservative paternal grandfather.

Incensed by the fact that his son had begun to wear 'Western clothes' and play cricket, Hassan's father pulled him out of the college and got him lectured by various clerics and *ulema* on how he was going against his faith by 'being overwhelmed by western lifestyle.' Hassan soon renounced everything that had attracted him at the college and became extremely conservative and religious. When Maududi was born (in 1903), Hassan pledged never to give his son a western education.

So Maududi received his early education at home through private tutors[30] who taught him the Quran, Hadith, Arabic and Persian. At age 12, Maududi was sent to the Oriental High School whose curriculum had been designed by famous Islamic scholar, Shibli Nomani. Apart from teaching Islamic law and tradition to the students, the school also taught Mathematics and English. Maududi then moved to an Islamic college, Darul Aloom, in Hyderabad. But he cut short his college education when his father fell ill and Maududi had to travel to Bhopal to visit him. In Bhopal, the young Maududi befriended Urdu poet and writer, Niaz Fatehpuri.[31]

---

[29] Muslim Education Quarterly Vol: 12, 1994, p.55
[30] Ibid.
[31] Masudul Hassan: *Syed Abul Ala Maududi and his Thought* (Islamic Publications, 1984) p.95

Fatehpuri's writings and poetry were highly critical of the orthodox Muslim clergy, and on a number of occasions various *ulema* had declared him to be a 'heretic.'[32] But Fatehpuri soldiered on and had already begun to make a name for himself in Urdu literary circles when he met Maududi. Inspired by Fatehpuri's writing style, Maududi too decided to become a writer. In 1919, the then 17-year-old Maududi moved to Delhi, where for the first time he began to study the works of Syed Ahmed Khan in full. This led to the study of major works of philosophy, sociology, history and politics by foremost European thinkers and writers.

In one of his articles for a newspaper, Maududi listed the names of those European scholars whose works and ideas he thought had shaped the rise of Western civilization.[33] The scholars that he mentioned in his list included German philosopher, Hegel; British economist, Adam Smith; revolutionary French writers, Rousseau and Voltaire; and pioneering evolutionist and biologist, Charles Darwin.[34] He began to shape a narrative through his newspaper and magazine columns in which he emphasized the need (for Muslims) to study and understand Western political thought and philosophy and to 'master their sciences.'[35] He wrote that one could not challenge anything or anyone that one did not understand.

All this while, Maududi was living the life of a studious young man and journalist who also enjoyed watching films in the newly emerging cinemas of India, and listening to songs. He married an independent-minded girl, Mehmuda, who was

---

[32] Irfan Ahmed: *Islamism and Democracy in India* (Princeton University, 2009) p.53

[33] Dr. Zakirullah Firdausi: *Political Ideology of Abul Ala Maududi* (Lulu Publications, 2014) p.15

[34] Entry on Maududi by Irfan Ahmed in *Princeton Encyclopedia of Islam.*

[35] Ibid.

educated at a missionary school in Delhi, wore modern dresses and owned her own bicycle.[36] She was under no condition to wear a *burqa*.[37] But Maududi did retain some link with his past as the son of a liberal-turned-conservative father. In his quest to revive the lost tradition of Muslim intellectualism, Maududi had also come close to India's main party of Sunni Deobandi Muslims, the Jamiat Ulema-i-Hind (JUIH). He was greatly dismayed by the collapse of the Ottoman Empire in Turkey, and he blamed Turkish nationalists for it. And when Mahatma Gandhi's Indian National Congress (INC) began to talk more aggressively about Indian nationalism, something snapped in Maududi. He had devoured dozens of books on Western philosophy and history, but when the Ottoman Empire was abolished by the Turkish nationalists, Maududi realized he had underrated the power of modern nationalism. This was one European concept he was not too familiar with. Disenchanted by the INC's Indian nationalism and JUH's alliance with the INC, Maududi retreated to the life of a husband who spent most of his time with his family, books, the occasional film and classical and semi-classical songs performed on stage.

In 1938, he bumped into Manzoor Nomani, an Islamic scholar who admonished him for distancing himself from his father's legacy and for not having a beard, and for living the life of a rudderless Muslim.[38] Already disappointed with the way the concept of nationalism was taking root in the minds of the Hindus and Muslims of India, Maududi retired to his library, but this time to study Islam in depth.

---

[36] Ibid.

[37] An enveloping outer garment worn by women in some Islamic traditions to cover their bodies when in public.

[38] Irfan Ahmed: *Islamism and Democracy in India* (Princeton University, 2009) p.54

He remerged with the theory that it wasn't really the greatness of modern Western thought that had been entirely responsible for the rise of European political power; but it was due to lack of conviction of the Muslims to practice their faith in the correct manner that had triggered their fall and made room for European powers to enter their domains and lives. In 1937, he vehemently attacked INC's nationalism, accusing it of trying to subjugate the Muslims of India. By the early 1940s he was being equally critical of Mohammad Ali Jinnah's All India Muslim League and of Muslim nationalism.

He declared the League to be 'a party of pagans'[39] and 'nominal Muslims'[40] who wanted to create a secular country in the name of Pakistan. However, Maududi did decide to leave India and head for a country which to him was an abomination and abode of nominal Muslims and the *jahiliya*. He began his political career in Pakistan in 1949, and it lasted till 1979, when he passed away from illness in a US hospital.

21st century politics in the Muslim world is not according the kind of enthusiastic reception that Maududi's ideas received in the second half of the 20th century. By the early 2000s, almost all experiments based on Maududi's ideas seemed to have collapsed under their own weight. The imagined Utopia turned into a living dystopia, torn asunder by violence perpetrated in the name of faith and triggered by a gradual retardation of social and economic evolution in a number of Muslim countries, including Pakistan.

This is ironic. Because compared to the blinkered mindset which his ideas seemed to have ended up creating within various mainstream regimes and clandestine groups in many Muslim countries, Maududi himself sounded rather broad-

---

[39] Ibid. p.62
[40] Ibid.

minded. Writing in flowing, rhetorical Urdu, Maududi echoed Syed Ahmad Khan by criticizing the Muslim clergy for keeping Muslims away from the study of Western philosophy and science. Maududi suggested that Western philosophy and science were at the heart of Western political and economic supremacy and needed to be studied so they could then be effectively dismantled and replaced by an 'Islamic society'. Here he was echoing the ideas of the pioneering pan-Islamist, Jamaluddin Al-Afghani. Maududi often castigated the *ulema* for 'being stuck in the past'[41] and thus halting the emergence of new research and thinking in the field of Islamic scholarship. In this context, he was reiterating Iqbal. Maududi was equally critical of modernist Muslims (including Pakistan's founder, Mohammad Ali Jinnah). He lambasted the modernists for understanding Islam through concepts constructed by the West[42] and for advocating that religion was a private matter.[43]

In a series of books, Maududi laid out his precepts of the modern-day 'Islamic State'. He was adamant about the necessity to gain state power to implement his principles of an Islamic State, but cautioned that the society first needed to be Islamized from below (through evangelical action) for the a state to begin imposing Islamic laws from above. He was the first Islamic scholar to use the term 'Islamic ideology.'[44] The term was later rephrased as 'Political Islam' by western scholarship on the subject.

---

[41] Abul Ala Maududi: *Come, Let Us Change This World* (Islamic Publications, 1980).
[42] Ibid
[43] Ibid
[44] Reinbard Scbulze: *A Modern History of the Islamic World* (I.B. Tauris, 2002) p.118

In 1977 when Maududi agreed to support the Ziaul Haq dictatorship in Pakistan, he was criticized for attempting to grab state power through a Machiavellian military dictator. Maududi's decision sparked an intense critique of his ideas by the modernist Islamic scholar, Dr Fazal Rehman Malik. Dr Malik described Maududi as a populist journalist, rather than a scholar. Malik suggested that Maududi's writings were 'shallow' and crafted only to bag the attention of muddled young men craving for an imagined faith-driven Utopia.[45]

Maududi's body of work is remarkable in its proficiency and creativity. And indeed, it is also contradictory. He used Western political concepts of the state to explain his idea of the Islamic State; and yet he accused modernist Muslims of understanding Islam through Western ideological constructs. He saw no space for monarchies in Islam, yet was entirely uncritical of conservative Arab monarchs.

Truth is, there was not one Maududi, but many. Elements of Leninism, Hegel's dualism, Afghani's pan-Islamism and various other modern political theories can be found in Maududi's thesis.[46] Perhaps this is why Maududi's ideas managed to appeal to various sections of society. From the urban Muslim middle-classes to modern conservative Muslim movements, all the way to the more militant reactionaries. But the question is, had Maududi been alive today, which one of the many Maududis he would have been most comfortable with in a Muslim world now crammed with raging dystopias?

****

---

[45] Fazalur Rhaman Malik: *Islam and Modernity* (University of Chicago Press, 1982)
[46] Entry on Maududi by Irfan Ahmed in *Princeton Encyclopedia of Islam.*

The Mu'tazilite in a Suit

Today the state of Pakistan, especially one of its sturdiest institutions, the military, is trying to rapidly alter its ideological make-up. The move is seeking a gradual departure from the mindset which drove and defined the country's military establishment for over three decades. Ever since the late 1970s, a concentrated effort was made by the dictatorship of General Zia to change the supposed 'Anglicized' nature of the armed forces and transform it into becoming an 'Islamic' one. And even though religious symbolism in times of war was often used by the institution in the past, under Zia, such symbolism became a mainstay, along with the state-backed proliferation of devout ritualism within the armed forces, achieved through allowing the wholesale entry of both political as well as apolitical evangelical outfits into the barracks.

The military's character was successfully transformed, and it was this transformation which was perceived to have made the institution stronger and more influential in the region. This largely misappropriated perception encouraged its continuation, despite the fact that it clearly began to struggle in finding relevance in a world where the Cold War had ended, and the Soviet Union had collapsed.

Its relevance then completely eroded in the post-9/11 world. What's more, the aforementioned perception had created a collective ego which soon began to challenge its own architects. The architects had settled for holding the perception as is, but the ego now wanted it to evolve even further. This ego's desire to do so now meant a war not only against the 'infidels', but against the state and society as well.

So what the Pakistan military establishment today is attempting to do is to construct a brand new narrative which could replace the one that has failed to find relevance in the post-9/11 scenario, and has in fact, become a major thorn in the side of the Pakistani state and polity. But it will require a strong new ideology as well, especially in a country whose polity and military have been heavily indoctrinated to understand Pakistan as an 'ideological state'. Part of the answer to this may lie in an interesting period of Pakistan's history. That period constitutes the Ayub Khan regime (1958-69). Much can be learned from it about what to do and what not to, in the context of what the military is now attempting to achieve.

Ayub Khan imposed Pakistan's first Martial Law in 1958 with the backing of an all-powerful president, Iskandar Mirza. Mirza and Ayub blamed rising corruption, a spiraling economy, and political chaos as reasons for the Martial Law. Both then went on to describe the 1956 Constitution as 'the selling of religion for political gains'. The Constitution had renamed the country, 'Islamic Republic of Pakistan'. Mirza and Ayub changed it to Republic of Pakistan. Both were of the view that Pakistan was created as a modern Muslim-majority state by Mohammad Ali Jinnah and not a theological entity.

Mirza was ousted by Ayub just 20 days after the coup, and Ayub became the president in 1959. Ayub's coup was a popular one. This gave him the leeway to aggressively deflect (through policy) all he thought was detrimental to a young country. He was allergic to leftists (who he believed were anarchic and disruptive expressions of progressive thought); and religious outfits repulsed him[47] (who he accused of being backward, archaic and ill-informed about Islam).

In a 1960 speech, Ayub claimed: 'Pakistan was not achieved to create a priest-ridden culture but it was created to evolve an

---

[47] R M. Sharma: *Representations of Gender, Democracy and Identity Politics in South Asia* (Sri Satguru Publications, 1996) p.42

enlightened society ...' He then added: 'In fact, it is a great injustice to both life and religion to impose on 20th century man the condition that he must go back several centuries in order to prove his credentials as a true Muslim ...'

In *Political & Social Transformation*[48], Dr. Anita M. Weiss writes that Ayub believed in a synthesis of modernist and traditionalist interpretations of Islam in order to make it compatible with changing modes of time. Ayub's policies, based on his understanding of Islamic Modernism, were seen as secular and Westernized by the religious parties, especially when he banned polygamy and when the 1962 Constitution formally renamed the country, 'Republic of Pakistan'. Then in 1964, he banned the Jamaat-i-Islami (JI).

But from 1965 onwards, Ayub's regime began to change complexion. This undermined his project of Islamic modernity. Dr. Sarfaraz Ansari gives three reasons for the project's rollback.[49] First, to get re-elected as president in 1965, Ayub allowed his information ministry to co-opt certain *ulema* who were then asked to negatively highlight the gender of his opponent, Fatima Jinnah. Secondly, after the 1965 war with India ended in a stalemate, it adversely impacted the country's economy. Ayub began to lose popularity and increasingly began to use religious rhetoric.

Muslim modernists began to abandon him, while the country's polity, now suffering from a stressed economy, began moving either left (Pakistan People's Party, National Awami Party, Awami League); or right towards religious outfits. Thirdly, by the time Ayub resigned in early 1969, many of his desperate ministers had begun mending fences with religious

---

[48] (Syracuse University Press, 1994) p.412
[49] *Forced Modernization and Public Policy* (Journal of Public Studies, Vol.18, Issue: 1).

outfits (to negate leftist opponents). But all this could not save Ayub's fall. A floundering economy and an attempt to repackage and repaint his stumbling regime with more 'pious' colours only ended up providing his opponents the space to make a re-entry into mainstream politics. The changing disposition of his regime was not very convincing and was seen as nothing more than a desperate ploy of a bemused government.

Nevertheless, before 1965, when Ayub was aggressively pushing forward his modernist agenda, the two men who were attempting to contextualize it through a rational reading of Islam for him were Ghulam Ahmad Parvez and Dr. Fazalur Rehman Malik. The conventional image of an Islamic scholar today in Pakistan is that of a man with a long beard, speaking Urdu in an Arabic accent, or a woman fully draped in a jet black *burqa*. This was not always the case. Dr. Fazalur Rehman Malik was a clean-shaven, lean man. He always looked sharp in his suits and ties. He was extremely well-informed and well-versed in Islamic literature, philosophy and history. At one point in time, he was actually on the verge of almost completely undermining the role of religious parties in Pakistan when he was forced to flee the country.

After studying Arabic at the Punjab University in Lahore, Rehman went to Oxford in the UK for further studies. He was teaching Islamic philosophy at McGill University in Canada when in 1961 he received an invitation from Ayub Khan to come to Pakistan and help him set up the Central Institute of Islamic Research (CIIR). Ayub, though a practicing Muslim who seldom missed saying his daily prayers, was not only averse to civilian politicians, but he also had a great disliking for the clergy. Initially he had fancied himself as a Pakistani Ataturk.[50]

---

[50] Husain Haqqani: *Pakistan: Between Mosque and Military* (Penguin Books).

With the ambition to create a Pakistan driven by his 'benevolent' military dictatorship built on state-facilitated capitalism, and a constitution culled from what he described to be the 'progressive and modernist Islam of Jinnah,' Ayub wanted the CIIR to help him achieve this through legislation. It was the CIIR under Dr. Rehman who advised Ayub to constitutionally curb the religious parties and their interpretation of Islam. Rehman then drew a social and political framework for making Pakistan a 'progressive, modern Muslim-majority state.'

Ayub did not act upon each and every aspect of Rehman's framework, but the workings of the CIIR certainly made the Ayub regime ban the JI in 1964.[51] The decision, however, was overturned by the Supreme Court. But Rehman was not really a fan of secularism. Instead he saw himself and his work to be a modern extension of the 'Islamic rationalism' of figures such as Sir Syed Ahmad Khan, Syed Ameer Ali, Maulana Shibli Naumani, Niaz Fatehpuri and the 9th century Muslim rationalists, the Mu'tazilites.

Rehman suggested that Pakistan, instead of attempting to become a militaristic bastion of Islam, should take the lead in engineering a Muslim polity which, through science and Islamic and secular scholarship, could successfully compete with the economic and technological prowess of the time's two superpowers: the capitalist United States and the communist Soviet Union.

The detailed research papers that the CIIR produced under Rehman's guidance emphasized the application of reason in the interpretation of the Quran, and the absorption of western science, philosophy and economics to help Islam (in Pakistan) survive as a progressive and flexible religion with the ability to

---

[51] Hayman, Ghayur, Khushik: *Pakistan: Zia and After* (Abhinav Publications, 1989) p.22

supplement economic, scientific and cultural progress instead of hindering or retarding society's natural evolution. However, when in a book he suggested that laws and society in Pakistan should be based on a rationalist and modernist interpretation of the Quran, and that Islamic traditions based on hearsay should only play a minimal role, he was fervidly challenged by his more conservative counterparts. The counterparts were also well aware of his advice to Ayub to ban religious parties.

Leading the attack on Rehman was Abul Ala Mauddudi, who demanded that Rehman be expelled from Pakistan and from the fold of Islam.[52] Then, in 1967, during a lecture that Rehman was delivering on Pakistan's then nascent state-owned TV channel, PTV, he suggested that drinking alcohol was not a major sin in Islam. Even though alcohol at the time was legal in Pakistan, the religious parties held a number of rallies against Rehman. Rehman, more or less, was basically repeating what early scholars of the Hanafi School of Islamic jurisprudence had already suggested. And, ironically, some 40 years after Rehman's musings in this context, and 30 years after the sale of alcohol (to Muslims) was banned in Pakistan (in 1977), the highly conservative Federal Shariat Court of Pakistan (FSC) finally decreed that, indeed, consuming alcohol was a minor sin.[53]

On May 28, 2009, the FSC declared that whipping for the offence of drinking was un-Islamic. It directed the government to amend the law (formulated in 1979) and to make the offence of drinking alcohol bailable[54] — even though the last person to be whipped for consuming alcohol was in 1981. In 1969 as Pakistan entered a turbulent period in which a far-reaching political

---

[52] AG Noorani: *Dr. Fazalur Rheman* (Criterion Quarterly, Vol.9, January, 2014).
[53] DAWN, May 29, 2009.
[54] Ibid.

movement led by leftist parties and student organizations forced Ayub to resign, Rehman continued being perused and harassed by the Islamic parties until he was left with no other choice but to leave the country.

He went to the US and distinguished himself as a highly regarded Professor of Islamic Thought and researcher at the University of Chicago. The 1970s and 1980s were also his most prolific years as an author in which he wrote some of the most influential books on modern Islamic thought. He never returned to Pakistan and died in Chicago in 1988.

****

The man who wasn't there

As mentioned earlier, the Ayub regime was repulsed by the politics of the left as well as the right. He had positioned the 'Pakistan ideology'[55] in the middle and/or as a moderate and progressive expression of Islam which was to launch Pakistan as a Muslim-majority state according to the economic and social dictates of modernity. He believed that the leftists were as detrimental to a Pakistan that he was trying to construct as were the conservative religious parties.

On October 31, 2015, during the first phase of the local bodies' elections in Sindh and Punjab provinces of Pakistan, I was going through the many images (of the event) that were being uploaded on my Facebook timeline. Since the populist

---

[55] A term first used in 1962 by Ayub, but it was nowhere in the founders' speeches. The term was also picked up by Jamat-i-Islami (JI) who, however, used it to counter Ayub's version with its own understanding of it. See also The Grand Concoction in *End of the Past*: Nadeem F. Paracha (Vanguard Books, 2016).

Pakistan People's Party (PPP) in Sindh and the centre-right Pakistan Muslim League-Nawaz (PML-N) in the Punjab were clearly sweeping the polls, most of the uploaded pictures were of workers and supporters of these two parties celebrating their big wins in the mentioned elections.

However, as I was flicking through these photos on my iPad, I suddenly came across pictures of two festive gatherings — one in Sindh and other in Punjab. In these pictures more than a dozen or so supporters were carrying posters of a bygone communist activist, Hassan Nasir. Intrigued, I messaged the young gentleman (on Facebook) who had uploaded the pictures. I asked him who the folks in the photos were. The young man was a Sindhi and a student at the University of Sindh in Jamshoro. He told me that he was a member of the Awami Workers Party (AWP) — a leftist grouping of various small Marxist outfits which had merged in 2010.

One of the photos was taken in the city of Okara in the Punjab, and the other in Naseerabad, a town in upper Sindh's Qambar Shahdadkot District. The AWP had won a seat in Okara, so the Okara photo was of young AWP workers celebrating their contestant's victory. The other photo was from Naseerabad where the AWP had won a couple of seats in the election. But I pondered, what was Hassan Nasir (who passed away in 1960) symbolizing in a gathering of a left-wing group in this day and age - 25 years after the demise of the Soviet Union and with it, of communism?

I had first come to know about Nasir when I was a college student in Karachi in the mid-1980s. Posters with his image had continued to crop up during the many movements that had emerged against the intransigent Ziaul Haq dictatorship. At the time, the posters were mostly being issued by left-wing student groups such as the National Students Federation (NSF), and parties such as the Mazdoor Kissan Party (MKP), and also the PPP.

In 1985, a MKP activist had told me that posters of Nasir had even emerged during the 1977 movement against the first PPP government of Z.A. Bhutto (1971-77). Some leftist groups, after being incensed by Bhutto's 'authoritarian personality' and his regime's 'betrayal of its socialist agenda', had joined hands with the right-wing alliance (the PNA) in a bid to topple Bhutto. Bhutto was eventually toppled in a reactionary military coup in July 1977.

Ironically, before this, Hassan Nasir's image had actually first been used on PPP posters during the 1970 election when the party was positioning itself as a socialist alternative to the religious right and the 'capitalist-feudal nexus.' So Nasir's face continued to crop up (as a symbol of defiance) in the early 1970s, the late 1970s, and the early 1980s. It continues to pop up even today. However, unlike Che Guevara (the celebrated Latin American revolutionary who was killed in 1967), and whose image too continues to be used by various protest groups around the world, Nasir's image is yet to get its very own 'post-modernist' makeover by also appearing on coffee cups and on baseball hats!

Hassan Nasir was born into an aristocratic Muslim family in Hyderabad Deccan, India. After finishing school in his hometown, Nasir got admission in UK's prestigious Cambridge University where he came into contact with various young British and Indian Marxists. On his return to India, and against his family's wishes, he plunged into a peasants' uprising against feudal lords and British colonial overlords in the Telangana region. When the movement collapsed after the departure of the British in 1947, Nasir decided to migrate to Pakistan. In 1948, he arrived in Karachi and joined the Communist Party of Pakistan (CPP).[56] His family stayed back in India.

Though just 22 years old at the time, he greatly impressed the CPP leadership with his profound knowledge of Marxism.[57] Soon, Nasir's revolutionary outlook and charisma made him popular among college students, peasants and factory workers in Karachi. In 1954, he was arrested by the government and forcibly flown back to India.[58] However, in 1955, he quietly slipped back in. Since the CPP had been banned in Pakistan in 1954, Punjabi and Urdu-speaking (Mohajir) leftists had begun to join progressive Sindhi, Baloch, Bengali and Pashtun nationalists in the National Awami Party (NAP). In 1957, Nasir was made the party's secretary general in Pakistan's largest city, Karachi. Officially he was an exile in India, but with the help of friends and sympathizers, he managed to operate secretly in Pakistan.

He turned his office into a busy working and planning area for students and trade unionists. His aristocratic background could have easily guaranteed him a rich and comfortable life in Karachi, but he chose to live among laborers in and around the make-shift shanty towns that had sprung up in the metropolis. In 1958 when Ayub Khan launched a military coup, he ordered a crackdown against leftists as well as the religious parties. Nasir went underground. Ayub, while being briefed by Karachi's police chief, lost his cool when Nasir's name came up. He is reported to have lashed out and shouted, 'How is that bloody communist still free?'[59]

---

[56] Daily Times, February 11, 2016
[57] Hasan Abidi quoted in Daily Times, February 11, 2016
[58] Shahid Saeed: Democracy's Martyr (The Friday Times, February 4, 2011).
[59] Jamal Naqvi; Humair Istiaq: *Leaving the Left Behind* (Pakistan Study Centre, 2014)

Nasir's activities and his popularity among the students and laborers had begun to greatly perturb the Ayub regime. Nasir was finally located, hiding in a shanty town in Karachi. He was picked up by the police and then taken in chains to a special cell that had been set-up by the police in Lahore's historical Lahore Fort.[60] Here Nasir was continuously tortured, beaten and refused food and water for days.[61] Then finally, he was slayed in his muggy, tiny cell. He was just 32. The Muslim aristocrat's son who had become a communist rebel was never seen or heard from again.

The press was told that Nasir had died in an accident. The news of his death left his father suffering a breakdown. His mother refused to believe that the body that the police had shown to the press was his. With Nasir's father indisposed, his mother travelled alone to Lahore to reclaim the body. 'This is not my son's body,' the ailing woman shouted and then fell to the ground. She was escorted out by the police and put in a waiting rickshaw.

She returned to India empty-handed. Till this day nobody is quite sure what happened to the young man's body and where is it buried. His father passed away and the family eventually lost its aristocratic status in India. The mother somehow survived his tragic demise till she passed away in the 1990s[62], convinced till the very end that the body which she had been shown was not her son's. Pakistan's leftists consider Nasir to be their first 'martyr'. That's why his face has continued to emerge on posters ever since the 1970s.

'He still symbolizes defiance and clarity of purpose beyond the political cynicism and rightest demagoguery of today (sic).'

---

[60] Tariq Ali: *Street Fighting Years* (Citadel Press, 1987) p.88
[61] Jamal Naqvi; Humair Istiaq: *Leaving the Left Behind* (Pakistan Study Centre, 2014)
[62] Kamal Asdar Ali (DAWN, November 8, 2015)

This is how the young man who had uploaded the pictures described Nasir when he wrote back to me. Well, as long as Nasir (like Che) too doesn't end up on coffee cups.

****

The Angst of Ecstasy

In December 2009 I stumbled upon a book which left me greatly intrigued. I had discovered it at a book store in Karachi. It was lying just behind a book on Stalin that I had originally picked up from the shelf. It looked really old and was called *Labbaik* (I am present). I picked it up and blew away that ubiquitous Karachi dust from its crumbling cover. The book was in Urdu and just had the title and the author's name on it. It was authored by one Mumtaz Mufti. I didn't know who the gentleman was but later discovered that he was a respected short-story writer who had been influenced by famous psychologist, Sigmund Freud. But from the 1960s onward he had become an ardent admirer of Sufism[63] under the guidance of another famous Urdu writer, Qudrat Ullah Shahab. *Labbaik* is about Mufti's maiden trip to Makkah to perform Hajj in 1965. Mufti had written this book when matters of faith in Pakistan had not been completely subjected to various social and political complications. And what a read it turned out to be. Mufti writes that in 1965 (a few months after the end of Pakistan's second war with India) he was suddenly overwhelmed by the longing to perform the Hajj[64]. This surprised him because he was not a very observant Muslim. To him mere ritual had nothing to do with spirituality but he considered the Hajj to be more about spiritual self-discovery than rituals.

---

[63] The mystical strand of Islam.
[64] Annual Muslim pilgrimage to Makkah.

So off he went to Makkah on a Pakistan International Airlines (PIA) flight. With him on the plane were many common Pakistani men and women, all going to Makkah to perform the Hajj. Also on the flight was a group of clerics. Mufti writes that the common folk (and he) were filled with joy but the clerics were all stern-faced, as if lacking souls. 'They have nothing in common with us,' he grumbles.

But over the next few days in Makkah, Mufti's joy eventually evaporates and he is filled with a strange awkwardness and angst. He finds the streets of the holy city echoing with chaos where someone is always trying to sell something or the other. In Mina (where the pilgrims go to hurl stones at 'Satan'[65]), Mufti is struck by an unbearable feeling of anxiety and vulnerability, and overawed by a sense of dread. He doesn't like the people of Mina. He believes they have been living under the shadow of the devil for far too long.

After completing the ritual, he settles in the office of his tour guide. Here he bumps into an acquaintance of his who had travelled to Makkah with his wife. The man begins to complain (to the guide) that a lady who had befriended his wife on the trip can now be seen with a man. 'We don't know who the man is,' says the complainant. 'Can you change our room and give us another room, away from the one where the lady is staying? She is destroying the sanctity of our visit.'

Hearing this, Mufti sees the common Pakistani whom he had praised on the plane for being full of joy and soul, now turning into a stern faced and soulless cleric. 'Let it be, brother,' Mufti tells the agitated man. 'Why are you forsaking the joy of Hajj for something you are not sure of?'

---

[65] Depicted by a set of rugged ancient pillars made of stone.

Whereas much of the book is about how Mufti first differentiates between the common Muslims and the soulless clerics, and then points out how common people too have the capacity to mutate into becoming like the clerics, in the final chapters Mufti is left emotionally ravaged when he realizes that he too is not immune from the traits he is lambasting. This realization is most painful and takes place in a mosque in Makkah where he had gone to offer prayers. While praying he begins to hear voices criticizing him for the way he looks and practices his faith. He turns around but can't figure out where the voices are coming from.

It soon transpires that the voices are emitting from his own head, criticizing him and even complaining how bad he smelled. He tries to ignore them, but is left feeling so agitated that he gets up and runs away. The judge had become the judged. One of the voices had complained how Mufti had the audacity to enter the mosque while smelling so bad. Mufti writes that he began to actually be able to smell himself and was repulsed by the experience.

Back in Pakistan he relates the episode to his mentor, Qudrat Ullah Shahab, and stretches one of his hands out towards Shahab, asking him to smell it. But Shahab could not smell anything. Mufti suggests that the smell was symbolic of the stench of hypocrisy that he smelled on others but was now himself engulfed by; and that moral judgments made by a mere mortal like him plague the human soul with something that the person in question will not like and will hide from, but continue to be repulsed by for the rest of his life.

CHAPTER 6

STATE OF FLUX:
ADVENT OF THE PAKISTANI NATIONALIST
DEBATE IN THE PUBLIC SPHERE

Paralleling the start of the celebrated students' movement in the United States and Europe which began taking shape in 1964-65, the spark in Pakistan in this respect was set alight by the aftermath of Pakistan's 1965 war against India. The official media (radio and press) had thumped in a skewed perception of the war, proclaiming that the country's armed forces had dealt India a hard, decisive blow.

But when the Soviet Union brokered a peace treaty between the two warring countries in the former Soviet city of Tashkent, the opposition political parties in Pakistan claimed that 'Pakistan had lost on the negotiation table what its forces had won on the field.'[1] There were demonstrations against the treaty by various student groups. These student activists would go down in history as the 'Tashkent Generation.'[2]

---

[1] Philip E. Jones: *The Pakistan People's Party-Rise to Power* (Oxford University Press, 2003).

[2] *Student Politics in Pakistan-A Celebration, Lament & History*: Nadeem F. Paracha (IWrite Journal, 2009)

The commotion also triggered a rather robust intellectual epoch in the country's history. Polemical debates flared up between the Islamic parties and those on the left. The Islamic outfits and leftist forces had managed to come to the fore with the decline of the Ayub government. At the core of the debate was the question, what it meant to be a Pakistani and/or what was Pakistan as a state and polity?

The religious groups suggested that the people should strive to turn Pakistan into an Islamic state because it was on the basis of Islam that the country had separated from the rest of India. To the Jamat Islami (JI), for example, the story of Pakistan began not during the Pakistan Movement, but with the invasion of Sindh by Arab commander Muhammad bin Qasim in the 8th century CE, who had defeated the region's Hindu ruler, Raja Dahir. On the other hand, Sindhi scholar and nationalist, G. M. Syed declared that to the Sindhis, Muhammad bin Qasim was the usurper and Raja Dahir the hero.[3]

However, one of the most captivating narratives to come out of the aforementioned debate emerged in 1967. A hybrid ideology called 'Islamic Socialism' started to become popular among many young Pakistanis and left-leaning intellectuals. Though not entirely indigenous to the region (South Asia), this ideology was adopted by the Pakistan People's Party (PPP), a party formed in December 1967 by Z A. Bhutto.

Bhutto was a bona fide politician. The idea of forming his own party was first suggested to him by a Marxist ideologue, J A. Rahim.[4] Both decided to form a leftist party to challenge the Ayub regime which they accused of promoting 'crony

---

[3] Ishtiaq Ahmed, *State, Nation and Ethnicity in Contemporary South Asia* (Continuum International Publication, 1998) p. 284

[4] Phillip E. Jones: *The Pakistan People's Party: Rise to Power* (Oxford University Press, 2003) p.109

capitalism.'[5] Almost immediately, three tendencies emerged in the PPP. A radical left-wing - led by an assortment of socialists, Leninists and Maoists - advocated a revolutionary 'people's movement' for the implementation of direct democracy; radical land reforms; and widespread state ownership of major industries. The right-wing of the party that was dominated by 'progressive' members of the landed elite and some 'liberal' Islamic elements, advised gradual reforms and the democratic demarcation of the provinces based on language and ethnicity. Between these two wings was a moderate faction dominated by a group of intellectuals calling themselves, 'Islamic Socialists.'

Bhutto had described himself as a social democrat[6] who held a sympathetic view of socialist ideologies. But he also prided himself as being a passionate Pakistani nationalist. When religious parties began a concerted campaign against the PPP – accusing the party of being dominated by communists out to destroy the Islamic fabric of the country's society [7] - Bhutto turned towards the party's Islamic Socialists to counter the onslaught.

The Islamic Socialist group in the party was being led by intellectual, poet and politician, Hanif Ramay. Ramay and a group of scholars had been formulating Islamic Socialism as a political theory ever since the 1950s.[8] And it is this expression which Bhutto chose to counter his critics with on the religious right, and to explain the PPP's left-leaning economic program. Ramay and his group were not exactly the originators of this term. It had already been used in the region before Pakistan's creation and also

---

[5] Ghulam Kibria: *A Shattered Dream: Understanding Pakistan's Underdevelopment* (Oxford University Press, 1999) p.50

[6] Ponna Wignaraja, Akmal Hussain: *The Challenge in South Asia* (United Nations University Press, 1989) p.227

[7] Piloo Modi: *Zulfi My Friend* (Thomson Press, 1973 [first edition]) p.166

[8] Phillip E. Jones: *The Pakistan People's Party: Rise to Power* (Oxford University Press, 2003) p.223

elsewhere in the Muslim world. What Ramay can be credited for is his attempt to mold it in the context of Pakistan and then in the context of the PPP's political and economic programs. Islamic Socialism was explained (by the PPP) as a fusion of modern socialism and the Quranic concept of egalitarianism.

In his various writings on the subject, Ramay was of the view that one of the very first expressions of such a fusion appeared in Russia in the late 19th and early 20th centuries.[9] A movement of Muslim farmers, peasants and petty-bourgeoisie in the Russian state of Tatarstan opposed the Russian monarchy, but was brutally crushed. In the early 20th century, the movement went underground and began working with communist, socialist and social democratic forces operating in Russia to overthrow the monarchy. The leaders of the Muslim movement which came to be known as the Waisi,[10] began describing themselves as 'Islamic Socialists'[11] when a revolution broke out against the Russian monarchy in 1906.

During the 1917 Bolshevik Revolution that finally toppled and eliminated the Russian monarchy, and imposed communist rule in the country, the Waisi fell in with the Bolsheviks and supported Russian revolutionary leader, Vladimir Lenin's widespread socialist program and policies. However, after Lenin's death in 1924, the Waisi began to assert that the Muslim community and its socialism in Tatarstan were a separate entity compared to Bolshevik communism.

The movement that had formed its own communes became a victim of Stalin's radical purges of the 1930s and was eventually wiped out. One is not quite sure how the Waisi defined their

---

[9] Islamic Socialism: An Ideological Trend in Pakistan in the 1960s (The Muslim World, Vol.65, Issue: 3, 1975) pp.1-3
[10] Ibid.
[11] Ibid.

socialism in a country where (after 1917) atheism had become the state credo. It was left to a group of influential thinkers and ideologues in South Asia and the Middle East to finally give a more coherent and doctrinal shape to this ideological fusion. It emerged an off-shoot of Islamic Modernism.

****

Green Men, Red Dreams

Islamic scholar, Ubaidullah Sindhi, who was born into a Sikh family (but converted to Islam) in Sialkot, was a vehement agitator against the British in India. Hunted by the authorities during the First World War, Sindhi escaped to Kabul, and from Kabul he travelled to Russia where he witnessed the unfolding of the 1917 Bolshevik Revolution. He stayed in Russia till 1923 and spent most of his time studying socialism and discussing politics with communist revolutionaries. Though impressed by the chants of economic equality and social justice during the revolution, Sindhi dismissed communism/Marxism's emphasis on religious non-belief.

From Russia, Sindhi travelled to Turkey and it was in Istanbul that he began to give shape to his ideas of Islam and Socialism in a series of writings aimed at the Muslims of India. He urged Muslims 'to evolve for themselves a religious basis to arrive at the economic justice at which communism aims but which it cannot fully achieve.'[12]

The reason he gave for this was that despite the fact that he saw both Islamic and communist economic philosophies similar vis-à-vis their emphasis on the fair distribution of wealth,

---

[12] Dr. Shaukat Ali: *Islam and the Challenges of Modernity* (Quaid-e-Azam University, 2004) p.301

Sindhi believed that socialism, if imposed with the help of a more theistic and spiritual thrust, would be more beneficial to the peasant and the working classes (in South Asia) than irreligious communism.

During the same period (1920s-30s), another (lesser known) Islamic scholar in India got smitten by the 1917 Russian revolution and Marxism.

Hafiz Rahman Sihwarwl saw Islam and Marxism sharing four elements in common:[13]

1. Prohibition of the accumulation of wealth in the hands of the privileged classes.
2. Organization of the economic structure of the state to ensure social welfare.
3. Equality of opportunity for all human beings.
4. Priority of collective social interest over individual privilege.

The motivation for many of these themes Hafiz drew from the Quran, which he understood as seeking to create an economic order in which the rich pay excessive profits through voluntary taxes (*Zakat*) to minimize differences in living standards. In the areas where Hafiz saw Islam and communism diverge was in Islam's sanction of private ownership within certain limits, and in its refusal to recognize an absolutely classless basis of society. He suggested that Islam, with its prohibition of the accumulation of wealth, is able to control the class structure through equality of opportunity.

---

[13] Islamic Socialism: An Ideological Trend in Pakistan in the 1960s (The Muslim World, Vol: 65, Issue: 3, 1975) pp.1-3

Building upon the initial thoughts of Sindhi and Hafiz were perhaps South Asia's two most ardent and articulate theoreticians of the fusion of Islam and Socialism: Ghulam Ahmed Parvez and Dr Khalifa Abdul Hakim. Parvez was a prominent 'Quranist'[14] or an Islamic scholar who insisted that for the Muslims to make progress in the modern world, Islamic thought and laws should be entirely based on the modern interpretations of the Quran. Parvez maintained that Muslims should spend more time studying the modern sciences[15] instead of wasting their energies on fighting ancient sectarian conflicts or ignoring the true egalitarian spirit of the Quran by indulging in multiple rituals handed down to them by ancient *ulema*.

Apart from continuing to author books and commentaries on the Quran, Parvez wrote a number of articles which propagated a more socialistic view of Islam.[16] In a series of essays he used verses from the Quran, incidents from the faith's history, and insights from the writings of Muhammad Iqbal to claim:

- The clergy and conservative *ulema* had hijacked Islam.
- They are agents of the rich people and promoters of uncontrolled Capitalism.
- Socialism best enforces Quranic dictums on property, justice and distribution of wealth.
- Islam's main mission was the eradication of all injustices and cruelties from society. It was a socio-economic movement, and the Prophet was a leader seeking to put an end to the capitalist exploitation of the powerful Quraysh merchants in 7th century Makkah and the corrupt bureaucracy of Byzantium and Persia.

---

[14] The Voice of Islam Vol: 14, 1965. p.406
[15] The Pakistan Philosophical Journal Vol: 23. p.52
[16] Ibid.

- According to the Quran, Muslims have three main responsibilities: Seeing, hearing and sensing through the agency of the mind. Consequently, real knowledge is based on empirically verifiable observation, or through the role of science.
- Poverty is the punishment of God and deserved by those who ignore science.
- In Muslim societies, science, as well as agrarian reform should play leading roles in developing the economy.
- A socialist path is a correction of the medieval distortion of Islam.

Another scholar at the time who was using Iqbal's writings on Islam and the Quran to formulate the Islam-Socialism fusion in South Asia was Dr Khalifa Abdul Hakim. A philosopher, author and admirer of Muhammad Iqbal, Khalifa ventured into the ideological territory of Islam and Socialism a bit later than Parvez. A keen student of Islam (especially Sufism), Khalifa, after getting his PhD from the Heidelberg University in Germany,[17] authored a number of books on Iqbal's philosophy, Islamic thought, Rumi (Sufi poet and writer), and also translated the Hindu holy book, the Bhagavad Gita, into Urdu.[18] It was after the creation of Pakistan in 1947 that Khalifa began to seriously study Marxism and what it meant to a young 'third world' Muslim country such as Pakistan.

In his 1951 book, *Islam and Communism*, Khalifa saw the fusion of Islam and Socialism as a concept that harnesses the freedom of thought, action and enterprise characteristic of Western democracies by creating opportunities for all. Khalifa was basically explaining the fusion to be a kind of a spiritual and

---

[17] The Pakistan Philosophical Journal Vol.23. p.291
[18] Mahavir Singh: Asia Annual (Digitalized version, August 2008) p.8

theistic concept of the welfare state enacted in various Western countries from the 1930s onward. In *Islam and Communism*, Khalifa sees land as being the principle source of economic wealth and thus the moral basis for agrarian reforms in Pakistan.

However, most thinkers discussed above say very little about exactly how much of a role a government and state should play in matters of faith in societies run on the ideology and economic system prescribed by the fusion of Islam and Socialism. But Parvez does clearly suggest that an 'Islamic-Socialist' society run on the laws and economics derived from rational interpretations of the Quran and modern scientific thought would inherently become responsible, law-abiding and egalitarian and would not require the state to play the role of a moral attendant.

In other words, Islamic-Socialist policies would guarantee a progressive (if not entirely secular) Muslim-majority state and polity where the citizens are enlightened enough to make their own moral choices, and where the state sticks to looking after the citizens' economic interests and needs and in delivering justice. Parvez continues by suggesting that the state, however, can induce modernist interpretations of the Quran through verses on property rights, *Zakat*, justice and the rights of women.

Meanwhile, in the Middle East, the Islam-Socialism fusion tendency evolved into becoming a more nationalistic and revolutionary idea, mainly due to the creation of Israel (in 1948) and the expulsion of thousands of Palestinians from the area. A Christian Syrian philosopher, Michel Aflaq, is considered to be the modern originator of the Middle Eastern strain of this fusion which expressed itself as 'Arab Socialism' and 'Ba'ath Socialism.' Born into an Arab Christian family, Aflaq became a communist at college, but broke away from the communists to formulate a radical new Arab nationalist philosophy with another young Syrian, Salah ad-Din al-Bitar.[19]

After studying the economic and political decline of the Arab people, Aflaq and Bitar advocated the creation of a united Arab state. For this they recast Arab nationalism by infusing into it a heavy dose of socialist economic ideas and by evoking the 'Quran's revolutionary spirit' to counter injustice and inequality. Aflaq and Bitar claimed that this would lead to a renaissance in the Arab world, turning it into an economic and political power. Their emphasis on the word 'renaissance' (which in Arabic is 'Al-Ba'ath') gave birth to the term 'Ba'ath Socialism,' and soon both Aflaq and Bitar set out to define exactly how this form of socialism worked.

Ba'ath Socialism appealed to the unity of all Arab nations on the basis of language/culture (Arab) and on the faith which most Arabs followed (Islam). It suggested that the Arab nations were being undermined by five forces:

1. European colonialism (driven by capitalism).
2. Soviet Communism.
3. Decadent monarchies in Arab countries.
4. Religious conservatism within Arab societies.
5. The clergy and the *ulema* who were keeping these societies in the clutches of backwardness.

To Aflaq and Bitar, Ba'ath Socialism offered a path between Western capitalism and Soviet communism by suggesting that all Arab nations come together as one state under a single 'vanguard party' of Arab nationalists who would impose socialist economic policies; modernize society through education and science; and separate religion from the state, but continue being inspired by

---

[19] Sami M. Moubayed: *Steel and Silk* (Cune Press, 2006) p.213

the egalitarian concepts of Islam that would remain to be the faith of a majority of citizens in the united Arab state.

In spite of being secular, Ba'ath Socialism celebrated Islam as a 'proof of Arab genius',[20] and a positive testament of Arab culture. Ba'ath Socialism seemed to have arrived at a ripe moment in Arab history because from 1940s onward, a number of anti-colonial movements in Iraq, Egypt, Algeria, Yemen and Syria were all being led by outfits declaring themselves to be adherents of Arab Socialism. Arab Socialist and Ba'ath outfits came to power in many of these countries too.

The Asian country where the idea and concept of Islamic Socialism managed to seep into mainstream imagination was Pakistan. As mentioned earlier, two of the earliest scholars who had theorized about this concept (in South Asia) were Ghulam Ahmad Parvez and Dr Khalifa Hakim. During the secular military dictatorship of Ayub Khan, a group of intellectuals led by Hanif Ramay emerged in Lahore and began working on giving a more contemporary shape to the ideas of Parvez and Khalifa. The group also weaved in their thesis elements from Ba'ath Socialism in the context of a non-Arab Muslim country such as Pakistan.

The project included the publishing of a monthly Urdu literary magazine called *Nusrat* which, apart from publishing Urdu poetry, short stories, and literary commentaries on the works of Urdu poets and writers, ran pieces on the works of Ghulam Ahmed Parvez, Dr Khalifa and Michal Aflaq. After the 1965 Pakistan-India war ended in a stalemate, Ayub Khan dismissed his young Foreign Minister, Zulfikar Ali Bhutto (for showing dissent). Bhutto befriended a retired bureaucrat and veteran Marxist ideologue, J.A. Rahim, and both decided to form

---

[20] Katherine A. A. Zupan: *Philosophy for Breakfast* (Lulu Publications, 2012) p.76

a populist left-wing party to challenge the Ayub dictatorship. In 1966, Bhutto came into contact with Hanif Ramay who presented him his group's work on Islamic Socialism.

In a series of articles (by Ramay and Safdar Mir) in *Nusrat*, the writers explained (the PPP's) Islamic Socialism to mean:

- Elimination of feudalism.
- Elimination of uncontrolled capitalism and the encouragement of a system based on freedom of opportunity and/or an economic system closely monitored by the government and the state.
- Nationalization of major banks, industries and schools.
- Encouraging the workers to participate in the running of factories.
- Promoting democracy and the building of democratic institutions.

All this was then explained as a modern 20th Century extension of the principals of equality and justice as practiced by the first Muslim regime in Medina and Makkah headed by Islam's Prophet,[21] and of the egalitarian economic and social proclamations found in the Quran. PPP's Islamic Socialism denounced the conservative religious parties and the clergy as being representatives of monopolist capitalists, feudal lords, dictators and 'imperialist forces.'[22] It also accused them of being agents of backwardness and social and spiritual stagnation.

****

---

[21] Islamic Socialism: An Ideological Trend in Pakistan in the 1960s (The Muslim World, Vol: 65, Issue: 3, 1975) pp.1-3
[22] Ibid.

The Woman who would be King

The Ayub regime fell in early 1969, after pressure was exerted on him to resign by his own senior officers in the military when the movement against him had brought the country to a standstill. He handed over the reins of the government to a lumbering general, Yahya Khan. Yahya promised to hold a general election (Pakistan's first based on adult franchise); and release the students, workers and politicians arrested during the last days of the Ayub regime. The elections were to be held in late 1970.

The years between Yahya's take-over and the 1970 election was a period of a stalemate between three competing nationalist and ideological narratives. The weakest in this context was the one which had been formed during the height of the Ayub regime but had become largely unpopular with the rise of the other two narratives. The religious right had accused Ayub's narrative of being 'secular' and opposed to the idea of an 'Islamic Pakistan'. The religious right's narrative rejected the whole concept of Islamic modernism, terming it a concoction of 'westernized' and elite secular groups whose influence and power were at risk from the creation of an Islamic state. The third narrative which had gained strength during this period had come from the left. This narrative saw Pakistani nationhood and culture as being multi-ethnic and multicultural best served by democracy and socialism.

The country's economy had nosedived and fears of a civil war between the state and Bengali nationalists in East Pakistan were growing. The country's economy had come to a cessation, now being run (or lack thereof) by the dictatorship of a lumbering and idiocentric general. This curious period is best encapsulated by the sudden emergence of an extraordinary and enigmatic woman who rose from being the wife of a conservative man to becoming the most influential person in the Yahya regime – despite the fact that she never held any political office.

Her name was Aqleem Akhtar. In the late 1960s she began being called General Rani (the Queen General). Between 1969 and late 1971, she was considered to be perhaps the most powerful woman in Pakistan. A muse and mistress of Yahya Khan, and often the brains behind the colourful general's regime,[23] General Rani was the person bureaucrats and politicians approached whenever they wanted Yahya's attention and audience.

Born in the Pakistani city of Gujarat into a well-to-do but conservative family, Aqleem was married off to a policeman who was twice her age.[24] For years she played well the role of a good wife, bearing six children and never venturing out of the house without a *burqa*. Then one day in 1963, while holidaying with her husband over the cool hills of Murree, something snapped in her. Walking with her husband among the tall pine trees of the hills, a gust of wind blew the *burqa* from her face. Enjoying the wind softly breezing across her face, it eventually made the *burqa*-flap on her face flounce away. Agitated by her callousness, her husband admonished her. She stopped walking. She stared back at him and then casually proceeded to take off the *burqa* from the rest of her body. Then, after tossing it towards him, she walked away, asking him to wear it himself![25]

She also took the couple's six children with her but struggled to make ends meet when her parents insisted that they would only help her if she went back to her husband. Alone, with six

[23] Frontier Gandhi (Vol:3, Issue 31, 1973) p.10
[24] Aeysha Nasir: Night of the General (Newsline, May 4, 2002)
[25] Ibid.

kids and no job, Aqeel began plotting to get close to influential men. She started visiting those nightclubs in Karachi and other such clubs in Lahore and Rawalpindi which were frequented by the political, military and business elite of the country.[26] Finding the men bored with their wives she began arranging 'dance parties' for them.[27] For this pursuit, she recruited beautiful young women who had run away from their homes after facing poverty and harassment.

It was at a club that was frequented by the country's top military men in Rawalpindi where Pakistan's future dictator, General Yahya Khan, fell for her.[28] A compulsive drinker and womanizer,[29] Yahya began an affair with Aqleem sometime in 1967. But throughout her relationship with Yahya, she kept insisting that they were 'just friends.'[30] Nevertheless, when a movement between 1968 and 1969 forced Ayub Khan to resign as head of state, he installed Yahya Khan as the country's Martial Law Administrator.

It was at this point that Aqleem began being called (in the press), General Rani. It is believed that apart from looking after Yahya's ferocious appetite for whisky and women, she also began 'advising' him on political matters. Those who met her in those days described her to be far more informed and astute in the field of politics than Yahya.

Soon she was being visited by politicians, bureaucrats and military men, some asking her to arrange her now-famous dance parties for them, or get Yahya to meet them or do certain favors for them. One of her 'friends' was also Pakistan's legendary

---

[26] Zafar Iqbal: *Angoor Ka Paani Aur General Rani* (UNews December 16, 2013)
[27] Ibid.
[28] Aeysha Nasir: Night of the General (Newsline, May 4, 2002)
[29] Ali Bhutto Begins To Pick Up The Pieces (TIME, Vol.99, 1972).
[30] Aeysha Nasir: Night of the General (Newsline, May 4, 20

singer and actress, Noor Jehan.[31] She had approached Aqleem after the Income Tax Department had charged her for withholding thousands of rupees worth of income tax.[32]

Noor Jehan asked Aqleem to request Yahya to intervene. Aqleem did. Yahya asked the income tax people to back off[33] and then proceeded to begin an affair with Noor Jehan. Aqleem Akhtar, the woman who had rebelled against her husband's demeaning behavior towards her, and then was left with nothing more than six hungry children and no source of income, became a powerful and rich woman during Yahya Khan's short dictatorship (1969-71).

Her good fortune lasted till early 1972. Yahya, after leading Pakistan into a disastrous war against India and Bengali nationalists in former East Pakistan in December 1971, was disgraced when he was forced by the military and political parties to step down, and then put under house arrest. He died in seclusion in 1980.

Z A. Bhutto's PPP that had won the majority of seats in West Pakistan in the 1970 election took over the reins of power from the military. Bhutto at once began to arrest military men, bureaucrats and politicians who had supported Ayub and Yahya dictatorships. And even though it is believed that Bhutto too was on good terms with Aqleem, he did not hold back and asked the police to put her under house arrest.

During the Bhutto regime (1972-77), Aqleem was constantly shuttled between house arrest and jail. Her cases were challenged in the courts by famous lawyer, S M. Zafar.[34] She was finally

---

[31] Dewan Berindranath: *The Private Life of Yahya Khan* (Sterling Publishers, 1974) p.96
[32] Ibid. p.87
[33] Aeysha Nasir: Night of the General (Newsline, May 4, 2002)
[34] Zafar Iqbal: *Angoor Ka Paani Aur General Rani* (UNews December 16, 2013)

released from house arrest when in July 1977 General Ziaul Haq toppled the Bhutto regime in a military coup. But by then, she had lost most of her wealth and property and was back being a pauper again. In the early 1980s someone advised her to get into a new kind of business that had begun to thrive during the Zia regime: drug smuggling and trafficking.

It is believed that after having a falling-out with some of Zia's men, she was falsely charged for drug trafficking and jailed. She was bailed out by a few friends and the cases against her were quashed at the end of the Zia dictatorship in 1988. All her children had by then been settled, but Aqleem became a loner, living alone and disallowed (by her children) to speak to the media or anyone who was not family. She outlived most of her friends and foes, though. But it was largely a lonely existence. Suffering from cancer in the later days of her life, she quietly passed away in 2002 at the age of 70.

****

A Poet, his Demons and his Dog

In 1969, when Ayub resigned and the eccentric Yahya was at the helm of power, the country hung in a state of nervous limbo. There was a feeling that it was on the brink of something which could cause an unprecedented catastrophe. Lives of two people unfolded quite like the fate of their country from its inception in 1947 till Yahya's take-over in 1969. One was a brilliant Urdu poet, and the other, the sister of the founder of Pakistan, Mohammad Ali Jinnah.

In 2013, while aiding a young cousin of mine in her thesis on the origins of the Pakistani national anthem, I noticed the name Saghar Siddiqui in the footnotes of one of the many books that I was scouring to piece together a historical and political background of the anthem. The anthem's music was composed in 1948[35], a year after the creation of Pakistan. The lyrics, however, did not come till 1952, written by poet Hafeez Jalandhri.[36] This anthem was finally adopted by the state and government of Pakistan in 1954.[37]

The book in which one of the footnotes mentioned Saghar Siddiqui had simply skimmed over the fact that many men and women had attempted to author the anthem between 1947 and 1954. But why I got interested in Saghar's name here was because I knew him to be a famous Urdu poet who died in poverty. That's all I knew about the man, apart from a few verses from the poems that he wrote and which, over the years, were shared with me by some friends.

After coming across his name in the book, I did manage to recall some verses of his, especially this one: '*Dil mila aur gham shanaas mila/phool ko aag ka libas mila/ Har shanaawar bhanwar main dooba tha/Jo sitara mila udaas mila*' (Bestowed with a heart that is conversant with misery/a flower got a garment of fire/Every swimmer was shackled and drowned by the whirlpool/ Every star that I met was sad ...).

This amateurish English translation does not do justice to the melancholic imagery present in these lines. What was a poet known for his bleak imagery and utter heartbreak up to by once wanting to write the national anthem of a country where he would eventually die in poverty? Though Saghar's work is now easily available, there is precious little

---

[35] Raza Rumi: *Delhi By Heart :Impressions of a Pakistani Traveler* (HarperCollins, 2013) p.77
[36] Stacy Taus-Bolstad: *Pakistan in Pictures* (Twenty First Century Books, 2003) p.69
[37] Ibid.

information about the man himself, apart from some old newspaper clippings about his demise and some hastily authored biographies of the man.

Interestingly, in 2014 when I was in Islamabad for a media conference, I was introduced to a gentleman who I was told was the son of a cousin of Saghar's. The gentleman was a retired bureaucrat but was well versed in Urdu poetry. I almost immediately asked him about Saghar's ambition to author the anthem. According to the gentleman, Saghar came from a well-to-do middle-class family in the Indian town of Ambala. He was a prodigious lad who began writing poetry as a child. He was 19 when he migrated to Pakistan (in 1947) and settled in Lahore.

The sensitive and gifted teenager was excited by the prospect of becoming a citizen of a newly created country. He at once got down to writing a national anthem for it. Though he failed to get his version of the anthem accepted by the government, he moved to publish a well-received literary magazine. The magazine was a critical success but did not sell well. Disappointed, Saghar closed it down.

Unlike most people who had migrated to Pakistan from India, Saghar did not ask the government to settle him on the properties left behind by the Hindus and the Sikhs. Instead, he preferred to stay in cheap hotels. He paid his rent from the meagre amounts of money that he received from magazines for the poems which he wrote for them. But within a decade, his early, youthful enthusiasm for Pakistan had eroded as he saw corruption, nepotism and mediocrity being rewarded at the expense of creative talent.[38] Broke in more ways than one, and at a stage where even the fast-acting cheap whisky of

---

[38] Julian Columeau: *Saghar* (Nigarshaat Publishing House, 2014).

Lahore failed to keep him numb, Saghar discovered morphine.[39] He bought his daily dose from janitors at various hospitals of Lahore.[40]

What's more, when some contemporary poets used to find this thin addict outside their homes asking for money, they would give him a few rupees but only after he had written a poem or two for them. These poets would then sell the poems to magazines for a lot more money, and some even went to the extent of getting them published in their own names.

With friends and strangers alike exploiting his genius of writing the most evocative Urdu *ghazals*[41] to meet their own avaricious needs, Saghar plunged even deeper into despair.[42] Soon he was turned out by the cheap hotels he was living in. He ended up walking the streets of Lahore. A fan of his once wrote[43] how (in 1966) while he was driving down Lahore's Circuit Road, the radio in his car began to play a *ghazal* written by Saghar. As the fan was quietly rejoicing the power of Saghar's words, his eyes caught a fleeting glimpse of a thin man with unkempt hair and in tattered clothes walking aimlessly on the side of the road. It was Saghar. Before the world abandoned Saghar, Saghar had abandoned the world.

For years he could be seen walking and sleeping on the streets of Lahore, living on the food given to him by those who took him to be a beggar or a *fakir*. Amazingly, he continued to write powerful poetry despite the fact that he could hardly utter a single coherent sentence anymore. At times he would write his

---

[39] Poetry of Saghar Siddiqui (Native Pakistan, Oct. 27, 2014)
[40] Ibid.
[41] A South Asian poetic-form consisting of rhyming couplets and a refrain with each line sharing the same meter.
[42] Shoaib-ur-Rehman: French author pushes boundaries, writing in Urdu (Agence France-Presse, 2014).
[43] Bakir Ahmad: Saghar Ko Dekha (Urdu Digest, 1995).

poems, read them out loudly with a vacant look in his eyes, then tear the papers he'd scribbled these poems on, make a heap and set it all on fire.

During his years on the streets he had befriended a stray dog[44] with whom he shared whatever food that was handed to him by the shopkeepers. The dog would follow him and sleep beside him on any street corner Saghar would choose to sleep on. After 15 years of morphine addiction, and living on the streets, Saghar was found dead in one such street corner of Lahore. He had passed away in his sleep. He was just 46. The dog who was with him for more than six years never left the spot where Saghar died. Finally, almost exactly a year after Saghar's death, the dog too died [45] — on the same spot where Saghar had drawn his last breathe.

****

Sister Sorrow

One of the most fascinating characters in the initial saga of the painful birth of Pakistan is Fatima Jinnah, the frail-looking, graceful and yet gritty sister of the founder of the country, Mohammad Ali Jinnah. She was a passionate political worker, a determined activist for women's rights and a qualified dental surgeon to boot. After receiving a degree (in dentistry) from the University of Calcutta in 1914, she became a close counsellor and a trusted confidant of her brother. She enthusiastically backed him when (in the 1940s) he finally decided to maneuver his party towards a more polemical position on the question of the future of India's Muslims.

---

[44] Ibid.
[45] Ibid.

After the tense 1946 election in the Punjab, Jinnah's party became the main engine behind what would later come to be known as the Pakistan Movement. Miss Jinnah worked tirelessly for the movement and was able to win respect and recognition within and outside the Muslim League. However, after the movement was able to achieve a separate country in 1947, Miss Jinnah's existence as a Pakistani was wrought with disappointments, disillusionment and eventual isolation.

Much has been speculated about her life between 1947 and 1967 (the year she passed away). But one of the best and most authentic accounts of her disappointments arrived in the shape of a book which she wrote in 1955 (*My Brother*) but which was published 32 years later in 1987! Even though her status was immediately elevated to that of being a patriotic heroine after the creation of Pakistan, why did it take so long for her book to be available for public consumption?

The answer to this can be found in some of the contents of the book. In it she laments how her brother was quickly 'betrayed' by even some of his closest comrades who had worked with him during the Pakistan Movement. Jinnah had assumed the role of Pakistan's first Governor General in 1947. But he faced his first surprise when, after his famous Aug 11 address to Pakistan's Constituent Assembly (in which he declared his vision of Pakistan as being a progressive Muslim majority state), the bureaucracy (pressed by some of Muslim League's leading members), asked the country's nascent print media and radio to only publish and broadcast an edited version of Jinnah's speech.[46]

According to Miss Jinnah's book, her brother, who had been suffering from tuberculosis throughout the later stages of his

---

[46] IA Rehman (DAWN, August 14, 2013).

struggle for Pakistan, began to rapidly lose his health after 1947. In her mind this was due to the disappointments and the sense of betrayal he felt at the hands of some of his comrades. Miss Jinnah seemed particularly bitter towards Pakistan's first Prime Minister, Liaquat Ali Khan, who was perhaps Jinnah's closest colleague in the Muslim League. She wrote that her brother told her that many of his former colleagues were coming to meet him only to determine how much life there was left in him, implying that they were most probably waiting for him to quietly perish. In her book Miss Jinnah also laments how heartlessly her brother was picked up and put into an ambulance (to be taken to a hospital) and how the ambulance broke down in the middle of the road. Jinnah expired on September 11, 1948.

There might have been pressure from the government in disallowing Miss Jinnah to publish her book in 1955, but there is also ample evidence suggesting that it was Miss Jinnah herself who hesitated to get the book published. Pakistan was just 8 years old and Liaquat Ali Khan had been assassinated in 1951.

Author and intellectual, Khaled Ahmed, in his book, *Pakistan Behind the Ideological Mask*[47] quotes celebrated lawyer, Sharifuddin Pirzada (who was a secretary to Jinnah), in saying that when Ms. Jinnah appeared on Radio Pakistan to announce Jinnah's passing, the state-owned radio channel's director-general, Z A. Bokhari, got a call from a government official asking him to switch off her speech the moment she began criticizing the government's attitude towards the founder of the country and how he was left to die in an old ambulance.

She became a virtual recluse after Jinnah's demise, until in 1965 when she was pulled out of her self-imposed political retirement to challenge Ayub Khan in a Presidential election.

---

[47] Vanguard Books, 2001.

By 1965 Ayub's popularity had begun to dwindle a bit and his Presidential candidature was challenged by the Combined Opposition Parties (COP) — a group made up of certain left-wing parties (that were opposed to his staunchly capitalist policies), and right-wing religious outfits (opposed to the 'secular' disposition of his regime). COP sprang a surprise when it convinced Ms. Jinnah to become its candidate in the election. She initially hesitated, but then agreed.

Khan was expecting to sweep the election, but not anymore. Though he did go on to win the election, Ms. Jinnah defeated him in two of Pakistan's largest cities: Karachi and Dhaka. She also won in Hyderabad and narrowly lost in Peshawar. COP accused the regime of electoral malpractice, but Ms. Jinnah once again decided to retire to a life of a recluse.

Her last meeting with a noted politician was with Z.A. Bhutto when he was eased out (as foreign minister) from the Ayub regime. According to Stanley Wolpert (in his book *Zulfi Bhutto of Pakistan*)[48], when Bhutto was pushed towards political oblivion by Ayub in 1966, Bhutto, whose bungalow was close to Ms. Jinnah's (in Karachi), walked to her house and asked for her advice and guidance over a cup of tea. She sounded disillusioned and told Bhutto: 'I told you not to trust him (Ayub).'

A year later, she passed away at the age of 71 on July 9, 1967. The government announced her passing due to a heart-attack. But to this day a number of politicians, and even Jinnah's nephew Akbar Pirbhai, insist that she was murdered. She was 71 and is buried beside her brother's grave in his impressive mausoleum in Karachi. Ironically, Liaquat Ali Khan too is buried there.

---

[48] Oxford University Press, 1993. p.81

CHAPTER 7

GOING DOWN, SWINGING:
THE IMPLOSION OF MUSLIM MODERNISM
IN PAKISTAN AND THE BEGINNINGS OF THE
RIGHTWARDS IDEOLOGICAL DIVERGENCE

Muslim Modernism's last stand

On December 9 and 17 of 1970, Pakistan held its very first election on the basis of adult franchise. Participating political parties had been campaigning for the event ever since January 1970. Bhutto's PPP and Mujibur Rahman's Awami League (AL) were drawing the largest crowds in West and East Pakistan respectively. The Yahya Khan regime did not trust either of the two.

Even though Yahya's intelligence agencies had predicted a victory for Mujib's AL in East Pakistan, the same agencies had almost entirely rubbished the idea of Bhutto's PPP sweeping the polls in West Pakistan.[1] Hopeful of the election generating a hung verdict that would be in the interest of the military regime, Yahya nevertheless decided to not only support various 'industrialist and

---

[1] IM Sehgal (Defense Journal, Vol.11, 2007). p.10

feudal backed' Muslim League factions, but also gave a nod of approval to the Islamic parties, especially the JI.

All that was brewing on the fringes of the Tashkent Generation between 1966 and 1969, exploded onto the mainstream in 1970. During the PPP campaign, new-found youthful infatuations, such as radical leftist politics and revolutionary posturing, and their romance with the ways and culture of the working classes met with the street-smart moorings of the pro-Bhutto proletariat segments and the passionate music and mores of Sindh and Punjab's rural and semi-urban 'shrine culture.'

The shrine culture, the one related to the devotional and recreational activity around the shrines of ancient Muslim Sufi saints, had been existing in the subcontinent for almost a thousand years. The saints' Islam was evidently more accommodating. A largely permissive culture of ecstatic devotional music, innovative rituals and indigenous intoxicants started to take shape around the shrines, mostly involving peasants, the dispossessed, and, later, the urban *lumpenproletariat*.[2]

This culture was largely tolerated and even patronized by various Muslim dynasties which ruled the subcontinent, and by the end of the Mughal Empire in the mid-19th Century, it had become a vital part of the belief and ritual system of a majority of Muslims in the region. However, from the 1950s, urban middle-class Pakistan had begun to simply dismiss this culture as being the domain of the uneducated and the superstitious.

But just as the hippies of the West (in the 1960s) had adopted various exotic and esoteric Eastern spiritual beliefs to demonstrate their disapproval of the materialism and 'soullessness' of the Western capitalist system, young, middle-

---

[2]   Marxist term for the unorganized and apolitical lower orders of society.

class rebels of urban Pakistan increasingly began to look upon Sufism and the shrine culture as a way to make a social, cultural and political connect with the downtrodden and the dispossessed.

Such a connect became more interesting when bourgeois and petty-bourgeois youth supporting the PPP came into direct contact with the boisterous masses of rural peasants, small shop owners, and the urban working classes at PPP's election rallies. The latter brought with them the music, the emotionalism and the devotional sense of loyalty of the shrine culture. The cultural synthesis emerging from this fusion was a leading reason behind Bhutto's image leaping from being that of a 'brave patriot' (who as Ayub's Foreign Minister had stood up to his boss in 1966), to ultimately being perceived by his supporters as the embodiment of a modern-day Sufi saint.[3]

When the state-owned television channel, PTV, began showing clips of various 1970 election rallies, standing out in vibrancy and uniqueness were PPP gatherings. Dominated by Bhutto's animated and at times demagogic oratory, these rallies also became famous for almost always turning into the kind of boisterous and musical fanfares usually witnessed outside the many shrines of Sufi saints across the country. The country's urban youth culture, the one that had begun to emerge in the mid-1960s, was Pakistan's reflection of the era's youthful romance with leftist ideals and radical student action. Along the way, this culture started to elaborate this idealism through the bohemian antics of the shrine culture.

The ever-expanding milieu of this new urban youth culture had also started to adopt contemporary Western fashions. But it was yet to be fully impacted by the 'counter-culture' of the hippies making the rounds in the United States and Europe. But

---

[3] *Theology and Theory After Empire* ed. D. Joy and J Duggan (Springer, 2014) p.149

this started to change after 1970 – and fast. Though the beginnings of the hippie phenomenon in the West can be placed in San Francisco in 1966, middle-class Pakistan's knowledge of the phenomenon (till about early 1968) was at best superficial.

But when Pakistan became an intermediate destination of the famous 'Hippie Trail,'[4] cities such as Peshawar, Swat, Rawalpindi, Lahore and Karachi became important hippie destinations. After entering Iran (from Turkey), the Hippie Trail curved into Afghanistan, from where the hippies entered Pakistan (through the Khyber Pass in the KP province). They travelled down to Rawalpindi and then to Lahore from where they entered India (by bus). Many hippies also travelled all the way down to Karachi in the south of Pakistan to visit the city's sprawling beaches. Another popular destination for these traveling hippies in Pakistan were the various large Sufi shrines in Lahore and Karachi. Here they mingled with the shrines' many *malangs* and fakirs (spiritual vagabonds).

About the same time, middle-class Pakistani youth had also started to frequent shrines more often than before, especially on Thursday nights where (till even today) a number of shrines hold nights dedicated to the traditional sub-continental Sufi devotional music, called the Qawaali. It was at the shrines of Lahore, the beaches of Karachi, and at the bus stands of Peshawar and Rawalpindi, where most Pakistanis came into direct contact with the passing hippies. And as portrayed by the flamboyant attire of TV personality, Zia Mohiuddin, in 1970's famous PTV show, the *Zia Mohyeddin Show*, the 'radical chic'[5] and 'hippie attire' developing

---

[4] An overland route that thousands of travelling hippies (from Europe and the United States) started to take on their journeys towards India and Nepal.

[5] Term coined by journalist Tom Wolfe in his 1970 essay to describe the adoption and promotion of radical political causes by fashionable icons.

in the West started to also catch the fancy of young middle-class Pakistanis. By the early 1970s, young men's hair that had remained somewhat short till even the late 1960s, started to grow longer (with thick sideburns); and women's *kameez* (traditional Pakistani shirts), grew shorter in length.

Sure of triggering a cultural and political revolution in Pakistan, young West and East Pakistanis joined a large number of their countrymen as they turned out to vote in the country's first 'real elections' in 1970. These elections, though held under a military dictatorship, are still hailed by a majority of Pakistani political commentators to have been the most free and fair held in the country. The results were stunning. Bhutto's PPP (in West Pakistan) and Mujib's Awami League (in East Pakistan), almost completely eclipsed the old guard of Pakistani politics. The results of the election came as a shock to the military regime of Yahya Khan and the Islamic parties.

Winning 162 National Assembly seats (out of a total of 300), Mujib's Awami League should have been invited to form Pakistan's first ever popularly elected government. But since Mujib and his party were squarely made up of Bengali nationalists, Yahya (in unison with Bhutto) hesitated. Next in line to form the government was Bhutto's PPP that had won 81 seats. What happened next is a thorny and controversial issue in the country's political history. Some commentators have blamed Yahya for pitching Bhutto's ego against Mujib's, while others accuse Bhutto of manipulating Yahya into keeping Mujib out. Pakistanis have yet to decide upon a convincing closure on the issue.

A clear fissure appeared on the issue between youth in West and East Pakistan even though they had been on the same page during the protest movement against the Ayub dictatorship in 1968-69. Energized by the election results but frustrated by the establishment's apparent reluctance to hand over power to the

Bengali dominated majority in the Parliament, Bengali nationalist groups started to violently agitate against the military regime of Yahya Khan. They had also accused the military of using intimidating tactics that, by 1971, were said to have become specifically brutal.

The turmoil soon mutated into yet another India-Pakistan war (in December 1971). But unlike the 1965 war that had resulted in a stalemate, this time the Pakistani troops were decimated by their Indian counterparts who were supported by militant Bengali nationalist groups (and vice versa). As Mujib was released from a West Pakistan jail to travel back to East Pakistan (via London), and take charge of the newly created Bangladesh, Bhutto was invited by a group of disgruntled officers [6] to take over the reins of what was left of Pakistan.

The radical environment created by the students movement in the late 1960s did manage to trigger a drastic change, but this change (i.e. the break-up of the country), was certainly not the one hoped by the seekers of change. Bhutto reiterated his party's commitment to introduce sweeping socialist reforms and give the country an elaborate constitution. If one reads through the economic numbers and stats of Pakistan between 1972 and 1974, the Bhutto regime (till then) did a rather remarkable job, considering the fact that it had inherited a country and an economy ravaged by a resource-depleting war. It is also true that during the first few years of the Bhutto regime, the nation's mood had successfully been transformed, as the country looked forward to a new Pakistan.

Of course, political conflicts between Bhutto and opposition parties continued making the news, but by and large, Pakistanis had decided to settle down and do whatever they could to restore

---

[6] V. Selochan: *The Military and Democracy in Asia and the Pacific* (ANU E, 2004) p.19

their pride after the East Pakistan debacle. As the opposition parties got bogged down by PPP's majority in the Parliament and by its burgeoning street power, the only worthwhile middle-class opposition faced by the Bhutto government came from JI's student-wing, the Islami Jamiat Taleba (IJT). Bhutto faced even more desertions from what was once his natural constituency (the progressive students), when between 1973 and 1974, he launched a purge within the PPP, expelling a number of the party's foremost leftist ideologues.[7] In a 1973 cabinet meeting he lambasted the 'agitprop activities' of the party's radical left faction and, ironically, declared that 'most of our troubles come from the left.'[8]

A large-scale move towards Islamic student groups on campuses during the Bhutto era was a way to express a gripe against the powerful Bhutto regime in the absence of a more united opposition in the Parliament. In fact, some observers have now even accused Bhutto of following Egyptian president, Anwar Saddat's example of encouraging the mushrooming of right-wing Islamic student groups on campuses to neutralize the hold of various left-wing student parties that had turned against him. However, the shift in the ideological mood of student politics of the time did not in any way reflect the populist cultural zeitgeist for which the Bhutto regime is fondly remembered.

The society maintained a liberal aura, as nightclubs, bars, horse racing, and cinemas continued to thrive and mushroom, and religiosity largely remained a private matter – even though the government and state of Pakistan had started to use religious symbolism more often than before, especially as a way to drown

---

[7] O. Noman: *Pakistan: Political and Economic History* (Routledge, 2013) p.103
[8] Ibid.

out the emerging post-1971 notion that Jinnah's 'Two Nation Theory' that had given birth to Pakistan had collapsed after the separation of East Pakistan. This tendency is quite apparent in the new Constitution which was passed by the National Assembly in 1973.

According to Mubarak Ali:

The Constitution of 1973 was declared after the defeat of the Pakistan in 1971 and the independence of Bangladesh. The new constitution incorporated Islamic provisions in order to win the support of religious parties and groups. It declared Islam to be the state religion.

It also announced the determination to strengthen bonds with the Muslim world. Further, it required that both the president and the prime minister must be Muslims.[9]

The scenario in this context was quite like the manner in which the Muslims of India had initially reacted after the collapse of Muslim power in South Asia in the 19th century. They had begun to identify with Muslim empires outside of the region to overcome their sudden sense of becoming a defeated people in India.

Pakistan's tourism industry witnessed an unprecedented boom during the Bhutto era, and the country's film industry reached a commercial peak. By now flamboyant fashions in attire and personal grooming that had been rapidly taking shape in the West – 'bellbottoms,' colourful shirts, long hair, chunky necklaces, platform shoes, etc. – arrived in full force and were enthusiastically embraced by the urban youth. And so did the traditional *shalwar-kameez* among men. Once considered to be the dress of the working-classes, Bhutto began to wear it regularly during his rallies, turning it into a populist fashion statement.

---

[9] Dr. Mubarak Ali: *Pakistan in Search of Identity* (Aakar, 2011) p.33

Western fashion and countercultural antics became all the rage among the urban youth, but this youth's desire to have a spiritual and cultural connect with the masses via the shrine culture remained afoot. Along with beer-serving roadside cafes in Karachi, shrines too became a favourite haunt for students, theatre artistes and painters. For the Pakistan film industry, the Bhutto era proved to be a commercial bonanza as the industry managed to generate dozens of hits between 1970 and 1977.[10] To accommodate the large number of films being produced (mainly in Lahore), the quantity of cinemas also increased across the country, with the largest one appearing in 1976 and appropriately named, Prince Cinema.

By the mid-1970s, the film industry was producing an average of 25 to 30 (Urdu) films a year.[11] The study of Pakistani cinema of the 1970s in comparison to Indian cinema of the period makes for an interesting case of contextual contrasts. Both the industries at the time were generating films of similar production quality but (after 1973), when Indian prime minister, Indira Gandhi's heavy handed policies and the rising incidents of corruption in her government triggered a full-fledged protest movement (the 'JP Movement'), Indian films became more socio-political in context, throwing up its version of the 'angry young man,' epitomized by actor Amitabh Bachchan's brooding roles in various Salim-Javed scripted films.[12] Nothing of the sort happened in Pakistani films of the time. In comparison to India, which eventually went into a convulsive political and economic turmoil when Indira declared a state of emergency in 1975, Pakistan's economy, comparatively speaking only, remained

---

[10] Mushtaq Gazdar: *Pakistani Cinema: 1947-97* (Oxford University Press, 1997).
[11] Ibid.
[12] Nikhat Kazmi: *Ire in the Soul* (HarperCollins, 1996) p.29

fairly stable[13] and the country's politics were firmly in the hands of a prime minister who was hardly ever challenged by a disunited and fragmented opposition. Even an anti-government insurgency by various Marxist-nationalist Baloch groups in the mountains of the arid province of Balochistan (1973-77), remained somewhat circumstantial in the major cities of Pakistan (except Quetta).

So what were Pakistani films about during the 1970s – a time when the local film industry had hit a commercial and creative peak? Though a bulk of them remained to be modern re-workings of the conventional sub-continental romantic farce, the subtext of the films, however, became a lot more social. One of the themes in Pakistani films of the time that managed to attract large audiences was a look at class conflict and class consciousness through romantic affairs between a man and a woman. The Pakistani film heroines started appearing in roles reflecting a more independent and outspoken streak to the point of rebelling against their conservative parents by getting involved (and then marrying) 'lower middle-class' men.

The flamboyant dynamics of 1970s' amorousness with various social aspects of liberalism generated a rather crackling cultural aura when it came together with Bhutto's sprawling populism. But the phenomenon also set into motion an anxious discourse (especially among the urban petty-bourgeoisie) enquiring about the limits of the emerging trends. This discourse (about a particular kind of fear) is clearly present in many of the time's Pakistani films, most of which were scripted and directed by people with strong petty-bourgeois backgrounds.

This fear reflected a concern about a society getting carried away by the tides of the time and in the process eroding the

---

[13] S. Akbar Zaidi: *Issues in Pakistan's Economy* (Oxford University Press, 2005) p.104

comforting economics and sociology of the 'joint family system' which, many feared was gradually being replaced by the 'Western' notions of social and domestic independence. The liberal-populist zeitgeist was also blamed (mainly by the more conservative sections of the urban middle-classes), for encouraging the youth to undermine the importance of Islam in the Pakistani society.

A 1978 study stated that more Pakistanis had visited Sufi shrines than mosques between the late 1960s and 1977 – a trend that would squarely change in the next decade and beyond. But the concerns and fear in some segments of the society of the erosion of the country's traditional family and moral structures remained largely veiled underneath the bombastic antics of the populist orotundity of the Bhutto regime and era. These fears only surfaced onto the mainstream either through certain 'social films' – that nonetheless remained highly showy in look – or through the rhetoric of the religious parties.

But the Bhutto regime's message in this respect was rather ambiguous. In spite of the fact that the cultural policies of the government clearly encouraged and fattened the free-wheeling zeitgeist of the period, some of the regime's political maneuvers, however, actually ended up strengthening a counter-narrative. For example, after the 1971 break-up of Pakistan and the war with India, the discourse about Pakistani nationalism became much more introverted. As author and academic, Rubina Saigol, rightly observed,[14] the shock and horror of the defeat in East Pakistan led to the reconstruction of ideological boundaries in a much more narrow form. A militaristic and negative nationalism, which saw enemies on every border, was constituted. This nationalism was not so much for progress or development as

---

[14] *Enemies Within and Enemies Without*: Futures, Vol.37, Issue: 9. 2005.

much as it was against Pakistan's myriad enemies, now supposedly lurking behind every door.[15]

The Divergence

The ambiguity of the Bhutto regime in this context was also apparent on the state-owned PTV. The 1970s are remembered as being the 'Golden Age of Television' in Pakistan[16], but many of the popular TV serials also addressed the same fears highlighted by certain 'social films' of the era. Though a majority of these TV serials either insinuated the government's populist/socialist overtones (1974's *Khuda Ki Basti*); or were a celebration of various apolitical liberal fads of the time (1974's *Kiran Kahani*, *Uncle Urfi*); there were also plays which addressed the dichotomy that emerged when the government-sponsored populist-liberalism clashed head-on with the new reactive narratives being built by the state after 1971.

Confident of being re-elected as prime minister, Bhutto announced new parliamentary elections in early 1977. By now aware of the middle-classes' growing disenchantment with his regime, Bhutto was still sure about his popularity among the urban working classes and small farmers and peasants in rural Pakistan. Whereas the once pro-Bhutto left (in urban Pakistan) had started to raise the tone of their grumblings against Bhutto's 'betrayal of PPP's original socialist agenda,' the conservative sections from the same class who had remained subdued during much of Bhutto's regime, suddenly found themselves galvanized on a common political platform.

This platform was shaped by a 9-party political alliance made up of the country's various politico-religious parties and

---

[15] Ibid.
[16] Newsline, Vol.19, 2007.

some small anti-Bhutto secular groups. The alliance was given a simple name: The Pakistan National Alliance (PNA). Subsequently, the PPP's manifesto for the 1977 election was a far cry from its manifesto for the 1970 election. To begin with, the word 'socialism' now played only a minor, obligatory role in the document. Though still calling itself an 'egalitarian' and 'poor-friendly' party, the terms 'Islam' and 'God' now took up more space in the PPP's new manifesto and rhetoric than before.

PNA's manifesto on the other end not only attacked the 'economic and political fall-outs of the regime's socialist policies,' its leaders denounced the Bhutto regime's 'liberalism' as well, which they blamed for 'spreading obscenity,' 'crime' and 'drunkenness' among the youth. PNA aggressively stated its goal to replace Bhutto's 'unIslamic policies' with those based on what PNA called, *Nizam-e-Mustapha*[17] (or laws and policies 'based on the Quran and *Sunnah*).

The bottom line, however, was, that the PNA was first and foremost a desperate alliance of various anti-Bhutto/anti-PPP parties and politicians who managed to detect the paradigm shift taking place in the ideological make-up of the urban middle-classes and the petty-bourgeoisie of the country. A paradigm shift in urban Pakistan's ideological and political milieu was certainly afoot and economics had a lot to do with it. Soon after 1974, the Bhutto regime was replete with difficulties and challenges, particularly in matters of the economy. Economic trends on the international level were hardly conducive for any third world economy to grow and prosper.[18] Devastating floods in 1976 and a world recession between 1975 and 1977 due to OPEC's unprecedented hikes in oil prices severely depressed the demand

---

[17] Dr. Mubarak Ali: *Pakistan in Search of Identity* (Aakar, 2011) p.33
[18] S. Akbar Zaidi: *Issues in Pakistan's Economy* (Oxford University Press, 2005) p.104

for Pakistani exports, affecting industrial output.[19] Unlike the Ayub regime, the Bhutto government did not play the role of sugar daddy to the industrialists. Consequently, the gap between Bhutto's economics of 'socialist' reformism and the interests of the industrialists increasingly grew apart. So it was not surprising to see large and medium level traders, businessmen and industrialists putting all their weight behind the PNA.

In March 1977, the people of Pakistan once again went to the polls (the first time after the historic 1970 election). Initial results showed the PPP sweeping the National Assembly elections. However, the PNA leadership accused the regime of mass rigging. It boycotted the Provincial Elections and announced a series of protests. Just as left-wing student organizations had triggered the anti-Ayub movement in the late 1960s, the movement against Bhutto was set off by the right-wing IJT, the student-wing of the JI. Most of the country's politicized campuses that had been bastions of leftist politics till about 1973, now erupted to the call of the IJT. PNA protests were mostly driven by students, small traders and shopkeepers and backed by the industrialists.

The protesters, upset by a recession and accompanying inflation, attacked bars, nightclubs, wine shops, cinemas and billboards exhibiting Pakistani liquor brands. They denounced them as symbols of the 'unIslamic Bhutto regime'.[20] The PNA leadership maintained that not only had the Bhutto regime's socialism undermined Islamic culture and law, it had also failed to offer relief to the poor. Fearing a military coup by the Army, Bhutto decided to hold talks with PNA leaders and if need be, hold fresh elections. For this, he also agreed to close down

---

[19] Ibid.
[20] S Vali Nasr: *Islamic Leviathan: Islam and the Making of State Power* (Oxford University Press, 2001) p.99

nightclubs and bars, outlaw gambling at horse racing, clamp down on 'obscenity' and make the Muslim holy day of Friday a weekly holiday (instead of Sunday).

But just as a compromise between Bhutto and PNA was in sight, Bhutto's own hand-picked military general, Muhammad Ziaul Haq, toppled the regime in a coup and imposed Martial Law on 5th July, 1977. Pakistan's urban classes had once again triggered a drastic change that was not necessarily constructive.

****

The Nietzschean Qawaal

One South Asian music genre which rapidly rose to become a favorite of Pakistanis in the 1970s was the Quwaali. Qawaali in South Asia was inspired by the devotional music of Sufi orders of Persia and Turkey[21] in which the beauty and power of the Almighty and his creations were sung to the tune of hypnotic music and whirling dances. The genre came to be known as Qawaali when, from the 12th century onward, it came into contact with the classical music traditions of South Asia and the devotional music of the dominant religions found in the region.[22]

Here it adopted the many musical instruments developed by Amir Khusro, the brilliant 13th century musician and poet in the courts of India's Muslim Delhi Sultanate. In Persia and Turkey, the Qawaali had been largely restricted to expressing the inner workings of Sufi orders. But by the 16th century (in South Asia), Qawaali also began to reflect the emotive and devotional dynamics of the populist culture and milieu that had begun to

---

[21] Ibid.
[22] G. Gorlinski: *100 Most Influential Musicians of All Time* p.317

develop around the cults of living Sufi saints, and more so, around the shrines of the saints.

These shrines, which today can be found across both India and Pakistan, were (and still are) visited not only by the region's Muslims, but also by Hindus and Sikhs. There's a history of theological conflict between Sufism and the more orthodox strands of Islam in which the Sufis rejected the strict ritual and doctrinal regimentation of Islamic orthodoxy, accusing it of divorcing faith from its spiritual core and soul. The orthodox Muslim *ulema* and the clergy retaliated by condemning Sufism for introducing 'negative' ritualistic innovations (*biddat*) in the faith.[23] They also scorned at the culture that began to develop around Sufi shrines in which common peasants and homeless men and women indulged in music and drugs. The Sufis responded by suggesting that the shrines were the only places in the realm where men and women of all creeds, castes and classes were welcome, and where the poor could find some food and shelter.

Muslim domains of the region, from the Delhi Sultanate to the Mughal Empire, employed a number of Islamic scholars and *ulema*. But knowing well the influence and the popularity that the Sufi saints enjoyed among the masses, the Sultans and Emperors were more inclined towards favouring the saints.[24] However, not all Sufi orders were always entirely copious and accommodating. Nevertheless, the popular memory in this context is still more of Sufi saints who had abandoned the world of material well-being and power politics, and isolated themselves to acquire a unique spiritual link with the Almighty.

---

[23] Asghar Ali Engineer: *On Developing Theology of Peace in Islam* (Sterling Publishers, 2003) p.109
[24] Richard D. Hecht; Vincent F. Biondo: *Religion, Everyday Life & Culture* (ABC-CLIO, 2010) p.101

Views of most ancient Sufis reach us through the poetry that they wrote and then composed with the help of certain *ragas*.[25] This points to the fact that these Sufis were mostly poet-musicians.[26] Some of their thoughts are clearly subversive and anti-establishment. Many of them claimed to have had a special spiritual connection with God. It is often believed (by their devotees) that they struck this link by roaming among the masses and then, after transcending regimented religious rituals, they retreated inwards to reach those parts of their minds and hearts that were not so well known or explored.[27] From here, they claimed, they could actually experience the presence of the Almighty – a presence whose power and beauty may render a mortal man senseless, and annihilate his ego, but also (and thus) make him one with his beloved Creator.

The annihilation process in this context (*fana*) was the price the saints were willing to pay and often (in their poetry) described the process as a passion-play demonstrated by a lover willing to annihilate his lesser self to be close to his elusive, pristine beloved.[28] Sufi musical and literary genres are abundant with such narratives. These narratives and imageries, when they became a centerpiece of Qawaali, suggest that after transcending conventional religious ritualism, the medium used by Sufi saints to make that ultimate link with the Almighty was beautiful poetry sung to the tune of mesmerizing music.

According to the same narrative, the Sufis who had made that link, seemed intoxicated by their distinct, all-encompassing love of the Almighty; like a man drunk on wine

---

[25] Conversation with late Musadiq Sanwal (Poet, folk musician & journalist) 2011.
[26] Ibid.
[27] Ibid.
[28] N Hanif: *Biographical Encyclopedia of Sufis* (Sarup & Sons, 2000) p.344

and (thus) unhindered by the inhibitions imposed by those who limit a man's potential to fully realize the spiritual and intellectual faculties[29] that the Almighty has bestowed him. This is another aspect of the Sufi narrative that the Qawaali enthusiastically embraces. But this aspect of the Qawaali purposely and teasingly remains ambiguous. For example, a verse of such a Qawaali which directly praises the consumption of wine, is then followed by a verse that treats the act of this consumption (and its effects) as a metaphor of a brazen love for the Almighty.

The Qawaali remained to be a popular musical genre with the masses in South Asia. But its first contemporary manifestation as a commercially viable art-form emerged in Pakistan in the 1970s. Its popularity in this respect was squarely based on the rise of two qawaals: Aziz Mian and the Sabri Brothers. These two not only aroused a keen interest in Qawaali across the classes, but also became two of the most commercially successful qawaals whose exploits were later matched by the mighty Nusrat Fateh Ali Khan in the 1990s.

Their greatest achievement was to ignite a passion for Qawaali among urban audiences[30] who had largely abandoned the traditional Farsi (Persian) Qawaali of the Muslim imperial courts, and the Punjabi Qawaali of Sufi shrines in rural and semi-rural areas of the Punjab province of Pakistan. In this regard, what Aziz Mian and the Sabri Brothers also did was to fully form Qawaali sung in Urdu[31] – Pakistan's national language. Qawaali was already a popular music genre in rural Punjab. It was mainly performed at Sufi shrines. Moving ahead, the Sabri

---

[29] Ibid.
[30] Conversation with late Musadiq Sanwal (Poet, folk musician & journalist) 2011
[31] Ibid.

Brothers and Aziz Mian created an urban audience for Qawaali. The audience they appealed to belonged to the urban middle and lower-middle-classes.

The first to experiment with the idea were the Sabri Brothers, led by Ghulam Farid Sabri and Maqbool Ahmed Sabri. They recorded *Mera Koi Nahi Hai Terey Siwa* ('I have no one but you') for EMI-Pakistan in 1958. Sung in Urdu, the qawaali is an intense ode to the Almighty. It was an instant hit and was received well by urbanites who were reintroduced to a genre of South Asian music which, over the decades, they had largely divorced themselves from.

At the time of the release of the Sabri Brothers' first famous Urdu qawaali, Aziz Mian was a 16-year-old school boy with a knack for always getting into trouble, and indulging in acts of petty vandalism and brawling.[32] Many years later most of his concerts would often fall apart and turn into drunken brawls. Aziz Mian would purposely work up the audience into a state in which many in the crowd would end up losing all sense of order and control. He would explain this as a stage from where the brawling men could hurl themselves into a state from where they could then leap further and strike a direct spiritual link with the Almighty.[33] A journalist reviewing one such Aziz Mian concert in Karachi in 1975 (for Dawn newspaper) described him as 'the Nietzschean qawaal.'

By the late 1970s, Aziz Mian would become an iconic quwaal in Pakistan. Rather an iconoclast, because of the way he often shattered various long-held traditions of the Qawaali. In the process, he developed and honed a style that was all his own. He came from a musical family and was already learning eastern

---

[32] Tariq Masood: *Aziz Mian* (Temco International, 1995) p.39
[33] RB Qureshi: *Sufi Music in Pakistan: Sound, Context & Meaning in Quwaali* (Cambridge University Press, 1987).

classical music when he arrived with his family in Pakistan from
India in 1947. Whereas the Sabri Brothers had settled in Karachi,
Aziz Mian's family lay its new roots in Lahore. Aziz Mian's
parents became regular visitors to the city's famous shrine of
Sufi saint, Data Ganj Baksh. Aziz Mian would often accompany
them. But Aziz Mian had a troubled youth. At an early age, he
had begun to smoke and became hooked to tobacco-laced *paans*
(beetle leaf). He would also often get into trouble for committing
acts of hooliganism as a teen. Worried by his behavior, his father
encouraged him to learn Qawaali from a group of established
qawaals who regularly performed Punjabi qawaalis at the Data
shrine. Aziz Mian agreed. But a he also decided to join a college
in Lahore where he continued to get into trouble. Though a
rabble-rouser and restive, he was considered a bright student by
his teachers.

In 1963, he got admitted to the Punjab University from
where he bagged a master's degree in Urdu literature and also
studied Arabic and Persian. It was here that he decided to
become a dedicated qawaal. He later told an interviewer, he saw
singing qawaalis as the only way he could have fulfilled his
restless quest to find some spiritual meaning in his riotous
existence. He began to perform in front of small crowds at
private functions.

Visitors at the Data shrine would often see a young man with
long, unkempt hair, colourful *kameez-shalwar* and wild eyes,
pacing up and down. It was Aziz Mian. To them, he could as
well have been one of the many *fakirs* who are often found at
Sufi shrines in South Asia. But, of course, he was different. He
was articulate in his speech, and could speak fluent Punjabi,
Urdu, Persian and English. In those days (mid/late 1960s), Aziz
Mian was mostly singing traditional folk qawaalis in Punjabi and
in Persian; but after listening to the Sabri Brothers sing in Urdu

(on radio) and then seeing them slowly attracting a whole new audience, Aziz Mian became restless again.

He didn't want to sing traditional qawaalis anymore. He received qawaali lyrics from some lesser-known Urdu poets, but he rejected them, suggesting that the lyrics did not reflect the nature of his quest. He tried to get in touch with the poets who were authoring Urdu lyrics for the Sabri Brothers, but he wasn't taken seriously. Then in 1969, while sitting at the Data shrine, Aziz Mian began writing lyrics himself.

A decade later, while performing the qawaali that he had written at the shrine, Aziz Mian told the audience: 'It was an evening just like this one. I was sitting at the Data shrine and conversing with God. I was praying for my well-being, when suddenly I began to be showered by a burst of words. I forgot what I was praying for and started to write down the emerging words right there.'[34] Thanks to the growing popularity of the Sabri Brothers, EMI-Pakistan had already given Aziz Mian some studio time to cut an album. But it would be the qawaali that he wrote at the shrine and then set to music that would go on to become his breakthrough moment.

The qawaali was titled *Mein Sharaabi* (I am a drunkard). On *Sharaabi* (first released in 1972), Aziz Mian also discovered and stamped a style of writing and singing that he would retain for the rest of his career.[35] He embraced the approach of the 'quarrelsome Sufis' of yore, who, in their peculiar states of mind, would hold brassy dialogues with God, punctuated with a series of paradoxical questions. Aziz Mian would start slowly, break into a catchy chorus with his 'qawaali party' (qawaali group), and then suddenly break out with a series of argumentative verses in a blistering display of speed-talking. He

[34] 1982 footage (on YouTube).
[35] Phillip Sweeny: *Dictionary of World Music* (Virgin, 1991) p.148

would address God, complaining how he loved Him but felt that he wasn't being loved back; or why a perfect entity such as God would create an imperfect creature such as man.

Aziz Mian was a heavy drinker and like various famous Sufi poets he often used the state (and concept) of drunkenness as a metaphor for the inexplicable effect the love for the Almighty had on him.[36] But he would also praise alcohol on its own terms. With the success of the *Mein Sharaabi* album, Aziz Mian rose to become one of the region's leading qawaals. As mentioned earlier, many of his concerts used to disintegrate into becoming drunken brawls when Aziz Mian would work up the audience to such a frenzy that many among the crowd would lose all sense of order. Aziz Mian saw the commotion as a reflection of his inner self and/or of a state of turmoil that eventually leads a man to annihilate internal inhibitions and pave the way for him to construct a special bridge which connected him with the enigmatic beauty and power of the Almighty. A pristine order and calm after deliberate chaos.

Both Aziz Mian and the Sabri Brothers also benefited from the cultural policies of the populist Bhutto regime. The policies instructed state media to regularly telecast folk music and Qawaali on TV and radio, especially during a weekly show (on TV) called *Lok Virsa*.[37] *Lok Virsa* was also responsible for introducing (to mainstream audiences) folk musicians such as Mai Bhagi (Sindhi), Faiz Mohammad Baloch (Balochi), Tufail Niazi (Punjabi), Allan Fakir (Sindhi), Reshma (Sariki), Pathanay Khan (Sariki) and Zarsanga (Pashto).

Compared to Aziz Mian, the Sabri Brothers were a lot more melodic and hypnotic in their style. Soon, a rivalry began to

---

[36] Ibid.
[37] Uxi Mufti: *Folk Heritage of Pakistan* (Institute of Folk Heritage, 1977) p.27

develop between them because both were catering to the same market. It was a brand new market centred in the urban areas. The Brothers would often mock Aziz Mian for being vehement and lacking melody. But Aziz Mian went on honing his unique style. Aziz Mian and the Sabri Brothers both stood for the same Sufi traditions and narratives that had developed in the region. But the Brothers disapproved of Aziz Mian's open praise of intoxicants in his qawaalis (even though alcohol was often consumed at the Sabri Brothers' concerts as well).

The Brothers thought Aziz Mian was uncouth and exploiting the Qawaali genre for quick fame. The rivalry between Aziz Mian and the Sabri Brothers took a more aggressive turn when, in 1975, both released their biggest hits to date. Aziz Mian extended *Mein Sharaabi* by adding another 30 minutes to the qawaali until it became an almost 50-munute-epic called *Teri Soorat* (your face)/ *Mein Sharaabi*. The album, released by EMI-Pakistan, sold over a million copies (LPs and cassettes) within a matter of months.[38]

The same year, the Sabri Brothers released *Bhar deh jholi* ('Fill my bag') which also became a massive seller, especially when it was chosen as a song for a 1975 Urdu film, *Bin Baadal Barsaat* (The Cloudless Monsoon), starring famous Pakistani film actor Muhammad Ali and actress Zeba. The Brothers appeared in the film, singing the qawaali at a shrine where Ali's character is shown with his wife (Zeba), pleading the Sufi saint buried there to ask God to grant them a child. The Pakistani film industry was peaking in the mid-1970s. So Aziz Mian too appeared in a film called, *License*. In it, he could be seen performing an abridged version of *Mein Sharaabi*. In early 1976, Prime Minister Zulfikar Ali Bhutto, invited Aziz Mian to

---

[38] Conversation with former head of EMI-Pakistan, Arshad Mehmood, in 2015, Karachi.

perform for him in Islamabad and share a drink. Aziz Mian gladly obliged. The same year, while commenting on the Brothers during a concert, Aziz Mian lamented that they were too conventional and that their spiritual connection with the Almighty was not as stark as his.

Slighted by Aziz Mian's comments, the Brothers released a thinly veiled taunt at him in shape of a qawaali titled, *O' sharabi, chor dey peena* ('Oh, drunkard, stop drinking'). The qawaali became an immediate hit, sung in the typically steady, controlled and hypnotic style of the Brothers, and then varnished with a bit of tongue-in-cheek humor aimed at Aziz Mian.[39] In a live bootleg recording of the qawaali[40], one of the brothers can be heard poking fun at 'drunkards' (Aziz Mian). He is doing this in a tongue-in-cheek manner because he is clearly conscious of the fact that the audience too was enjoying their drink. Consequently, the other brother laughingly suggests, 'but, of course, no one drinks here (in this concert hall).'

Aziz Mian was quick to retaliate. He wrote and recorded *Hai kambakht tu nein pe hi nahi* ('unfortunate soul, you never even drank!'). In it, he derided the Brothers for being deprived of understanding and experiencing the 'spiritual dimensions of being drunk.' The retaliatory qawaali starts with Aziz proudly owning up to liking his drink, then suggests that those who didn't drink and gave lectures while indulging in other misdeeds, were hypocrites. All the while, he continues to taunt the Brothers for never having experienced spiritual intoxication.

In the long climax of the qawaali, Aziz Mian's taunting turns into angry sarcastic jibes thrown at the Brothers, as he dismisses them for not understanding his intoxicated love for the Almighty

---

[39] While performing the qawaali live, the Brothers would often apply 'comical music' while singing about a drunkard.

[40] Recorded in Dubai in the mid-1980s.

because they have no clue what it meant or felt like. According to EMI-Pakistan, which released both the records, Aziz Mian and Sabri Brothers sold over two million LPs and cassettes in 1977 alone.[41] Fans from both the camps would often throw words and verses from the two qawaalis at each other.

Pakistani Qawaali had reached a commercial peak and then went global when Aziz Mian and the Sabri Brothers began touring outside Pakistan, enthralling audiences in various countries, including the US, UK, France, Germany, the Soviet Union and Iran. Then, Aziz Mian suddenly fell on the wrong side of the law. In April 1977, sale of alcoholic beverages (to Muslims) in Pakistan was banned.[42] In July 1977, the Bhutto regime fell in a reactionary military coup orchestrated by General Ziaul Haq. During the Zia dictatorship (1977-88), Aziz Mian's concerts were often raided by the police and the people there arrested for 'drunken behavior.'

In 1980, Aziz Mian began adding more conventional qawaalis to his set, but he always wrapped up his concerts with *Mein Sharaabi*. However, he would usually launch into the qawaali by first jokingly addressing the crowd (in Punjabi): 'I'm about to sing *Mein Sharaabi* (the crowd would roar). But you people don't have to worry. They'll arrest me, not you!' The crowd would burst into laughter.

On a number of occasions Aziz Mian was approached by the anti-Zia student and political outfits to write and sing a qawaali against the Zia regime. But he shied away. Instead, he decided to add extempore lyrics to his famous qawaalis. These additional lyrics spoke about how men intoxicated by their love of God and

---

[41] Conversation with former head of EMI-Pakistan, Arshad Mehmood, in 2015, Karachi.
[42] Hayman, Ghayur, Kaushik: *Pakistan: Zia & After* (Abhinav Publications, 1989) p.28

justice stood up to tyrants who had no understanding and appreciation of this unique kind of love.

In 1982, during a small concert in Karachi where Aziz Mian had been invited to perform, he noticed some policemen inside the venue. Believing that they would begin harassing the gathering the moment he launched into his *Sharaabi* qawaali, he decided to test the patience of the cops by singing what ended up becoming the longest qawaali recorded in the history of the genre.[43] Beginning the concert with his 1979 hit, the passionate *Allah Hi Jannay Kon Bashar Hai* ('Only God knows who is human'), he then launched into *Hasshar Kay Roz Yeh Poochon Ga* ('On the Day of Judgment, I shall ask') – a qawaali that went on for 115 minutes![44] Recorded at the venue and then released, the epic qawaali talks about God inquiring man about his (man's) hypocrisies. Aziz Mian taunts the puritans who call him a drunk. He suggests that in reality, they were the ones who were drunk on things which were far more sinister. Things like power, hypocrisy and prejudice.

By the time the Zia dictatorship folded (August, 1988), Pakistan's 'Golden Age of Qawaali' was at an end. Frustrated by not being able to play enough concerts and record a lot more albums in the 1980s, Aziz Mian's drinking problem worsened. In the late 1980s, the supremacy of both Aziz Mian and the Sabri Brothers was successfully challenged by a little known qawaal who would (for a while) go on to regenerate the Qawaali genre in Pakistan, and turn it into a popular global phenomenon. Nusrat Fateh Ali Khan had arrived.

Immensely talented, Nusrat took the melodious subtleties of the Sabri Brothers and the lyrical spiritual paradoxes aired in Aziz Mian's qawaalis and fused them into a style which

---

[43] MA Sheikh: *Music in Pakistan* (Xlibris Publications, 2012) p.72
[44] Ibid.

was flexible enough to be adopted and related on a more universal level. Nusrat Fateh Ali's 1993 epic, *Tum Aik Ghorak Danda Ho* (You Are an Enigma) adopts Aziz Mian's style of arguing with God, and fuses it with the Sabri Brothers' hypnotic melodicism. But unlike Aziz Mian, Nusrat did not write his own lyrics. Nusrat Fateh Ali dominated the qawaali scene across the late 1980s and 1990s, selling albums and playing to packed audiences around the world. But like Aziz Mian, Nusrat too had a deep 'love affair with drink.' He died of liver failure in 1997.

In 1994, Ghulam Farid, leader of the Sabri Brothers, passed away. Aziz Mian continued to perform throughout the 1990s, but the rise of a new batch of qawaals led by Nusrat Fateh Ali never allowed Aziz the space to make his comeback and regain the popularity and commercial success which he had enjoyed between 1972 and 1982. Exhausted and ailing with a failing liver, in 2000, he agreed to honour a contract to perform concerts in Iran. However, halfway through the tour, he passed away. He was 56.

****

The Fall Guy

In 1966 when Zulfikar Ali Bhutto was pushed out from his post as Foreign Minister by the Ayub Khan regime, he found himself in political wilderness. He had even decided to quit politics and leave the country.[45] The feeling of disaffection in him was such that at one point he walked out of his house in Karachi's Clifton area (70 Clifton), and strolled into the opulent Mohatta Palace that is about a 100 meters from 70

---

[45] Stanley Wolpert: *Zulfi Bhutto of Pakistan* (Oxford University Press, 1993) p.23

Clifton.[46] At the time the Mohatta was the residence of Fatimah Jinnah, the aging sister of the founder of Pakistan, Mohammad Ali Jinnah.

Ms. Jinnah had contested the 1965 presidential election against Ayub Khan. But she had retired into seclusion after she was narrowly defeated by the fetching Field Marshall. Bhutto was part of the Ayub government during the election and had enthusiastically aided Ayub in his electoral campaign against Ms. Jinnah. Nevertheless, when Bhutto arrived at her doorstep, feeling abandoned, Ms. Jinnah agreed to meet him and her parting words to him were: 'I told you never to trust Ayub.'[47]

Bhutto had opposed Ayub's ceasefire agreement with the Indian Prime Minster when the 1965 Pakistan-India war reached a stalemate. The war was largely initiated by Bhutto's analysis which hypothesized that the Indian military was vulnerable after it was defeated by the Chinese army in 1962.[48] Ayub accused Bhutto of misleading him, and Bhutto came out to claim that 'Ayub had lost the war on the negotiating table'.[49] Bhutto enjoyed a sudden surge of popularity among students who were angry at the ceasefire agreement. But after his ouster from the Ayub regime, Bhutto was just a young former foreign minister who had gained the admiration of some sections of the youth. This support was likely to wither away if not cultivated from a political platform.

So Bhutto first tried to make his way into Council Muslim League - the Muslim League faction that was opposed to the League's faction being led by Ayub (the Convention Muslim

---

[46] Phillip E. Jones: *Pakistan People's Party: Rise To Power* (Oxford University Press, 2003)
[47] Ibid.
[48] Ibid.
[49] Ibid.

League). But Bhutto's meeting with the Council League leadership did not go anywhere, mainly because the party was being headed by established Muslim League veterans.

After noticing the era's rise of leftist sentiments among the youth around the world, Bhutto sensed the same phenomenon unfolding in Pakistan. Encouraged by the support he had received from the student community after the 1965 war, Bhutto now began to contemplate joining the time's largest left-wing party in Pakistan, the National Awami Party (NAP).[50] But here too he failed to bag an important spot because NAP already had a number of established leaders in its fold.

The resultant despondency drove Bhutto to leave Pakistan for the UK. There he began receiving letters from J. A. Rahim. Rahim was a retired civil servant who had been a surreptitious member of the clandestine Communist Party of Pakistan (CPP).[51] Rahim advised Bhutto to form his own party. Bhutto met Rahim and explained to him how Pakistan was ripe for the emergence of a populist progressive party.

Like Bhutto, Rahim too possessed a sharp intellect and was extremely well-read. But he was also a trained Marxist ideologue and theoretician. A Bengali[52], he had studied Philosophy and Political Science at university and then gone on to receive an additional degree in Law. As a university student, Rahim had taken part in the movement which had given birth to Pakistan in 1947. In Pakistan he joined the new country's fledgling civil service. He also covertly became a member of

---

[50] Ibid.
[51] JH Korson: *Contemporary Problems of Pakistan* (Brill Archives, 1974) p.32
[52] JA Rahim was a Bengali from the Bengali-majority East Pakistan, a region that separated from the rest of the country in 1971.

the Communist Party of Pakistan.[53] But he chose to be politically sedentary, until he saw how Bhutto was hailed as a hero by the youth in 1965.

At the time, Bhutto had a rather superficial knowledge of Marxism, but he was impressed by how Rahim had used Marxist analytical tools to justify the emergence of a populist socialist party in Pakistan. Consequently, in 1967, Rahim became one of the founding members of such a party: The Pakistan People's Party (PPP). Bhutto was elected the party's chairman.

Rahim was also the main author of the party's first manifesto.[54] Other contributors included Dr Mubasher Hassan (left-leaning economist), Hanif Ramay (the intellectual who introduced Bhutto to the concept of 'Islamic Socialism'),[55] and Bhutto himself. Rahim, Hassan and another socialist leader, S. Mohammad Rashid, were the main architects behind organizing the PPP across cities, towns and villages of (mainly) West Pakistan. They used various Maoist and Leninist organizational methods in this regard, setting up numerous party offices; forming youth, peasant and labour groups; and striking alliances with radical left-wing student outfits and trade unions.

Rahim also authored much of the party's literature (in English) which was translated into Urdu and in regional languages. The PPP swept the 1970 election in West Pakistan's two largest provinces, Sindh and the Punjab. It became the country's ruling party in December 1971 after East Pakistan broke away to become Bangladesh. Bhutto became President and then Prime Minister.

---

[53] Phillip E. Jones: *Pakistan Peoples Party: Rise To Power* (Oxford University Press, 2003)
[54] Tariq Ali: *Street Fighting Years: An Autobiography of the Sixties* (Verso, 1987) p.318
[55] Phillip E. Jones: *Pakistan Peoples Party: Rise To Power* (Oxford University Press, 2003) p.223

Rahim was made a federal minister. Along with other upper PPP ideologues, Rahim immediately initiated the party's project to turn Pakistan into a socialist economy. However, by 1973, when a dramatic increase in oil prices by oil-rich Arab states triggered a global economic crisis, Bhutto began to drastically scale back his government's socialist initiatives. Bhutto was more of a populist pragmatist than a socialist. From 1974 onwards, he moved slightly to the right and sidelined the party's left ideologues. Some of them were even ousted. Rahim was asked to become Pakistan's Ambassador to France. But in 1975, Rahim was back and sitting in the drawing room of 70 Clifton with some other ministers. Bhutto used to often invite his ministers and party leaders for dinner but would not meet them till very late in the night. Rahim, now in his 70s, got agitated and complained, 'I am not waiting for the Maharaja of Larkana!'[56] [57]

He then stood up and left. The very next day an armed party of Bhutto's special security force raided Rahim's house, dragged him out, punched and kicked him, and then threw him in jail.[58] Bhutto accused Rahim of insulting his (Bhutto's) ethnicity[59]. However, Bhutto soon released him, apologized and asked him to return to France as Ambassador. Rahim passed away in 1977, the year Bhutto's regime fell in a reactionary military coup. Rahim's son welcomed the fall.[60]

It is surprising that not much has been written about the man who transformed Bhutto from being a lost politician into

---

[56] Stanley Wolpert: *Zulfi Bhutto of Pakistan* (Oxford University Press, 1993) p.240

[57] Bhutto hailed from the Sindhi town of Larkana. Maharaja in Urdu and Hindi means king or prince.

[58] I H. Burney in Outlook (Vol: 3), 1974.

[59] Bhutto was Sindhi-speaking.

[60] Abdul Qayyum: *Three Presidents, Three Prime Ministers* (Dost Publications, 1996) p.129

becoming a powerful partisan force, and then helped him form one of the largest political parties in Pakistan. During Bhutto's last days in his death cell (in 1979), one of the things Bhutto is said to have regretted most was his fall-out with his former mentor. But the mentor was no more. And after April 4, 1979, neither was Bhutto. He was hanged through a sham murder trial by the military regime.

****

The Conflicted Romantic

The 1970s are remembered as the 'Golden Age of Television' in Pakistan, in which the state-owned PTV produced a sequence of quality serials and music programming. Though (in that era), most of the TV serials in Pakistan either insinuated the Bhutto government's 'socialist' and populist overtones, or were an apolitical celebration of the various liberal notions of the period; there were also teleplays which indirectly addressed the perceived dichotomy which emerged when the government-initiated populism clashed head-on with a new reactive historical narrative being built by the state after the violent separation of East Pakistan in 1971.

The frontline figure in this context was intellectual and playwright, Ashfaq Ahmed. A serial based on his teleplays called *Aik Mohabbat, Sau Afsanay* (One Love, Many Stories [1975-76]), celebrated the liberal signs of the times and the sense of freedom being exhibited by the middle-class youth. But the bottom-line of almost each and every play of the serial was always a plea to balance modern notions of liberalism with the country's traditional religious moorings. But the problem was, nobody was quite sure exactly what this traditional religious stock constituted. Pakistan was (and still is) a diverse populace of various ethnicities, Islamic sects and sub-sects, and 'minority religions'. So much so that (as proven by the violent 1971 Bengali nationalist movement in former East Pakistan) one's ethnic roots had begun to matter more than the concoction of a singular version of faith and nationhood shaped by the state at the time of Pakistan's creation in 1947.

Ashfaq's balancing pleas emerged from his Sufi bent. For a while he was a supporter of Bhutto's socialist initiatives, so he would first rip into the supposed 'hypocrisies of the modern bourgeoisie' before advising an equilibrium between modern materialism and traditional eastern spiritualism. This is clearly visible in one of his most popular TV plays, *Dada Dildada* (The Hearty Grandfather [1976]).

It is a story of a loving and liberal grandfather and his favourite grandson (played by the late Zafar Masood) who (with his long hair, flamboyant personality and liberal ideas), is the stereotypical 1970s urban middle-class youth. The grandfather (Dada) loves to drink and the family is happy radiating within the comfort of their bourgeoisie cocoon, until the grandson falls seriously ill. The helplessness of the 'liberal' belief system is then supposedly exposed when the doctors fail to cure the grandson and the family (especially the doting grandfather) starts to crumble.

Ashfaq alludes that the glue which was keeping the family together was of superficial nature because it had actually detached the family from its traditional spiritual anchorage. In a scene inspired by Mughal Emperor Babar's sacrificial undertaking — in which to save his son Humayun's life, Babar is said to have given up alcohol[61] — the grandfather prays to God

---

[61] Harivansh Rai Bachchan: *In the Afternoon of Time* (penguin Books, 1998). p.266

that his life be given to the grandson and for this he was willing to give up drinking.

The grandfather then enters the grandson's bedroom where the young man lies dying. There the grandfather starts to walk slowly around the grandson's bed until he stops and sits on the edge of the bed. The next thing we see is the young man opening his eyes. He is cured. When he approaches the grandfather, the old man has quietly passed away.

Ashfaq Ahmed's TV plays of the era were a lot more literary compared to the hyperbolic nature of the time's 'social films;' but the question is, was Ahmad also critiquing Bhutto's populism, blaming it for encouraging the disengagement between Pakistani youth and religion? The Bhutto regime seemed to have perceived Ashfaq as attacking bourgeois-capitalist values, whereas to Ashfaq, he was simply ordaining 'genuine Sufism' in the vulnerable minds of modern young people (of the era).

But his critique seems to have had a more pronounced scheme, because during the conservative set-up under the Ziaul Haq dictatorship in the 1980s, Ashfaq Ahmed's TV plays actually became the social and intellectual validations of Zia's convoluted 'Islamisation' agenda. Ashfaq Ahmed who had been inspired by the 1940s' 'Progressive Writers Movement' in South Asia, had, by the 1960s, begun to abandon the Movement's Marxist and Freudian themes. But his teleplays of the 1970s appeared to have largely supported the populist discourse of the Bhutto regime, even though the plays had increasingly become critical of the social outcome of the liberal aura that the Pakistani society was emitting (at least on the surface) during the mentioned decade.

Eventually, Ashfaq also emerged as one of the first popular TV playwrights to become conscious of a dichotomy (this time during the Zia regime) which saw the middle classes become 'pious' and, simultaneously, overtly materialistic. Observers believe that after experiencing bitter disappointment with the Z.A. Bhutto regime, Ashfaq Ahmed himself wanted to tackle the social and cultural dichotomies emerging from Zia's Islamisation-meets-capitalism maneuvers.

By now Ashfaq had started to dabble heavily into Sufism. His teleplays became longwinded and somewhat complicated commentaries on the psychological tensions in the society arising due an awkward merger of materialism (*maa'dah pasandi*) and spiritualism (*roohaniat*). Fakirs danced in most of these teleplays, as urban middle-class families were shown stricken with various psychological and spiritual ills after letting their materialistic desires override their spiritual instincts.

These plays were a symptom of yet another important development. Even though the shrine culture that was glorified by these plays was, in the political context, more associated with Bhutto's populism, however, beginning in 1981, it had started to be co-opted by the Zia regime. In the 1950s, Pakistan's 'social films' had largely portrayed the Islamic cleric (*maulvi*) as an uncouth, illiterate and exploitative scoundrel[62] (mostly in films by famous Expressionist film director, Luqman).

Teleplays in the 1970s continued the tradition, with 1974's Nijat (Riddance) that was penned by Ashfaq, going as far as to explore the sexual tautness a young village cleric goes through in everyday life, crammed between his primal instincts and his puritanical indoctrination. However, beginning in 1980, the Zia regime 'advised' PTV to

---

[62] Ziauddin Sardar: *Critical Muslim 3* (Oxford University Press, 2013)

discourage the practice of showing the cleric the way he had been perceived by the bulk of Pakistani writers.

From then onward the cleric in PTV teleplays not only became a recurring character, but he suddenly became a wise old man with a white beard, praying-beads in hand, and blessed with a soft and empathic disposition. As PTV was announcing the arrival of the good *maulvi* on the mini-screen, the character of the *pirs* (spiritual leaders directly associated with Sufi shrines) became largely villainous. They were now shown as men who exploited the superstitious and illiterate peasants.

To take the mantra of 'Islamisation' to the middle-classes, PTV, apart from using the symbol of the wise and polite cleric in its teleplays, also began introducing conservative Islamic televangelists who had the ability to punctuate their commentaries with English words and terms. The impression being given was that of a preacher who could use and understand English and was, thus, 'educated' and 'civilized,' even though the contents of the lectures of these preachers remained to be highly conservative, and, of course, in line with Zia's Islamisation discourse.

Ashfaq's job now was to present the cleric as someone who was as equipped to run a shrine as he was a mosque. The line between the Sufi and the cleric began to blur in his plays during the Zia regime. Ashfaq lured the bourgeoisie away from the supposed 'irreligiosity' of the 1970s with Sufi-themed plots of spirituality, and once their interest was aroused, the same plots then put them on a path of middle-class piety which attempted to work as a reconciliation between religious devoutness and modern material aspirations. To him this was a balancing act. To his critics it was nothing but a way to excuse moral and material hypocrisy. Ashfaq's influence as a playwright began to wane after the 1980s. He passed away in 2004, outliving both Bhutto and Zia.

****

Girl in a Volcano

When one enters into a conversation about Pakistan's Urdu poetesses, he or she usually can't talk beyond the brilliance and poetic charms of women such as the elegant Parveen Shakir, the fiery Fehmida Riaz and the redolent Kishwar Naheed. Though many do know about one Sara Shagufta as well, somehow a lot of local literary critics feel a sense of dread, confusion and even frustration while critiquing her poetry.

Sara's work has attracted highly polarized responses. Some have called her the Virginia Woolf of Pakistan, while others scorn at her for being a self-obsessed rambler.[63] One of the reasons behind the contrasting responses that her work has provoked is, perhaps, to do with how she suddenly exploded as a poet after living a pretty ordinary life of a housewife.

Sara Shagufta was born in Gujranwala in 1955. She wrote poetry only fleetingly as a teenager, going through the motions of schooling and willingly being prepared by her parents to one day become a good wife. What was unknown to her parents was that her obedience was an unconscious attempt on her part to ruthlessly repress a rather volcanic emotional side of her personality which would surge much later.

When she first got married in 1972 at the age of 17, she tried her best to become the good wife. But her volatile (albeit

---

[63] Amrta Pritama: *Life & Poetry of Sara Shagufta* (B. R. Publication, 1994) p.97

self-repressed) personality, and intelligence somehow offended her husband.[64] The marriage didn't last long and she moved on to marry a second time, this time on her own accord. But when the couple's child died at birth, the husband blamed Sara.[65] This is the moment when what she had been repressing for years finally flared up. It was a rebirth of sorts but an extremely painful one. The emotional volcano in her had been simmering for far too long. She stormed out of the marriage. According to her biographer, she began to 'use the lava that poured out as ink with which she wrote some of her most controversial and intense poetry.'[66]

For the next decade or so she would write manic, provocative and yet overtly sensitive poems, and at the same time search for a man who would sacrifice his ego to empathize with her stirred state of mind and sense of love. She rapidly fell in and out of love, marrying twice more but storming out of these marriages as well. When the military general Ziaul Haq toppled the Bhutto regime in July 1977, Sara turned political.

Though her poems were still mostly about misunderstood women and a longing to be loved and understood despite her turbulent emotional state and sense of individualism, she plunged into political activism, taking part in various anti-Zia rallies and movements.[67] In the early 1980s, Sara was arrested at a time when the military regime was jailing poets, student activists, journalists and intellectuals.

- Many chose to escape into exile, but Sara decided to stay. Sara's fourth marriage too crumbled. Pressed to the brink by her constant

---

[64] Ibid.
[65] Sara: A Play by Mahesh Dattani (Media Publicist, April 1, 2010).
[66] Amrta Pritama: *Life & Poetry of Sara Shagufta* (B. R. Publication, 1994)
[67] Ibid. p.96

emotional, intellectual and now political tribulations, she finally ran out of the emotional and creative enclaves that she had constructed for herself to retreat into. On the night of March 1984, she committed suicide by swallowing poison. She was just 29. Moved by Sara's death, another famous Urdu poetess, Parveen Shakir, wrote a poem lamenting Sara's untimely demise. Ironically, Shakir too would die young. She was killed in a car crash in Islamabad in 1994.

****

Man, Feminist, Donkey

When the concept of 'women's lib'[68] began to take root as a movement in the late 1960s and 1970s (in the West), a number of urban middle-class Pakistani women too began to echo the movement's mantras and rhetoric. Some of these women would eventually go on to form various women's organizations which directly challenged what, according to them, were 'anti-women laws' of the dictatorship of General Ziaul Haq (July 1977-August 1988).

But one of the first prominent feminists in Pakistan was actually a man! He was the famous film comedian and director, Rangeela, who became the paramount Pakistani filmmaker to fully express the concerns and beliefs of the 1970s' 'women's lib movement'. And he did it through a big-budgeted feature film which he directed, produced and acted in. The film was called *Aurat Raj* (Women's Rule). It was released in 1979 but bombed at the box-office, despite the fact that it was made and released in an era when the Pakistan film industry was still thriving and the country's cities and towns were peppered by hundreds of cinemas.

---

[68] Women's liberation (aka Women's lib).

Aurat Raj was just too ahead of its time (in the context of Pakistani cinema);[69] and Rangeela had to edit out a number of even more interesting ideas from the film because by the time the film was released, a reactionary dictatorship had come in. Nevertheless, Rangeela not only managed to make the film, but also got the distributors to release it in cinemas across the country.

In the 1970s, a majority of Pakistani films had actually ridiculed the antics of the period's women's lib movement. But Rangeela decided to turn the tables and satirize those who were ridiculing the movement, especially men. Rangeela did not come from an educated or liberal background. He was a half-literate man who, before becoming an actor, had eked out a meagre living by painting billboards. In the 1960s he managed to rise as a film comedian, known for his awkward slapstick antics devoid of any wit whatsoever. His strange frame - big head, small body, thin legs and the odd sounds which emerged from his gaping mouth - were enough to make filmmakers cast him to provide a few laughs in their otherwise more 'serious' farces.

Bored with this slapstick routine and frustrated by the way filmmakers were constantly typecasting him, Rangeela formed his own production company. He started to direct and produce his own films and the first three released by his company (between 1969 and 1972) all scored big at the box-office. He continued to appear as a comedian in his own films as well, but he gave himself a more central role in the plots and also introduced himself as a soulful playback singer.[70]

With three major hits, his production company was suddenly flooded with millions of rupees. But he was still not satisfied.

---

[69] Mushtaq Gazdar: *Pakistani Cinema – 1947-97* (Oxford University Press, 1997)
[70] A playback singer is a singer whose singing is pre-recorded for use in movies, especially in India and Pakistan.

Restless as he was, he decided to put almost all of his earnings into an ambitious project which sought to bring to the big screen a Pakistani/Urdu version of Anthony Quinn's 1956 Hollywood epic, *The Hunchback of Notre Dame*.

Playing the misunderstood hunchback himself (in a fictional Island kingdom), Rangeela was gutted when the film performed dismally at the box-office. What's more, he had lost almost all the money which his production company had made during the previous three years. He had to revert back to picking up stereotypical slapstick roles again to survive as a professional actor. It was during this period that he managed to bag a lead role in a film called *Insaan Aur Gadha* (Man and Donkey). Directed by Syed Kamal, the film went on to become a major hit, putting Rangeela in the limelight again.

In *Insaan Aur Gadha*, we see a donkey praying to God to turn him into a human being. When the donkey does turn into an (albeit awkward) man (played by Rangeela), he faces situations that make him ask God to turn him back into a donkey again. Tired of existing as a man, he holds a political rally in which only donkeys participate. He makes a hilarious speech there decrying the moral, social and political hypocrisies of human beings.

Here the film was clearly satirizing populist leader and fiery orator, Zulfikar Ali Bhutto. The scene takes a sardonic swipe at the inanity of the masses who fall for the rhetorical charms of popular leaders. The Bhutto regime banned the film[71] believing that the scene was a parody of Bhutto's speech-making style, which it was. Though Rangeela had been a passionate supporter of Bhutto, he had become disillusioned with the elected prime minister. However, the ban was soon lifted and the film was again allowed to run after vanishing from the cinemas for a few weeks.

---

[71] The Herald Vol. 36, 2005. P.76

The bankruptcy and collapse of Rangeel's production company did not stop him from dreaming big. After managing to recover some of the money he had lost, Rangeela rebuilt his production company. In 1978 he again began plotting a film that would make him stand out as a film-maker. It was at this point that someone told him about an idea of a story that the famous Pakistani novelist, Shaukat Thanvi, had once mentioned about a world in which societies were entirely matriarchal.

Excited, Rangeela decided to expand the idea into a film. He signed up a number of the time's famous actors and actresses and completed the film by early 1979. Once again Rangeela invested all of his earnings into an off-beat project. The distributers were shocked at what they saw: A scathing satire on male-dominated societies. The film also parodied the concepts of heroes and heroines in Pakistani films, and was sympathetic to the radical feminist point of view.

The film is actually like no other ever made in this country. It has a wife (played by Rani) of a flamboyant male chauvinist (played by Waheed Murad) who treats women like objects. The wife finally puts her foot down and organizes a women's movement in the area. The movement dramatically spreads and mobs of women begin to get hold of oppressive men and beat them up in the streets.

The government intervenes and decides to hold an election to resolve the issue. The election is swept by the Aurat Raj Party (Women's Rule Party) and the womenfolk gain political power. Rani becomes the country's new leader and purchases a special bomb from a foreign country. The bomb is special because after exploding it turns all men into women. All the women are elevated to the social and political positions which were once dominated by the men, and the men are relegated to wearing women's clothes and pushed into occupations and duties which are stereotypically associated to women.

What follows is a hilarious, biting satire which mocks male chauvinism, social conservatism and female stereotypes constructed by the popular media in a patriarchal society. The film was so visually and conceptually startling (for its time) that the audiences were not sure exactly how to respond. Rangeela once again went bankrupt.

In a 1990s essay of hers, the well-known TV producer, Shireen Pasha, wrote that some very good films began to flop from the late 1970s onward. According to her one of the reasons was a demographic shift in the country's film audiences. As the populist and extroverted cultural zeitgeist of the decade began to recede and a more conservative mind-set began to take its place, the Pakistani films' middle-class audiences became introverted and stopped venturing to the cinemas.

Romantic and social films began to flop and action flicks became popular. So one can deduce that, though, Pakistani cinema's middle-class audiences (which constituted a huge female audience) would have been more appreciative of a film like *Aurat Raj*, those who actually went to see it belonged to an emerging new audience who had come to watch Waheed Murad as a shouldering Casanova and Sultan Rahi as the muscle man he would go on to become in the 1980s.

But what they got was Murad being beaten black and blue by Rani and Sultan Rahi in a blond wig, playing the role of a mustached mother-in-law! As for Rangeela, he never recovered from the loss he concurred from this cinematic debacle. He managed to remain afloat as a comedian for the next decade or so, but never again did he allow himself to dream this way. He died of liver failure in 2005.

****

Man who fell to Earth

As a kid in the 1970s, one of the first Urdu authors that I began reading was Ibn-i-Safi. Most Pakistani kids and young people in cities did the same and probably many still do. I don't anymore, now outgrowing the fantastic sounding cities and countries full of quirky spies, strange gadgets and racy plots that Safi created in his novels, making him one of Pakistan's biggest-selling Urdu novelists of all time.[72]

However, I returned to reading Safi again a few years ago when English translations of some of his many novels began appearing in local book stores. Though much of Safi's highly inventive style of writing largely gets lost in translation, it was nice to see someone actually attempting to introduce this most prolific and popular author to a whole new generation. More interesting, however, is the reality of Safi the man. A reality that is still not very well documented.

A majority of his fans simply know him through the colourful characters that he created, operating in an environment which Safi culled from the archetypical political paranoia of the Cold War years (a period during which Safi wrote his novels). Very few are aware that some of Safi's characters and plots may also have emerged from a serious bout of schizophrenia[73] that he suffered in the early 1960s. For a period of time, the mental illness rendered him incapable of writing anything at all[74], but he eventually recovered and actually converted some of the phantasms that he had confronted during his illness into new scenarios and plots in his comeback novels.

---

[72] Ziauddin Sardar: *Critical Muslims: Pakistan* (Oxford University Press, 2012) p.135
[73] The Son of Ibnne Safi: Anuradha Varma (The Times of India, May 23, 2011)
[74] Ibid.

Ibn-i-Safi was himself a fascinating character. Born in 1928 in Allahabad (in British India), Safi became part of the Progressive Writers Movement. It was a left-oriented endeavor which included a number of Urdu writers who fused Marxism with Freudian psychology.[75] Safi was constantly harassed by the British colonial authorities for his views. Even after the British left India in 1947, Safi continued to face harassment (this time from the Indian authorities).[76]

Warrants were issued for his arrest and this forced him to cross over into the newly formed Muslim-majority country, Pakistan. He became a school teacher here, but continued to write stories and articles for various Urdu magazines. In the 1950s, he took a literary detour and began to pen highly imaginative spy novels, though some of them he had already begun to write and plot in India.

From 1954 onward the pace of his writing doubled, and by 1960 he had authored dozens of novels, all taking place in the imaginary, fantastical world which he had created, and full of flamboyant and wise-cracking spies, beautiful women, strange-sounding villains, exotic places and odd gadgets. But as Safi came up with one exotic story after another, he also began to isolate himself from his immediate surroundings. He eventually collapsed within himself, suffering a crippling spell of schizophrenia. Incidentally at the time of his breakdown, Safi was working on a non-fiction book on human psychology called, *Aadmi Ki Jarien* (Man's Roots). He never finished it.

In 1960 his career seemed to be as good as over when he was put on heavy tranquilizers. The hyperkinetic genius had

---

[75] Sobia Karim: *Progressivism and Modernism in Urdu Literature* (American Journal of Contemporary Research, 2012).
[76] Ziauddin Sardar: *Critical Muslims: Pakistan* (Oxford University Press, 2012) p.135

crossed that thin line into a territory roundly described as 'madness.' He hid in his room, refusing to come out, as strange-sounding men plotted and conspired against him from subterranean bases (all in his head). After a stint in hospital where he received treatment through electric shocks,[77] Safi was shifted back to his home where he was patiently nursed back to health by his wife and a family *hakeem.* [78]Amazingly, just three years later, he was back writing again.

The demand for his spy novels reached new heights in Pakistan as well as India. He kept producing them with incredible speed. By the early 1970s, he was dishing out an average of three to four novels a year, setting new standards in the genre of racy Urdu spy fiction. In another interesting twist, in 1973, the Pakistan military actually invited him on a few occasions to lecture new recruits on the 'art of espionage'.[79]

During my research on him (for this book), I stumbled upon an old 1973 newspaper cutting (from a local Urdu daily) that had a photograph of Safi lecturing a group of military recruits in Islamabad. In the short report that accompanied the photograph, an officer is quoted as saying that it was 'Safi Sahib's unique understanding of the politics of the Cold War that made them [the military] invite him to deliver a few lectures'.

Being Pakistan's best-selling author, one of Safi's books was also turned into a film by Hussain Talpur (a maverick film-maker nicknamed, 'Maulana Hippie'). However, the film, *Dhamaka* (Explosion), released in 1974, bombed at the box-office as the director simply failed to convincingly

---

[77] Rashid Ashraf: Inbn-e-Safi: Beyond Borders (Business Recorder, July 23, 2011)
[78] A traditional practitioner of herbal medicine.
[79] Azfar Nisar; Aeysha Mehmood: *Identity Formation in Detective Fiction in Pakistan* (Journal of Pakistan Studies Vol:4, 2012) p.38

translate Safi's animated words and imagery on the big screen. But despite being a bestselling author, a lot of his fans believe Safi made half the amount of money that he should have. This was mainly due to the shadiness of some of his publishers, and his own lack of understanding of the financial sides of his profession.

In 1977, a TV series based on some of his novels was produced by the country's state-owned TV channel, PTV. However, its run was disallowed when during the same year the government of the populist Z.A. Bhutto was toppled in a military coup. The reason given by the in-coming military regime was that the series was 'vulgar'.

In 1978, Safi, who had continued to be on medication ever since the early 1960s, fell ill again. His legendary productivity as a writer slowed down and by 1979 he was bedridden, as publishers fought around him over how much money was made from his books. Then in 1980 he passed away, dying quietly and finally getting the rest that he had longed for decades. He left behind an enormous body of work that is still being reproduced. He was 52.

****

The Pakistani Calypso

The flamboyant zeitgeist of the 1970s in Pakistan also determined how the country's sportsmen carried themselves. Pakistan became a hockey power in this decade and its hockey teams of the period were often made up of men who were boisterous and highly animated. Same can be said about the country's cricket team, especially the one which began to develop from the mid-1970s onward. One of its most intriguing characters in this regard was Wasim Hassan Raja.

Pakistan has produced a number of brilliant cricketers. But none has been as impalpable and (to his captains) as frustratingly talented as Wasim Hassan Raja. Just before the 1987 Cricket World Cup when the then Pakistan cricket captain, Imran Khan, was holding a large fundraiser for his planned cancer hospital in Lahore, the Pakistan team joined him on the stage. The host of the event, late comedian and actor, Moin Akhtar, went around with a microphone interviewing various players. When he reached Imran, he asked him who he thought was the most talented player he's ever played with.

Imran smiled, and while pointing towards Wasim Raja's younger brother and cricketer, Ramiz Raja, said: 'His brother, Wasim. He was hugely talented, but very erratic.' Another Pakistani cricketing great, Javed Miandad, agreed. He explained Raja as a 'breathtaking stroke maker.'[80] Imran, in his book, *An All Round View*, wrote that Raja never did justice to his stunning talents as a batsman.

Coming from an upper-middle-class family of Lahore, Raja made his Test cricket debut for Pakistan in 1973 at the age of 20, selected because of his prodigious cricketing talents. Imran wrote (in the aforementioned book), that when he used to see Raja bat in the nets at the time, he was floored by how hard Raja stroked the ball and with such ease and style.

But throughout his career, Raja remained to be a nonconformist and a loner. He continued to have a problematic relationship with almost all of his captains and with the Pakistan cricket board. Perhaps the only captain who was able to

---

[80] Gideon Haigh: *Silent Revolutions: Writings on Cricket History* (Black Inc. 2006) p.306

somewhat nurture his talent well was Mushtaq Muhammad, under whom Raja played some of his finest cricket.

In 1975 former West Indian captain and batsman, Rohan Kanahi, wrote that he was highly impressed • by the swashbuckling batting style of Raja. But he was perplexed to see Raja sitting alone at the bar during a party at a business tycoon's house in Karachi's Old Clifton area. 'He (Raja) was not very easy to talk to,' he told a journalist after the party. 'He was very private and detached from the rest of the team.'[81]

But the crowds loved him. During the second Test match against the visiting West Indies team in 1975, while fielding near the boundary line, Raja baited a section of the large crowd at Karachi's National Stadium by teasingly threatening to unzip his fly.[82] Outraged, the conservative Urdu press accused him of being drunk on the field, which, most probably, he was. But Raja responded by cracking a hard-hitting century. So that was that.

Pushed in and out of the team due to his cavalier approach, Raja was dropped from the squad after the first Test match during the 1976 series against the visiting New Zealand side. His name was missing again from the 18-member squad that was announced for Pakistan's twin tours of Australia and the West Indies. Both teams at the time were considered to be the best in the world.

On the insistence of captain, Mushtaq Muhammad, Raja was finally given a place in the touring squad. But in spite of performing well in the side games, Raja could not find a place in the playing XI in the 3-Test series against Australia (and which

---

[81] Told to me by Muhshtaq Haleem a friend of various West Indian players who were on that tour.
[82] I am a witness to this. I was present in the stands watching the match as an 8-year-old. I had gone to the stadium with my elder cousins. To them Raja was what Shahid Afridi would become to Pakistani cricket fans almost 30 years later.

Pakistan drew 1-1). Just before the third and last Test of the series, Raja had scored a scorching century against a tough Queensland side. But when the night before the Test he was told by the team manager (Col. Shujah) that he will not be picked for the match, Raja went on a rampage.

Always a reckless drinker but painfully introverted, Raja decided to express his rage by smashing all the mirrors in his hotel room with a half-empty whiskey bottle.[83] He then stumbled into the hotel lobby, slurring abuses at Col. Shujah.[84] A few Pakistani players who were having a drink at the hotel bar panicked. They immediately approached Mushtaq, and it was left to the captain to cool Raja down. The fact was that Col. Shujah had actually wanted Raja in the playing XI, but it was Mushtaq who decided to play Haroon Rashid instead.[85]

Raja during his tirade had also demanded to be sent back home. But did not remember saying this the next morning. When the news reached the Pakistan cricket board, it decided to recall Raja to Pakistan as a disciplinary measure. Mushtaq vetoed the decision. Raja finally got his chance on the West Indies leg of the tour, on faster wickets and against an even quicker set of bowlers. In a closely contested 5-Test series that the Windies won 2-1, Raja stacked over 500 runs, cracking one century; 5 fifties; and hitting 14 sixes – a world record at the time.[86]

A Pakistani player[87] fondly remembered how Raja (during the fourth Test) sat in the dressing room in his shorts, then casually walked out to smoke a cigarette with some West Indian

---

[83] Mushtaq Mohammad: *Inside Out* (Uniprint, 2006)
[84] Ibid.
[85] Ibid.
[86] The record was equaled by England's Kevin Pietersen in 2006.
[87] Told to me by a former Pakistani player who was on that tour. Name of the player is withheld on request.

fans, came back, padded up, went in and hit the fearsome fast bowler, Joel Garner, for a first ball six over long-off!

Almost a decade later, famous Caribbean cricket commentator and journalist, Tony Cozier, wrote that (during the 1977 series) Raja had become extremely popular with the West Indian cricket fans who had dubbed him the 'Pakistani calypso.'[88] In his 2006 autobiography, Mushtaq Mohammad wrote that he continued to tolerate Raja's 'many eccentricities' because he was performing brilliantly.

After five top Pakistani players (including Mushtaq) opted to play for Kerry Pecker's World Series Cricket[89] in Australia (and were consequently banned by the Pakistani board), Raja's name came up as a potential replacement for Mushtaq as captain. But his volatile personality and cavalier approach made the board give the position to wicketkeeper Wasim Bari. Raja was made Vice-Captain.

When the banned players returned for the 1978 series against India, Raja was dropped. He had batted carelessly during the late 1977 and mid-1978 series against England. But most other Pakistani batsmen had failed as well and this is why the banned players were recalled. However, Raja found himself back in the team for Pakistan's exhaustive six-Test tour of India in 1979. Asif Iqbal replaced Mushtaq as skipper.

Asif had no clue how to handle the team's two brilliant but mercurial players: fast bowler Sarfaraz Nawaz and Raja. Asif had a falling out with Nawaz who refused to play under him. But Asif decided to take Raja along. Sarfaraz was an extrovert. He

---

[88] Calypso is a popular style of Afro-Caribbean music that originated in Trinidad and Tobago during the early to mid-20th century.

[89] Kerry Packer was an Australian media tycoon who formed his own rebel cricket league which was not recognized by the official international cricket body. Players who played for this league were banned by their respective cricket boards.

was boisterous, confrontational and loved to stay out late, visiting bars and clubs. Raja on the other hand was an introvert, moody and private.

As Pakistan's top order batsmen all struggled on the Indian tour and the team's premier fast bowler, Imran Khan, found himself struggling to fix a troubled back and fending off reports about him having a torrid affair with Bollywood actress, Zeenat Aman, Raja decided to have a ball. Pakistan lost the series 2-0, but Raja scored over 500 runs, throwing caution to the wind and always in danger of being dropped for not heeding the captain's advice. But he was the only one scoring big runs for a befuddled Pakistan side.

TV viewers were often amused by the sight of Asif almost pleading with Raja to stay put on the wicket and hold the fort. But Raja would keep swinging hard and connecting, and then almost always fall to reckless shots. During a side game on the same tour (which was being televised in Pakistan), Raja enthralled a large crowd with a few lusty sixes. He then lost his wicket in trying to play another heavy stroke. As the TV cameras followed him walking back to the pavilion, an Indian fan came running towards him to shake Raja's hand. Raja stretched out his hand, then suddenly dropped it and gestured as if he was about to go straight for the fan's testicles! The fan jerked back and fell over. The stadium erupted with laughter. The camera quickly panned away.

Raja carried his good form under new captain, Javed Miandad, even though Miandad confessed that it was always tough to rein-in Raja's impulsiveness and detached demeanor.[90] Veteran sports journalist, Iqbal Munir, explained Raja as an 'angry young man,'[91] who was always hard to

---

[90] Javed Miandad; Saad Shafqat: *Cutting Edge* (Oxford University Press, 2004).
[91] SAMMA TV interview, 2006.

understand, and, in fact, actually did *not* want to be understood.[92] Raja hardly had any close friends in the team. The only player he did somewhat get along with was fast bowler, Sarfaraz Nawaz, himself a volatile and erratic figure. Along with Imran Khan, Raja was the other man in the side at the time famous (rather infamous) for having multiple affairs. However, in 1981, he decided to tie the knot when he fell for a British woman. The couple wedded in 1981 and Raja invited only a handful members of the Pakistan team. He conveniently forgot to invite Sarfaraz.

But instead of being offended, Sarfaraz in an interview to Pakistan's monthly magazine, Herald, said that he planned to gatecrash the wedding because 'this was one wedding he would never want to miss.'[93] He added: 'How can one not go to Wasim Raja's wedding? It's almost unimaginable to see him sitting there like a responsible husband-to-be!'[94]

Raja continued to baffle the selectors and captains and constantly lost his position in the side until he finally bid farewell to cricket in 1986. Apart from having another successful series in 1984 (against India), Raja stopped reacting the way he used to when being dropped. It seemed his volatile temperament was neutralized when his younger brother, Rameez, entered the squad. He was more than happy to see his younger brother come good, even though Rameez was not half as talented as Wasim. However, he was considered to be a more dependable batsman and a lot more 'normal.'

Imran Khan suggested that Wasim Raja was brimming with extraordinary talent, but his detached attitude, and his temperamental and loner personality stopped him from realizing

---

[92] Ibid.
[93] Herald (May, 1981)
[94] Ibid.

his true potential and become a constant part of the team.[95] After quitting cricket, Raja moved to the UK to become a teacher. He returned as a coach of the Pakistan national cricket squad. But his stint as coach (in the early 1990s), was terribly short. Brilliant left-arm fast bowler, Wasim Akram, later wrote[96] that Raja (as coach) was extremely moody, temperamental and would often get angry 'for no reason at all' [97] Akram thought Raja was an unpredictable grouch.

Raja again returned to the UK and settled there permanently with his wife and two sons. He was often invited to officiate Test matches as a referee, but he also resumed his career as a teacher of mathematics and geography. In 2006, while playing a friendly match for Surrey's over-50 IX, Raja suddenly collapsed. He was immediately rushed to a hospital where he was declared dead on arrival. He was just 54.

****

Pandora's Men

The legacy of Pakistan's former Prime Minister, Zulfikar Ali Bhutto, is a mixed bag of praise, platitudes and panning. Whereas, on the one hand, he is hailed as being perhaps the sharpest and most dazzling politicians ever to grace the country's political landscape, he is also slammed for being a megalomaniac and a demagogue, readily willing to sideline his democratic principles in his pursuit to retain political power.

Applauded for successfully regenerating a demoralized and fractured country's pride (after the 1971 East Pakistan debacle),

---

[95] Imran Khan: *All-Round View* (Chatto & Windus, 1988)
[96] Wasim Akram: *Wasim* (Piatkus Books, 1998)
[97] Ibid.

and igniting within the working-classes a sudden sense of political consciousness, Bhutto is also remembered as the man who (to remain in power) continued to play footsie with reactionary political outfits and (thus) ultimately betraying his own party's democratic and socialist credentials.

Not only did he attract fierce opposition from the right-wing parties, but the left and liberal sections of the Pakistani intelligentsia have also come down hard on him for capitulating to the demands of right-wing outfits on certain issues. With the ever-increasing problem of religious bigotry and violence that Pakistan has been facing ever since the 1980s, many intellectuals, authors and political historians in the country have blamed the Bhutto government's 1974 act of constitutionally redefining the status of the Ahmadiyya community as the starting point of what began to mutate into becoming a sectarian monstrosity in the next three decades.

The Ahmadiyya community was (almost overnight) turned into a non-Muslim minority in Pakistan. Many observers correctly point out that by surrendering to the demands of the religious parties in this context (especially after they had resorted to violence), Bhutto unwittingly restored their confidence and status that were badly battered during the 1970 election.

But I believe panning Bhutto for introducing constitutional expressions of bigotry has become too much of a cliché. It's become a somewhat knee-jerk reaction, and an exercise in which the details of the 1974 event have gotten lost in the eagerness of repeatedly pointing out the starling irony of a left-liberal government passing a controversial theological edict.

I will not go into the theological aspects of what was then called 'the Ahmadiyya question,' because I am not academically qualified to do that. Nevertheless, it is important that one attempts to objectively piece together the events that led to the final act. Events that seem to have gotten buried underneath layers of polemical diatribes exchanged between orthodox Muslim scholars and those associated with the Ahmadiyya community; and also due to the somewhat intellectual laziness of the secular intelligentsia that has exhibited a rather myopic understanding and judgment of and on Bhutto's role in the episode. My take on the issue is by no means an attempt to judge the theological merits or demerits of the bill that constitutionally relegated the Ahmadiyya community as a non-Muslim minority. Mine is just an attempt to bring to light certain events that culminated in the demotion of the Ahmadiyya community.

To do so I did go through some literature produced by orthodox Sunni and Shia *ulema* and by those associated with the Ahmadiyya community during the commotion, but the literature is largely theological in nature. So I have ignored it because I lack the theological training to comment on it, and anyway, it is hardly helpful in understanding the day-to-day on-ground happenings which led the Bhutto government to turn a demand of his right-wing opponents into a legislative ruling.

Instead, my findings in this respect are squarely based on, and culled from the writings of historians and authors who, I believe, have transcribed the history of the event in the most objective and informed manner. I have also used a plethora of information available in the day-to-day reporting of the commotion by certain Urdu and English newspapers of the time (especially between May and July 1974).

As we have already discoursed elsewhere in this book, a series of modern, as well as puritanical reformist Muslim movements emerged after the complete fall of the Muslim Empire in India in the mid-1800s. The Ahmadiyya movement was one of them. The Ahmadiyya community was founded in 1889 by Mirza Ghulam Ahmad, who claimed he was under divine instruction to fulfil the major prophecies present in Islamic and other sacred texts regarding a 'world reformer' who would unite humanity.[98] He announced to Christians awaiting the second coming of Jesus, Muslims anticipating the Mahdi, Hindus expecting Krishna, and Buddhists searching for Buddha, that he was the promised messiah for them all,[99] bespoken by God to rejuvenate true faith.

When Mirza died the Ahmadiyya split into two sects: the 'Qadianis' and the 'Lahoris'.[100] The Qadianis claimed that Mirza was a messiah, and declared that Muslims who did not accept him as such were non-Muslims.[101] Claiming divine prophecy is regarded to be a major sin by a majority of Muslims, even though the Lahori faction believes that Mirza never claimed prophethood.[102] Orthodox Muslim sects in South Asia believe that he did.

As the 19th century reformist movements competed against each other to organize the Muslim community in India, they often clashed among themselves. In their polemical publications, they denounced their counterparts as either being 'bad Muslims' (*fakir*) or outright heretics/infidels (*kafir*). For example, the Sunni Muslim reformists emerging from seminaries in the Indian city of Deoband (the 'Deobandis') denounced another Sunni Muslim sub-sect, the 'Barelvis,' of introducing questionable innovations in the practice and rituals of Islam. The Barelvis, a less puritanical Sunni sub-sect, responded in kind. Both, however, were on the same page when it came to Shia Islam and accused the Shias of heresy.

[98] M G. Ahmad: *The Heavenly Decree* (Islam International, 2006) p.i
[99] Ibid.
[100] J Azuma: *My Neighbor's Faith* (HarperCollins, 2009) p.61
[101] From a 1914 article by Abul Kalam Azad quoted by Z Aziz in *The True Succession: The Founding of the Lahore Ahmadiyya Movement* (A.A.I.I.L, 2014) p.101
[102] J Azuma: *My Neighbor's Faith* (HarperCollins, 2009) p.61

Till about 1913, the Ahmadiyya movement was seen as a spiritual and evangelical branch of the modernist reformist Muslim initiatives triggered by the likes of Sir Syed Ahmad Khan and Syed Ameer Ali. In fact, till the early 1900s, a number of Indian Muslim intellectuals considered Mirza Ghulam Ahmad as a modern redeemer of faith in India.[103] Contrary to popular belief, agitation against the Ahmadiyya movement (by the orthodox Muslim sects and sub-sects in India) did not emerge immediately after the formation of the community in 1889. The more vocal accusations against the community first arose 24 years later in 1914 when an influential Ahmadiyya leader, Mirza Muhammad Ahmad, began to publicly declare that Mirza Ghulam Ahmad was a messiah and those Muslims who disagreed with this were at fault.[104]

This split the movement, with the so-called 'Qadianis' sticking to Mirza Muhammad Ahmad's assertions and the 'Lahori' faction denouncing him and accusing him of inferring something that Mirza Ghulam Ahmad did not claimed. Nevertheless, the schism within the Ahmadiyya community and Mirza Muhammad Ahmad's unabashed claims left the movement vulnerable against accusations of being heretical. The accusations began to pile up in earnest from 1915 onwards and by the 1940s the orthodox *ulema* began to pressurize the Muslim leadership in India to address the 'Ahmadiyya question.' Interestingly, the Ahmadiyya movement allied itself with Jinnah's All India Muslim League (AIML). During the crucial 1946 election in the Punjab, the main opposition to the Ahmadiyya came from Islamic groups allied to the Indian National Congress (INC); or from Islamic scholars who did not recognize the League to be the sole representative of Indian Muslims.

---

[103] SA Vahid (ed): *Thoughts and Reelections of Iqbal* (Lahore, 1964) p.297
[104] M Ahmad: *A Mighty Striving* (2012) p.234

The League at the time was a mixture of Muslim modernists, secular democrats, pro-Jinnah *ulema* and even some Marxists. The pro-League *ulema*, however, advised Jinnah to dissociate himself from the party's Ahmadiyya members because Islamic outfits that were being backed by the INC were using the issue to question the party's Muslim credentials. Jinnah ignored the suggestion.[105]

In 1951, three years after the creation of Pakistan, the government initiated an intense crackdown against left-leaning officers in the military, the Communist Party of Pakistan (CPP) and its affiliated trade, student and labour unions. This created just enough of a space for some radical rightist forces to seep in. This opportunity was further widened by the disintegration of the ruling Muslim League that was by then plagued by infighting, corruption and exhaustive power struggles between its main leaders. In 1953 after smelling an opportunity to reinstate their political credentials, the Jamaat-i-Islami (JI) and the Majlis-i-Ahrar gladly played into the hands of the then Chief Minister of Punjab and veteran Muslim Leaguer, Mian Mumtaz Daultana, who was plotting the downfall of his own party's prime minster, Khuwaja Nazimuddin.[106]

Harboring a burning ambition to become the prime minister after former Prime Minister Liaquat Ali Khan's assassination in 1951, Daultana was bypassed when the League chose the Bengali Nazimuddin as PM who Daultana had considered to be incompetent. As Chief Minister of Punjab, Daultana was being criticized for the rising graph of unemployment and food shortages in the province.[107] Anticipating protests against his

---

[105] Ibid. p.491

[106] MJ Nelson: *In the Shadow of Shariah* (Hurst Publishers, 2008) p.122

[107] V. Grover; R. Arora: *Political System of Pakistan* (Deep & Deep, 1995) p.158

provincial government's failure to rectify the economic crises in Punjab, Daultana began to allude that the economic crises in the province were mainly the doing of outsiders.[108]

The Ahmadiyya had played a role in the creation of Pakistan and were placed in important positions in the country's military, bureaucracy, the government and within Pakistan's still nascent business class. Daultana did not accuse the Ahmadiyya directly. Instead, he purposefully ignored[109] and even gave calculated support to JI and the Ahrar who decided to use the crises in the Punjab by launching a campaign against the Ahmadiyya community, demanding its excommunication from the fold of Islam.

As JI and Ahrar members went on a rampage destroying Ahmadiyya property in Lahore, Daultana was able to shift the media's attention away from his provincial government's economic failures. But his triumph was short-lived. The Nazimuddin government with the help of the military crushed the movement and rounded up JI and Ahrar leaders. It then went on to dismiss Daultana. The demand to throw the Ahmadiyya out of the fold of Islam was rejected.

The crackdown against the protesters and the arrest of the movement's main leaders (on charges of instigating violence against the state) seemed to have buried the Ahmadiyya question once and for all. No significant move to reignite the issue was made for the next 20 years. But when the move did come, it took everyone by surprise.

Ahmadiyya had overwhelmingly voted for the Pakistan People's Party (PPP) in the Punjab province during the 1970 election. The community was well entrenched in the country's

---

[108] Ibid.
[109] Report on the Court of Inquiry Constituted Under Punjab Act-II on the 1953 Punjab Disturbances (Published in 1954)

economy and had not faced any major acts of persecution from the orthodox Islamic parties and the *ulema* ever since 1954. On May 22, 1974, some 160 members of JI's student-wing, the IJT, boarded a train headed for Peshawar in the former NWFP. On its way to Peshawar, the train stopped for a while at the Rabwah railway station. The city of Rabwah was predominantly an Ahmadiyya town. The community's spiritual headquarters were also located here. As the train stopped at Rabwah, IJT students got out and began to raise slogans against the Ahmadiyya[110] and cursed the community's spiritual figurehead, late Mirza Ghulam Ahmad (during the sloganeering). According to the IJT members, however, they did this because members of the Ahmadiyya community were forcibly distributing 'propaganda pamphlets' to the passengers.[111]

The train then left the station taking the charged students to Peshawar. No untoward incident was reported apart from the slogan-chanting. However, when the incident was related to some Ahmadiyya leaders in Rabwah, they ordered Ahmadiyya youth to reach the station. After finding out that the students would be returning to Multan from Peshawar on the 29th of May, dozens of young Ahmadiyya men gathered at the station. When the targeted train came to a halt, the men fell upon the bogeys carrying the IJT members. A fight ensued and 30 IJT men were severely beaten for insulting the spiritual sentiments of the Ahmadiyya.[112]

A non-Ahmadiyya man who witnessed the commotion at the station told reporters that both the incidents (the slogans and the retaliation) were unprecedented. 'Someone wanted this to happen,'

---

[110] Hassan Abbas: *Pakistan's Drift into Extremism* (Routledge, 2015) p.82
[111] Ibid.
[112] Anwar H. Syed: *The Discourse & Politics of Z A. Bhutto* (McMillian Press, 1992)

he said, without saying who that someone was.[113] Interestingly, whereas the first incident had only been briefly reported by the newspapers, the news of the attack on IJT was prominently displayed in the country's Urdu press. JI demanded that the culprits of the attack be apprehended or the party would hold countrywide protest rallies. Police arrested 71 Ahmadiyya men in Rabwah and the Punjab government headed by the PPP's Chief Minister, Hanif Ramay, appointed KM Samadani, a High Court judge, to hold an inquiry into the incident.[114] But this did not stop the JI from launching a protest movement. It was soon joined by other opposition parties which included the centre-right Muslim League, the right-wing Majlis-i-Ahrar and even the centrist Tehrik-i-Istiqlal headed by Asghar Khan. Also joining the protests were various bar associations of the Punjab, orthodox ulema and clerics.

They demanded that Ahmadiyya members be removed from the bureaucracy and government; Ahmadiyya youth outfits be disarmed; and that Rabwah be declared an 'open city' because it had become 'a state within a state.'[115] The protests turned violent and spread across various cities of the Punjab. Mobs attacked houses and businesses owned by the Ahmadiyya. Dozens of members of the Ahmadiyya community lost their lives, mostly in Gujranwala and Sargodha.[116]

The leaders of the protest movement then demanded that the Ahmadiyya be excommunicated from the fold of Islam. On June 4, while speaking on the floor of the National Assembly, Prime Minister Bhutto refused to allow opposition members to speak on the Ahmadiyya issue.[117] He accused the opposition of being

---

[113] Morning News (May 25, 1974).
[114] Anwar H. Syed: *The Discourse & Politics of Z A. Bhutto* (McMillian Press, 1992)
[115] Ibid.
[116] Ibid.
[117] DAWN June 5, 1974.

'hell-bent on destroying the country.' His party had an overwhelming majority in the assembly and protests from the members on the opposition benches were briskly relegated.

Then, when the riots escalated, Bhutto gave the Punjab CM the green signal to use force to quell the riots. The police came down hard on the rioters and managed to reduce the intensity of the turmoil after a week. On June 14, opposition parties called for a wheel-jam strike. It was successful in the Punjab and in some cities of the former NWFP, but was largely ignored in Sindh and Balochistan.

On June 19, newspapers quoted Bhutto as saying that the government was committed to protecting the lives and property of all Pakistanis and that his government was even willing to use the army for this purpose. He was reminding the opposition how the army had brutally cracked down against anti-Ahmadiyya rioters in 1953. Bhutto then appealed to the opposition that the 'Ahmadiyya question' can be settled in a more 'civilized manner' without resorting to violence and bigotry. He said now was not the right time.[118] He appeared on TV and radio and insisted that he will not allow 'savagery and cannibalism'. He said the Ahmadiyya issue had been around for 90 years and could not be solved in a day. He suggested that the issue be referred to the Advisory Council of Islamic Ideology (ACII) - a non-legislative advisory body that was formed by the Ayub Khan dictatorship in the early 1960s and was mostly headed by liberal Islamic scholars.

After the June 14 strike, Bhutto allowed the issue to be discussed in the assembly and told the press that his party members in the House were free to vote on the issue according to their individual conscience.[119] Jamiat Ulema-i-Islam (JUI) chief,

---

[118] Morning News, June 20, 1974.
[119] Anwar H. Syed: *The Discourse & Politics of Z A. Bhutto* (McMillian Press, 1992)

Maulana Mufti Mehmood, who was heading the opposition's stand on the issue, responded by accusing Bhutto of trying to put the Ahmadiyya question in cold storage. 'A mere resolution in the assembly will be an eyewash,' he told reporters. 'Bhutto is trying to sweep the issue underneath the carpet.'

Religious parties, the JI, the JUI and the Barelvi Jamiat Ulema-i-Pakistan (JUP) had formed an 'Action Committee' with the centre-right Pakistan Democratic Party (of Nawabzada Nasarullah) and Pir Pagara's Muslim League faction. They called it Qadiyani Muhasbah Committee (Committee for the Exposition of Qadyanism). Opposition parties such as the left-wing National Awami Party (NAP) remained silent. Mufti Mehmood demanded that a bill be passed in the assembly that would once and for all declare the Ahmadiyya community as a non-Muslim minority. JI's Mian Tufail demanded the same and warned Bhutto that 'his double-talk on the Ahmadiyya issue would trigger his downfall.' The centre-right PDP also joined in the chorus and demanded that a bill be introduced in the Parliament declaring the Ahmadiyya as non-Muslim. Opposition parties and clerics again threatened to take to the streets to force the government to introduce the suggested bill.

Bhutto maintained that declaring the Ahmadiyya a minority and pushing them out from state and government institutions would be detrimental to the economy and political stability of the country. He also protested that the issue was a religious one and hence the National Assembly should not be used to resolve it. The religious parties disagreed. They reminded him of the constitution that all the political parties had approved only a year earlier (1973). They told him that the constitution had declared Pakistan an Islamic Republic so how could he claim that a religious issue had no place in the National Assembly?

It was at about this time that some advisors of Bhutto warned that if the crises was allowed to simmer or sidelined, the party might lose some assembly members in the Punjab[120] who were sympathetic towards the demands of the opposition. On Bhutto's orders, one of his ministers, Kausar Niazi, led a government delegation that held a series of meetings with the *ulema* belonging to Sunni (both Deobandi and Barelvi) sub-sects, and the Shia sect. They agreed to form a parliamentary committee to look into the demands of the parties that were leading the anti-Ahmadiyya movement.

The government convinced the members of the committee that the spiritual leader of the Ahmadiyya community also be given the opportunity to present his thoughts and opinion on the issue. After weeks of intense discussions between the parliamentary committee, the *ulema* and the head of the Ahmadiyya community, the committee decided to finally introduce the bill in the assembly.

Sections of the press stated that a majority of PPP legislators were unwilling to vote for the bill. But even though the report that was prepared by the committee was never made public, parts of it were leaked to the legislators. The report allegedly recorded the head of the Ahmadiyya community telling the committee that he only considered those who were Ahmadiyya as Muslim.[121] On Sept 7, 1974, the bill was passed and the Ahmadiyya became a non-Muslim minority.

The violence came to a halt after the passage of the bill, but a large number of Ahmadiyya who were actively involved in the fields of business, teaching and the civil service began to move out of Pakistan, leaving behind the less well-to-do members of

---

[120] Ibid.
[121] Ibid.

the community who till this day face regular bouts of violence and harassment.

In another series of ironies, in 1977, the parties that had rejoiced the excommunication of the Ahmadiyya in 1974 were out on the streets again, this time agitating against the very government and man who had agreed to accept their most assertive demand. In the final act of this irony, in April 1979, the same man was sent to the gallows (through a sham murder trial) by the military dictatorship of Ziaul Haq.

In 1984, the Zia dictatorship further consolidated the state's stance against the Ahmadiyya by issuing an ordinance (Ordinance XX) which prohibited the Ahmadiyya from preaching or professing their beliefs. The ordinance that was enacted to suppress 'anti-Islamic activities' forbids Ahmadiyya to call themselves Muslim or to pose as Muslims. Their places of worships cannot be called mosques and they are barred from performing the Muslim call to prayer, using the traditional Islamic greeting in public, publicly quoting from the Quran, preaching in public, seeking converts, or producing, publishing, and disseminating their religious materials.

****

The Misunderstood Maulana

Though, just for a while, the Bhutto government had become gallant in the eyes of the religious sections of the country, within this government was an anti-hero, who, incongruously, was also an Islamic scholar. Minister of Religious Affairs in the Z.A. Bhutto government, Kausar Niazi, has often been mistreated by history. Many local historians have charged him for influencing some of the Bhutto government's many controversial policies, especially the one that supposedly 'resolved the long standing Ahmadiyya question'. A number of former members of Bhutto's PPP have squarely blamed Niazi for influencing Bhutto regarding the thorny matter. In the 1950s and the 1960s, Kausar Niazi was a prominent member of the JI. In 1953 he was arrested and jailed by the government for taking part in the violent anti-Ahamdiyya riots in Lahore. Niazi was also highly vocal in his support for JI's criticism of the 'secular' Ayub Khan dictatorship (1958-69).[122]

However, after Ayub Khan eased out his young foreign minister, Z.A. Bhutto, in 1966, Niazi supported Bhutto. When Bhutto formed his own party in 1967 (the PPP), the JI denounced the PPP of being a party of communists who were being backed by the Soviet Union to 'destroy Islam in Pakistan'.[123] After disagreeing with JI's line of attack against Bhutto, Niazi broke away from JI. He was consequently invited by Bhutto to join the PPP. Bhutto was searching for a religious scholar to join his party, someone who could retaliate against JI's diatribes against the PPP. Niazi's entry into the PPP was not welcomed by the PPP's leftist ideologues.[124] But Bhutto overruled their concerns, suggesting that Niazi fully backed the party's socialist program. Niazi was given the party ticket to contest the 1970 election from a constituency in Sialkot. This constituency had a large Ahamdiyya population.

But Niazi, now positioning himself as a 'progressive Muslim scholar' and a firm advocate of the PPP's socialist manifesto, decided to hold a series of meetings with the leaders of the

---

[122] Dalip Mukerjee: *Quest For Power* (Vikas Publishing House, 1972) p.70
[123] R K P Multani: *Islamic Fundamentalism in South Asia* (Summit Enterprises, 2007) pp.153-154
[124] Husain Haqqani: *Pakistan: Between Mosque and Military* (University of Michigan, 2008) p.107

Ahamdiyya community. He convinced them that the PPP would never allow the religious parties to outlaw the Ahmadiyya from the fold of Islam and that the PPP was the community's only hope against excommunication. The Ahmadiyya community, before getting Niazi's assurances, had already reached an understanding with the leaders of the socialist National Awami Party (NAP).[125] The NAP too had promised the community that it would keep the religious parties from reviving the anti-Ahmadiyya campaign.

Niazi succeeded in making the Ahmadiyya community choose the PPP over NAP and vote for the PPP across Pakistan. This also helped Niazi to win the election from his Sialkot constituency where he received over 90,000 votes. Niazi became an advisor in the Bhutto cabinet, and in 1974 he was made a federal minister (Minister of Religious Affairs). This was also the year when the religious parties had revived their campaign to oust the Ahmadiyya community from the fold of mainstream Islam.

After much ruckus in the streets and the parliament, Bhutto decided to allow the religious parties to table a bill for the constitutional excommunication of the Ahmadiyya from Islam. Bhutto asked the PPP legislators to vote (for or against the bill) according to their own conscience. Some Punjab-based PPP legislators along with the religious parties and conservative Muslim League (ML) factions voted to declare the Ahamdiyya a non-Muslim minority. The NAP abstained from voting but did not air its disapproval. NAP's leader, Wali Khan, was still simmering from the manner in which the Ahmadiyya leaders had broken their understanding with NAP, and had, instead, favoured the PPP during the 1970 election.

---

[125] Humair Ishtiaque: *Story Untold* (Pakistani Study Centre, 2012)

Eminent lawyer, Barrister Azizullah, wrote in his diary that when he asked Wali Khan why NAP had remained quiet on the issue, he was told (by Wali): 'Let them (the Ahmadiyya) go to the ones they voted for ...'

What was Niazi's stand on the issue, a man who in the 1950s had agitated against the Ahamdiyya? Ironically, Niazi actually advised Bhutto not to turn the bill into law.[126] Niazi's opposition in this regard is explained in a bit more detail by the respected Pakistani columnist and intellectual, late Khalid Hassan, in a letter that he wrote to one of his readers many years later.[127] He wrote: 'If there was one man in the Bhutto cabinet in 1974 who was opposed to declaring the Ahmadiyya a minority, it was Maulana Kausar Niazi. He told me this himself.'

Hassan recalled Niazi telling Bhutto, 'please do not pursue this 80 years old problem. As far as the clerics are concerned, one cleric can't bear to stand behind another to say his prayers. Let them decide on their own; the government should stay away from this matter ...'[128] But Bhutto, concerned that his inaction on the issue would destabilize his government, ignored Niazi's advice.

Niazi lost his place in the PPP when Bhutto was toppled in a military coup in 1977. Niazi was accused by Bhutto's widow, Nusrat Bhutto, of 'being the establishment's man'. In 1978, Niazi formed his own faction of the PPP, the Progressive Peoples Party. The party did not last and Niazi retired from politics. He returned in 1990 as a member of National People's Party (a party formed by his former PPP colleague, Mustafa Jatoi who was eased out from the PPP by Benazir Bhutto in 1987). Kasuri was

---

[126] Husain Haqqani: *Pakistan: Between Mosque and Military* (University of Michigan, 2008) p.109
[127] Portions of the letter published on Telegraph.co.uk April 16, 2009.
[128] Ibid.

finally welcomed back into the PPP in 1993 by Benazir when she became Prime Minister for the second time. But Kasuri passed away only a year later in 1994.

****

Shortly Naked

The 1970s are remembered as a decade of cultural flamboyance in which lifestyle liberalism dominated the social discourse across the world. Pakistan was no exception. By 1975 cinemas and nightclubs in the country were reporting record profits,[129] and tourists were thronging the streets of Karachi, Lahore, Gilgit, Peshawar and Swat.[130] The swinging times managed to somewhat overshadow the political and economic turmoil the country had found itself in after the 1971 war with India. The country's urban cultural scene also began to incorporate patrons from classes that were below the so-called elite sections.

For example, in the 1970s, apart from the already established nightclubs such as Oasis and Playboy (in Karachi), bars and clubs also sprang up in the city's Saddar area and on Tariq Road[131] which specifically catered to middle and lower middle-class clients. When in 1975 Pakistan's first 'Adults Only' film, *Dhulan Aik Raat Ki* (Bride for a Night) became a massive hit, three Karachi-based journalists[132] managed to get a license from the government to publish Pakistan's first ever Urdu 'sex magazine.'

---

[129] Shah Alam Khan: *Tourism in Pakistan: 1975-77* (Pakistan Ministry of Tourism, 1977) p.15
[130] Ibid.
[131] Jonathan Shapiro Anjaria, Colin McFarlane, Huma Yousaf: *Urban Navigations: Politics, Space and the City in South Asia* (Routledge, 2013) p.304
[132] Names withheld on request of two the journalists. The third passed away in 2009.

American 'adult magazines' such as Playboy and Penthouse were only available from some booksellers who used to smuggle them into the country from the US and UK and sold them at a price only affordable to a limited number of Pakistanis. The journalists decided to start publishing a Pakistani Playboy that would be in Urdu and cost only Rs. 2 a copy. Called *Ishtraq* (partnership), it appeared on the newsstands in January 1976. Though not published on glossy paper and only publishing black and white pictures, every month the magazine carried a few political articles, some steamy short stories, and images lifted from Playboy and Penthouse photo shoots. It also had a column on 'sexual advice' in which readers' questions were answered by psychologists.

Ishtraq was an immediate hit, but only available in the big cities. By November 1976 its circulation had risen from 9,000 copies per month to almost 30,000, despite the fact that the publishers had jacked up its price in July 1976 from Rs.2 to Rs. 4. The magazine was, however, banned and its license revoked when opposition leaders forced a cornered Bhutto regime to close down nightclubs and bars in April 1977.

Interestingly, the magazine's license was renewed in late 1978 by the reactionary Ziaul Haq dictatorship. But the magazine was only allowed to function as a social lifestyle monthly. It was banned again in 1979 when it ran a completely apolitical story about a journalist's experience of going out to buy a goat for that year's Eidul Azha.[133] The story mentioned how the journalist was made to check the goat's teeth. This, Zia's Information Ministry claimed, was a taunt at Ziaul Haq's ubiquitous grin! The ministry immediately cancelled the magazine's license again.

---

[133] Conversation with one of the publishers in Karachi, September, 2007.

The journalists were all 'blacklisted' by the dictatorship. The ban on them to work in a newspaper was lifted in 1980 and all of them joined mainstream Urdu dailies. Copies of old *Ishtraq* issues were ordered (by the government) to be burned, even though some of them continued to be sold (in secret) for a while at an old books market in Karachi's congested Bolton Market area. This is where I got my copy from (as a 15-year-old teen) in 1981. Unfortunately, I lent it to a friend at college in 1985, who then lent it to a cousin of his who never returned it. What a loss.

****

The Missing Star

Pakistan is not exactly known for producing international tennis stars. But recently Aisam-ul-Haq has done well to represent the country as its most well-known tennis player. But long before Aisam, Pakistan had managed to produce a tennis player who not only became one of the first Pakistanis to play at the prestigious Wimbledon tournament, but also played a number of matches against famous international tennis stars, such as Jimmy Corners and Arthur Ash.

It is thus sad that the name of this player has gone missing from the memory of a majority of Pakistanis. The truth is, he too went missing. He suddenly vanished, as if into thin air. His name was Haroon Rahim, and for almost a decade he was one of the most respected and well known Pakistanis in the international tennis circuit. He first entered the limelight when he represented Pakistan in the Davis Cup at the age of 15 (in 1967).[134] A tennis prodigy, Rahim rapidly rose to become

---

[134] Haroon's Suggestions: The Statesmen, Vol. 23, 1977.

Pakistan's No: 1. At age 20 he was given a scholarship by the University of California (UCLA) where he became the captain of the university's tennis team and partnered future World No:1 Jimmy Connors[135] in many tournaments.

Rahim remains to be the only Pakistani player to have made it to the quarterfinals of the highly competitive US Open (in 1975). It was due to him that various famous tennis stars visited Pakistan for matches in the 1970s.[136] But his personal life wasn't always this glorious. Though coming from a well-to-do family, Rahim was constantly rebelling against his family's patrician background. He began to spend more time in the United States. In 1978, while at the peak of his game, Rahim met and married an American woman.[137] This did not go down well with his family who refused to acknowledge the union.

Angered by the reaction of his family, he cut off all ties with them.[138] Not only that, he also quit tennis and simply disappeared. He was just 29 at the time. Some believe that he joined a roving cult in California, sold all his possessions, and changed his name and appearance.[139] This is also the time when his family stopped their search for him. He was never heard from (or seen) again, even though his family believes he's still living in the US (under a new name and identity).

****

---

[135] Ibid

[136] World Tennis, Vol. 28, 1980. p.16

[137] Haroon Rahim: The Unknown Hero: Maira S. (Pakistan 360 Degrees, December 11, 2010).

[138] Ibid.

[139] An acquaintance of Haroon's brother told me that this was never the case. He said that the family knew where he was till the early 1980s, even though he severed all ties with them. None of them have spoken or heard from him for over three decades now.

Cooler Sahib

In July 2015, while driving over the Clifton Flyover in Karachi - a good part of which runs past the shrine of Sufi saint Abdullah Shah Ghazi - I thought I saw a *malang* (spiritual vagabond) whom I once knew. He was lying on the footpath on the right of where the flyover ends. I slowed down the car to take a closer look and indeed it was him, even though he must have been in his 70s now. I hadn't seen him for over 23 years, but remembered well his face, and, especially, his name: Khassu.

I pulled the car closer to the footpath on which he was blissfully taking a nap. I rolled down the car window and shouted, 'Khassu! Khassu!' But Khassu just wouldn't respond. I tried to park my car beside the footpath so I could get down, but a line of vehicles had begun to mound behind my car, with their drivers honking like their lives depended on using their car horns in the most deranged manner possible. I instinctively turned left towards the centre of the road and drove away. A week or so later, I went looking for Khassu again but he was nowhere to be found.

Until about 1995 there used to be a block of apartments just behind the Abdullah Shah Ghazi shrine. The apartment block had a huge parking lot. Some friends of mine and I often went there to play cricket. This was between the mid-1980s and early 1990s. The apartments began being torn down after 1995 and today an imposing 62-storied building stands on that plot.

In the late 1980s my friends and I would frequently visit the Shah Ghazi shrine (mostly out of curiosity); especially on Thursday evenings when a concert of qawaali used to be held there. I wonder if they are still held there now, but till the early 1990s, qawaalis were a regular fixture at the shrine every Thursday evening from 10 pm onwards.

Here is where we first met Khassu. I think it was in 1987, and we had just entered our 20s. Khassu was there, always in a green flowing kurta,[140] a multicoloured fakir cap,[141] a greying stubble and lots of metallic bangles on his wrists. He never spoke a word, unless he was at the qawaali (which he usually was). As the music and the chanting would start to reach a swirling crescendo, Khassu would spring to his feet and begin employing a fascinating, anarchic dance (dhamaal)[142:] all the while shouting 'haq, haq, haq Allah!' After the qawaali he would immediately retreat back into his forlorn state, quietly sharing a sulfi[143] with us.

One day a friend of mine asked another *malang* what Khassu's story was? He told us that Khassu was left at the gate of the shrine when he was a child (that must have been some time in the late 1950s). He'd been living here ever since. The *malang* told us that Khassu was not always this quiet. Then a most remarkable story followed when he said, 'Khassu is waiting.'

Waiting for what? We had asked.

'For Cooler Sahib …' he replied. He actually meant Colour Sahib.[144] Who was Cooler Sahib?

From Urdu, the *malang* suddenly switched to speaking in Punjabi: 'Cooler Sahib was a dear friend (of the vagabonds of the shrine). Especially of Khassu. Khassu still waits for him.'

Where did Cooler Sahib go?

'To his maker, the Almighty,' the *malang* had told us.

So why was Khassu still waiting for him?

---

[140] A loose upper garment traditionally worn by men and women in South Asian countries.

[141] Colourful cap made with patches of cloth of different colours.

[142] A popular form of dance (usually performed when in a trance) in Pakistan.

[143] A kind of a pipe from which drugs such as hashish are smoked.

[144] Sahib means Mister in Urdu and Hindi.

'Cooler Saab told him he will be back to finish a *draaing* (drawing) he was making for Khassu,' the *malang* explained. 'But he never came back. We heard he had died. But Khaasu never believed it. He is still waiting for him.'

Over the next few months we discovered that 'Cooler Sahib' was none other than one of Pakistan's foremost painters, Ahmad Parvez. Born in Rawalpindi, Parvez began his career as a painter at the Punjab University. A restless soul, he soon moved to London in 1955. In the late 1960s, he returned to Pakistan and moved to Karachi. Across the 1970s he rose to become one of the country's premier artists and a huge influence on the then thriving art scene of the city. In spite of being surrounded by admirers, Parvez remained to be a restive and impatient man.

His lifestyle became increasingly erratic. Nonchalant about being hailed as a genius by art critics in the UK, US and Pakistan, and able to sell his work easily, a contemporary noted that Parvez treated money 'as if he hated it'.[145] Parvez was given to rampages and turbulent interactions.[146] In the 1970s, Parvez was a frequent visitor to the Abdullah Shah Ghazi shrine,[147] and could often be seen there with a hashish joint in hand. Critics and contemporaries of Parvez suggest that most of the money that he made was spent on alcohol. Sick of the company he was attracting, he began frequenting various Sufi shrines of Karachi. He became a regular visitor to the Shah Ghazi shrine. Art critic, Zubaida Agha, in an essay on Ahmed Parvez wrote that the more fame Parvez gathered, the more erratic and 'unhealthy' his lifestyle became. By the late 1970s he was almost permanently

---

[145] Remembering a maestro: Salwat Ali (DAWN, Sept. 15, 2013).
[146] Ibid
[147] In Pakistan, Everybody Must Get Stoned: Mariya Karimjee (Global Post, Feb. 27, 2013)

staying on the grounds of the shrine. This is when he must have struck a friendship with Khassu.

A Lahore-based artist, Maqbool Ahmed, who was a student at the Lahore College of Arts in the early 1980s, once told me how when as a teen he came to Karachi (from Quetta) to meet his idol, Ahmed Parvez, he was shocked at what he saw: 'This was in 1978. Parvez was a mess. He didn't even acknowledge my praise and presence. He was an extremely troubled man, but no one seemed to understand why this was.'[148]

Maqbool said Parvez could have made millions (of rupees): 'He did make money but it seemed he wasn't interested. He behaved as if he was selling his soul to people who had no clue what his art was all about.' Maqbool then wondered: 'perhaps it was this guilt that drove him into the hands of the *malangs*?'

Even when the government bestowed upon him the prestigious Pride of Performance Award, Parvez continued with his self-destructive lifestyle. And then it happened. And no one was surprised. In 1979, he was found dead in a room that he had rented at the now-defunct Bombay Hotel, near the I.I. Chundrigar Road in Karachi. Lamenting Parvez's self-imposed isolation and destructive lifestyle, an art critic writing for Dawn in 1979 wrote: 'Ahmed Parvez still had another 20 years of genius left in him. But then, perhaps, it was this genius that so tragically sealed his fate'.

I now know that his friend Khassu is alive. Though he was asleep when I last saw him, it did seem he was still waiting for Cooler Sahib. And for that '*draaing*' he was promised 36 years ago.

---

[148] Conversation with artist, Maqbool Ahmad, in 1989, Karachi.

CHAPTER 8

METAMORPHOSIS: PAKISTANI NATIONALISM TRANSMUTES - FROM MUSLIM TO 'ISLAMIC'

In one of his initial addresses to the nation on PTV after July 1977, General Ziaul Haq suddenly cut away from his written speech, looked up into the camera and claimed that he knows why most people have stopped watching Pakistan Television (PTV): '*Mujay patah hai log ab TV kyoon nahi daikhtay. Chiriaan jo ourr gain"* (I know why some people have stopped watching TV now. All the birds have flown).'

At once a list was drawn by the new Information Ministry of men and women who were to be banned. A number of actors, actresses, producers and playwrights were barred from appearing on PTV (because they were deemed as being 'pro-Bhutto'). The list also contained names of certain Pakistani films, songs and PTV teleplays that were not allowed any re-runs because they were either labeled as 'obscene' and 'vulgar' or 'politically subversive.'

For example, songs like Naheed Akhtar's *Tutaru Tara Tara* and Alamgir's *Daikha Na Tha* were judged to be 'obscene,' while plays such as Shaukat Siddiqui's *Khuda Ki*

Basti (God's Colony, a 1974 play based on Siddiqui's novel about poverty and crime in Karachi's slums) were not allowed a rerun because the new censor board thought the play glorified socialism - an ideology the new regime reasoned was 'atheistic'.

The Ministry of Information also ordered the destruction of all recorded speeches of former Prime Minister, Z A. Bhutto from PTV's archives and video library, and disallowed the usage of the words 'Bhutto', '*Jamhooriat*' (Democracy) and 'socialism' in plays, talk shows and news bulletins on PTV[1] and Radio Pakistan.

Most urban middle and lower-middle-class Pakistanis began adapting to the changing cultural and political paradigm, largely depoliticizing themselves in the process, perhaps as a defense mechanism to ward off the questions of social morality that they were now facing in an era of outward exhibition of religious piety and a behind-the-scene dash for the sudden opening of worldly opportunities. As a consequence, some stark social and political fissures started to emerge within these classes.

After the folding of the decade of 'socialism' and ideological tussles of the 1970s, urban Pakistan saw itself embracing an anarchic form of capitalism enjoined by a convoluted strain of puritanical Islam and a somewhat incongruous sense of moralism. The contradictions in this context were consciously repressed, with much of the urban society preferring large degrees of pragmatism to deal with the changing scenario, convincing itself that its material survival now depended on its active engagement with the emerging zeitgeist, no matter how contradictory it might have seemed to the society's previous middle-class sensibilities.

---

[1] B Hassan: *Uncensored* (Royal Books, 2000) p.10

The era of populist social and political extroversion had finally come to a close, giving way to a an introversion that had little to do with reflection, and more with a need to hide one's political and social self in an era of sweeping religious propagation and reactive legislation that were directly opposed to the 1970s' populist bearings. This can be located in how the Pakistani society responded to a curious episode which in 1979.

In July 1979, America's National Aeronautics and Space Administration (NASA) announced that its 'Skylab' satellite that had been orbiting the planet since 1973 had developed a fault and was expected to fall over Earth. NASA was not sure exactly where it will crash, but experts believed that the burly satellite was likely to fall either over Australia or over the Indian subcontinent. Though the same experts also stated that the satellite would start to burn after entering Earth's atmosphere and most probably end up in the sea, the story took a life of its own in Pakistan.

The state-owned PTV started to run regular bulletins on the latest whereabouts of the Skylab, usually read by Azhar Lodhi, a newscaster who would go on to become a ubiquitous presence on PTV across the Zia years. Lodhi would maintain a gloomy tone in the bulletins, and then start to punctuate them with equally somber pleas for prayers. Suddenly, most Pakistanis who till then had taken the affair lightly, began applying apocalyptic overtones while speaking (to PTV and newspaper reporters) about the event. Many, including members of the urban middle-classes, even went to the extent of wondering whether the fall of the Skylab (on Pakistan) may trigger the beginning of the Day of Judgment (*Qayamat*)[2].

An anxious strain of panic and fear cut across the Pakistani society. But it was as if the military regime was purposefully

[2] Newsweek, Vol.94, Issue:2, 1979

using the occasion to instill fear into the people's minds by allowing Lodhi to use an apocalyptic tone and pleas for prayers, perhaps alluding that in such a testing hour, Pakistan required a pious and Islamic regime.

In those days, more Pakistanis were still visiting shrines than they were mosques[3], with much of the middle-classes going to the mosques only on special occasions such as the two Eids (celebratory Muslim holidays), and sometimes for the traditional Muslim day of collective prayers on Fridays. However, with Zia's laws starting to come into force, and PTV doubling the number of Islamic programs in its transmission, many young middle-class Pakistanis saw themselves being led (mostly by fear) towards mosques as Lodhi continued to dramatically announce the closing in of the falling Skylab.

The Skylab eventually fell (on July 12, 1979) over the ocean and the deserts of Australia, and once the feared Day of Judgment did not come, the episode was quickly forgotten. The event elapsed but the apocalyptic outlook that it had prompted in the Pakistani society lingered, and it was this grim point of view that worked well for the Zia dictatorship to intensify its so-called 'Islamic' maneuvers and appeal.

The society - especially the urban middle-classes - seemed to have started to collapse inwards, becoming more stoic and introverted in nature in the face of the rapid political, social and cultural changes that had begun to take shape from 1977 onwards.

When General Ziaul Haq toppled the Bhutto regime in July 1977, he had promised to hold fresh elections within 90 days. Instead, he went on to rule the country as a military dictator for 11 years. Zia began to undo the policies of the Bhutto regime and introduced a number of draconian laws (in the name of faith). His

---

[3] Naveeda Khan: *Beyond Crisis: Re-evaluating Pakistan* (Routledge, 2012) p.470

regime was then showered with millions of dollars and riyals by the United States and Saudi Arabia who wanted him to turn Pakistan into a launching pad for an insurgency against Soviet forces that had occupied neighboring Afghanistan in 1979.

This war and the large amounts of American and Saudi aid that followed helped Zia strengthen his grip on power and also stabilize the country's economy that witnessed a boom of sorts under him.[4] The tenancy of the Zia regime was overtly conservative, and the policies which he formulated gradually began to almost completely change the cultural and political dynamics of the society. Nevertheless, the economic boom under him ran parallel to the mushrooming of a rather anarchical form of capitalism and a two-fold growth in institutional corruption and crime. Between 1977 and 1983, his regime faced multiple movements led by left-leaning and progressive political parties. But by the mid-1980s, the resultant violence triggered by these movements began being dwarfed by vicious conflicts between various ethnic groups. It was also in the mid-1980s that the extremist and sectarian organizations that were formed by the state to fuel the mujahedeen insurgency in Afghanistan began to turn inwards and would go on to become a major issue for the state of Pakistan in the coming decades.

Due to the regime's policies, the Pakistani society retracted. From being populist/extroverted it became conformist/introverted. The country's once-thriving film industry collapsed and other art-forms such as folk music, Qawaali and theatre also began their collective decline. However, despite the regime's reactive tone, PTV somehow continued to produce quality programming.

Pakistan cricket and squash that had begun to ascend in the world arena in the late 1970s continued their rise. But from the

---

[4] Yasmeen Mohiuddin: *Pakistan: A global studies handbook* (ABC-CLIO, 2007) p.108

mid-1980s onward, Pakistan hockey began to experience a steady decline. By the time of Zia's demise in 1988, the Pakistan society stood considerably transformed. Interestingly, regarding the time's conservative zeitgeist and Zia's intransigent policies, all that was sowed during this period would not come into full fruition till after Zia's demise. These seeds would begin to sprout events and effects from which Pakistan is yet to recover.

****

The boy who stormed Heaven

In 2010, I met a carpenter named Mateeullah (aka Matee Ghara). 'Ghara' in Urdu means carpenter. Matee at the time seemed to be in his early 70s. He was from my ancestral hometown, Makhad in the Attock District of Pakistan. Matee was hired as a carpenter by my paternal grandfather in the early 1960s to work in the textile mill which my grandfather and his brothers were setting up in Karachi at the time.

Matee Ghara quit the job at the factory in the late 1960s when I was born. He remembered me well, even though I had no recollection of him. Matee had quit because he had managed to bag a job in Makkah, the Muslim holy city in the Kingdom of Saudi Arabia. However, I did remember him once visiting my grandfather sometime in the mid-1980s. But when I mentioned this to him, he became sad. Surprised by his reaction, I asked whether I had prompted a memory he'd rather not talk about.

'No, no, *puttar* (son) ...' he responded in Punjabi. 'I had come to your grandfather to ask him to help me look for my son, Munir.'

I asked him what happened to his son.

'He was beheaded in Saudi Arabia ...' He replied, his voice heavy with grief.

He then added: 'But at the time (in the early 1980s), I did not know this. The Saudis refused to tell me and the Pakistani Embassy told me they had no clue where my son had vanished. It was only some years later that we found out that he had been executed in Riyadh ...'

Matee Ghara, an expert carpenter, had quit his job in Karachi and moved to Makkah with his wife and three young sons. In 1969, he bagged a job at a fledgling furniture factory in Makkah which was owned by a minor Arab prince and managed by a former Pakistani trader. Matee was one of the earliest Pakistanis to travel to an oil-rich Arab country for work.

'There were hardly any Pakistanis in Saudi Arabia when I reached there,' Matee had told me. 'That country was still barren with very few buildings and roads.'

But all this was about to change. In 1964, when one of the more enterprising sons of the founder of the Saudi monarchy became king, he came in with a vision to transform Saudi Arabia into a powerful political player in the world; an ambition built upon the wealth that the desert kingdom had begun to pile after oil was discovered here in 1938. That son was Faisal. He had replaced his brother, King Saud, who had ascended to the thrown in 1953 after King Abdulaziz (the founder of the Saud monarchy) had passed away. Faisal had been critical of his brother Saud, often accusing him of floundering Saudi money, and mismanaging the country's economy.[5] In 1963, Faisal pulled off a quiet palace coup which sidelined his brother.[6] By 1964, Faisal was the new King of Saudi Arabia.

---

[5] Middle East Record Vol: 1, 1960. p.372
[6] Anwar Haroon: *History of Saudi Arabia and Wahabism* (Xlibris, 2014) p.205

Faisal was perturbed by the fact that even though his kingdom was made up of lands and sites from where Islam had originally emerged (in 7th century CE), the Muslim world (at the time) was being dominated by men such as the 'secular' Egyptian ruler and leader, Gammal Abul Nasser; and by left-leaning ideologies such as Ba'ath Socialism and Arab Nationalism that had glued together socialist concepts with populist nationalism and Islamic symbolism.[7]

As a response, Faisal welcomed members of Egypt's radical Muslim Brotherhood who had either escaped or were expelled from Nasser's Egypt. Faisal planned to counter Arab Nationalism by promoting his version of pan-Islamism, and for this he was willing to use his kingdom's oil wealth. But such plans would take some time to materialize. So, Faisal began to concentrate on his other idea to counter Nasser. He began to 'modernize' Saudi Arabia.

He allowed a large number of American and European companies and technicians to set up shop in the kingdom and build for him modern highways, boulevards and buildings. This move by him was denounced by the powerful religious figureheads who had been empowered by his father, Abdulaziz. Though American and British technicians and businessmen (especially those related to the oil industry) had often visited Saudi Arabia during Abdulaziz's time as well, the number of westerners visiting and working in Saudi Arabia increased dramatically during the Faisal era.

Faisal was desperate to modernize Saudi Arabia because Nasser in Egypt and secular Arab regimes in Iraq, Syria, Algeria and Tunisia had all described Saudi Arabia as 'a regressive feudal/tribal backwater' (that was ill-suited to represent the

---

[7] Gad Silbermann: *A study of the ideology and policy of Arab socialist regimes* (Academic Committee of Middle East, 1973) p.4

Muslim world in an era of modern progress).[8] But Faisal had to be careful about how much he could modernize Saudi Arabia. His father had constructed a monarchy with the help of insurgents made up of fanatical Bedouins called the Ikhwan (the brotherhood).[9] Abdulaziz had used the Ikhwan to defeat rival tribes and the Jordanian Hashmite ruler of Makkah in 1926 to become king of a land he renamed Saudi Arabia (after the Saud tribe that Abdulaziz belonged to).[10]

The Ikhwan were followers of a particularly strict and puritanical strand of Islam which some call 'Wahabism.' In the 1930s when oil was discovered in the land and Abdulaziz began receiving Western businessmen and technicians, the Ikhwan accused him of betraying their trust by 'dealing with the devil.'[11] Abdulaziz tried to appease the Ikhwan by insisting that Saudi Arabia was to be an entirely 'Islamic abode' with strict *sharia* laws, and that for Saudi Arabia's new-found oil wealth to be managed well, he needed western expertise and personnel.

But the Ikhwan were unmoved. They threatened to break away from the orbit of the Abdulaziz monarchy and attack the westerners for 'polluting the holy land.' Abdulaziz was alarmed by the reaction and asked British warplanes stationed in Iraq to bomb Ikhwan strongholds near the Saudi-Iraq border.[12] Hundreds were killed in the bombing, prompting an all-out revolt by the Ikhwan against the monarchy. Then, Saudi troops and the Ikhwan came face-to-face in a decisive battle around the

---

[8] Gerhard Böwering, Patricia Crone: *Princeton Encyclopedia of Islamic Political Thought* (Princeton University Press, 2013) p.486

[9] *The Role of the Ikhwan under Abdul Aziz Al-Saud: 1916-34* (University of Durham, 1999)

[10] Ibid.

[11] Ibid.

[12] Ibid.

oasis of Nejdi. Saudi troops armed with latest British weapons mercilessly cut down the Ikhwan and crushed the rebellion.[13]

The few Ikhwan members who managed to survive the rout were allowed to lead quiet lives in the desert. One such man was Mohammad bin Seif.[14] In the 1920s, he had been a commander in Abdulaziz's Ikhwan troops. Seven years after the Ikhwan defeat at the hands of the Saudi army, Seif got married and was blessed with a son. He named him Juhayman. After crushing the Ikhwan, Abdulaziz permitted the formation of a powerful group of clerics who would advise the monarchy on implementing Islamic laws. But the group was not permitted to ever criticize the monarchy. It was led by a blind cleric called Bin Baz.[15]

Nevertheless, in the 1940s, Bin Baz expressed his concern about how the holy land was being allowed to receive 'infidels' (westerners).[16] He was promptly arrested and jailed. He was soon released and, ironically, was made the regime's official religious figurehead after he agreed not to criticize the monarchy.[17] He was, however, allowed (and even encouraged) to deliver fiery sermons in the grand mosque of Makkah against 'communists', whom he believed had taken over the minds of the Muslims in other Arab countries. He also often raged against 'the obscenities of modernity' that were never to be allowed to enter the holy land.

So when Faisal began his modernization project, the powerful Bin Baz was not amused. Faisal largely ignored Bin Baz as long as he didn't pose any direct threat to the Saudi monarchy. Matee Ghara remembered visiting the grand mosque

---

[13] Jenifer Reed: *The Saudi Royal Family* (Infobase Publishing, 2009) p.35

[14] Ibrahim Abu-Rabi: *Intellectual Origins of Islamic Resurgence in the Modern Arab World* (SUNY Press, 1996) p.74

[15] Simon Ross Valentine: *Wahabism in Saudi Arabia and Beyond* (Oxford University Press, 2014) p.160

[16] Ibid.

[17] Ibid.

in the late 1960s and hearing Bin Baz speak. Matee told me: 'Baz was not very happy with Faisal. He never denounce him directly, but kept saying that the holy land was being turned into a playground of the devil.'

In the next few years (i.e. by the early 1970s), Saudi cities began to change and grow. More and more foreigners (including South Asians and Africans) started to arrive (for work), and brand new roads and buildings emerged. The number of people visiting Makkah to perform Hajj also doubled.

Matee told me: 'Faisal was very popular among most Saudis, especially young Saudis. But we, Pakistanis, and people from other poor Muslim countries who had settled in Saudi Arabia also loved him dearly. He was creating new jobs and my three sons got a good education in an Iranian school, even though we were Sunnis. But in those days (Iran was under the Shah) and Iranian schools only taught non-religious subjects. There was no Pakistani school in Saudi Arabia at the time.'

In 1973, when Matee's oldest son Munir turned 16, his mother implored him to get his religious education from a Pakistani Islamic evangelist. The evangelist had been invited by the Saudi regime to set up a religious school for South Asian Muslims in Makkah. Of course, the idea was to impart the Saudi version of the faith to the children of Pakistani and Indian Muslim families working in Saudi Arabia.

'Munir began attending this school (in 1973),' Matee informed me. 'But slowly, he began to question the way we had been practicing our faith. He told us that Pakistanis didn't know anything about Islam. I was doing well and my family was now settled, so I just thanked the Almighty *(Rab)* and ignored Munir.'

He continued: 'But I became angry when one day, he (Munir) insisted that his younger brothers be taken out from the Iranian school. I asked him where else will they study. They were not allowed to go to Saudi schools and, anyway, they didn't know how to speak or understand Arabic. The western schools set up by European and American ex-pats were too expensive. But Munir said they (his brothers) didn't need to learn nonsense and told me to put them with him in the school that he had begun to attend (on his mother's insistence). He said religious studies are all a person needs. The tension between him and me became so strenuous over this issue that I pulled my other sons out of the Iranian school and sent them back to Pakistan to live with their grandparents in our village. There they went to a government school for a while, but dropped out and became petty farmers ...'

Saudi Arabia enjoyed a windfall of profits when it increased oil prices after the 1973 Egypt-Israel War.[18] Nasser in Egypt had passed away in 1970 and his successor, Anwar Sadat, enjoyed a sudden burst of popularity when Egyptian and Syrian forces managed to achieve some victories against Israeli forces with Soviet-made jets and artillery. However, the United States quickly reinforced Israeli forces and they rebounded by pushing back the combined Egyptian-Syrian armies. This was Faisal's moment to strike and emerge as the Muslim world's leader. He stopped oil supplies to the US and other European countries supporting Israel. The US economy, heavily dependent on Saudi oil, began to buckle.[19] The US was thus forced to ask Israeli forces to fall back. Faisal slowed down oil production and tripled the price of oil, enjoying massive profits.[20]

Watching Faisal emerge as a hero (and now loaded with a windfall of 'Petro-Dollars'), Egypt's Sadat began to warm up to him. Faisal promised to reconstruct Egyptian economy but only if Sadat would let go of 'Nasserism.' Almost immediately, Sadat

---

[18] Robert Sexton: *Exploring Economics* (Cengage, 2014) p.392
[19] Rushefsky: *Public Policy in the United States* (M E Sharpe, 2008) p.56
[20] Karen R. Merrill: *The Oil Crisis of 1973-74* (Bedford/St. Martin's, 2007)

expelled Soviet military and technical advisors from Egypt and broke away from the Soviet camp.[21] He also allowed the expelled members of the Muslim Brotherhood to return to Egypt.

Matee remembered all this: 'Much later, we found out that most of Matee's acquaintances at the school belonged to the Muslim Brotherhood. Some of them were his teachers. They were recruiting Pakistanis to set up Muslim Brotherhood branches in Pakistan. But those who tried were arrested by the Bhutto regime. Munir told us Bhutto was playing a double game. On the one hand (like Sadat), he had come under the influence of Faisal, while on the other hand (unlike Sadat), he wasn't allowing organizations like the Muslim Brotherhood to operate in Pakistan. Munir was very angry. He said Bhutto was willing to allow Palestinian outfits like the PLO to open offices in Pakistan and that the PLO was not Muslim. But he believed that Sadat too was not sincere…'

Munir was not a fan of King Faisal either. Matee told me that (according to Munir), Faisal was throwing around money to make his regime politically influential in the Muslim world, but doing nothing for religion: 'I started to become very concerned about Munir,' Matee said. 'At the school, Munir was learning no skills.'

Matee added: 'I asked him what he wanted to do, and how he will support himself and his future wife and children. But he just didn't care. He also told us not to indulge in indecencies like watching TV, listening to the radio and all. I got really sick of it and told him there was not much happening in Saudi Arabia anyway. TV just had Bin Baz lectures and the radio was all in Arabic. He was unmoved and kept at it until one day I went to his school and told the principal (an Egyptian), that I wanted to pull out my son from the school. Two days later, I was visited by two Pakistanis and

---

[21] P.R. Kumaraswamy: *Revisiting the Yom Kippur War* (Routledge, 2013) p.47

a Bangladeshi and warned that my action of pulling out my son would be seen as a rebellious act against the regime. They asked me to be grateful that my son was being put on the correct path. Then another two days later, a hefty Saudi man came, and, in broken Urdu, told me to let my son be and never admonish him. I was stunned. I didn't know who this Saudi was.'

In 1975, Faisal was assassinated. According to the official version, he was killed by a 'deranged' young cousin of a man who had been shot dead by Saudi police during a riot in 1965.[22] The riots had started in Riyadh by the followers of Bin Baz when Faisal had launched Saudi Arabia's first TV station. However, conspiracy theorists suggested (and they still do) that Faisal was murdered by the American CIA because the US government was simmering after the way Faisal had used the power of oil to browbeat the West.[23]

'There was great sadness all over,' Matee remembered. 'He (Faisal) was such a good man. Had he lived, Saudi Arabia would be so different. Pakistanis were treated in the friendliest manner during his rule. We were treated very badly after he passed away.'

How did Munir react, I asked him.

'By then (1975), we hardly saw him. One day he came home and said that Faisal had destroyed Saudi Arabia. He said he had made it corrupt. But what perturbed me most was when he said that now the holy land will be cleansed from all corruption. I asked him did he mean the new king, Khalid (Faisal's brother). He just scoffed me ...'

Juhayman, the son of the defeated Ikhwan fighter, was born in the late 1930s. He lived with his parents as a Bedouin in the desert. He was never formally educated but did receive some

---

[22] Alexei Vassiliev: *King Faisal: Personality, Faith & Times* (Saqi Publications, 2013)
[23] Ibid.

religious education. He grew up hearing stories of how the Ikhwan had laid down their lives to bring the Saud family to power and then how they were wiped out by the same family.[24] Juhayman joined the Saudi Guardsman as a truck driver.[25] The Guardsmen were a small government force positioned in the Kingdom's far-flung areas. On the side, Juhayman ran a tiny clandestine business, smuggling in cigarettes (on camels) from Kuwait.[26] In 1973, he quit the Guardsmen and came to Medina, where he lived in a small rundown apartment. He began to regularly visit the Islamic University in Medina, where Bin Baz would often deliver his fiery sermons. By now, Baz had become the most influential cleric in the Kingdom, though he was still on the payroll of the monarchy. During the Faisal regime, Baz would only indirectly criticize Faisal's modernization project. When Khalid took over as King, his younger brother, Crown Prince Fahad, put more wheels on the project that Faisal had started, and initiated the emergence of shopping malls in Makkah and Medina and American soap operas on Saudi TV. Fahad also gathered a reputation of being a 'playboy prince'.[27]

Baz was livid. In his lectures at the Islamic University, he began to directly attack Khalid and Fahad. He went to the extent of asking the government to ban cigarettes and even clapping in public![28] Faisal had allowed Saudi women to work in offices. Khalid accelerated this policy, leaving Baz complaining that

---

[24] Thomas Hagghammer, Stephane Lacroix: *The Meccan Rebellion* (Amal Press, 2011)

[25] Yaroslav Trofimov: *The Siege of Mecca* (Knopf Doubleday Publishing Group, 2008)

[26] Ibid.

[27] Fahad's First Months as King: Mark Weston (Wiley, 2011).

[28] Yaroslav Trofimov: *The Siege of Mecca* (Knopf Doubleday Publishing Group, 2008)

'this act (of allowing women to work) was inspired by Satan.'[29] But since most of Baz's audiences (at the University) were made up of exiled Muslims from other countries and a few disaffected Saudis (like Juhayman), Khalid did not take any action against him. In 1976, Baz decided to form a missionary organization that pledged to halt the wave of 'abominations' being introduced by the monarchy, and to reinstate the 'true faith of the Saudis in the holy land.'

The outfit was called Dawa Salafiya[30] and it began to recruit and send missionaries across the Kingdom. Juayman became one such missionary. He rose quickly through the ranks of the outfit. By 1977, the Dawa had become a powerful missionary outfit, headed by Baz, and having in its ranks thousands of Saudis. But it also included Yemenis, Pakistanis, Muslim Indians, Bangladeshis, Sudanese, Somalis, Egyptians and even a few Afro-American Muslim converts.

Matee told me: 'Years later we discovered that Munir too had joined Baz's organization. It (the organization) was recruiting common Saudis and young non-Saudi Muslims working in Saudi Arabia, but they also began visiting religious schools like the one attended by my son; and (with the help of the school's administration), the organization began to attract educated young men like Munir. We hardly saw him anymore. We had no clue what he was up to.'

In 1978, Juhayman had a falling out with the Dawa.[31] He criticized Baz for continuing to be on the payroll of the monarchy. Baz explained to him that the monarchy might be

---

[29] Ibid.
[30] Kai Bird: *Divided City: Coming of Age between the Arabs and Israeli* (Simon & Schuster Publications, 2010).
[31] Yaroslav Trofimov: *The Siege of Mecca* (Knopf Doubleday Publishing Group, 2008)

corrupt and the princes may be playboys, but the monarchy remained to be a barrier against communism and secularism in the region. Juhayman scoffed at this and quit the organization. With him also went some other members of the organization, one of them (perhaps) Munir.

Juhayman now began to write and publish long rants against the 'corruption of the monarchy,' the sacrilege of the holy land by Saudi princes, and 'their infidel guests,' and also about how clerics like Baz were not practicing what they were preaching. Juhayman soon came under the radar of the Saudi police, especially when he began to talk to the members of the Egyptian Muslim Brotherhood (settled in Saudi Arabia) about how they planned to topple Sadat. Most of Juhayman's followers were young Saudis who had come from poor Bedouin families. They had arrived in the Kingdom's big cities to benefit from the rapid pace of economic modernization but had been left feeling alienated and disorientated. Others came from working-class groups of non-Saudi Muslims from various South Asian and African countries.

In late 1977, Juhayman formed a clandestine organization. He told his followers to shun all material luxuries. The members also let their hair and beards grow, and walked around in dusty white robes preaching 'the true word of God.'[32] They destroyed their identity cards and formed communes in Makkah, Medina and Riyadh, where they lived, ate and prayed together.

The Saudi government finally acted and arrested some members of Juhayman's group. But Bin Baz came to their rescue and ordered their release. The Saudi regime obliged.

---

[32] Ibid.

Then, in November 1978, the brother of one of Juhayman's closest aids, Mohammed Abdullah al-Qahtanithat, began to allude that his brother was the Mehdi[33] (the mythical warrior-savior who according to some non-Quranic Islamic traditions would appear to spread God's laws on Earth). Juhayman went along with the façade. It was helpful to his cause. It gave his movement a messianic sheen. Juhayman began to tell his followers to prepare for a showdown with the unholy forces of tyranny, obscenity and greed.

The group began to amass weapons. The weapons were first stolen from the armories of the Guardsmen by Juhayman's followers in the paramilitary outfit.[34] Then more rifles and machine guns were smuggled in from Yemen. Bombs and even more guns were bought from the black market[35] that was then crammed with weaponry smuggled in from Lebanon, a country which had collapsed into a lethal civil war.

In late 1978, Juhayman quoted an obscure hadith foretelling the arrival of the Mehdi who would fight anti-Islam forces from the Grand Mosque in Makkah. The Mosque was located at the location of the most sacred Islamic site, the Ka'aba. On November 29, 1979, as the grand mufti of the mosque was preparing to lead the morning prayers that were being attended by thousands of Muslims from across the world, Juhayman led some 500 of his followers, all heavily armed, and barged into the mosque, seizing it.

His followers who entered the mosque also included a dozen or so veiled women who had joined his movement. Juhayman cut off the telephone lines, allowed many worshippers to leave

---

[33] Ibid.
[34] Thomas Hagghammer, Stephane Lacroix: *The Meccan Rebellion* (Amal Press, 2011
[35] Ibid.

the mosque, but retained hundreds of others as hostages. He put expert marksmen on the roofs who then easily repulsed the Saudi regime's first attempt to take back the mosque. Dozens of Saudi policemen and troops were cut down by heavy machine gun fire from Juhayman's men.[36]

Matee was in Riyadh at the time. He told me: 'I was in Riyadh for some work. My wife called at a relative's apartment where I was staying. She told him she could see black smoke rising from the Ka'aba. But then the line got disconnected and my relative just couldn't call her back. The phone lines went dead. Then we began to hear murmurings about an attack on Ka'aba. I was scared. Nobody was saying a word about it on the TV or the radio. I hurried back to Makkah on a taxi driven by a Pakistani. He told me the airports were being shut down. When I reached home the next day, indeed, I too could see black smoke rising from the site of the mosque and the Ka'aba from my apartment window. Then police vans appeared and began announcing that everyone should remain indoors. I panicked. I thought of Munir. I knew he prayed regularly at the mosque. My wife begged me to fetch him. I ran down and headed towards the school. It was sealed and being guarded by Saudi soldiers. One officer told me to go back because there was no one there. I began to shout, 'Munir, Munir! The soldiers started to push me inside a waiting army truck, but I dodged them and ran back home ...'

The Saudi regime summoned its leading religious figurehead, Bin Baz, and other official clerics to issue a *fatwa* against the attackers, which they did.[37] With a *fatwa* in hand (sanctioning Saudi soldiers to enter the holy premises with weapons), troops moved again to retake the mosque.

---

[36] Lawrence Wright: *The Looming Tower* (Knopf Doubleday Publishing Group, 2006)
[37] Yaroslav Trofimov: *The Siege of Mecca* (Knopf Doubleday Publishing Group, 2008)

But once again they were repelled by machinegun fire and grenades. Dozens more lay dead. The Saudi regime began to panic. It blacked-out all news coming out from the besieged kingdom.

Matee told me: 'For days the whole country just stood still. The TV and radio went blank. We couldn't even tune into the BBC (radio). Phones were dead. All we heard was gunfire. Nobody spoke. Nobody was allowed to speak. But one day, our phone suddenly rang. The operator said the call was from Pakistan. It was my mother. The phones were back on. She asked us what was happening. We told her we had no clue. She said that the American Embassy in Islamabad had been burned down. I was shocked. Was it the Americans attacking the Ka'aba? The phones went dead again.'

Pakistan's state-owned TV channel the PTV was telecasting a cricket Test match between Pakistan and India being played in the Indian city of Bangalore on the day of the siege. The transmission was suddenly interrupted and the newscaster, Azhar Lodhi, appeared on the screen. In a somber tone, he announced the attack on Ka'aba without giving any details about the attackers. PTV did not return to the Test match; instead it started to run recitations from the Quran.

PTV had the details of the attack, but on the advice of Zia's military regime it did not announce that the attackers were all Muslim. Pakistanis tuned into BBC Radio's Urdu service that quoted the official Iranian media that was now under the control of an Islamic revolutionary government in Tehran. The reported quote suggested that the attack was the work of the 'American-Zionist lobby.'

The very next day, large rallies condemning the siege appeared in major Pakistani cities. The biggest rally took place in the country's capital, Islamabad. It was a spontaneous gathering held outside the American embassy building. It suddenly turned violent when some students made fiery speeches, blaming the United States for the attack on the Ka'aba. The gathering soon turned into a rampaging mob which forced its way inside the embassy's compound and offices.[38] The mob was acting upon what it had heard on the BBC believing that the Iranian quote which the radio network had used was actual news.

The Iranians were well aware of the reality behind the takeover of the mosque by Saudi fanatics. But they used the opportunity to embarrass both the Americans and the Saudi monarchy by claiming that it was part of a US plot to 'occupy' Makkah. The Zia regime, unimpressed by American criticism of its takeover (in 1977), and facing American sanctions, did not reveal the details of the attack to the public at large.

Suddenly, unchecked by the Zia regime, the news broadcast by Iranian radio that was then reproduced by some Urdu newspapers in Pakistan was used as a plank to organize a sit-in outside the US embassy in Islamabad. The sit-in was then infiltrated by some boisterous young men who instigated the gathered people to attack the embassy. The mob surged forward towards the embassy, setting it on fire. The attack lasted for hours, but the police stayed put.[39]

Pakistan Army helicopters hovered over the burning building and only landed on the roof of the crumbling structure after the mob had already killed two Americans and two Pakistani employees of the embassy. Two protesters also lost their lives in the chaos. The violence and the rallies finally came to a sudden halt once the Zia regime decided to release the full details of the attack in Makkah.

---

[38] A Day of Terror Recalled: Cameron W. Barr (Washington Post, Nov. 27, 2004)
[39] Ibid.

After three more raids by Saudi forces were repulsed by Juhayman's men, the Saudi regime contacted the French for help.[40] The Saudis had earlier declined Jordanian and Pakistani offers to use their armies to enter the mosque.[41] The French sent three senior commandos of the French army to oversee a plan to break the siege.[42] Saudi troops, now working under the instructions of the French military experts, tried again. After days of intense fighting, Saudi troops finally managed to break through. Over 255 people died. This included dozens of pilgrims who were being held inside the mosque as hostages. Over 500 were injured. 127 Saudi soldiers were killed.[43] Though most of Juayman's men were also killed, Juayman and 67 of his followers who survived the counterattack were arrested. In January 1980, they were all beheaded.

Surprisingly, instead of cracking down on anarchic religious outfits, King Khalid did what his father Abdulaziz had done after crushing the Ikhwan. Khalid, too, further empowered the Kingdom's official hardline clergy. The idea was that this would absorb (and neutralize) any fanatical outbursts against the monarchy. But in the coming years, this policy would once again backfire when it failed to halt the emergence of extremist outfits generated by the Saudi monarchy's curious mixture of officially peddling a puritanical strand of the faith, its appeasement of those who proliferate this strand, and its desire to achieve rapid economic modernization without implementing any social and political reform.

---

[40] Yaroslav Trofimov: *The Siege of Mecca* (Knopf Doubleday Publishing Group, 2008)
[41] Ibid.
[42] Dr. John Calvert: *Islamism: A Documentary and Reference Guide* (Greenwood Publishing Group, 2006) p.178
[43] Yaroslav Trofimov: *The Siege of Mecca* (Knopf Doubleday Publishing Group, 2008)

Out of the 500 or so of Juhayman's men who had seized the mosque, more than 70 percent were Saudi men. The rest belonged to countries such as Sudan, Yemen, Somalia, Egypt, India, Bangladesh and Pakistan. There were a few African-American converts as well.[44] Matee never believed his son was involved, until he was finally informed (three years after the attack) that Munir had been arrested and beheaded: 'When the dust settled, I went looking for Munir again. After months, the Saudis released the list of those killed in the attack. Munir's name was not on the dead pilgrims' list. But the Saudis never fully released the names of the militants who were killed inside the mosque or were beheaded by the government. Munir was nowhere. I pleaded with the Pakistani Embassy in Riyadh and then the Pakistan government to help me find my son, but they said they had no information about him.' Matee returned to Pakistan in 1985.

According to what Matee found out, Munir had been introduced to Juhayman's group by an Egyptian teacher of his at the school. The teacher had been a member of the Muslim Brotherhood and had arrived in Saudi Arabia as an exile in the 1960s. He quit the Brotherhood in the late 1970s and became a recruiter for Juhayman. Matee Ghara had told me: 'I don't know what role Munir played in all this. My wife kept waiting for him. She said, '*Janat toh maa kay pair talay hoti hey* (Heaven is underneath a mother's feet); what was my son doing looking for it in the ways of a mad man?''

She passed away in 1994, still hoping that one day her Munir may just come back to her. He didn't.

****

---

[44] Ibid

The Gentleman Fanatic

The armed forces of Pakistan were largely a secular lot till the 1970s. But from the late 1970s onward they were systematically 'Islamized'; especially during the dictatorship of General Ziaul Haq. Historians commenting on the phenomenon have pointed at Zia's admiration of famous Islamic scholar, Abul Ala Maududi.[45] It is true that Zia was an avid fan of Maududi's writings, but it was not exactly on Maududi's thesis that Zia initiated his 'Islamisation' process in the country's armed forces.

It were the thesis and theories of a relatively lesser known and obscure figure upon which Zia almost squarely designed his 'Islamic reformation of the Pakistan Army.' His name was Brigadier-General S K. Malik.[46] In 1975 at the height of Z A. Bhutto's populist regime, Malik quietly published a book called *The Quranic Concept of War*.[47] S K. Malik had begun writing it in 1974 as a reaction to the Pakistan military's defeat against India in 1971. When he discussed his project with Zia (who was an inauspicious Lieutenant General at the time) the latter was highly impressed by Malik's thesis.[48] He encouraged him to publish it in the form of a book. One is not sure whether Bhutto (an avid reader) ever got to read Malik's book which Zia had begun to distribute among the officers. I believe he didn't because Malik's theory was squarely against any metaphorical interpretation of the Quran,[49] especially of the verses that deal with the concept of holy war. To Zia, however, such thinking was necessary to infuse a more faith-based streak in

---

[45] Husain Haqqani: *Pakistan: Between Mosque & Military* (Carnegie, 2005) p.139

[46] JC Myres: Review of Malik's Quranic Concept of War (Startegic Studies Institute)

[47] Ibid.

[48] B. Prakashan: The Organizer Vol: 53, 2001. p. xlviii

[49] Bhutto was more in favour of the rationalist reading of the Quran.

the armed forces[50], an institution that he believed had been softened because it was steeped in the ideals of 'modernist Islam,' and was too colonial and 'westernized' in its outlook and mannerisms.

Various economic and political factors contributed to the July 1977 military coup that Zia pulled off against the Bhutto regime. Zia rode in on a wave of protests by political parties who had been expressing urban middle-class frustrations, and the interests of the trader and industrial classes that had been directly affected by Bhutto's (albeit half-baked) socialist maneuvers.

These classes had agreed to let the religious parties take the lead against the Bhutto regime.[51] So when in July 1977 Zia toppled Bhutto, he adopted the anti-Bhutto movement's religious tenor. As mentioned earlier, though most political historians have suggested that Zia planned his coming 'Islamic rule' on the models of 'Islamic governance' theorized by Maududi, his main inspiration in this context largely came from S K. Malik's book. Not surprisingly, in the second year of his dictatorship in 1979, he sanctioned the mainstream publication of the book and also wrote the book's foreword. Zia initially used Malik's thesis to 'Islamize' the Pakistani army, and then to turn the concept of *jihad* into a national policy. He also helped popularize the book among Afghan, Pakistani and Arab mujahedeen who had all gathered on the Pakistan side of the Pak-Afghan border to lead guerrilla raids into Afghanistan against Soviet forces.[52]

He made sure that the book was made available in all leading bookstores of the country. By 1986, the book had been translated into Arabic, Urdu and Persian (from English).

---

[50] JC Myres: Review of Malik's Quranic Concept of War (Startegic Studies Institute)

[51] A. Mahmood: Globe 12 June, 1997. p.17

[52] Dr. S Gorka: Grandmasters of Jihad (The Jihad Report, May 16, 2015).

General Zia embraced Malik's expansive understanding of jihad.[53] Malik explained it as a duty extending to soldiers, as well as citizens. Zia accepted Malik's redefinition of 'defensive jihad' to include the removal of any obstacles and resistance to the spread of Islam. According to Malik, even passive resistance to the advancement of Islam was 'legitimate grounds for an armed attack.'

Malik in his book suggests that war should dictate policy and not the other way round. Meaning that war or jihad should work as a pre-emptive tool against 'anti-Islam forces.' It didn't matter whether these (perceived enemies of faith) were hostile or not. According to Malik, Islam permits this.[54] As Malik went to great lengths to prove this by dissecting various verses of the Quran, it is this aspect of the book that is most popular with many Islamist groups today. Malik completely rejected any allegorical or metaphorical understanding of the Quran and refused to study it in a more contextual manner. He simply intellectualized the literalist reading of the Muslim scriptures in the light of a standing army of an Islamic country that should always be ready to wage war against hostile and passive, real or imagined enemies. Malik then goes on to advocate that every Muslim citizen of an Islamic country should think like a 'holy warrior.' Thus, many experts now believe that Zia used Malik's thesis to also justify the alliances he made with militant sectarian and Islamist forces that sprang up during his regime. But what about the author himself?

Malik retired from the military to concentrate on becoming a scholar. Perturbed by the criticism the armed forces were being subjected to after the 1971 East Pakistan debacle, he had set out to answer the military's critics, but ended up constructing an

---

[53] Patrick Poole's review of Malik's book in PJ Media, January 2007.
[54] Ibid.

entirely reactive response. He first came up with his thesis in 1974 in a world in which Islamists and religious extremists were still obscure characters in Pakistan, found only on the far fringes of society and politics. Thus, he was largely writing a cathartic tirade as a man deeply disturbed and depressed by what had taken place in 1971.

He didn't seem to be a very ambitious man. He never gave any interviews or ever became a prominent member of Zia's government. He remained almost entirely in the background. My research did suggest that he was a moderate Muslim, but by 1974 had become highly religious and somber. When or where was he born and when did he die, no one seems to know for sure. I believe, such a private and unambitious character could not have been writing a highly volatile book by consciously aiming to radicalize the military and the civilians and then foreseeing the emergence of sectarian and Islamist violence on a global scale.

His was a reactive and angry tirade against what he thought were the enemies of his beloved armed forces. He was rigid and myopic in his study of religious texts because to him the military's supposedly lax and liberal approach towards faith had made it weak. I do wonder though, what he would have thought about his work today when quotes from his book regularly appear in 'jihadi literature'[55] that not only advocates but boasts of committing terrible violence on civilian and military targets alike and then justifies it as something sanctioned by the scriptures?

Would Malik be elated, or distraught by the manner in which his reactive diatribe that he molded and presented as a scholarly study was first used by a manipulative military dictator to justify

---

[55] Patrick Poole's review of Malik's book in PJ Media, January 2007.

his hold over power, and then cherry-picked by militants and their apologists to rationalize nihilist violence?

****

The Tragic Pretenders

Ziaul Haq faced (and survived) a number of protest movements, two military coup attempts, and at least one major assassination attempt. This attempt was made by the members of an enigmatic urban guerrilla organization called the Al-Zulfikar. It was made at a time when 'Islamic militancy' (in Pakistan) was unheard of and radical belligerency was associated more with far-left groups.

On 7 September, 2015, I received an e-mail from a Pakistani who claimed to be living in a European city. He wrote that he had read my Sunday column in Dawn (of 6 September, 2015), part of which was about how several members of the now defunct urban guerrilla group, the Al-Zulfiqar Organization (AZO), who had reached Libya and Syria (from Kabul), were never heard from again. He insisted that 'a lot of the boys who ended up in Libya and Syria, did not vanish.' According to him, some were still living in the mentioned countries, while many also managed to get political asylum in various European states. He was once part of the AZO too. He shared dozens of photos that he had taken of 'the boys' and of himself in Tripoli (Libya) and Kabul in the early 1980s. He claimed he was now settled in a European city.

His narrative was that AZO and its activities were demonized not only by the Zia dictatorship, but also by men such as journalist and author, Raja Anwar. Now this is the ironic bit. Anwar remains to be the only author who has written a detailed account of the life and times of the AZO (in *The Terrorist Prince*). The irony is that he too was once a member of the AZO, and, yet, many of his former comrades and even some respected journalists have continued to dispute the authenticity of the information that he provides in his book.

Anwar was a leftist student radical during the students and workers movement against the Ayub Khan regime in the late 1960s. He then went on to join ZA Bhutto's populist Pakistan People's Party (PPP) when it came to power in December, 1971. He was made an Advisor on Youth Affairs by Bhutto.[56] After the Bhutto regime fell in a military coup in July 1977, and Bhutto was arrested, Bhutto's wife, Nusrat Bhutto, gave Anwar the responsibility of setting up party cells[57] which could be activated to hold spontaneous protests against the Zia regime. During a number of such protests, some young PPP supporters even set themselves on fire (in Lahore and Rawalpindi).

Anwar is from the Punjab city of Rawalpindi. In his book, he reminds the readers that most of the young men who went up in flames to protest against Bhutto's arrest (and then trial) belonged to working-class Punjabi families. Bhutto was a Sindhi, and it seems Anwar made sure to point out that Bhutto's most diehard supporters at the time resided in the Punjab. He continues to mention this throughout his book and it is only in the latter half of the tome that it becomes clear why he does this. He denounces AZO chief, Murtaza Bhutto (ZA Bhutto's eldest son), as being a 'Sindhi feudal' who didn't care much about his Punjabi supporters. After Bhutto was hanged through a contentious trial in April 1979, Anwar writes that the police was hot on his (Anwar's) heels, and he escaped to Munich, Germany. From

---

[56] Raja Anwar: *The Terrorist Prince: The Life & Death of Murtaza Bhutto* (Verso, 1997) p.xi
[57] Ibid. p.23

there he flew to Kabul, where he joined Murtaza and his brother, Shahnawaz. The brothers had formed a small urban guerrilla outfit called the People's Liberation Army (PLA). Kabul was chosen by the brothers because in 1978, Afghanistan had witnessed a coup d'état set in motion by the covert supporters and members of the country's two main communist parties inside the Afghan armed forces.

Murtaza and Shahnawaz were in London when their father was hanged, whereas their mother and sister (Benazir) were in jail in Pakistan. The brothers had organized rallies in London to put pressure on the Zia government, but after failing to get the dictator to halt Bhutto's execution, Murtaza went into a rage and decided to topple Zia through guerilla warfare. Anwar writes that Murtaza first approached radical Libyan leader, Muammar Gaddafi, for financial and logistical support. Gaddafi had been on very good terms with ZA Bhutto.

When Bhutto was on death row, Gaddafi had sent Libya's Prime Minister to Pakistan on a special plane and asked Zia to put Bhutto on that plane and allow it to fly him (Bhutto) to Libya.[58] Zia refused and ordered the plane to fly back. Gaddafi then sent a 'secret message' to Bhutto's wife stating that he was willing to send in special commandos to break Bhutto out from jail.[59] Gaddafi planned to use Palestinian fighters associated with Yasser Arafat's Palestine Liberation Organization (PLO) for the mission. The message was conveyed to Bhutto by his wife, but Bhutto rejected the 'offer' by stating that he didn't want to escape and seek refuge in another country.[60] After Bhutto's execution, Gaddafi set up a drill camp near Tripoli to train early

---

[58] I A Tirmazi: *The Profile of Intelligence* (Library of Congress, 1995).
[59] Ibid.
[60] Nusrat Goes With Many Historic Secrets: Hamid Mir (The News, October 24, 2011).

AZO recruits in guerrilla warfare.[61] The training was imparted to the young Pakistanis by PLO men.

Anwar, in his account, claims that PLO had also agreed to supply arms to AZO. AZO was still called Peoples Liberation Army. The ship in which the arms were being smuggled (from Beirut to Tripoli) was intercepted by Israeli authorities and the weapons confiscated. Another source of possible support and funding that Murtaza explored was the ruling family of the United Arab Emirates (UAE). The royal family too had been on good terms with the Bhutto clan. After Bhutto's execution, it had offered political asylum to Bhutto's wife and children.[62] Anwar writes that the UAE monarchy was willing to help Murtaza, but after Murtaza published his organization's first communique, the UAE monarchy balked.

The communique described PLA (now renamed AZO) as a 'Marxist-Leninist movement' at war with the 'illegitimate regime of Ziaul Haq'. A prince and minister from the UAE's ruling family told Murtaza that the UAE did not want anything to do with a communist organization. Also, the UAE ruling dynasty was not on very good terms with Gaddafi who till then had been the main backer of the AZO. In Kabul, Murtaza was left to lean (for logistical support) entirely on the Kabul regime and on Gaddafi. The Kabul government accepted to back AZO as long as it was useful to dent the Zia regime which, with the help of the Americans and the Saudis, had begun to facilitate the formation of various anti-Soviet mujahedeen groups on the Pak-Afghan border. Soviet troops had entered Afghanistan in December 1979 and by early 1980 anti-Soviet Afghan insurgents had begun to gather on the Pakistan side of the border.

---

[61] I A Tirmazi: *The Profile of Intelligence* (Library of Congress, 1995)
[62] Syed Shabbir Hussain: *Ayub, Bhutto & Zia* (Sang-e-Meel Publications, 2000) p.270

By the time Anwar reached Kabul (in early 1980) AZO had already lost almost its entire first batch of fighters. These were young men who had been supporters of the PPP and were trained in Tripoli and in Kabul. When they were sent back to Pakistan to carry out bank robberies (to raise funds for the outfit), some had been killed (by the police), while others were arrested. They also assassinated a civilian member of the Zia regime, but botched an attack on one of the judges who had sent Bhutto to the gallows.

In 1981, a second batch of young men reached Kabul through Pakistan's anarchic tribal areas. They were helped on the way by Pashtun members of a small militant Maoist outfit, the Mazdoor Kissan Party (MKP).[63] Between 1968 and 1974, the MKP had fought a guerrilla war against the police in the Charsaada District of Khyber Pakhtunkwa (KP) province. Again, most of the new entrants were members of the PPP's student wing (PSF), and some also belonged to another left-wing student outfit, the NSF. Most of them arrived from the cities and towns of the Punjab and KP and from Sindh's capital city, Karachi. They were all under 25 years of age. One such new recruit was former President of PSF in Karachi, Salamullah Tipu. Tipu came from a lower-middle-class Urdu-speaking family in Karachi.[64] He went to a local school and then joined the army as a teen in the late 1960s.[65] He was, however, dismissed for 'bad behavior'.[66] He joined a college in the early 1970s and was recruited by the student outfit of the right-wing Jamat-i-Islami, the IJT.[67]

[63] Raja Anwar: *The Terrorist Prince: The Life & Death of Murtaza Bhutto* (Verso, 1997) p.44
[64] Laurent Gayer: *Karachi: Ordered Disorder* (HarperCollins, 2014).
[65] Ibid.
[66] Raja Anwar: *The Terrorist Prince: The Life & Death of Murtaza Bhutto* (Verso, 1997)
[67] Conversation with former progressive student leader, Akram Kaimkhani, in London, 2011.

Tipu befriended some members of the left-wing NSF who convinced him to quit the IJT. In 1974, he walked out of the IJT to join NSF. A firebrand and always spoiling for a fight, he became a muscleman for the NSF.[68] However, in 1976, when NSF refused to give him a ticket to contest that year's student union election at his college, Tipu switched sides again and joined the PSF. He quickly rose through the ranks of the organization, and in 1978 he was made the President of the PSF in Karachi. According to Anwar, Tipu did not play any significant role in the anti-Zia protests that the PPP and PSF organized when Bhutto was in jail. There is only scant information on him during this period.

In late1980, after witnessing the IJT using sophisticated weapons during the increasing episodes of campus violence, Tipu began to form an armed wing within the PSF. The IJT at the time was supporting the Zia regime. Then, in early 1981, when an anti-Zia rally at the Karachi University turned violent, the protesting students tried to set fire to a vehicle belonging to an army officer. The IJT was against the protest and some of its members rushed to the scene to stop the agitation.[69] IJT's chapter at Karachi University helped the police nab some of the agitating students. One of the arrested was Akram Kaimkhani.[70]

I met Kaimkhani in London in 2011. I was visiting the School of Oriental & African Studies (SOAS University) as a guest speaker and bumped into Kaimkhani who was in the audience. He is settled there for the last three decades and hasn't returned to Pakistan. Kaimkhani told me that there was a protest against Zia at the Karachi University and it was triggered by the presence of an army officer on the campus: 'He (the officer) was

---

[68] Ibid.
[69] Laurent Gayer: *Karachi: Ordered Disorder* (HarperCollins, 2014).
[70] Ibid.

just there to either pick or drop a relative, but some students got agitated by his presence because Zia's regime was going after the progressive groups,' Kaimkhani explained.

He added: 'I was there just raising slogans. But after the officer's vehicle was torched, I was nabbed by some members of the opposing student group, beaten up and handed over to the police!'

Kaimkhani's classmate and friend at the university, Abbas Nasir[71], who today is settled in Spain with his wife and children, agrees.

Abbas told me: 'At the university I was not associated with any particular student outfit. But my sympathies were clearly with the progressive groups. Kaimkhani was a good friend. He wasn't a radical, but like me sympathized with the progressive student outfits. I was there when the officer's jeep went up in flames. I'm not sure who torched it. It was all very chaotic. The next day we heard that the protest had been attacked by some IJT guys, and that Kaimkhani had been nabbed by the cops. He was good friends with Tipu. Tipu respected him a lot. So when Tipu got to know what had happen, he rode into the university and (with his group) began hurling abuses at some students gathered outside an IJT camp. Then suddenly there was sound of gunfire. Bullets began to fly to and fro. The shootout was between Tipu's group and a couple of IJT fellows. In the end, an IJT member was killed. We never saw Tipu again after that.'[72]

The weapons that Tipu and his group used against the IJT (that day) had actually been stolen by Tipu from IJT men.[73]

---

[71] Abbas Nasir rose to become a prominent journalist in Karachi and then Editor of Pakistan's largest English language daily, Dawn (2005-2011).

[72] Conversation, Karachi, 2012.

[73] Laurent Gayer: *Karachi: Ordered Disorder* (HarperCollins, 2014).

Tipu had raided a van carrying a cache of pistols and AK-47s only days before the incident at the university. The van was being driven by members of the IJT when Tipu and some of his friends 'raided it.'[74] But after the shooting, with the cops looking for him, Tipu escaped to Peshawar and from Peshawar he walked across the Pak-Afghan border and entered Kabul.

Anwar's account suggests that after two AZO men had botched an assassination attempt on Zia in Rawalpindi, he (Anwar) had a falling out with Murtaza. Murtaza got Anwar thrown in a jail by the Afghan intelligence agency, KHAD, accusing him of being 'Zia's agent.' But why did Anwar have a falling out with Murtaza?

This question was also asked by eminent scholar and intellectual, late Eqbal Ahmad, in a detailed critique of Anwar's book that he wrote for the *London Book Review* in 1998.[75] Ahmad also correctly points out that he (Anwar) is at best vague about of the issue. But Anwar does mention that after a botched operations by AZO men in Pakistan, he advised Murtaza to return to Pakistan and help his mother and sister who had formed a multiparty alliance against the Zia regime (the Movement for the Restoration of Democracy or the MRD). But why would Murtaza get him thrown in jail just for saying just that?

The person who emailed me (henceforth the Email Man) wrote that Anwar was suspected by Murtaza of 'being Zia's agent.' He claimed it was on Anwar's information (that he provided to his supposed 'handlers' in the Zia government) that some AZO men were arrested in Pakistan. However, this is exactly what Anwar too alludes to in his book, but with a twist. He suggests that Murtaza was becoming 'increasingly paranoid,'

---

[74] Ibid.
[75] I am destiny: Eqbal Ahmad (London Book Review, 18 June, 1998).

and when Anwar insisted that AZO should launch a political struggle against the Zia regime, Murtaza accused him of being Zia's agent and convinced the Afghan intelligence agency to throw him in jail.

But had KHAD really been convinced that Anwar was Zia's agent, it would have certainly executed him. But it didn't, even though Anwar lingered in a jail cell for another three years before he was allowed to leave Kabul. Unable to return to Pakistan after his release, Anwar flew to Germany where he got political asylum. He returned to Pakistan after Zia's demise in 1988 and rejoined the PPP. He contested an election from Rawalpindi on a PPP ticket but lost. In 1995, he quit the party and joined the centre-right PML-N. He published his book in 1997, just months after Murtaza was killed in a controversial police encounter in Karachi.

The Email Man claimed that Anwar's book can't be accurate because he was in jail between late 1980 and 1984. 'He was an outsider. He was not committed to the cause,' the Email Man lamented in one of his correspondences. Much of Anwar's book is based on what he was told by Tipu who had become Anwar's cellmate in 1984. Tipu too had had a falling out with Murtaza and was being tried (by KHAD) for the murder of a man in Kabul. He was bitter towards Murtaza and thus, one can assume that much of what he told Anwar in that cell was a mixture of truths and half-truths.

In his extensive review of Anwar's book, Eqbal Ahmad wrote:

'It was Murtaza Bhutto who, for reasons Anwar does not make clear in his book, had him thrown into the notorious Pul-i-Charkhi prison of Communist-ruled Afghanistan. The Terrorist Prince is a bitter, largely secondhand account of Murtaza's People's Liberation Army, later named al-Zulfiqar ...'

This is the crux of the argument of Anwar's critics as well. Though some of his former comrades have accused him of being 'Zia's agent,' most others have simply lamented that by lambasting Murtaza in his book, he had disrespected the memory of the dozens of young men who were killed, hanged or arrested (by Zia) during AZO's so-called 'revolutionary struggle.' But to be fair to Anwar, his anger towards Murtaza is largely due to how Anwar began to see him. He described Murtaza to be an arrogant and reckless man who played with the lives of naïve young idealists. In his book, Anwar also derides Murtaza's mother (Nusrat) and sister (Benazir) who he accuses of alienating and ignoring young activists who had somehow managed to survive Murtaza's reckless adventurism and Zia's hangmen.

The Email Man, however, insisted that most AZO men had complete faith in Murtaza and it were 'suspicious people' like Raja Anwar who 'have been used' (by whom?) over the years to sketch a demonic portrait of Murtaza. Murtaza's daughter, Fatima Bhutto, in her book, *Songs of Blood & Sword*, presents a vivid account of her father's life in exile. Interestingly, she does not refer at all to Anwar's book. She is, however, particularly harsh towards her aunt, Benazir.

Surviving members of the AZO too have been extremely critical of Benazir. In March 1981, when Tipu (and two other AZO men) hijacked a PIA plane from Karachi, Benazir publically denounced the hijacking[76] and asked her brothers to end their adventurism (because it was harming the movement which she had begun against Zia on the streets of Pakistan). EmailMan is not a big Benazir fan. In his correspondence with me he went on to claim that over a dozen AZO men who had travelled to Austria in 1984 were arrested by the Vienna police

---

[76] Benazir Bhutto: *Daughter of the East* (Hamilton, 1988) p.147

on the information provided by Benazir. To him, Benazir was hell-bent on damaging Murtaza's movement (to safeguard her own political interests).

I had interviewed Benazir in 1993 for an English weekly and asked her about such accusations that had resumed in the press on the eve of Murtaza's return to Pakistan the same year. She had said: 'All I wanted my brothers to do was to return to Pakistan and fight with me against Zia. I publically rejected his (Murtaza's) tactics because they were harming the democratic struggle which we had started in Pakistan. His ways gave Zia the excuse to jail, torture and hang anyone he wanted. So many young men went to the gallows just for politically opposing Zia. They were not criminals or terrorists. I had no clue what he (Murtaza) was up to or where his people were. All I knew was that his tactics were not correct ...'

When Anwar was about to be released from the Kabul jail, Murtaza had gotten KHAD to throw Tipu in the same cell (in 1984). In a 2004 interview which I conducted of a cousin of Tipu's (for a research paper), he told me that Tipu's family still lies low. His parents and siblings were not harassed by the police after Tipu was reported to have died in Afghanistan. But they just simply buried his memory. It was a painful memory.

During the hijacking, Tipu's father was picked up by the police and asked to talk to his son. Tipu refused to talk to him.[77] After the episode, Tipu's family never heard from him again. His cousin (who was a teenager at the time) told me: 'He lost his way. He was a very emotional man (*jazbati admi*). After the hijacking, his family was avoided like a disease. Their neighbors refused to talk to them, cops kept an eye on them, and the PPP disowned them!'

---

[77] Conversation with a cousin of Tipu's in Karachi, 2004.

In the end, even Murtaza didn't want anything to do with them because (according to Fatima Bhutto[78]), Tipu was most likely 'Zia's agent.' Fatima was told by her father that the hijacking was entirely planned and executed by Tipu most probably on the behest of Zia's agencies. Even Benazir in her 1988 autobiography, *Daughter of the East*, is not sure what to make of the hijacking. She publically denounced it but says that (later on) she wondered exactly what the real motive was behind the hijacking. She alluded that most probably Tipu and his men had been 'allowed' to hijack the plane (by Zia), so he (Zia) could use it as an excuse to ruthlessly crush the 1981 MRD movement against him.

However, it is a now a matter of record that when Tipu and his men got the pilot to land the PIA plane at Kabul Airport (from Karachi), Tipu was in direct contact (on wireless) with Murtaza. Anwar quotes Tipu as saying that Murtaza came to visit him and had even hugged him. Tipu's idol at the time was the notorious playboy-terrorist 'Carlos the Jackal'[79] who had worked with radical Palestinian groups and for various left-wing militant outfits in Germany, Italy and France.

Anwar writes that Tipu saw the hijacking as a 'great revolutionary act' and in his excitement shot dead a Pakistani passenger after accusing him of being part of the Zia regime. He wasn't. Tipu told Anwar that he informed Murtaza that the man was claiming to be someone who had actually worked for Z A. Bhutto, but Murtaza had kept accusing the besieged passenger of being 'Zia's man.' The man was shot dead by Tipu after the Zia regime refused to discharge the political prisoners that Tipu had demanded should be released from Pakistani jails.

---

[78] *Songs of Blood and Sword* (Nation Books, 2011).
[79] Conversation with a cousin of Tipu's in Karachi, 2004.

Anwar quotes Tipu as saying that the man was killed on Murtaza's instructions, whereas Fatima claims that Murtaza had no clue what was transpiring inside the plane. She insists in her book that the hijacking was entirely the doing of Tipu, and Murtaza was actually taken aback by it. The truth may lie somewhere in between because Anwar suggests that AZO was desperately trying to get direct support from the Soviet intelligence agency, the KGB, and for this Murtaza had been desiring to pull off a dramatic act.

Anwar also suggests that the hijacking may not have been Murtaza's idea, but since Tipu wanted so much to become 'a star revolutionary,' he gifted Murtaza the spectacular act that he was looking for. The KGB had decided not to deal with AZO directly and had asked KHAD to facilitate the organization. But after the murder of the Pakistani passenger, KGB advised the Kabul regime to ask the hijackers to leave Kabul.

Tipu and his men forced the pilot to fly the plane to the Syrian capital, Damascus. Syria was being ruled by another of ZA Bhutto's friends, Hafizul Asad who, like Gaddafi, was also anti-Zia. The Zia regime finally agreed to release the political prisoners which AZO had demanded, but only after Tipu threatened to kill the American and European passengers on the plane.

The released men were all political captives who had been rotting in Zia's jails. Akram Kaimkhani was one of them. In his 2011 conversation with me in London, Kaimkhani told me that not all the prisoners wanted to leave: 'We were planning to fight it out in Pakistan, but even those who didn't want to leave, they were hastily bundled onto a chartered plane and flown to Damascus. Zia was in a hurry to use this episode to begin a fresh crackdown against his opponents.'

Some of the released political prisoners joined the AZO in Kabul, while others settled in Libya and Syria. Some managed to find political asylum in various European countries. Tipu returned to Kabul, while the other two hijackers flew out to Libya[80]. None of them ever returned to Pakistan.

After the hijacking, Murtaza shifted to an apartment in Damascus. Though he was still AZO's chief, Tipu became the organization's main man in Kabul. As most of the AZO men continued to live in the congested AZO headquarters in Kabul, Tipu was given a furnished apartment by KHAD and a brand new car. He, however, became even more reckless. He would get drunk and race his car up and down Kabul's main roads, harassing bystanders.[81] Head of KHAD, Najibullah, admonished him for 'resting on his laurels.' And after Najib threatened to expel him from Kabul (apparently on Murtaza's insistence), Tipu told Najib: 'I am the real communist. Murtaza is a feudal. I am the true revolutionary ...!'[82]

According to Anwar, Murtaza was not happy about Tipu's new-found 'star status'. Tipu told Anwar that 'out of jealously' Murtaza got him implicated in a murder case in Kabul. This happened after Tipu laid out his plans to attack US and Israeli embassies in certain European countries. He then shared with Murtaza his grandest plan, that of assassinating Zia during the dictator's official trip to India. The idea was not shared with Najibullah because the Soviet Union was close to India and had a Pakistani head of state been assassinated in India, this could have implicated India or even started a war between India and Pakistan.

---

[80] Both were Tipu's childhood friends and belonged to PSF.
[81] Raja Anwar: *The Terrorist Prince: The Life & Death of Murtaza Bhutto* (Verso, 1997)
[82] Ibid.

Tipu travelled to New Delhi where Zia was on an official visit. According to Anwar, Murtaza gave Tipu the contact number of a man who was to supply him with the weapon that was to be used to assassinate Zia.[83] Tipu never got the weapon. He returned to Kabul fuming. Again, quoting Tipu, Anwar writes that Murtaza told Tipu that a certain man was responsible for the botched operation. Taking this as a signal to act against the man, Tipu shot him in a suburban residential area of Kabul. But there is also another version of the story.

According to newspaper reports of the period, the AZO had broken into two factions. One faction was being led by Tipu and the other by Murtaza's close confidant, Sohail Sethi.[84] During an armed clash between the two groups, a member of the Sethi faction was killed.[85] To his horror, Tipu was immediately arrested by the Kabul police and thrown in jail. In mid-1984 he was sentenced to death and executed by a firing squad. He was 28 years old. By the time Tipu was executed, Anwar had already been released by KHAD. He left for Germany. After Tipu's demise, Murtaza mostly operated from Damascus and the remaining AZO men were asked to leave Kabul by KHAD.

Some returned to Pakistan only to be arrested and jailed, while some, with great difficulty, managed to reach Tripoli. Qaddafi had closed down the training camps there. So the men stayed in Tripoli as second-class citizens. The few lucky ones managed to find political asylum in some European countries. During the commotion between the Tipu and Murtaza/Sethi factions, a group had already been dispatched to the Austrian city of Vienna, where it was to storm and take over the Israeli embassy. The other option was to attack a gathering of

---

[83] Ibid.
[84] South Asia Report, Issue: 278, 1983.
[85] Ibid.

western diplomats. But as the infighting within AZO was raging in Kabul, all members of the group were arrested by the Vienna police and given long jail sentences between 15 to 25 years each.

These young men, after conducting reconnaissance of the Israeli Embassy and figuring out how they would storm it, had suddenly stopped receiving any new instructions from Kabul. Soon, much of their time was spent drinking beer and sleeping in parks and in cheap hotels. Not knowing what was transpiring in Kabul, they were finally apprehended by the police along with the cache of arms which they were carrying.

In 1985, AZO began receiving its third batch of fighters. Most of these were young Sindhi-speakers from the interior of the Sindh province. Some of them were arrested and executed by the Zia regime when they returned to Pakistan to assassinate a pro-Zia politician in Karachi. Anwar claims that by 1985, the AZO had become a militant Sindhi nationalist outfit. Also in 1985, Murtaza's brother, Shahnawaz, was allegedly poisoned to death in Cannes, France. Benazir in her autobiography believes that Shahnawaz's Afghan wife was somehow involved and (thus) working on the instructions of the Zia regime. Murtaza folded the AZO in 1990 and returned to Pakistan in 1993. Some observers suggest that his return was 'facilitated by those who wanted an open confrontation between Benazir and him.' Benazir was in power when Murtaza landed in Karachi. He was immediately taken into 'protective custody.'

Though the AZO had folded, its name was constantly used in 1990 by Sindh's Chief Minister, Jam Sadiq Ali, who unleashed the police against the PPP on the pretext that many of its workers were working for the AZO.[86] However, when in

---

[86] JPRS Report issue: 92110, 1992

1992, the military began a 'clean-up' operation in Sindh, it went after the militants of Karachi's largest party, the Mohajir Qaumi Movement (MQM) which was in an alliance with Sadiq's provincial government in Sindh. The AZO's name suddenly vanished from the newspapers.

The curtain had come down on the Soviet Union, the Afghan conflict was coming to an end (for the time being at least) and left-wing militant outfits were being disbanded all over the world. In 1993, Murtaza arrived in a very different Pakistan. Zia was no more, Murtaza's sister was in power, and a new kind of militant was emerging. A militant who justified his violence not through Marxist dialecticism or by quoting Lenin, Mao or Marx, but by claiming that his/her actions were being ordained by the Almighty himself.

In 1996, Murtaza was killed in a controversial police encounter near his late father's house in Karachi. The once dreaded AZO became just another annotation of history.

****

Three Men and a Saint

The Sindh province of Pakistan is considered to be one of the most pluralistic regions of the country. It is also called the 'land of the Sufi saints'[87], and its habitants take great pride in the fact that Sindhis have continued to follow a more flexible and 'spiritual' strand of Islam. Between the 1930s and mid-2000s, the existential narrative that furnished the Sindhi identity in Pakistan was this: Sindhis were of a land that was largely shaped by the deeds of hundreds of Sufi saints who preached tolerance

---

[87] MW Jotwani: *The Sufis of Sindh* (Publications Division, 1986) p.36

and co-existence here, and were suspicious of those who were stripping Islam of its mystical essence and replacing it with a creed based on a rigid worldview and an obsession with rituals.

This narrative was essential for Sindhis because it helped them find an anchor for their ethnic identity and sense of history; especially in a country where (according to them) the state was attempting to undermine centuries-old ethnic identities[88] through a largely cosmetic ideology assembled by a myopic understanding of the ethnic, religious and sectarian complexities of Pakistan.

The 19th century British traveler, Richard Burton, in his prolific accounts of Sindh, described the province to be one of the calmest regions of British India, with its own unique blends of faith.[89] Writing in the mid-1800s, Burton described Sindh as a land dotted by numerous shrines of Sufi saints, frequented in large numbers by both the Muslim as well as the Hindu inhabitants of the region. He described the Sindhi Muslims to be somewhat different (in their beliefs and rituals) from the Muslims of the rest of India. According to Burton, even the Hindus of Sindh were different because their Hinduism was more influenced by Buddhism.[90] When Punjab was being ripped by violent and gruesome clashes between the Hindus, Sikhs and Muslims during the partition of India in 1947, Sindh remained largely peaceful.[91]

Sindh's British Governor at the time, Francis Mudie, reported that the Hindus of Sindh were likely to stay behind (in Pakistan) because there was no chance of communal violence in

[88] MJ Chitkara: *Jeeay Sindh* (APH Publishers, 1996) p.4
[89] Christopher Ondaatje: *Sindh Revisited: A Journey in the Footsteps of Captain Sir Richard Francis Burton* (Long Riders Guild Press, 2006)
[90] Ibid.
[91] Rita Kothari: *The Burden of Refuge* (Orient Longman, 2006) p.78

the province which had exhibited 'great communal harmony'.[92] However, after some Hindu places of worship were attacked in Karachi in 1948, Hindu Sindhis began to leave in droves. This is when Sindhi intellectuals and political thinkers such as Ibrahim Joyo and GM Syed began to shape a meta-narrative of Sindhi identity, because to them, the departing Hindus were first Sindhis and then Hindus; and that their departure had weakened Sindh's demography and economy.

After the creation of Pakistan (and then the demise of its founder, Mohammad Ali Jinnah), the Pakistani state began in earnest its long-drawn project to cut through the country's ethnic complexities by constructing and then imposing a monolithic narrative of Pakistani nationhood. This attracted the scorn of the country's various ethnicities who dismissed and rejected the state's idea of nationhood. They believed it contradicted the notions of nationhood and faith enshrined in the historical DNA of their respective ethnicities.

Between 1958 and the early 1970s, GM Syed immersed himself in the study of the religious, social and political histories of Sindh. In 1966, he created *Bazm-e-Sufian-e-Sindh*,[93] an intellectual initiative which also included a number of other Sindhi scholars. Syed and these scholars publish papers and books which helped form the doctrinal basis of modern Sindhi nationalism. This nationalism described the Sindhis as being the descendants of the natives of the Indus Valley Civilization. It saw Sindhis as people whose social, political and religious consciousness were influenced by various religions and cultures which had arrived and established themselves in the region in the last 5000

---

[92] Essay by Vazira Fazila in *Interpreting the Sindh World: Essays of Society and History* (Oxford University Press, 2010).
[93] The Case of Sindh (Naeen Sindh Academy, Karachi (Year NA).

years. It added that this aspect of Sindh's history, along with the Muslim Sufi saints who began to arrive and settle in Sindh after the 8th Century CE, helped shape the Sindhi society in becoming inherently tolerant and pluralistic,[94] and repulsed by those strands of the faith which eschewed tolerance.

Syed's works gave Sindhi identity a historical and religious context that also helped shield the Sindhi society from being affected by the disastrous sectarian and extremist fall-outs of the various religious experiments conducted by the state and governments of Pakistan. Though Syed failed to transform his scholarly impact into political mileage (for himself), another Sindhi, ZA Bhutto, who was accused by Syed of being a stooge of the 'establishment',[95] recognized the impact Syed had had on the Sindhi mindset.

In 1975, when Bhutto's party, the PPP, was in power and he was ruling as the country's first elected prime minister, he appropriated Syed's narrative by organizing a large government-backed conference on Sindh (in Karachi)[96], in which Sindhi scholars were invited to officially adopt what Syed had already initiated, but in the cultural context only. Ironically though, in 1972, Syed's Sindhi ethnic party, the Jeeay Sindh (JS), had demanded the separation of Sindh from Pakistan and Syed had been arrested. Bhutto wanted to neutralize separatist feelings in his home province by tying Syed's enormous thesis and narrative of Sindh's religious and cultural history to that of the Pakistani state's.

It was during the 1975 conference that Syed's idea of Sindh historically being 'the land of the Sufis' was first recognized and

---

[94] GM Syed: *Religion & Reality* (Fiction House, 2012).
[95] M Soalech Korejo: *GM Syed: An Analysis of His Political Perceptive* (Oxford University Press, 2000) p.xxii
[96] Hamida Khuro, Anwar Mooraj: *Karachi: Megacity of our Times* (Oxford University Press, 1997)

promoted by the state.[97] It was then turned into an official narrative (through state-owned media), but only after stripping off the Sindhi nationalist/separatist aspect which Syed had attached to this narrative. Thus, it was after 1975 that the expression 'Sindh is a land of Sufis' was given official currency. Bhutto, besides trying to neutralize Syed's political impact in the province, used the conference to further beef up his regime's concept of the populist 'Third World Socialism' by combining it with Syed's thesis on Sindhi Sufism.[98]

On the day Bhutto was hanged in April 1979, Syed commented that the 'the (Punjabi-dominated) establishment doesn't realize that today it hanged its most loyal servant.'[99] Yet, most of the movements and protests against the Zia dictatorship took place in Sindh. And during perhaps the largest movement (the 1983 MRD uprising in the interior of Sindh), Syed did not take any part. When he was asked why his party had decided not to take part in a movement that was being brutally crushed by the 'establishment', Syed said: 'Zia is making our job easier by leading the break-up of Pakistan.'[100]

Zia was killed in August 1988 when (allegedly) a bomb went off on the C130 plane he was traveling on. The PPP (now led by Bhutto's young daughter, Benazir Bhutto) had managed to retain its influence and popularity in Sindh, whereas the Sindhi nationalists by then had become a fractured and fragmented lot. Jeeay Sindh had broken into various factions and many Sindhi nationalists had also joined Murtaza Bhutto's urban guerrilla outfit, the Al-Zulfikar (AZO).

---

[97] Ibid.
[98] Essay by Oskar Verkaaik in *Interpreting the Sindh World: Essays of Society and History* (Oxford University Press, 2010).
[99] Asian Survey, Vol: 2, 2002. p.225
[100] Movement for the Restoration of Democracy: Abdul Qadir Mushtaq (GC University, Faisalabad, 2015). P.118

Despite the fact that the PPP had managed to dominate the political proceedings in Sindh, GM Syed continued to be revered as a sage by the Sindhis. Dutch academic, Oskar Verkaaik, during his field study in Sindh in 1989-90 [101], saw shops which had portraits of ZA Bhutto hanging on the walls right beside those of GM Syed with the words '*Sain Latif' jo pyaro'* (Sindhi for Shah Latif's beloved) written over them. 18th century Sufi saint, Shah Abdul Latif Bhittai was declared as 'Sindh's patron saint' in Syed's initial narrative. The declaration was made official by the federal government in 1975.

Sindh's existential disposition shaped by the likes of GM Syed and then pragmatically adopted and reengineered by Bhutto had survived Zia's intransigent ideological onslaught. But even though Sindh managed to withstand the many waves of religious extremism and radicalization in Pakistan, from the mid-2000s onward, the province began to witness episodes of religious bigotry and violence. In the last five years or so, attacks on Hindu places of worship and on men who had allegedly committed 'blasphemy', have been reported from the 'land of the Sufis.' The quantity of such incidents in Sindh is still lower when compared to those taking place in the Punjab and the Khyber Pakhtunkhwa provinces, but the incidents seem to generate more debate because they took place in Sindh.

Sindh's sprawling cosmopolitan capital, Karachi, is a staggering melting-pot of various ethnicities, religions, sects and sub-sects; but its general pluralistic disposition is often tainted by its darker sides, seething with ethnic tensions, violent criminal gangs and administrational chaos. What's more, entering the chaos here were also various groups of militant sectarian and extremist organizations who began to take over

---

[101] Oskaar Verkaaik: *Migrants & Militants: Fun and Urban Violence in Pakistan* (Princeton University Press, 2004)

several congested swaths of the city from the early 2000's.[102] But the rest of Sindh, till only a few years ago, was being explained as being perhaps the country's last major bastion of sectarian and religious harmony. So what happened?

Three views have recently cropped up to explain the rising incidents of religious bigotry in Sindh.

- Many Sindhi nationalists have accused the state of using extreme groups in Sindh to neutralize Sindhi nationalism.
- The second view suggests that when Sindh suffered serious damage from the devastating 2011 floods in the province, some well-organized militant religious organizations set-up 'relief camps' in the flood-hit areas. But when the floods receded, these organizations stayed back and began to build madrasahs[103] from where they are indoctrinating young Sindhis from poverty-stricken backgrounds.
- The third view sees the PPP – the party which has been sweeping elections in Sindh for over 40 years – of being unable to detect the intensity of the problem, and now suffering from complacency. Those holding this view also blame the failed economic policies of the PPP governments here, which are making many poor young Sindhis fall into the trap being laid by the extremist organizations.

However, there are also those who believe that bad economics is not the main issue (at least in this regard). Just before the 2013 election, Faiz Qureshi, a retired Sindhi civil servant told a local news channel: 'Sindhis are not fools to keep voting for the PPP despite of that party leaving them hungry and

---

[102] Extremist Group Expands its Reach: Saeed Shah; Shaoib Hassan
[103] Islamic seminaries.

desperate.' He then added: 'this (the gradual rise of religious discord) is a completely new phenomenon in Sindh. The PPP just doesn't know how to tackle it.'

Some economists have credited the many PPP governments in Sindh for helping shape a growing Sindhi middle-class. Political economist, Asad Sayeed, claims that to most Sindhis, the PPP remains to be the only party which helps them keep pace with the economics related to federal-level politics. He suggests, 'the PPP remains to be their (the Sindhis') main link with the federal government and bureaucracy in Islamabad.'[104]

Some three years ago, author and columnist, Ayesha Siddiqua, explained in an article[105] how she had witnessed the emergence of madrasahs in upper Sindh. To her, the sudden growth of madrassas in the province is not a coincidence. She believes they are being set up for reasons that are far more ominous than just being reactions to bad economics. The interior of the Sindh province has the fewest number of madrasahs, especially the kind which sprang up in the Punjab and KP from the 1980s onward and were used as indoctrination centres for young men willing to fight 'infidels' in Afghanistan.

But Sindhis were never part of any *jihad* (state-sponsored or otherwise). So, who is joining these seminaries? A TV host at a Sindhi TV channel Awaaz (Voice) recently told me: 'It's confusing. Most Sindhis are still PPP voters and followers of Syed Sain (GM Syed). Most of them are still pluralistic and visit Sufi shrines like they always did. The problem is that the new generation of Sindhis have lost its bearings.'

When I asked him to elaborate, he added: 'Till even a decade ago, most young Sindhis used to either join the student-wings of the

---

[104] Conversation with Saeed in Karachi, February, 2015.
[105] The Madrassah Mix: Ayesha Siddiqua (Dawn, March 1, 2015).

PPP or that of a Sindhi nationalist party. But the generation today has become anarchist. One really doesn't know where they stand.'

He continued: 'The PPP has grown lazy. It keeps its voters happy with certain economic schemes but fails to understand so many complexities which have cropped up in the Sindhi society. Many young Sindhis today are not being educated about their people's history the way they used to. Look at the Sindhi nationalists. They've split into a thousand factions!'

The PPP-led Sindh government organized a Sindh Festival in 2014. It was the brainchild of Bilawal Bhutto, the son of former chairperson of the PPP, late Benazir Bhutto. To him the festival was the PPP's way of revitalizing views about Sindh's Sufi heritage among the new generation of young Sindhis. When I asked the Sindhi journalist about this, he said: 'As an idea, it (the festival) made sense. But it won't do much. Because some Sindhis have learned from the rest of Pakistan that land and other petty disputes can now be solved by accusing ones opponent of religious sacrilege.'

The same year (2014), a Hindu place of worship was torched in Bhutto's hometown of Larkana. The majority of Sindhis I managed to talk to after the Larkana incident exhibited a genuine concern. Most were of the view that something of the scale of Syed's narrative would be required to once again shield Sindh from the scrooge of sectarianism and extremism that has ravaged Pakistani society and polity for decades now. They believe Syed's works should be popularized among the new generation of young Sindhis. But since the PPP is still the largest party in the province, they think that its next foray should be an intellectual one. It should provide a platform that should engineer a narrative based on the modern-day understanding of Sindh's heritage and that it (the narrative) should then be circulated among the young people of Sindh through educational institutions.

The Mohajirs (Urdu-speakers) constitute the second largest ethnic community in Sindh. They are sprinkled across the province, but they are a majority in the province's capital, Karachi.[106] A large Mohajir population can also be found in Sindh's second largest city, Hyderabad. Unlike the country's other ethnic groups, Mohajirs are not 'people of the soil' and/or they have roots in areas that are outside of what today is Pakistan.

A majority of them arrived from various Indian villages, towns and cities (especially from North India). 'Mohajir' in Urdu means 'refugee', and that's what they were called when they migrated to Pakistan in 1947. Most of them were Urdu-speakers, but also included Guajarati-speakers. A bulk of them settled in Karachi and by the early 1950s, they had become a vital part of the otherwise Punjabi-dominated ruling elite of Pakistan – mainly due to the high rate of education found among the Mohajir community; its urbane complexion; and the fact that many of them had the required expertise to run the new country's nascent bureaucracy and (urban) economy.

Socially, the Mohajirs of Sindh were urbane, but politically they sided with the country's two major religious parties, the JI and the Jamiat Ulema Pakistan (JUP).[107] The dichotomy between the Mohajirs' social and political dispositions was a result of the community's sense of insecurity that it felt in a country where the majority of its inhabitants were 'people of the soil.' The Punjabis, Bengalis, Sindhis, Baloch and Pakhtuns already had dedicated constituencies in the new country based on their ethnic histories and distinct languages.

---

[106] According to the 1998 Consensus Report, the Mohajirs constitute 48% of Karachi's population.

[107] Newsline, Vol: 18, October 2010.

The Mohajirs didn't. They were refugees. So, out of this sense of anxiety, on the one hand, they excelled in the building and running of the nascent country's state and government institutions (except the military which was dominated by the Punjabis); and on the other hand, they politically allied themselves with religious parties and the state of Pakistan which wanted to eschew and undermine the ethnic diversity of the country to mold a more monolithic concept of Pakistani nationhood.[108]

This curtailed any chance of the Mohajirs to earnestly integrate with and adopt the ways of the Sindhi-speaking majority of Sindh. Also, since the Mohajir community had risen to become part of the country's early ruling elite, the Sindhis began to see the Mohajirs as cultural, economic and political invaders who wanted to sideline the Sindhis in their own land.[109] But by the time the country got its first military rule in 1958 (Ayub Khan), the Mohajirs had already begun to lose their influence in the ruling elite.

With the radical Baloch, Bengali and Sindhi nationalists distancing themselves from the state's narrative of nationhood (and remaining well outside of the ruling elite), Ayub (who hailed from Khyber Pakhtunkhwa), slowly began to pull the Pakhtuns into the mainstream of Pakistan's economy and politics. For example, famous Pakhtun nationalist leaders such as Wali Khan too decided to 'bargain with the establishment after the 1971 East Pakistan debacle' [110] and this also facilitated the gradual entry of the Pakhtuns into the ruling

---

[108] See also 'The Great Concoction' in *End of the Past:* Nadeem F. Paracha (Vanguard Books, 2016).

[109] Peter Janke: *Ethnic and Religious Conflicts* (Dartmouth, 1994) p.177

[110] Jamal Naqvi: *Leaving the Left Behind* (Pakistan Study Centre, University of Karachi, 2013).

and economic elites of the country. By the late 1960s, the Mohajirs had decisively lost their place in the ruling elite.

When a Sindhi, ZA Bhutto, became the country's prime minister, the Mohajirs feared that they would be further sidelined, this time by the economic and political resurgence of Sindhis under Bhutto. In response to this apprehension, the Mohajirs participated in droves against the Bhutto regime during the 1977 anti-Bhutto movement orchestrated by the Pakistan National Alliance (PNA).[111] PNA's key drivers were the country's three main religious parties: JI, JUP and the JUI, though it also had in its fold Pir Pagara's conservative Muslim League faction and Asghar Khan's centrist Tehreek-e-Istaqlal. PNA accused Bhutto of rigging the 1977 election and the violent movement that it initiated made way for the country's third Martial Law (General Ziaul Haq).

But taking part in the PNA movement did not see the Mohajirs finding their way back into the fold of the ruling elite, even though the JI became an important player in Zia's first cabinet. Disillusioned by the results of the movement, some Mohajir politicians came to the conclusion that the Mohajirs had been exploited by the religious parties [112] and it was the shoulders of the Mohajirs that these parties had used to climb into the corridors of power.

It was this feeling which triggered the formation of the All Pakistan Mohajir Students Organization (in 1978) and then the Mohajir Qaumi Movement (MQM) in 1984. Its founders, Altaf Hussain and Azim Ahmed Tariq, decided to organize the Mohajir community into a cohesive ethnic whole. For this, they felt the need to break away from the Mohajir

---

[111] Journal of South Asian & Middle Eastern Studies: Vol: 23, 1999. p.51
[112] Altaf Hussain: *My Life's Journey: The Early Years 1966-1988* (Oxford University Press, 2011)

community's tradition of being politically allied to the religious parties, and politicize the Mohajirs' more pluralistic social disposition. The Mohajir dichotomy between social liberalism and political conservatism was thus dissolved and replaced with a new identity-narrative which concentrated on the formation of Mohajir ethnic nationalism pitched against the 'Punjabi establishment' as a whole [113] and against the political muscle of the religious parties in urban Sindh.

The MQM eventually broke the electoral hold of the religious parties in Karachi and succeeded in organizing and reinventing the Mohajirs of Sindh as a distinct ethnic group. By 1992, the MQM had become Sindh's second largest political party. Its rise created severe cleavages in Karachi's traditional political landscape that had been largely dominated by parties such as the PPP, the JI and JUP.

As Karachi's economics and resources continued to come under stress due to the increasing migration to the city from within Sindh, KP and the Punjab provinces, corruption in the police and other government institutions operating in Karachi grew two-fold. The need to use muscle to tilt the political and economic aspects of the city towards a community's interests became prominent.

Thus emerged the militant wings in the city's prominent political groups,[114] whose members, even by the early 1990s, had begun to moonlight as fraudsters and violent criminals. These cleavages saw the MQM ghettoizing large swaths of the city's Mohajirs in areas where it ruled supreme. The results were disastrous. This replaced the pluralistic and enterprising disposition of the Mohajirs with a besieged mentality, which, in turn, began to express itself in a rather violent manner, attracting

---

[113] Oskar Verkaaik: *A People of Migrants* (VU University Press, 1994) p.1
[114] Laurent Gayer: *Karachi: Ordered Disorder* (HarperCollins, 2014).

the concern and then the wrath of the state. Between 1992 and 1999, the MQM faced three full-fledged operations by the military, police and para-military forces. The operations and the violence did not fragment the party because the Mohajir nationalism that it had molded remained intact. But the experience did leave the MQM leadership to further elaborate and define the Mohajir nationalist narrative.

In 2002, MQM began to regenerate itself when it decided to end hostilities with the state by allying itself with the General Musharraf dictatorship (1999-2008). Musharraf had posed as a liberal, and it was during this period that the MQM began to expand the concept of Mohajir identity and nationalism. The party had already weaned the Mohajir community away from the concept of Pakistani nationhood propagated by the religious parties. Now it added two more dimensions to Mohajir nationalism which worked side-by-side. Altaf Hussain began to explain the Mohajirs as 'Urdu-speaking Sindhis' who were connected to the Sindhi-speakers of the province through a spiritual bond inspired by the teachings of Sindh's patron saint, Shah Abdul Latif. This was MQM's way of resolving the Mohajirs' early failures to fully adopt Sindhi culture. But Sindhi nationalists saw it as just another cynical political move.

The other dimension that emerged during this period among the Mohajir community (through the MQM) addressed the disposition of Mohajir identity in the Mohajir-majority areas of Sindh. This dimension saw MQM make Mohajir nationalism and identity (regarding Islam) to be understood as a modern reworking of the 'modernist Islam' of 19th century Muslim scholar, Syed Ahmed Khan, and his 'Aligarh School of Thought'.

So, whereas Sindhi nationalism had formulated a pluralism based on the teachings and histories of Sufi saints, Mohajir nationalism began to express its pluralism as a modern reworking of the 'rational Islam' of Syed Ahmed Khan, which sees spiritual growth as a consequence of material progress. However, this still didn't dent the party's militant propensities.

Now coming back to the 2014 festival conceived and organized by Bilawal Bhutto, he was trying to reassert the popular perception that Sindhi culture was historically pluralistic, tolerant and deeply rooted in the traditions of Sufism. Bilawal used this acuity and its many artistic, literary and social expressions to explain what he thought could be used as a cultural model (across Pakistan) to overwhelm the extremist mindset that has been ravaging the country for so many years now. But unlike GM Syed, Bilawal was not just talking about an inherent and 'indigenous pluralism'.

Syed's 'indigenous pluralism' had meant a society that was informally spiritual but civically materialistic; and (thus) whose economic, political and social interests were best served by keeping its religious beliefs within the confines of the mosque and/or the Sufi shrine.[115] He thought this was vital because religious orthodoxy when used as a political tool becomes a weapon in the hands of forces that try to seize and neutralize a pluralistic society (like Sindh) by imposing a cosmetic homogeneity through monolithic concepts of society, culture and faith.[116]

For example, to Syed and his contemporaries in Sindh's intellectual circles, the kind of faith which was being advocated in Pakistan was alien to the Islam that had been practiced by Sindhi Muslims of the region for a thousand years. Syed's indigenous pluralism was also suspicious of Western capitalism, but not in an intransigent manner. He suggested addressing the

---

[115] GM Syed: *Religion & Reality* (Fiction House, 2012).
[116] Ibid.

onslaught of 'soulless modern materialism' on a social level with the help of Sindh's traditional disposition and its inherent spiritual psyche.[117]

But today Sindh is changing. The Sindhi-speaking middle-class has expanded in the last three decades. Syed is still revered in the province, but he is not as relevant as he was till about the early 1980s. But the PPP still is.

Apart from being popular among Sindhi peasants and the working-classes, the PPP offers the emerging Sindhi-speaking middle and lower middle classes opportunities to attempt fulfilling their upwardly mobile ambitions. Sindhis still see the PPP as the only nationwide party that is not only close to their ethnic roots, but is their best mode to keep in touch with the economics and politics tied to federal-level politics. Thus, voting for the PPP (by the Sindhis) is now more of a pragmatic move than an ideological one.

But the emergence of a larger Sindhi-speaking middle-class has also triggered social strife in the province. The youth among this section of the Sindhi-speakers see the PPP as a dinosaur associated with the politics of their parents. However, there is still no effective alternative to the PPP here. The PPP has continued to neutralize the Sindhi nationalists who have little or nothing substantial to offer anymore to the new Sindhi-speaking youth in terms of this youth's more universal ideas of upward mobility.

Other parties such as the centre-right Pakistan Muslim League-Nawaz and the populist Pakistan Thereek-e-Isnaf are largely seen in Sindh as squarely peddling the interests of non-Sindhi businessmen and bourgeoisie. But even though religious parties have remained to be weak in the province, certain social

---

[117] Ibid.

and economic fissures being caused by the rapid emergence of Sindhi-speaking middle-classes has witnessed a very non-Sindhi phenomenon of religious radicalization creeping in.

This is still a new phenomenon among Sindhi speakers. But one can relate it to the manner in which Punjab's middle and trader classes became overtly conservative from the late 1970s onward, due to their growing exposure and engagement with conservative oil-rich Arab societies in the Middle East, and due to the economic benefits which they enjoyed during the Zia dictatorship in the 1980s. Of course, the Sindhis (from any class) did not enjoy such benefits during the Zia government.

But a series of PPP provincial regimes in Sindh ever since the 1970s have helped shape the Sindhi middle-classes. They have become more influential in impacting the electoral and economic dynamics of Sindh. Conscious of this, Bilawal's Sindh Festival was planned as a two-pronged strategy: First, to furnish Bilawal's idea of a 'progressive Pakistan', and second, to check the trend of urbanization in Sindh from going the way urbanization went in the Punjab (in the political context). The cultural activities that were on display during the Sindh Festival suggest an understanding (or need) on Bilawal's part of an urbanization trend that should produce a progressive workforce and an economic, political and religious culture based on a healthy respect for diversity; instead of a culture based on economics tied to the politics of faith and sects. Of course, many aspects of Bilawal's thinking have a lot to do with youthful optimism and (for want of a better word) well-intentioned social engineering.

But PPP's rejuvenation can now only be convincingly cemented if the party's next step is steeped in an ideology that, though futuristic, is still rooted in the party's past of being a large, all-encompassing progressive entity close to its founder's fusion of populist politics and GM Syed's meta-narrative and imagery of Sindh being inherently the 'land of the Sufis.'

****

The Flasher

In 1983, a movement against the Zia dictatorship began to spiral out of control and threatened a full-scale civil war in Pakistan's Sindh province. Dozens of civilians were killed, hundreds arrested and many escaped into the thick forests near the cities of Dadu and Moro. Many (eventually) become bandits.[118] A movement that had begun as a nationwide anti-Zia agitation, mutated into a civil war of sorts between Sindhi nationalists and the state. The movement was eventually crushed with the help of the army. One of the most intriguing characters of the movement was a middle-aged Sindhi man reportedly belonging to a small Maoist party, the Awami Tehreek (AT).

His sudden claim to fame had to do with just one act of his: In September 1983, he had jumped in front of an armored limousine in which Zia was travelling (in Dadu), lift the *dhoti* [119] that he was wearing, and flash his privates for the dictator to see, all the while shouting (in Sindhi), *'bhali karey aya, bhali karey aya'* ('welcome, welcome').[120] He was arrested and never seen or heard from again.

Though protests against Zia had begun almost immediately after his military coup in July 1977, his regime's harsh measures

---

[118] The Marxist Review: Vol: 18, 1985. p.65
[119] The dhoti is a traditional men's garment, worn in the Indian Subcontinent mainly by Punjabi and Sindhi Pakistanis and Bengali people (In Bangladesh and India).
[120] K R. Malkani: *The Sindh Story* (Sindh Academy, 1984)

against any and all obstruction did not allow opposition groups to organize themselves in a more coherent and systematic manner. The beginning of the anti-Soviet insurgency in Afghanistan in early 1980 had meant that the Zia regime was poised to attract recognition from the United States and become its vessel to carry the large military and financial aid that the US and Saudi Arabia pledged to back the insurgents in Afghanistan. But it would take another few years for Zia to use this patronage to strengthen his position.

The Movement for the Restoration of Democracy (MRD) was formed in 1981.[121] It was a multiparty alliance initiated by the PPP. The MRD included the centre-left PPP; the center-left, Pakistan National Party; the far-left, Awami Tehreek; the far-left, Qaumi Mahaz-i-Azadi; the far-left Muzdoor Kissan Party; the centre-left National Democratic Party; the centrist Tehreek-i-Istaqlal; the centre-right Pakistan Democratic Party; the centrist Muslim League (Malik Qasim faction); and the right-wing Jamiat Ulema Islam, which was also the only mainstream religious party opposing Zia.

The movement kicked off in early 1981, but it took another two years for MRD to gather a more substantial momentum. However, by 1983, Zia had consolidated his position and revived the economy. Yet, this revival, which was largely built upon the substantial flow of US and Saudi aid, brought with it a new kind of institutional corruption,[122] and the mainstreaming of radical clerics who were propped up by the state to recruit and indoctrinate young Pakistanis and Afghans for the insurgency against Soviet forces in Kabul.

---

[121] Stephen P. Cohen: *The Idea of Pakistan* (Brookings Institution, 2004) p.136

[122] Outlook Traveler Vol: 8, June, 2008. p.132

The country's largest and most populated province, Punjab, was a bastion of the PPP ever since the late 1960s. The party led by a Sindhi (ZA Bhutto) had swept the election in the province in 1970 and then again in the (latter annulled) 1977 election. To dent PPP's support base in Punjab, Zia (an immigrant Punjabi), began to overtly patronize those sections of Punjab that had been adversely affected by the Bhutto regime's haphazard 'socialist' policies. Such sections included prominent business groups. Zia's economic policies were also designed to attract the support of Punjab's urban middle and lower-middle-class traders and shopkeepers.

Zia then gradually aligned these sections with certain radical religious outfits that he had begun to foster. Thus, an economic revival witnessed during the Zia regime was accompanied by a burst of religiosity within Punjab's bourgeoisie and petty-bourgeoisie. The MRD leadership reacted to this by deducing that the fruits of the economic revival witnessed (after 1980) were mostly falling in the hands of central/urban Punjab's industrialist and business communities and the trader classes;[123] whereas rest of the country (as well as working-class and rural Punjabis) were being ravaged by economic exploitation, the rising rates of crime and corruption, and the growing incidents of sectarian violence. On August 14, 1983, the MRD launched a movement against Zia.

The movement kicked-off simultaneously in Sindh and the Punjab, but it failed to gather much support in the latter province. Soon, it became restricted to Sindh, where at one point, it began to look like it would turn into a full-blown Sindhi nationalist movement. MRD activists and youth belonging to the student-wings of MRD parties and various left-wing Sindhi nationalist groups plunged into the fray and

---

[123] Impact International: Vol: 13-14, 1983. p.107

disrupted everyday life in Sindh. Sindh's metropolitan capital, Karachi, too, witnessed widespread protests by journalist, student and women's organizations, but compared to the rest of the province, Karachi remained relatively unruffled.

In the interior of Sindh, the situation eventually became too hot for the police to handle and Zia had to call in the army. Dozens of MRD supporters were killed in the ensuing violence. By September 1983, the movement had become a militant Sindhi nationalist expression when Punjab failed to rise. Zia had managed to change the political and social complexion of Punjab by initiating the gradual process of drying up the support that the PPP had enjoyed in that province.

Apart from the fact that there was already anger among the Sindhis against the hanging of a Sindhi prime minister, contributing to the violence in the province in 1983 was the feeling that Sindhis, as well as the Urdu-speakers (Mohajirs) in Sindh's provincial capital, Karachi, were being 'invaded' by elements that were posing a threat to their economic interests.[124] From 1982 onward, Karachi began receiving large numbers of Afghan refugees, some of whom came for the sole purpose of setting up illegal drug and weapons businesses in the city. This trend would go on to trigger the vicious circle of ethnic violence in Karachi from 1985 onward.

Secondly, Zia began to allot land in interior Sindh to Punjabis who were encouraged (by the regime) to migrate from Punjab to Sindh.[125] Zia did this to create a constituency for himself in Sindh. But what he received was resistance and resentment from the Sindhis and Urdu-speaking traders and members of the Sindhi

---

[124] Struggle for Democracy in Sindh (Berkely Journal of Social Science, Vol: 1, June 2011)
[125] Ibid.

landed elite. In Karachi, Memon[126], Sindhi, and Urdu-speaking traders and businessmen formed an organization called the Maha Sindh[127] to 'protect the interests of Sindh's Mohajirs and Sindhis'. But this organization was mostly centred in Karachi. It soon became an entirely Mohajir vehicle and would partly evolve into becoming the Mohajir Qaumi Movement (MQM) in 1984.[128] But the reaction to the regime's maneuvers in this context was more violent in the interior of Sindh, where protesters turned militant and military troops had to be called in in to quell the turmoil.

Begun on August 14 1983, the MRD Movement had started to whirl out of control by early September, not only for the Zia dictatorship but for the main MRD leadership as well. In August, Sindh's capital, Karachi, had witnessed court arrests and protest rallies on a daily basis by labour unionists, student leaders and anti-Zia politicians. But in September, the focus of the movement had shifted to the central and northern parts of Sindh that got caught up in a whirlpool of violence.

The MRD movement here had begun to take the shape of a Sindhi nationalist uprising bordering on an insurgency against the state. Faced by a volley of questions (mainly from foreign journalists), Zia decided to prove that 'only a handful of troublemakers' were involved in the violence.[129] He announced that he would go on a whirlwind tour of Sindh to attest that he was as popular there as he believed he was in the Punjab. So he took off from Rawalpindi in his big military aircraft (C-130) to Sindh's capital, Karachi.

---

[126] *Memon* people are a collection of ethnic groups from the northern part of the Indian Subcontinent, and now mostly settled in Pakistan's larghest city, Karachi.
[127] Struggle for Democracy in Sindh (Berkely Journal of Social Science, Vol: 1, June 2011)
[128] Ibid.
[129] DAWN, September 1, 1983.

Zia's plane landed at the Karachi International Airport, and from Karachi, he planned to fly to Hyderabad with his posse. With him was also a crew from the state-controlled Pakistan Television (PTV) which was to cover the general's 'successful tour of Sindh.' After arriving in Karachi, Zia briefly talked to a select group of journalists and reiterated his views about the situation in Sindh, insisting all was well, and that the MRD movement was the work of a handful of politicians who were 'working against Pakistan.'[130]

He sounded confident about the success of his visit to the troubled spots of Sindh. This confidence was not only generated by what he was hearing from his advisers but also because by the time he reached Sindh's second largest city, Hyderabad, he'd already had telephonic conversations with Sindh's most respected Sindhi nationalist leader and scholar, GM Syed.[131]

Syed told reporters: 'It (the MRD Movement) is a PPP-led movement and it has nothing to do with Sindhi nationalism. PPP is just trying to grab power.'[132] The decision to ignore the 1983 MRD Movement would eventually cost Syed his political career. Syed's logic behind opting to not to take any part in the movement seems to be linked to his perception of the PPP being a party that was used by the 'Punjabi ruling elite'[133] to keep nationalist sentiments in Sindh at bay. This narrative was well known by Syed's admirers. Yet, what shocked many of them was not really the act of Syed not taking part in a PPP-led movement, but the fact that Syed was actually responding to Zia's friendly overtures towards him. Syed's apologists have suggested that he did this to neutralize the PPP's influence in

---

[130] Ibid
[131] JPRS Report: Issue: 92, 1992. p.42
[132] Ibid.
[133] MS Korejo: *GM Syed* (Oxford University Press, 2000) p.81

Sindh so he could construct a movement on his own terms. So Syed sat quietly, watching the MRD movement in Sindh fast becoming a Sindhi nationalist uprising – without him.

By September, the movement had begun to slip away from the hands of the top leadership of the PPP and of other component parties of the MRD. PPP chairperson, Benazir Bhutto, released a statement from her jail cell urging Punjab to rise if it wanted to save Pakistan from breaking up.[134] She was getting nervous. The movement was now almost entirely being navigated by the local leaders of PPP's youth-wing; Maoist outfits such as Awami Tehreek, Qaumi Mahaz-i-Azadi and Mazdoor Kissan Party; left-wing student organizations such as the revamped Democratic Students Federation (DSF); and a breakaway faction of the Jeeay Sindh Tehreek. Back in Hyderabad, Zia spoke about the inherent patriotism of all Sindhis. By this, he meant not only indigenous Sindhis, but also the Urdu-speakers (Mohajirs), and the Punjabis settled in the province (called 'New Sindhis'). Radical left-wing Sindhi nationalist, Rasool Baksh Palejo, scoffed at Zia's comment.

Palejo, though not a GM Syed disciple, echoed Syed's original narrative about Mohajirs. In the 1960s, Syed had accused the Urdu-speakers of coming to Sindh (as migrants from India), but behaving like those Europeans who had invaded the lands of the 'Red Indians' in the Americas[135] and had treated them shabbily. Palejo's rebuff did not go down well with the Mohajir members of the various small left-wing parties and youth outfits that were taking part in the movement.

Aamer Zain, a young Urdu-speaking activist of the DSF in the Sindh city of Khairpur, was quoted in a pro-PPP Sindhi newspaper as saying: 'With all due respect to Palejo Sahib, I am as much a

---

[134] Benazir Bhutto: *Daughter of the East* (Hamilton, 1988).
[135] Ashraf Tariq: *Panic in Karachi* (DHN International, 1999) p.88

Sindhi as he is, otherwise why would I be risking my future, and everything else by taking part in this movement …?' On 15th September, Zain was arrested by the police during a violent rally in the Sindh city of Nawabshah and severely tortured.

In 1983, there was no MQM. There were just two tiny Mohajir nationalist organizations with not much influence. There was also the student outfit, All Pakistan Mohajir Students Organization (APMSO), but it wasn't as prominent as it would become after 1985. The Mohajir community largely sat out the MRD movement.

The Sindhi nationalists' biggest grudge during the MRD movement, however, was against the Punjabi settlers. Sindhi nationalists had been accusing the Zia of sending and settling ambitious Punjabi traders and agriculturalists in Sindh to prop up a constituency for himself in the province. The nationalists claimed that these settlers were taking over Sindhi businesses and jobs[136] and siding with the pro-Zia feudal elite to repress Sindhi nationalism. One of the most prominent among these feudal leaders was Pir Pagaro.

From Hyderabad, Zia began his tour of the troubled interior of the Sindh province. He particularly wanted the cameras to capture his tour of Dadu and Moro, the two cities most affected by the movement. It was decided by his security team that he would use a helicopter to fly there. His aides seemed a tad fidgety and nervous. The thick forests around Moro and Dadu had become sanctuaries for hundreds of activists escaping Zia's forces. Another rallying point for the activists were the many big and small shrines of Sufi saints across Sindh. As Zia sat in the helicopter, waiting to land in Dadu, some of his security advisers shared with him his regime's latest triumphs in the area.

---

[136] Struggle for Democracy in Sindh (Berkely Journal of Social Science, Vol: 1, June 2011)

Hundreds of 'troublemakers and traitors' had been arrested and eliminated, he was told, and a plan was also afoot to flush out 'rebels' hiding in the shrines and the forests.

Most of Sindh's influential *pirs* (spiritual leaders) were opposing Zia. They had thrived during the Bhutto regime, especially the powerful Pir of Hala. So Zia contacted Pir Pagaro and requested him to use his influence to make the keepers of the Sufi shrines reject 'Sindhi rebels'. Pagara tried but failed. One September evening in 1983, Pakistanis watched a video clip on the state-owned PTV's 9pm Urdu news bulletin which showed Zia descending from a helicopter and being greeted by a dozen or so smiling men in Sindhi caps. He had reached Dadu. Viewers were told that Zia was 'warmly greeted by patriotic Sindhis in Dadu.'

The next day, however, when Pakistanis tuned into BBC Radio's Urdu service at 8pm, the newscaster, after detailing the nature of the day's rallies, protest marches, and violence in Sindh, also added a brief report about a more amusing episode. This report became a topic of glee at the Karachi Press Club that was heavily involved in accommodating the journalists who were taking part in the movement.

This is what happened: As Zia's helicopter landed on a helipad in Dadu, he was greeted by a few men wearing Sindhi caps. He was then escorted towards a bulletproof limousine that was followed by jeeps carrying armed security personnel. He was expecting the roads of Dadu to be lined up with Sindhis cheering his arrival. In fact, he was sure that his aides had done well to organize a colourful show for the TV cameras to capture.

His motorcade moved into the city on its way to a building where he was expected to speak to the press. To his satisfaction, he did find a sprinkling of people on the roadsides, holding small

Pakistani flags. But then, suddenly, his speeding limo swayed to the right, closely avoiding hitting a stray dog that had appeared, as if out of nowhere. It was no ordinary dog. It had been pushed in front of the general's motorcade by the same small roadside crowd. On the dog's body the following was scribbled (in Sindhi) with red paint. It read: 'Zia is a dog.'

The journalists and the BBC correspondent accompanying the motorcade were not sure what Zia's reaction to this was. As the motorcade moved on, a donkey was seen being made to run on the edges of the scruffy Dadu road that Zia's limo was travelling on. The poor beast was being chased by a group of small kids and on its body too, the red paint screamed Zia's appellation. So much for the show of pomp and popularity Zia was expecting from his aides.

The general's limo now gathered even more speed, until it came to a bumpy portion of the road. Here, it slowed down. In front of the limo was a jeep packed with police guards. The jeep came to an abrupt halt and the cops rushed out, brandishing their rifles. A middle-aged man, hiding in a tree had suddenly jumped down and landed (on his backside) right in front of Zia's limo. The man was wearing a traditional Sindhi dress that also included a *dhoti*.

Before the guards could grab him, he lifted his *dhoti* and exposed his privates, all the while shouting (in Sindhi) '*Bhali karey aya! Bhali kary aya!*' (Welcome! Welcome!). He was grabbed, pulled to one side of the road and beaten, as Zia's limo screeched away. Nobody quite knows what happened to the flasher after he was arrested. But Zia did decide to suddenly end his 'famous' tour of Sindh the very next day – terming it a 'great success.'

Two factors prevented the movement from turning into a full-scale civil war. First was the calling in of the Pakistan Army whose prowess was just too overwhelming to challenge by the rather anarchic and disjointed nature of the agitation. Though the movement had been initiated by an organized alliance of anti-Zia parties, it soon swirled out of the immediate orbit of the alliance's top leadership and began being steered by the leaders and workers of small Maoist outfits and the student-wings of the parties that were part of the MRD.

By September 1983, the movement did not have anyone piloting it from a central command point, and the violence which followed was largely triggered by spontaneous rallies and agitation organized by anti-Zia groups stationed in various cities and villages of north and central Sindh. There was hardly any co-ordination between such groups, and no central or joint leadership. Every group followed its own particular party's local leader who had eventually lost contact with the main MRD leadership which was either operating from different cities, villages or towns; or had been arrested.

Though the Zia regime confidentially saw the movement as an insurgency, it really wasn't. The bulk of the agitation constituted protest rallies. Even in the rallies which turned violent, the protesters were armed with just stones and bricks. Episodes of armed violence only took place when the police tried to enter the forests of Moro and Dadu to flush out the activists who had escaped into the woods. And even then, the armed retaliation did not come from the escapees, but from the hardened highway bandits who already had their bases inside these forests. However, over the next few years, many of the escapees were recruited by the bandits and became notorious highway men.

Secondly, MRD's senior leadership too prevented the movement from turning into an all-out insurgency. The movement was originally launched to trigger nationwide protests against the regime and force Zia to resign (so fresh elections could follow). But when the movement mutated and became a radical expression of Sindhi nationalism in Sindh, the main MRD leadership held itself back to reorient the movement (which it finally did in 1986).

In 1997, an activist of the JUI (the only religious party that was part of the movement), wrote a telling account of what happened to the movement. Though the book (written in Urdu)[137] is largely about his time in various jails of Sindh during the movement, his observations about his jail mates reflect the anarchic nature of the movement. He was arrested in 1983 from Karachi and was locked in a tiny jail cell in Hyderabad. He was first accused of being a 'Soviet agent', and then of being a member of the clandestine left-wing urban guerrilla outfit, the Al-Zulfiqar. After realizing the absurdity of accusing a member of a right-wing religious party of being a communist, the police booked him for taking part in 'anti-state activities'. He was constantly tortured, along with the young men who kept being thrown in the same jail. His jail mates included members of the PPP's student wing; young Sindhi nationalists; and fiery Maoists. He wrote that though they were taking part in the same movement, they often held each other in contempt.

As for the flasher, the most popular theory about him is that he was a peasant in a village near Dadu who had managed to get one of his sons educated. His son had travelled to Karachi for further studies (at the Karachi University). Here, he first joined the student-wing of the Jeeay Sindh Tehreek and then the progressive student alliance, the United Students Movement (USM). He was arrested in 1981 after a serious

---

[137] English translation by Dr. Haroon Ahmad (2001)

episode of violence between the USM and JI's student-wing erupted at the Karachi University. He was still in a Karachi jail when his father performed the flasher stunt in September 1983. It is believed that the stunt was the idea of the Dadu chapter of the Maoist Awami Tehreek.[138] No one knows what happened to the man after he was arrested, but his son was released after Zia's demise in 1988.

****

The Wizard of Leaf

In January 2016, I reconnected with a friend of mine who I hadn't met for over 30 years. He somehow got my cell phone number and invited me to his son's wedding. Even though I could not go to the wedding, another call by him got us talking about the past.

I had first met him in the small town of Moro in the Naushero Feroze district of Sindh in 1986. I was studying at a college in Karachi at the time and had accompanied a posse of young anti-Zia activists travelling onward to Nawabshah to organize a rally for Benazir Bhutto who had returned from exile to challenge Zia's dictatorship. Benazir had managed to hold a large rally in Lahore and then in Karachi's Lyari area, before she was arrested and put under house arrest. I was in Moro when she was taken in. We were staying in the backyard of an old shrine of a Sufi saint, where we were often met by a group of men who belonged to the Awami Tehreek (AT).

When the rally which we were supposed to help organize was cancelled, we spent much of our time lazing around the

---

[138] Told to me by a former Awami Tehreek activist in 2004.

courtyard of the shrine, discussing politics and drinking some wonderful home-made 'apple wine' provided by a cousin of one of the lads who ran a liquor store in the area. This is where I met Haroon, a young Sindhi nationalist who was a couple of years older than me. He had arrived with the AT activists. While exchanging pleasantries with me, he almost immediately noticed that I was perhaps the only non-Sindhi in the group. He said, 'You speak Urdu like a Mohajir, but you dance like a Punjabi ...'

Taken aback, I asked him what he meant by 'I danced like a Punjabi?'

It turned out he had seen me the evening before, participating in the freewheeling Sufi folk dance, the *dhamaal*, at the shrine. I chuckled and told him I was just having some fun and couldn't understand how my dance was 'Punjabi'. But I did tell him that he was correct about my Urdu accent: 'My father is a Punjabi, and my mother is a Mohajir. But I am a true Karachiite ...'

Haroon just nodded his head, as if he already knew that. He had been in jail in Dadu ever since 1984, and had been released (on bail) just a few days before our meeting. He was severely tortured there, and he proudly showed us the cuts and wounds he had received on his back, shins and parts of his head during his time in a cell. As we got talking over some tea and cigarettes, I kept asking him what he had meant by 'I danced like a Punjabi.' He finally smiled wider than he usually did, and said: 'Punjabis do the *dhamaal* in a particular manner. They are more uninhibited, whereas we Sindhis remain more restrained. But though you were doing the *dhamaal* in a most free and uninhabited manner, you are actually a very reserved person, right?'

I just shrugged my shoulders. He smiled widely again: 'But, my Punjabi-Mohajir brother, whenever you go to Multan or

Lahore or any city of the Punjab, do notice how their (the Punjabis') style of dancing is changing. They are now dancing the way Zia wants them to.'

I protested: 'I was in Lahore when BB (Benazir) arrived from exile. Thousands of Lahoris turned up. Many of them danced exactly the way you saw me dance …'

Haroon was unmoved: 'But no other people have experienced the intensity of Zia's Martial Law the way us Sindhis have.' Before I could add my bit again, he said a rather curious thing: 'There is actually a way we can make others feel this intensity …'

From his pocket he took out a small pack. In it were dried leaves: 'Do you know what this is?' He asked. 'Of course,' I replied. '*Bhang*. I have had it on a couple of occasions,' I added. *Bhang* is a preparation made from a hallucinogenic plant (cannabis) and is traditionally used in South Asia.[139]

'This is how we make others feel the intensity of Zia's rule in Sindh,' Haroon explained.

By now I had begun to laugh: 'Through *bhang*?'

'No ordinary *bhang*,' Haroon retorted.

Well, that evening our group was treated to Haroon's *bhang*. We gladly took it, vigorously mixed with icy water. It took about 50 minutes to kick in, and when it did, my God! Within the next few hours, most of us were convinced we had gone mad. We would laugh, cry, sulk for no apparent reason; try to hide from the most terrifying hallucinations, and make teary-eyed pleads to Haroon to get us committed to a hospital. The next morning, after the hallucinatory nightmare was finally over, I told Haroon: 'I now understand.' He just let out a loud laugh and said

---

[139] Tod Mikuriya: *Excerpts from the Indian Hemp Commission Report* (Last Gasp Inc. 1994) p.38

something in Sindhi, which I was later told had meant: 'Tyranny breeds insanity.'

When Haroon had told me that this was how they (the Sindhis) made others realize the intensity of Zia's regime (in Sindh), he wasn't really making it all up. The *bhang* that he had had with him was made from an extraordinary strain of the cannabis plant which had appeared in Sindh in 1981. It was aptly called 'Martial La' (Martial Law). It grew in the wild around the forests along the towns of Dadu and Moro, or maybe someone had planted it there. It was first introduced into the 'market' in 1983 during the peak of the violent MRD movement against Zia.

No one knows who gave it its name ('Martial La'). Haroon moved to the Middle East in 1991 and I lost contact with him, until in late 2015, when I received his call. He worked as a nurse in a hospital in Qatar, and then after completing his MBBS from a university in Cyprus, he became a physician and settled in Greece. There he married an Iranian lady, had four kids, and was in Pakistan to get one of them married.

I couldn't go to the wedding (because I was travelling at the time); but I did remind him how he had made me almost lose my mind with 'Martial La'. He laughed: 'Look at it this way, Paracha. Something good also came from it.'

I asked him what?

'When the next time you do the *dhamaal*, notice yourself,' he said.

'I haven't done the *dhamaal* in ages,' I replied.

'Yes,' he said, 'but now when you do, you will do it like a Sindhi!' He laughed again.

I chuckled too: 'Thus spoke a citizen of Greece. What do Greeks know about the *dhamaal*? Come back to Pakistan, *saain*.'[140] I taunted him.

Haroon went quiet for a bit. Then in a serious tone, said: 'Remember, *saain*. Tyranny breeds insanity.'

This time, however, he said this in Punjabi.

****

A Last Piece of Chocolate

The 1980s were a disastrous decade for Pakistani cinema. As if all of a sudden, Urdu films that till 1979 had been doing good business rapidly started to lose their main (middle-class) audiences. This was also the time when the practice of turning cinemas into 'shopping plazas' also kicked in, with Karachi's famous Naz Cinema becoming the first casualty. One of the primary reasons for this was the social and cultural introversion that the country's urban middle-classes had started to slide into ever since the late 1970s. This can also explain the rapid proliferation of the VCR – a machine that kept many Pakistanis, including regular cinema goers - comfortably stationed in their homes and enjoying smuggled Indian films on video tapes away from the cultural, social and political fall-outs of Zia's rampaging 'Islamisation project'.

A shop from where I usually buy my cigarettes in Karachi, once had a fading poster of bygone Pakistani film star, Waheed Murad, pasted on a wall. I had been noticing the poster ever since I first began buying my cigarettes from this place almost 20 years ago. I know the shop owner well. Today he is a white-

---

[140] Saain is Mister in Sindhi.

haired man in his late 60s and his name is Yameen. He owns three more such shops in the area and has done well for himself and his family. He lives in a 3-bedroom apartment with his wife and 3 children (two sons and a daughter). The sons are college graduates. One of them looks after two of Yameen's shops, while the other son works in the sales department of a tea company. In early 2015, Yameen's daughter completed her intermediate from a local college.

Yet, despite the fact that I have known Yameen for over 20 years now, I had no idea that before he set up his first shop in Karachi's Boat Basin area 31 years ago, he used to be a barber. I came to know about this only recently after I finally asked him about the fading, dusty Waheed Murad poster in his shop. He began to giggle: '*Arey, aap nahi jaantey ...?*' (You still don't know about this?).

One of Yameen's employees, Kudrat, smiled as well: '*Yaar, Paracha Sahib, aap nein Yawar Bhai ki dukhti rug par haath rak diya hai ...*' (You have hit a sore nerve).

It turns out that the poster is over 40 years old! Yameen bought it from a street vendor in 1974 when he was in his early 20s. He was a huge Waheed Murad fan. At the time Pakistan's film industry was thriving and Waheed Murad was one of its biggest stars. Yameen had joined an uncle's barber shop in Karachi's Guru Mandir area after he dropped out from school.

'I had become a barber because of Waheed Murad,' he told me. 'His hair style was all the rage in those days. Women were crazy about him and all the men wanted the barbers to give them the Waheed Murad Cut ...'

In 1979, Yameen managed to set up his own barber shop. But four years later, he suddenly sold it to a friend and used the money to set up a cigarette shop in the city's coastal Clifton area.

Wasn't the barber shop doing well?

'The shop was doing very well,' Yameen replied. 'I was making good money from it.'

But then why suddenly sell it?

'*Murad Sahib ki wafat hogayee thi* ...' (Waheed Murad died), Yameen explained.

After Murad's demise, Yameen stopped going to the cinemas, and, anyway, by then the country's Urdu film industry had already begun its downward slide and the extroverted and populist characteristics of the pre-1980s' society had begun to fold inwards.

'One day, just like that, I quit being a barber,' Yameen explained. 'I was heartbroken by his (Murad's) death. But more saddening was the fact that people simply forgot about him. He had brought such joy and colour to so many Pakistanis, but very few mourned his death.'

When Pakistan's film industry began its decline, a number of actors and filmmakers who had been reaping fame and fortune suddenly found themselves abandoned. Some took to drinking and slipped into obscurity; some compromised their egos (and fee) and began doing TV serials; while others ventured into taking roles in loud, kitsch Punjabi films whose stock and popularity rose rather bizarrely in the 1980s.

The tragedy of the once idealized film stars suddenly losing all their sheen in Pakistan is most strikingly exemplified by the fate of a man who for more than a decade was the country's leading silver-screen icon: Waheed Murad.

From the mid-1960s till about 1977, it seemed as if anything Murad touched turned to gold. His hairstyle after 1967 was repeatedly copied by young men, and his lively romantic roles turned him into a heartthrob of millions of college girls and housewives. He would only accept roles of polished and gentle romantic men who wore their hearts on their sleeves and demonstrated their optimistic disposition with an unabashed rejection of both irony and cynicism. He was endearingly dubbed 'the chocolate hero.'[141]

But when things in the industry received multiple jolts after a reactionary 1977 military coup in Pakistan, Murad became the calamity's first casualty. As Murad's contemporaries, such as Mohammad Ali, actually turned rightwards to start making films that accorded with the 'correct moral lines' laid down by the in-coming dictatorship, Murad's romantic heroes who would dance, sing and shed tears at the drop of a hat, suddenly went out of vogue. Murad tried to reinvent himself as a character actor. But the image of a jolly romantic attached to him was just too overwhelming for anyone to take his more grounded roles seriously.

Even though another contemporary of his, Nadeem, was still dishing out hits till 1979, Murad began being ignored by the filmmakers. The fall from where he was till 1977 was just too sudden and rapid. Perplexed and bitter, the man whose car (in 1971) was once mobbed by dozens of college girls in Karachi and literally painted red with lipstick (à la Rajesh Khanna)[142], slipped into an existentialist void further magnified by heavy substance abuse.

When he appeared on a TV show in 1982, Murad looked exhausted. With bags of dark circles underneath his eyes, he sounded like a man on the verge of a breakdown. His wife of many years had temporarily left him when some film producers offered Murad to return to the big screen in the role of a hero (on the condition that he would clean up his act). Murad agreed.

---

141 Illustrated Weekly of Pakistan: Vol: 22, Issue: 1-9, March 1, 1969. p. 28
142 Fame & Fidelity: Mustansar Husain Tarar (DAWN, March 11, 2007)

But in 1982's minor hit, Aahat (Instinct), he seemed to be playing himself - a broken man surrounded by empty whiskey bottles, medicines and shattered pieces of what was once such a radiant life. But destiny had marked him to fall even further. In early 1983, while driving under the influence of anti-depressants, he smashed his car into a tree, leaving a deep scar across the right side of his face.[143] After the accident, he tried to find solace in his two children and more (empty) promises by film producers, who had to keep saying 'yes' to a man who had helped them make millions of rupees in the past. But, of course, they were in no mood to hire him again. Theirs was just a gesture of pity.

Then finally it happened. In 1983, the now 46-year-old former star, heartthrob and cinematic Midas, was found dead in a bedroom of a friend's house.[144] The cause of death was said to be an overdose of an assortment of psychotropic medicines. Many believed that he had ended his own life. There was no post-mortem report. But some Urdu newspapers reported that at the time of his death, pieces of paan (betel leaf) were found in his mouth mixed with tobacco and some 'unknown substance.'[145] A film critic lamented that it weren't the pills and substance abuse which killed Murad. 'It was a broken heart which took his life.'

When I told this to Yameen, he agreed: *Bilkul!* (Indeed).' But then suddenly Yameen withdrew and quietly walked out of the shop. His employee gestured to me with his hands that he (Yameen) would be alright. But he did add: '*Kaha tha na, Paracha Sahib, Yameen Bhai ki dukti rag par haath rak diya aap nein ...*' (I told you, you had hit a sore nerve).

---

[143] Khurram Ali Shafique: *Waheed Murad: His Life, Our Times* (Liberdux Publications, 2015)
[144] Ibid.
[145] Waheed Murad (uedubiograpghy.com)

Two days later when I visited the shop again, I noticed the poster had been peeled off. I asked Kudrat about it and he said, Yameen had pulled it off.

And where was Yameen, I asked.

'Wo retire hogaye hein' (He has retired), Kudrat informed.

****

The Middle-Aged Angry Man

With the arrival of the VCR, the erosion of the fame and fortunes of the once thriving Pakistan film industry in the early 1980s became starker than ever. The other culprit pushing the industry towards financial and creative ruin was the cumbersome cultural restrictions imposed by the Zia dictatorship. But the truth is that after 1979 the country's film scene seemed exhausted and unable to compete with the sudden flow of Indian films being smuggled in (on video tapes). It also failed to work around the challenges posed by Zia's new censor policies.

Had the industry been as robust as it was till the mid-1970s, it could have salvaged at least some of its influence and impact. Instead, it just began to feebly wither away. But when most Pakistani film historians talk about the downfall of the local film industry (from the 1980s onward), they are mostly lamenting the collapse of the once flourishing Urdu film scene.

The thing is that this collapse did not suddenly leave a large number of personnel who were associated with the industry, unemployed, even though many famous names associated with Pakistan's Urdu cinema did tumble down from the pedestals that they had once been put upon by their many fans. But it is true that the fatal combination of the arrival and proliferation of the VCR, Zia's smothering policies, and the film industry's own creative bankruptcy triggered a mass exit (from the cinemas) of the Urdu films' core audiences. Though a number of cinemas too began to close down, many continued to operate successfully (at least in the 1980s) and before the emergence of multiplex cinemas in the 2000s.

So if the industry had collapsed, then how were the cinemas (which hadn't closed down) still functioning, and, more so, why didn't the crumbling industry see a flood of men and women lose their jobs? Well, many did, but then there were also those who simply moved towards an emerging cinematic phenomenon that would go on to actually keep hundreds of men and women from the industry engaged and employed.

This phenomenon was the unique Punjabi film genre, triggered by the release of *Maula Jatt* in late 1979. Though during happier days Urdu films were the industry's primary product, Punjabi films too did well. But Punjabi movies of the 1960s and 1970s were largely soft romantic yarns, with melodious tunes and sodden plots. *Maula Jatt* changed all that. It introduced the gritty and amoral imagery and tone of the violent 'Spaghetti Westerns'[146] woven into characters inspired by the myth of the Punjabis being a martial race[147]; and plots interlaced with messianic folk heroics taking on the oppressors in Punjab's rural settings.

It is also true that (by the late 1980s) the success of *Maula Jatt* (and the local cinematic formula that it introduced) eventually mutated, and unleashed dozens of Punjabi films that became no more than throwaway self-parodies. So much so that till this day,

---

[146] Spaghetti Western, also known as Italian Western or Macaroni Western (primarily in Japan), was a broad subgenre of rugged Western films that emerged in the mid-1960s in the wake of Sergio Leone's film-making style and international box-office success.

[147] The concept of Punjabis (and Pashtuns) being martial races was first constructed and popularized by British Colonialists in India in the 19th and early 20th centuries.

this formula and perception of Punjabi cinema is roundly satirized. Unfortunately, the under par cinematic byproducts which followed in the wake of *Maula Jatt*'s success erased some crucial and rather noble aspects of this Punjabi classic. Aspects such as, how it actually saved the Pakistan film industry from suffering a complete collapse, and consequently, kept hundreds of men and women associated with the local film industry employed. And the truth is *Maula Jatt* is nothing like the loud, cynical and meaningless filmic Punjabi yarns which it eventually inspired across the 1980s. On the contrary, it is a rather intelligent exercise in commercial film-making, studded with some excellent performances, thoughtful plotting, imaginative direction, and sharp, snappy dialogue. It quite clearly radiates a pioneering spirit (for its time), and is quite conscious of this fact.

Just as the Pakistan film industry was beginning its long decline, *Maula Jatt* struck gold, becoming a huge success. Its box-office triumph even sprinted past Urdu cinema's biggest hit (till then) i.e. 1977's *Aaina*.[148] *Maula Jatt* enjoyed the full patronage of a new breed of Pakistani cinema fans. As the urban middle-classes retreated, their place in the cinemas was taken by the urban working classes and rural peasants, many of whom had been vitalized by the populist zeitgeist of the 1970s Bhutto era (1971-77), and whose families had benefitted from the emerging trend of Pakistani labour travelling to oil-rich Gulf states for work.

What is also forgotten about *Maula Jatt* is that it had a subversive soul, and yet managed to play across cinemas to large audiences during a period of intense dictatorial persecution and moral policing. How did that happen?

Maula Jatt was lavishly studded with bawdy female dances, stylistic action sequences, and snappy dialogue, turning the

---

[148] Arjun Singh Jai: *Popcorn Essayists* (Westland Books, 2011)

then struggling 41-year-old actor, Sultan Rahi, into a popular mainstay. He also became Pakistani cinema's first famous 'angry young man.'[149] Also gaining popularity (and notoriety) through the film was veteran villain, Mustafa Qureshi, whose role as the violent but introspective and almost philosophical, Noori Nath, would see him play Rahi's nemesis in a number of similar Punjabi films throughout the 1980s.

The film's theme of an angry young man in a Punjab village taking on oppressive feudal lords and eventually his main nemesis - the cool, calculating psychopath Noori Nath - went down well with the film's largely urban working-class and rural audiences. But when hordes of working-class Pakistanis and peasants started venturing into cinemas to watch the film, the censor board suddenly stepped in and demanded that the director take out certain scenes from the film.[150]

According to the film's producer, Sarwar Bhatti, the Zia regime had by then established a working relationship with various members of the 'landed gentry' in rural Punjab. It was alarmed by what it perceived was the film's 'anti-establishment' tone.[151] To the censors, the audiences were identifying the villains in the film as caricatures of factory owners, feudal lords (chaudhrys) and the Punjab police.[152]

---

[149] The *angry young men* were a group of mostly working and middle class British playwrights and novelists who became prominent in the 1950s and writers who were characterized by a disillusionment with traditional British society. Explosive characters played by Indian film actor, Amitabh Bachchan, in various films of the 1970s introduced and popularized the idea of the angry young man in South Asian films.

[150] Ayesha Jalal: *Struggle for Pakistan* (Harvard University Press, 2014) p.247

[151] Mushtaq Gazdar: *Pakistani Cinema: 1947-97* (Oxford University Press, 1997) p.163

[152] Ayesha Jalal: *Struggle for Pakistan* (Harvard University Press, 2014) p.247

The censor board ordered the producer to tone down the film's content through a re-edit and which Bhatti promptly did. But a large number of cinema owners still had with them the original print of the film, and they continued running it[153] despite the fact that they had been provided a freshly censored print. *Maula Jatt* eventually ran for more than two years, racking a huge profit for its makers and in the process keeping the disintegrating Pakistan film industry afloat for at least another 10 years.

However, Rahi, who rose to become the biggest box-office attraction in the 1980s and almost single-handedly kept the industry rolling, was shot dead in 1996. The police report suggested that he was killed by bandits on a Punjab highway where his car had stopped due to a flat tire.[154] But ever since his death three other theories have emerged. One claims that he was shot by a group of men who had some property dispute with him; or they hired a gang of criminals who were being patronized by some higher-ups in Punjab's provincial government.[155] The other theory suggests that Rahi, who was born into a Christian family but had become a Muslim in the 1960s[156], was planning to re-convert to Christianity and that those in the know ambushed him (for this reason).

Nevertheless, till this day his death remains to be shrouded in mystery (and varied theories). With him also went the Punjabi film industry and genre which Maula Jatt had set into motion.

****

---

[153] Cinemaya issue-6, 1988, p.56

[154] Omar Kureshi: *The Other Side of Daylight* (Interglobe, 1998) pp.565-67

[155] Ibid.

[156] Asif Mal, Global Cristian Voice, September 5, 2013.

The Jovial Subversives

Almost everyone in Pakistan knows about *Fifty-Fifty* — the satirical skit show that debuted in 1978 on the state-owned Pakistan Television (PTV), and ran till 1984. The show's legacy has been such that it is not only instantly recalled by those who saw it first-hand on their TV sets, but also by those who were either too young at the time or not even born.

The show was still attracting a large, loyal viewership when its creators decided to call it a day. In 1988 Shalimar Recording Company (SRC) released the first official VHS release of the show which was a compilation of some of its most popular skits. The release was converted to DVD in the 1990s and this took the show into the 2000s, a period when skits ripped from these DVDs began to be uploaded on various websites (especially YouTube).

Fifty-Fifty never really went away. Its uploaded episodes on websites still get a large number of clicks and its DVDs remain to be best-sellers. *Fifty-Fifty* has a rather curious history. It debuted in 1978, hardly a year after the arrival of the intransigent Zia regime. The show emerged when this regime had begun to embark on a banning spree, cancelling TV shows, films and songs it deemed 'immoral' or 'detrimental to the well-being of the country'.[157]

And yet, PTV somehow managed to launch a social satire show helmed by a maverick producer, Shoaib Mansoor, who was still in his early 20s and almost entirely inexperienced. In an interview which he gave to an English daily in the 1990s,[158] he suggested that despite the fact that a dictatorship had taken over in July 1977, the situation (in 1978) was still fluid and one could make his or her way on TV with ideas which a few years later would become almost taboo.

---

[157] Press Foundation of Asia, 1979. p.198
[158] The News International

As a college student, Mansoor had been a fan of *Such Gup* and *Taal Matol*, the two satire shows penned and produced by Shoaib Hashmi (for PTV) in the early 1970s. One of the main cast members of Hashmi's shows was actor, singer and composer, Arshad Mehmood. Mansoor befriended Arshad and both began to visit the house of Anwar Maqsood whose main claim to fame till then was the fact that he used to write the script for PTV's flamboyant variety programme, *The Zia Mohyuddin Show* (1970-73).[159]

Mansoor and Arshad began to talk about producing their own satire show and call it *Fifty-Fifty*.[160] Highly impressed by Hashmi's satirical style, they began to look for a writer who could match his panache. Mansoor was convinced that Maqsood was that writer. Maqsood agreed to do the script but by the time the show was given the go-ahead by PTV, General Ziaul Haq had overthrown the government of Z.A. Bhutto.

So Maqsood had to tailor the script according to the new regime's dictates and 'advices'.[161] The regime was not to be spoken of (in a satirical manner) and nor were the policies that it was introducing in the name of morality and faith. Maqsood instead turned his guns squarely towards the bureaucracy, the Pakistan film industry (that had begun its decline), and popular sports such as cricket and hockey.

A cast of relative newcomers was assembled and these included small-time stage comedians such as Ismail Tara, Majid Jahangir, Zeba Shahnaz, Ashraf Khan and Sakhi Kamal. A tall hefty man who used to work for a travelling agency also became a regular, and so did experienced actor, Latif Kapadia. Soon, the then unknown (but future comedy stars) such as Umer Sharif and Bushra Ansari too begin to sporadically appear on *Fifty-Fifty*.

---

[159] *42 Golden Years of PTV* (Special show on PTV, 2006).
[160] Third World International Vol: 10, 1979. p.91
[161] Ibid.

Anwar Maqsood became a regular too, often appearing in skits where he played a serious looking man interviewing a wide variety of idiosyncratic characters that he had penned. Some performers from Shoaib Hashmi's defunct shows too migrated to *Fifty-Fifty*, including Arshad Mehmood. The show debuted in late 1978 to instant acclaim. Though it began by satirizing the incompetence of the bureaucracy and the volatile nature of the country's cricket and hockey cultures, Maqsood began to devise methods through which he could trick the censors. He would use a subtle and dry style of wit to critique the regime which the members of the censor board would often fail to pick.

For example, during the show's second season in 1979, Maqsood and Mansoor were able to slip in a skit that (on the surface) was about a crooked cloth merchant bemoaning a police raid on his shop. However, the merchant (played by the versatile Majid Jahangir), also talks about a cream he had been applying on the 'long painful marks' (*'lumbey, lumbey nishan'*) on his back. With this skit, Maqsood slyly managed to satirize the dictatorship's controversial ploy of publicly flogging petty criminals to insert a sense of fear in the society. Many years later, Mansoor told a newspaper that the censors failed to pick this up, but Zia did! Zia was a regular viewer of the show, and would often call Mansoor on the phone to discuss his (Zia's) observations. The first time this happened was right after the episode that had the cloth merchant skit.

Fifty-Fifty also became one of the earliest in Pakistan to satirize the influence of 'Arabisation' in the country — especially after hundreds of Pakistanis (from the late 1970s onward) had begun to travel (for work) to oil-rich Middle-Eastern countries. In a 1980 skit of the show, an Arab sheikh is shown having tea at a café. One by one he is approached by Pakistani men of all classes and professions, asking him for a job in his country. They also express how close they are (in habits) to the Arabs, until another man appears and tells the aspirants that the Sheikh was actually a PTV actor playing the role of an ancient Arab warrior in a TV series. He also admonishes them, telling them, 'what's wrong with being a Pakistani, that you all are groveling at the feet of a sheikh …!'

The show also often lamented (albeit in a satirical manner) the decline of the local Urdu film industry and the rise of the loud and 'crude' Punjabi films. To highlight the supposed absurdities of Punjabi cinema, the show produced what is perhaps its most popular skit in which it created a trailer of a Punjabi film but with dialogues that are fused with English (*Bashira in Trouble*) – maybe to satirize the impact of loud rural themes on the more urbane audiences; or maybe even the fact that these Punjabi films had liberally adopted imagery of Hollywood westerns.

When phone calls from Zia became too frequent and the team had to quietly listen to his rambling critiques, Maqsood decided to quit.[162] Some believe he also had a falling out with Mansoor. Mansoor, Ismail Tara, Majid Jahangir, Zeba Shehnaz and Ashraf Khan now began to script the show, but when spontaneous lobbies close to the regime began to bemoan the way it was mocking Punjabi and Pashtu speakers, the members decided to call it a day (1982).

An intense letter-writing and call-in campaign from fans forced PTV to revive the show in mid-1983. But soon the show's two top performers, Majid Jahangir and Ismail Tara, had an altercation and Jahangir stormed out. Phone calls from Zia resumed, leaving Mansoor wondering why the head of the state was always stuck in a room watching TV! Then a lobby demanded that the show stop making fun of Urdu-speakers

---

[162] Ibid.

(Mohajirs). Exhausted and frustrated, the team decided to wrap up the show once again in 1984, this time for good. However, most cast members of *Fifty-Fifty* who began as unknowns went on to become stars.

Many continue to insist that the reason the quality of writing, direction and acting on the show was so high was mainly due to the fact that the actors, writers and the director of the show had to continuously be on their feet and devise intelligent ways to dodge an extremely suspicious censor board, and a dictator who thought he was an insightful critic. A joke is still popular among the show's team. It goes something like this: decades after the show ended, a man who (in 1979) was on the censor board, suddenly began to smirk. When someone asked him why he was smirking, he replied: 'I just understood an (anti-Zia) joke that Anwar Maqsood had written in 1978; and which, I had allowed to air thinking it was about a goat!'

****

The woman who lost herself

'A real genius,' is how famous author and playwright, Ashfaq Ahmed, once described Pakistan's TV and film actress, Roohi Bano. Bano was the most sought-after TV actress in Pakistan in the 1970s and early 1980s. Along with Uzma Gillani and late Khalida Riasat, Bano defined the art of serious acting for a host of Pakistani TV actresses to come. But Bano remained to be the finest in the league because even though she also acted as a heroine in a few films and took some light roles on TV as well, producers struggling to bring to the mini-screen plays by intellectual heavyweights such as

Ashfaq Ahmed, Bano Qudsia and Munnu Bhai, always chose her as their leading lady.

The reason was simple: She could seamlessly immerse herself in roles authored to construct complex psychological and emotional characters. That's why her most compelling moments can be found in TV plays scripted by Ashfaq Ahmad in the 1970s and early 1980s – a time when the author himself was struggling to come to terms with his own intellectual disposition and existential crisis.

At the time, very few of Bano's fans knew that the psychologically scarred roles that she was playing so convincingly were also starkly reflecting what was going on in her own life: broken relationships, increasing bouts of paranoia and sudden fits of depression. She felt betrayed and manipulated and then in a rush of blood, she got married.[163]

Not much is known about her marriage except that it produced a son. A few years later, she divorced and married again.[164] In 1986 this marriage too ended in a divorce.[165] By the late 1980s, Bano, who had been such a popular and respected mainstay on TV, was only rarely seen on the mini-screen. It transpired that she had been facing serious psychological and emotional issues throughout the 1970s; and in the mid-1980s she even had to be committed to a psychiatric hospital for treatment.[166] The irony was that Bano herself held a Master's degree in Psychology. She was still only in her 20s when she began suffering psychiatric problems. These hastened her disappearance from the screen.

---

[163] Asiaweek, Vol: 12, 1996. p.31
[164] Ibid.
[165] Ibid.
[166] Sad but true: Adnan Lodhi (Express Tribune, August 13, 2015).

Her condition only worsened when TV plays began facing heavy censorship during the Zia dictatorship and she kept turning down 'sanitized roles'[167] (even though she continued to do plays authored by Ashfaq Ahmed). In 1981 she lashed out at Zia for banning the wearing of the South Asian women's dress, the *sari*, on TV. 'Sari is a graceful dress. I am myself quite fond of it,' she told a reporter.[168]

When Bano did return to the screen (in 1989), her fans could hardly recognize her. She seemed to have aged rapidly and looked exhausted. Her great comeback never materialized. After just a few plays, she went back on heavy medication and suffered another series of breakdowns. Then, in 2005, her son was shot dead (apparently by muggers).[169] She was committed to a psychiatrist facility in Lahore. She seemed to have been making a recovery, but her condition once again deteriorated when one of her doctors passed away.[170]

Today, she leads a reclusive life in Lahore. She does not mention her husbands at all but still seems to have fond memories of her days as a leading TV actress. Over the years, various TV producers tried to bring her back into acting, but eventually let go of the idea after claiming that 'she was not functional.'[171] In 2006, she was reported to have set a room in her home on fire because (according to her) 'it (the room) was full of painful memories.' In an interview[172], she said: 'At times I feel that I am one of my own impostors. It seems that I am impersonating a stranger; someone I no longer am.'

---

[167] Organizer Vol: 33, 1981. p.96
[168] Ibid.
[169] In and Out of Darkness: Shoaib Ahmad (Dawn, May 4, 2015).
[170] Ibid.
[171] Ibid.
[172] Newsline, January 2015

Bano continues to remain suspended in an uncertain state of purgatory, while her fans still long for that magical comeback which she was expected to make all those years ago.

****

A Tall Tale

According to the *Guinness Book of World Records*, the tallest living man in the world (between 1982 and 1998), was Pakistan's Mohammad Alam Channa.[173] Before his death in 1998, Channa was reported to be 7ft 8in tall, even though some believe he eventually reached a height of 8ft. Born in 1953 in the city of Sehwan (in Pakistan's Sindh province), Channa is said to have stood 6ft 4 inches by the time he was 18. He continued to grow taller till he was 26.[174]

Channa came from an impoverished Sindhi family.[175] He did not receive any noteworthy education. The male members of his family had traditionally served as minor keepers at the famous shrine of Sufi saint, Lal Shahbaz Qalandar, in Sehwan. Here is where Channa too spent most of his years, tasked to keep certain areas of the shrine clean.[176] The annual *urs* (death anniversaries) of Sufi saints across South Asia are celebrated in a rather festive manner because since Sufi saints are considered to be 'the beloveds of God', their departure from earth is seen by their devotees as a *visal* (or when they are finally united with their beloved). For centuries the *urs* of Lal Shahbaz has been a vibrant, festive and boisterous occasion.

---

[173] The Guinnes Book of World Records (Facts on File, 1994) p.59
[174] V C. Medvei: *The History of Clinical Endocrinolog* (CRC Press, 1993) p.375
[175] Ibid.
[176] All About Pakistan (website), July 2, 2015.

Ever since the 1950s, travelling circuses (in Sindh) have also become mainstays in the area around the shrine where the festivities take place. It was the owner of one such circus stationed outside the shrine during the *urs* of 1978 who offered Channa a job in his circus.[177] Channa was making just Rs.15 a week at the shrine. So when the circus offered him Rs.160 a month, he decided to immediately accept the offer. The circus turned Channa into a local star. He would travel with it across the length and breadth of Pakistan's arid Sindh province. In his circus act, all he had to do was to make an entry just when two short men dressed as jokers were going through their routine. He would walk in and proceed to lift up the jokers (who would pretend to run away from the giant). Channa would grab them and then put them on his shoulders.

In 1981 a man who had watched Channa at the circus wrote a letter to the editors of the *Guinness Book of World Records*. With the letter he also sent some photos of Channa he had taken at the circus.[178] Months later some officials from Guinness landed in Sindh's capital city, Karachi, and from there they reached Sehwan where they met and measured Channa. They measured him at being 7ft 7 inches. But it took another few years for them to enter Channa's name in the Guinness book as the tallest living human on earth.[179] The news was first broken by local Sindhi newspapers. It was then picked up by a number of large Urdu and English language papers and then finally read in the main 9 pm Urdu news bulletin on the state-owned PTV. Almost overnight Channa had become a well-known name. He

---

[177] Ibid.

[178] The man was from Pakistan's largest city Karachi. He was an official in a government department in that city and was in the town of Dadu for some work when he caught Channa's act at the circus.

[179] Asiaweek, Vol: 19, 1993. p.88.

began being chased by media personnel and onlookers wherever he went.[180] Distressed by the kind of attention he had begun to attract, Channa quit the circus and retreated to work at the shrine.

He was still working at the shrine when in August 1983, a widespread protest movement erupted across Sindh against Zia. To prove that the protests were largely the work of a 'handful of traitors', Zia decided to tour all the hot spots of the province. But he continued to face protests wherever his helicopter landed. In September 1983 after he had to hastily conclude one such trip, Zia's advisors in Sindh suggested that he met with 'Sindh's latest pride,' Alam Channa (for a photo session). Some government officials (escorted by a dozen or so policemen), quietly arrived at Channa's small house in Sehwan. They did not go to the shrine because the shrine had become a meeting point of anti-Zia activists.

Someone told Channa that cops were waiting for him outside his house. Channa was almost entirely apolitical so he could not understand why there were cops stationed outside his home. He stayed put at the shrine until told by a messenger that the government was inviting him to receive an award from the 'President.' Channa walked back home and met the officials, who asked him to accompany them to Karachi. He shrugged his shoulders and agreed. He was to be picked up the next evening and driven to Karachi.

However, once the officials had left, Channa and his family were visited by a group of Sindhi nationalists. They asked him about his meeting with the officials and then told that since Sindhis were being oppressed by Zia, he must refuse to meet him. Channa again shrugged his shoulders and agreed. The next morning he walked to work to the shrine as he always did. He

---

[180] Christine Osbourne: *Travels with my hat* (A Sense of Place Publishing, 2014)

stayed there doing his chores till late in the evening. The officials had arrived at his house, but after waiting in the area for hours, they returned to Karachi empty-handed.

No one knows what Zia was told. But it seems his obsession to meet the famous Sindhi remained intact. In 1985 Zia once again exhibited his desire to be photographed with Channa. By now Channa had begun to be invited to various events abroad. But when in Sehwan, he would still walk to the shrine and do exactly what he had always done. In March 1985, he was visited again by some government officials (this time without the police escort). They invited him to receive a special award from Zia during the parade ceremony on Pakistan's Republic Day on March 23. On 21st March he was driven to Karachi and then flown to Islamabad. There, during the award ceremony, and in front of thousands of spectators, he received a decoration from Zia and a photographer captured the occasion for the press. All leading Pakistani newspapers (and also UK's *Daily Telegraph*), ran the picture of Zia handing an award to Channa who had to significantly bend his back forward to receive it. The same photo was also run by many Sindhi papers, but with a different caption.

Instead of simply writing 'The world's tallest men, Alam Channa, receiving a special award from General Ziaul Haq', one Sindhi newspaper wrote (in Sindhi): 'Sindh still looks down upon Zia.' Nevertheless, the Zia regime gifted Channa a brand new Toyota car.[181] Channa continued to gather fame after Zia's demise in 1988. The post-Zia regimes of Benazir Bhutto and Nawaz Sharif too used Channa as a famous face of Pakistan. Channa went on to tour (on government expense) various Middle Eastern, Asian and European countries and the US. He was given a job by the first Benazir Bhutto government as a security guard

---

[181] Pakistan and Gulf Economist, Vol: 8, 1989. pp.27-39

in Karachi.[182] In 1989, while travelling in his Toyota car which was being driven by a friend, he met with an accident. The car was totally destroyed and Channa was seriously injured. His hip bone was shattered.[183] After a slow recovery in a government hospital, Channa, fed up with the kind of constant attention he had received in the city, returned to Sehwan.[184] But he never fully recovered from his injuries. At Sehwan his health began to deteriorate. He often became depressed and distressed, complaining he was happier being a non-entity. He would often talk about his days in the circus and refused to let go of his job at the shrine, despite the fact that he had begun to receive cash gifts from around the world. In 1998 his kidneys failed. The government decided to send him to the US and finance his treatment. But (in a US hospital) he slipped into a coma and soon passed away. He was 45. He is buried in Sehwan.

His son, now 27, has been appealing to the government ever since to help him fulfil the illiterate Channa's most fervent wish: To build a university in his beloved Sehwan.

****

Murder, he wrote

In November 1982, veteran British film director, Richard Attenborough, released his historical epic, Gandhi. Based on the life of Indian nationalist and spiritual figurehead, Mahatma Gandhi (1869-1948), the film was a box-office hit. In April 1983, when the film won eight Oscars at Hollywood's 55th

---

[182] Ibid.
[183] Ibid
[184] Christine Osbourne: *Travels with my hat* (A Sense of Place Publishing, 2014)

Academy Awards ceremony, the Pakistan government complained that the movie had undermined the role of Pakistan's founder, Mohammad Ali Jinnah and had even distorted his image. The film depicts Jinnah (played by Alyque Padamsee) as a snooty figure given to appeasing communal urges not because he believed in them, but because he was envious of Gandhi's populist appeal.

Certainly the film's writer, John Briley, and director, Attenborough, seemed to have largely based the characters of both Gandhi and Jinnah on how (till then) the state-backed Indian history had perceived these two men to be. Much of this history had been authored during the various Congress regimes that had come to power between 1947 and the early 1980s. In this version of history, and, consequently, the film, the Mahatma is portrayed as being a man who, if he wanted to, could have even walked on water; whereas Jinnah was painted as a character who was more passionate about his expensive suits than about Indian nationalism; and ultimately the man who used communal tensions to create a separate Muslim country just because he was resentful of Gandhi's fame.

Myths (both positive and negative) about important people are usually created to suit the agendas of those who want to gain mileage from the legacies of the departed. In the film, a scene shows Gandhi being ejected from a first-class railway carriage in racist South Africa after a white passenger objects to sharing space with a 'coloured' man (Gandhi). This is a myth which suited the Congress regime and its sympathizers in the Western press. The fact is, Gandhi's demand to be allowed to travel first-class (with white South Africans) was actually accepted!

The culture editor of The Telegraph, Martin Chilton, wrote[185]: '(This incident) rather than marking the start of a campaign against racial oppression, as legend has it, was the start of a campaign to actually extend racial segregation in South Africa. (The truth is) Gandhi was adamant that respectable Indians should not be obliged to use the same facilities as the blacks ...'

Historian and film critic, Alex von Tunzelmann, writing in The Guardian[186], noticed that the film also steers well clear of exploring Gandhi's thoughts on the Axis powers (headed by Nazi Germany), 'some of which might have made a Western audience choke on its popcorn!'[187]

Myths have tailed Jinnah for quite a while as well, especially after he, like Gandhi, passed away just a year after partition. To most official historians, Jinnah too would have been able to walk on water. Till the early 1980s, Jinnah was largely presented in Pakistan as someone big but distant, important but elusive. He was never quite explored as a personality.

The Zia regime after reacting to the way Jinnah was portrayed in the film Gandhi, decided to bankroll a high-budgeted epic on Jinnah. But nothing much became of the project because initial research and the resultant scripts kept portraying a Jinnah who was quite different from the version of him that had begun to be sketched and propagated by the Zia regime. From the impersonal, impalpable but almost numinous character drawn by the state before Zia, Jinnah had become (under Zia), a reactive ideologue who had worked tirelessly to construct an entirely theological state in South Asia. As a response, in 1985, renowned scholar and historian, Ayesha

---

[185] The Telegraph, 11 April, 2016
[186] The Guardian, October 14, 2009
[187] Ibid.

Jalal, published the seminal, The Sole Spokesman. In it she cut to pieces the images of Jinnah popularized by the Congress regimes in India, the film Gandhi, as well as the image of the founder of Pakistan being concocted and proliferated by the Zia dictatorship.

Revisionist historians had finally begun to appear in Pakistan, challenging the histories authored by state-sponsored historians. One of the first revisionists in this context was K.K. Aziz. Today, Aziz is a well-known name among academics and students of history in Pakistan. Many young people in this country are thankful to him for liberating them from the stranglehold of the slanted histories and ideological narratives that they were indoctrinated with at school and college.

In Pakistan, histories related to the ideological make-up of the country have been constantly mutating; a process in which, over the decades, every major political debacle has seen the insertion of a series of brand new half-truths in school textbooks.[188] This has entailed the extraction of facts that might contradict the state's rationale in explaining these debacles. It's an almost Orwellian process that (even till mid-1980s) was not fully studied or questioned, in spite of the fact that there was ample evidence available to challenge the spotty yarns and spins that had begun to enjoy a two-fold growth in the country's textbooks (especially after the 1971 East Pakistan tragedy[189] and then during the military dictatorship of Zia in the 1980s[190]).

The first noted Pakistani historian to pose a studied challenge in this respect was the enigmatic Professor K.K. Aziz.

---

[188] Radicalization of State & Society in Pakistan" Rubina Saigol (Heinrich Boll Stiftung, 2010.
[189] Ibid
[190] Ibid

His 1985 book *Murder of History* was one of the first studies that directly challenged the numerous claims made (about Pakistan's creation and ideological evolution) in school textbooks. Aziz's book failed to sell well when it was first published in 1985. But it did reach all those who (from the mid-1990s) would eventually initiate a robust inquiry into the material that was being taught to school children in the name of history and 'Pakistan studies'. Today *Murder of History* is one of the most popular books among local history buffs and has enjoyed numerous reprints.

But what made Aziz write it? First of all, he had closely witnessed the state's project to revise many parts of the history books being taught in schools after the 1971 East Pakistan debacle. Because (ironically) when this project was first initiated during the populist Z.A. Bhutto regime[191] (1971-77), Aziz was part of that government. But before all this, Aziz, after receiving a PhD from Manchester University (in the 1950s), had returned to Pakistan and became an active member of the time's 'progressive crowd'. But unlike the many poets, intellectuals and politicians which he befriended in Lahore's coffee houses,[192] Aziz decided to become a dedicated historian. By the early 1960s, he had already authored a number of books on the history of colonialism in South Asia. But more interestingly (in the late 1960s), he helped conservative historian, I.H. Qureshi, in authoring The Struggle for Pakistan — the book that would go on to inform the state-backed history of Pakistan (during the Bhutto and Zia regimes), and the tome that Aziz would eventually go on to deconstruct in Murder of History.

---

[191] The Threat of Pakistan's Revisionist Texts: Afnan Khan (The Guardian, May 18, 2009)
[192] KK Aziz: *The Coffee House of Lahore* (Sang-e-Meel Publications, 2008)

Aziz was teaching at a university in Khartoum (Sudan) when he was invited by the Bhutto regime to head the Pakistan Commission of Historical and Cultural Research (PCHCR). In 1974, he was given the task to shape and streamline the findings of the hefty Humoodur Rehman Commission[193]. The commission had conducted an extensive inquiry into the civil war in former East Pakistan and on the region's consequential separation from the rest of Pakistan in December 1971.

However, in 1977, just when he was about to convert his hectic research into a report and a possible book, Bhutto's regime was toppled by Zia. Zia immediately removed Aziz from the PCHCR and then got the police to raid his house[194]. All of his research material was confiscated. Heartbroken, Aziz moved back to Khartoum. But after Sudan too began to experience political turmoil, Aziz managed to bag a research chair at a university in Germany. It was here that he began to collect the material from which some of his most well-known books would emerge.

In 1985, he returned to Lahore and stayed with his brother-in-law who helped him publish *Murder of History*. Once again, this landed him in having a confrontation with the Zia regime. He was now struggling to make ends meet. No one was willing to publish him and he needed a proper facility where he could conduct his scholarly research and write his books. He was still staying with his brother-in-law in Lahore when in 1993 the second edition of *Murder of History* was published. This time the book did relatively well. Also, Benazir Bhutto's second government (1993-96) had come to power and she instructed the Pakistan Embassy in the UK to provide an office to Aziz and a nominal monthly wage.[195]

---

[193] Unsung scholar (Dawn, September 6, 2009).
[194] Ibid.
[195] For KK Aziz: F. Aijazuddin July21, 2009

He travelled to the UK and began work on at least eight books simultaneously.[196] In 1996 he lost his post at the Embassy when Benazir's second government fell.[197] With the help of some Pakistanis in the UK his stay in London was funded before this too fell away and he had to return to Pakistan. But in Lahore he had a falling out with his brother-in-law and stayed with a friend. During Nawaz Sharif's second government (1997-99), he again faced intellectual isolation and in 1999 packed his bags and left for the UK again. However, by then he had already managed to complete a number of books. The manuscripts of these books were left behind with various publishers who began to publish them. Though he had vowed never to return to Pakistan, in 2008, he landed in Lahore but died the next year due to illness.

As fate would have it, by the time Aziz decided to return, the reputation of this once isolated historian had been transformed and he was hailed as a thorough scholar and pioneering historian. *Murder of History* enjoyed its third reprint in 2010 and is now widely quoted by noted Pakistani and Western historians. Also, ever since his death, a series of books authored by Aziz in the 1990s have also appeared. The history sections of book stores across Pakistan now carry a number of works authored by Aziz; something that was almost inconceivable when *Murder of History* first appeared, systematically filling in the holes in the well-established national narratives with facts which were once considered to be off-limits.

****

---

[196] KK Aziz: *The Pakistani Historian* (Sang-e-Meel Publications, 2009)
[197] Ibid.

The Brainwasher

In March 2014, I was delighted to bump into Mukhtar. Mukhtar used to be one of my favourite barbers back in the 1980s when I was a college student. He used to work at a barber shop near my college in Karachi's busy Saddar area. He was a robust man in his 30s and hailed from the city of Gujranwala in the Punjab province. When I bumped into him at a chemist shop many years later, he looked very old and tired. But somehow he recognized me immediately. After hugging me, he touched my hair and laughed: 'So short,' he said (in Urdu). 'Nobody's giving you a Che (Guevara) style anymore?'

Mukhtar remembered how I had liked my hair to look 'radical' in those days; and since I used to lead a left-wing student group at college, he would often give me tips how to challenge the Zia dictatorship. The truth is, Mukhtar wasn't a particularly good barber. But I kept going back to him because of the way I had first discovered him. In fact, though in those days I was intensely lapping up the writings of Karl Marx and Mao Tse-tung and the poetry of Faiz Ahmed Faiz and other progressive Urdu poets, Mukhtar ended up becoming a mentor of sorts. This, despite the fact that he never attended school after he had dropped out when he was in the 7th grade. He got a sound beating from his father who was a lowly-paid clerk at a government office.

But Mukhtar was a stubborn and restless soul. When he left Gujranwala at the age of 19 (in 1973), he just had two wishes: To meet his hero, Z.A. Bhutto, and to get a break in films. His desire was to play the role of Major Aziz Bhatti in a Pakistani war flick. Bhatti was one of the most heroic figures to emerge during the 1965 Pakistan-India war, after he was killed in action. Instead, having no place to live and no job in Karachi, Mukhtar spent his nights sleeping in the city's public parks before he was recruited by a kind owner of a barber shop. The owner trained him and then gave him a job at his shop where Mukhtar rose from being the guy who used to sweep bundles of hair from the floor to becoming a popular barber in his own right.

Everyone knew he wasn't much of a barber. But he was a great conversationalist and his clients loved his jokes, comments and analysis on politics, cricket and films. I first visited the shop in 1984 when I was a first year student at a nearby college. While waiting my turn, I couldn't help but notice Mukhtar giving a stern-looking middle-aged man a haircut and humming verses from some obscure Urdu poem. All the while he kept winking and smiling at a colleague. The colleague smiled back but continued to gesture him to keep quiet. After the haircut, the stern-looking man got up, paid the shop owner and left. Mukhtar and his colleague burst out laughing only to be admonished by the owner: 'Mukhtar, your antics will make us all end up in Central Jail!'

I was next. '*Aap inqulaabi lagtey ho. Che cut doun aap koh*? (You look like a revolutionary. Should I give you a Che cut?)' He smiled. 'Give me any cut you like, comrade,' I replied, 'as long as you tell me what you were humming and why?' From Urdu our conversation switched to Punjabi. He asked: 'Are you interested in poetry?' But before I could answer, he added ... 'beyond Faiz Sahib and Faraz?'

I asked him what he had in mind. 'Did you know,' he replied, 'the annoying looking man to whom I was giving a haircut is a corrupt government official? Allah knows better, but some say he is also a spy of the government who spies in shops in this area. His salary isn't that much but he is loaded with black money. He also thinks he is a very cultured man. So whenever he comes here I start to hum Noon Meem Rashid's *Scheherazade*. Ever read it?'

I said I hadn't read Rashid much. He told me to read it and only then will I understand why he was humming it in front of the government official. Noon Meem Rashid was one of the most enigmatic poets to come out of Pakistan. After bagging a Master's degree in Economics from the Government College of Lahore, he had spent most of his life working as a civil servant, and even served at the United Nations. His emergence as a poet was slow mainly because he seemed to be leading two separate lives. One was of a 'normal' white-collar professional going about his business in an expensive three-piece suit. The other life was that of a highly esoteric poet challenging the conventions of Urdu poetry and *ghazal* [198] and having a robust (but secret) sexual lifestyle that was at best ambiguous. [199]

Writing about Rashid in the 1990s, respected literary critic, Professor Gilani Kamran, wrote that Rashid employed erotic *ghazal* phraseology for the interpretation of socio-political reality. It was only in the late 1960s, when Rashid was in his 50s, that he began being read widely by poetry fans in Pakistan. He also worked vigorously against the slipping in of Arabic influence in Pakistani culture and strived to retain the region's historical Persian influence. [200] It was at this juncture that he suddenly decided to move to the UK.

As a young man in the 1930s, Rashid was briefly associated with the radical Khaksar outfit [201], which was formed by Muslim scholar and activist Allama Mashriqi. The organization was

---

[198] A South Asian poetic form consisting of rhyming couplets and a refrain, with each line sharing the same meter.

[199] Styapal Abnand interview in ViewPoint (9 December, 2010).

[200] The Thousand Faces of Mirage: Syed Nomanul Haq (Dawn, October 12, 2014).

[201] The Universalist: Intizar Hussain (Dawn, April 26, 2015)

vehemently anti-British and was formed on quasi-fascist lines to oust the British colonialists from India through an 'Islamic revolution.' But Rashid had soon become disillusioned by the Khaksar and realized the 'futility of ideologies'.[202] He became entirely secular.

In 1975, he passed away. Just before his death, Rashid instructed his (second) wife and friends that instead of burying his body, they should cremate it. That's exactly what they did.[203] This made the religious lobbies in Pakistan ask the government to declare Rashid an infidel and ban the sale of books containing his poetry. But as fate would have it, his poetry enjoyed far more popularity and recognition after his death than it did when he was alive.

After my first encounter with Mukhtar in 1984, I managed to get my hands on a copy of Noon Meem Rashid's poems one of which was *Scheherazade*. He had written it a few years before his death in 1975. The poem is a surreal tale of a barber who has the ability to cut open the skull of his clients, wash their brains and put them back in. One day he was doing the same to a high-ranking minister when he was suddenly summoned by the king. He put the minister's brain down and rushed to attend the king's call. When he returned, he saw that the minister's brain had been eaten up by ants. So, to avoid persecution, he put a bull's brain in the minister's head. And voila! The minister emerged sounding wiser and more intelligent.

It's a vicious satire on the intellectual level of potentates. So Mukhtar (who never even finished school) used to hum this poem while giving the corrupt government official a haircut and get a kick out of the fact that the official had no clue what he was humming. I stopped visiting the shop after I finished college in

---

[202] Ibid.
[203] Ibid.

1987. In early 1994, when I went to the shop to meet Mukhtar, I was told that he had married the owner's daughter and left Karachi for Gujranwala.

I never saw him again until our reunion almost two decades later. He was still married and lived with his wife and one of his sons in an apartment in Karachi's Khada Market area. Now in his 60s, he looked fatigued. He said he'd been suffering from various ailments. He had two sons. One was settled in Oman and the other was a junior officer at a government bank in Karachi. I asked him whether he was still reading and humming Noon Meem Rashid. He managed to crack a tired laugh: 'No. But I would like to go the way Rashid went.' After I bid farewell, I wondered what he meant by that. But then it struck me what this once robust but now old and sad barber was really implying. Rashid had asked his wife to cremate his body. And that's what she did. I just shook my head and whispered to myself: 'Mukhtar Bhai. Still cutting open heads and replacing brains.'

CHAPTER 9

AND THE ABYSS STARED BACK:
THE CONSERVATIVE TRANSFORMATION OF PAKISTANI SOCIETY FROM BELOW

For the mid-1990s the so-called 'Islamization' process which was initiated from above (i.e. by the state and government), began becoming a project of the society below. But interestingly, just before this, an attempt was made (on a largely cultural level) to reverse the trends set by the Zia era. One interesting (and rather underrated) way to navigate the overall trajectory of the immediate post-Zia decade is a cultural phenomenon which emerged after Zia's demise in August 1988. Though almost entirely urban and middle-class in its make-up, it was an art-form that spawned a culture that was coxswained by the political, economic and social signs of the time. Its nature was largely iconoclastic, despite the fact that it became a corporate product, and, as a culture, it eventually became inflicted by a guilt which made it shrivel and then actually reject itself. In fact this too was coxswained by the topsy-turvy zeitgeist it was dancing with.

I was 21 when the campaigning for the 1988 election kicked off. And those who were old enough to remember will tell you how it turned into becoming one big street party. For example, in

Karachi, 'car rallies' (especially of young supporters of the PPP and the MQM), became a common sight in which young people and families would set out in their cars and on motorbikes, with party flags in their hands or on their respective transports. They would drive all around the city in convoys, blasting songs from car stereos, and chanting slogans.

Often such rallies of different parties would converge, and instead of shouting slogans against each other, they would join forces and start to chant pro-democracy slogans. Young men on motorbikes would pass by cops and taunt them by placing beer cans and vodka bottles on their heads, or blow hashish smoke in the cops' faces. The boisterous and celebratory nature of the rallies was such that the cops would either just stand there or do nothing, or some would actually join the ravers and start dancing with them. There was no serious violence between supporters of different parties or between the supporters and the cops.

This sudden celebratory outpouring of the youth onto the streets was an instinctive expression of a feeling; that of a weight being lifted from the collective consciousness of young Pakistanis who had been constantly herded by the departed Zia dictatorship to shed their political and creative passions and replace them with piety and penance. Many observers suggest that the wave of pop music acts which rose in Pakistan from 1988 onward was a direct outcome of the above-mentioned feeling. The outbreak of many pop acts at the time was at least one expression of the feeling of being liberated from the clutches of state-sanctioned ideas of morality, but there was an economic dimension to this phenomenon as well.

During the Zia dictatorship the country was covered in a façade of strict conservatism and an awkward moralistic pretense. But its urban underbelly was clogged with raising ethnic tensions, gang violence, corruption and state-sponsored terror partaken by Zia's various intelligence agencies to suppress dissent against the dictatorship. Ironically, it were tensions like these and a somewhat freak economic prosperity - triggered by a 'black economy' fueled by the unprecedented flow of aid coming in from the US and Saudi Arabia for the 'Afghan Jihad,' and the growing trend of drug smuggling[1] - which also propelled the gradual expansion of the country's urban middle and lower-middle-classes.[2] And it is the youth cultures which emerged from these classes that fired the first shots of the kind of pop culture, scene and music we now call, modern Pakistani pop.

Change was in the air. Tensions were running high and something had to give. This was the underlining feeling among the time's youth. They could not pin-point exactly what or how this change would happen, but the moment Benazir Bhutto returned from exile in 1986 and led a mammoth rally in Lahore, the country's major urban centres saw a quiet but certain outpouring of brand new pop bands who wanted to sound different from the time's pop scions.

Most of the new acts which began appearing after 1986 played at private parties and weddings and at college functions. A band called the Vital Signs became firm favourites in the period's college function circuit, even though the band never took itself seriously. Music was just a hobby. But all that changed when they were discovered by ace PTV producer and director, Shoaib Mansoor, a shy, introverted bohemian and a keen music lover. Wanting to cash-in on the charisma he found in the way the band looked and sounded, Shoaib asked them to record a national song he had wanted to air (as a video) on PTV. The song was *Dil, Dil Pakistan*.

---

[1] Asian Survey, Vol.31 (University of California Press, 1991) p.587
[2] Ibid.

It was released in the summer of 1987 as a video (directed by Shoaib), in which the Signs were shown singing the song over what looked to be a 'hill station' near Islamabad. It was an instant hit. It was the first time since the Zia regime had restricted the wearing of western dress on TV (in 1982-83) that young men in denims and leather jackets were seen (and allowed) on PTV. Shoaib had pulled off a quiet coup. And then Zia died.

In early 1989, the Signs recorded their debut album (for EMI-Pakistan) and also appeared in a teleplay on PTV written and directed by Shoaib Mansoor. The album was an immediate hit. But what really got this pop wave going was another Shaoaib Mansoor gem. He directed an indoor concert in Rawalpindi that not only included performances from the Vital Signs and a number of other new pop acts, but also by the famous pop duo of the 1980s, Nazia and Zoheb Hassan. After PTV aired the concert (calling the show *Music '89*), a PR firm in Karachi got the idea of holding what would become the country's first ever open-air music festival. The festival was held in February 1989 on the premises of a widespread amusement park (Funland) and was attended by over ten thousand young Karachiites. Famous philanthropist, Abdul Sattar Edhi, was invited as a guest and he made a rip-roaring speech. The bands playing at the festival were the hard-rocking Final Cut and the Barbarians and a very young and still unknown, Ali Haider.

After the success of *Music '89* and the festival, Jamat-i-Islami (JI) held a demonstration in Karachi, in which its leaders accused the new Benazir Bhutto government of promoting obscenity and secularism in the name of art. But the damage had been done. Between 1989 and 1990, EMI-Pakistan, apart from releasing the Vital Signs debut album, also released albums by another set of emerging pop stars such as Ali Haider and The

Strings. However, on the political scene, the euphoria that had swept across the nation after the arrival of democracy in 1988 had begun to corrode. Tensions between the PPP government and the right-wing opposition (the Islami Jamhoori Ittihad), and between the PPP and the MQM in Sindh, began to express itself in the shape of deadly clashes between the student-wings of the involved parties.

Ethnic violence began to raise its ugly head again and the young 36-year-old Benazir Bhutto was left lashing out in a chaotic manner at the obvious intrigues engineered by the remnants of the Zia regime within the country's intelligence agencies, the business community and right-wing political parties. She also struggled to keep a check on corruption and mismanagement by many of her own ministers.

Her government was dismissed by the President, and Nawaz Sharif's right-wing IJI was handed a cosmetic mandate to rule after winning a largely rigged election in 1990. Nawaz's IJI had promised to restore 'Ziaism'[3] and rid the country of the 'moral and economic corruption' of the fallen PPP regime. As Prime Minister, he ordered PTV to make sure that that all women who appear on the state-owned channel wore *dupattas* (head scarfs) over their heads. He also banned pop music from the channel. This could have effectively retracted the momentum of the emerging pop music scene in the country, but in 1990 the Benazir regime had already green-lighted the launch of a semi-private TV channel, Shalimar Television Network (STN).

Programming (between 5 pm and 12 am) on this channel was outsourced to National Television Marketing (NTM), a private content-generating company formed by advertising tycoon, Tahir Khan. In turn, NTM outsourced the creation of

---

[3] Khalid Mahmud: *Pakistan's Political Scene: 1984*-1992 (Rhhtas Books, 1992) p.183

entertainment programming (teleplays, music shows, etc.) to freelance directors and producers and then offered advertising slots to multinationals on NTM.

The experiment was an immediate success. PTV was right away put under pressure by NTM's superior entertainment programming and began to lose its monopoly over the viewers and advertisers. Also, Nawaz's restrictions on PTV did not apply to NTM. Apart from big-budgeted teleplays and serials, NTM also began to produce and run the country's first ever pop shows on TV. The two most popular among these were *Pepsi Top of the Pops* and *Music Channel Charts* (MCC).

Pepsi had begun to invest heavily in Pakistan in the 1980s, side-lining Coca-Cola. It was also the first major company to begin using cricketing stars in its advertising, and in 1991 it moved in to occupy the space and market created by the emerging new pop scene in the country when it signed up the Vital Signs. Whereas NTM's *Pepsi Top of the Pops* largely concentrated on promoting pop acts on Pepsi's payroll, MCC unleashed a plethora of brand new acts who, through their videos on the shows, experienced almost overnight success. In 1993 when the Nawaz regime too was dismissed by the trigger-happy President (Ishaq Khan) on corruption charges, Benazir's PPP won a narrow victory in the year's election and formed a new government at the centre.

Aptly, 1993 was a massive year for the local pop scene. Large pop festivals returned and the scene saw the release of a number of new albums by various bands and acts. According to EMI-Pakistan, it sold over millions of cassettes and CDs of local pop acts in 1993[4]. Two more record labels had also emerged, Sonic and Sound Master. Apart from Pepsi, the makers of

---

[4] CEO of EMI-Pakistan, Ameed Riaz, told me this in 1995.

Pakistani soft-drink, Pakola, too entered the field, signing up Ali Haider whose second album *Qarar* had sold over a million copies within weeks!

The success of MCC and its compilation albums gave bands such as Collage, Nadeem Jaffary, Arid Zone, Milestones, Sequencers and Fringe Benefits enough recognition to attract offers from concert organizers. On the festival front, the largest took place in 1995 at Karachi's KMC Stadium where over 10 thousand young men and women saw Vital Signs, Milestones and Awaz play for over five hours. The widening of the scene resulted in outcomes that further advanced the phenomenon.

Corporate interest in pop musicians grew as more and more multinationals began investing in pop acts for advertising purposes. This, and the fact that record labels had begun to pay chunks of money (as compared to tiny royalties) to the performers, saw a number of musicians finally managing to turn their art into a profession. Event management companies specializing in organizing pop concerts mushroomed, and so did high-tech recording studios with quality producers and engineers at the helm.

The second Benazir government also pitched in when as a policy it began to organize entourages of pop musicians, fashion designers and fashion models who were regularly sent on tours abroad so they could attract foreign investment for Pakistani cultural and textile industries. Vital Signs, Junoon, Awaz, Ali Haider, Saleem Javed and Hassan Jahangir were already veterans of foreign tours, playing in the US, UK and India.

Commercial and creative growth of the scene also encouraged aesthetic and stylistic diversifications. Whereas light pop acts such as Vital Signs matured and incorporated musical complexities into their compositions to explore more multifaceted themes and genres, bands such as Awaz, Sequencers and Fringe Benefits took off from where the Signs had left. Junoon arrived with the agenda to introduce the mainstream market with a fusion of riff-friendly hard-rock, Qawaali and Sufi folk music, giving birth to what came to be known as 'Sufi-Rock.'[5] Yattagan/Fakhar-e-Alam introduced 'Bhangra-Rap' into the scene, and Jazba adopted postures and elements from politically-attuned radical hip-hop acts such as Public Enemy.

In 1994, when the scene actually became larger than the market, a string of musicians who failed to break into the mainstream formed a parallel scene. Bands emerged in Lahore and Karachi who were largely inspired by the Grunge Rock outbreak in the US (in the early 1990s). They began to play and record their songs in basements, garages or in front of small gatherings of fans who could not relate to the dynamics and aesthetics of the mainstream scene.

The mainstream did not take the parallel scene as a threat at first, but when a large 'underground' concert was held at Lahore's Al-Hamra Theatre in 1995, the English press began to give space to bands such as The Trip, Mind Riot, The Anonymous, Coven, Brain Masala, etc. Though, hardly any of these bands were able to release an album in the mainstream market and usually distributed their songs on cassettes at concerts, in their interviews they began to badmouth the mainstream scene and acts, sometimes calling them 'corporate bastards' that would be wiped out 'through an underground music revolution!'

Of course, this was sheer rhetorical posturing, but somehow it did manage to leave Pepsi and some mainstream acts feeling concerned and even offended. For example, *Pepsi Top of the Pops* tried to co-opt some of the 'parallel acts' by covering an

---

[5] The author coined this term in 1993 in an article in The News International.

underground concert in Lahore. But the show only ended up editing out most of the interviews that the show's VJs conducted of the musicians that were playing there.

But the commotion was short-lived. The parallel scene eventually withered away at the coming in of yet another wave of pop acts in 1996, this time through the new NTM show called *VeeJay* (hosted by comedians Faisal Qureshi, Ahmed Parvez, Ahsan Rahim and female pop star, Hadiqa Kayani). Many performers who had arrived during the first wave (1988-92) and the second (1993-96), had become established stars. But there were also those who simply vanished, some due to the way they were mismanaged by record labels and some losing their way due to alcohol and drugs. The third wave unleashed by *VeeJay* turned Hadiqa into a star. Acts such as Abrarul Haq, Sharique Rumi, Javad Ahmed and the satirical Dr. Aur Billa also emerged. In late 1996 the second Benazir Bhutto government fell, this time dismissed by its own handpicked President (Farooq Laghari). The charges were the same: mismanagement, corruption and a failure to halt ethnic violence in Sindh.

Nawaz Sharif's Pakistan Muslim League-Nawaz (PMLN) returned to power after the early 1997 election. Complaining that the Benazir government had turned Pakistan into a den of decadence, PM Nawaz once again clamped a ban on pop music on PTV. But in his new moral crusade, Nawaz lost the plot completely. If the second Benazir government was corrupt, his was even more suspect. When the press began to highlight this deviousness, he decided to muzzle it through intelligence agencies, threats and various other acts of coercion.

But Pakistan's pop scene had already reached its nadir. Instead of levelling out, it began to wither away. Two main reasons contributed the most in factoring its eventual slow-burn, one economic and the other social. By 1997 the local pop market had been stretched to the limit, and, consequently, it eventually suffered a tear. New acts who had come in on the third wave could not create a new market but were only successful in cannibalizing the market share of the various acts who had arrived during the second wave.

Falling sales saw certain established pop stars gradually move towards a peculiar social phenomenon that had begun to emerge amidst urban middle-class Pakistanis; a phenomenon that was the opposite of the cultural zeitgeist of the late 1980s and early 1990s.

A number of Islamic outfits had already made in-roads by riding on Zia's 'Islamisation' process in the 1980s. But since most of them were highly militant, it were the evangelical movements that managed to reap the most success within the country's uncertain social and cultural milieu. The largest among them was also the oldest. The ranks of the *Tableeghi Jamat* (TJ), a highly ritualistic Deobandi evangelical movement, swelled. But since the TJ was more a collection of petty-bourgeoisie cohorts and fellow travelers, newer evangelical outfits emerged with the idea of almost exclusively catering to the growing 'born again' trend that had begun to mushroom within the county's middle and upper-middle classes from the mid-1990s. Three of the most prominent organizations in this context were Farhat Hashmi's Al-Huda, Zakir Naik's 'Islamic Research Foundation' and Babar R. Chaudhry's Arrahman Araheem (AA).

All three also benefited from another unprecedented trend which began to emerge within the urban middle-class youth of Pakistan: Never before did young Pakistanis exhibit so much interest in religiosity as did the generations which grew up in much of the 1990s and (and almost all of the early 2000s). This exhibition of religiosity also began to influence the showbiz and sporting circles. Many of Pakistan's once flamboyant cricketers began joining the TJ and in the late 1990s AA became an attraction for a number of pop starts and TV personalities.

Naik, Hashmi and Chaudhry were all constructing feel-good narratives and apologias for the educated urbanites so that these urbanites could feel at home with religious ritualism, attire and rhetoric, while at the same time continue to enjoy the fruits of amoral modern economic materialism and frequent interaction with (Western and Indian) cultures that were otherwise described as being 'anti-Islam.'

By the late 1990s, the pop scene had almost completely lost steam. A majority of major bands broke-up and many promising acts and groups who had rode in on the largest of the waves (the second), simply withered away. As the scene (and the country's economy went into a tail-spin in 1998), multinationals began to pull back their money from the scene and a lot of studios and record labels closed shop.

Though Nawaz was toppled in a military coup in late 1999 by General Pervez Musharraf, who presented himself as a liberal and a patron of the arts, the post-9/11 scenario in Pakistan turned extremely violent. The growing violence from militant Islamist groups made it almost impossible for pop concerts to be held, so much that we now have a generation that has very little or even no memory of a time when the country actually had a vibrant pop scene and large music concerts were a norm for young Pakistanis.

Just as the Ayub Khan coup in 1958 had (initially) been popular, the military coup pulled off in 1999 by General Pervez Musharraf too was largely received with a sigh of relief and even joy by most Pakistanis. Tired of the political chaos, corruption, intrigues and ethnic and sectarian violence that had plagued the 1990s, Pakistanis looked forward to a period of some sort of stability.

In the first five years of his dictatorship, Musharraf managed to inject this sense of stability. Ethnic violence greatly receded, the economy bolstered, various radical religious and sectarian organizations were banned and neo-liberal capitalist maneuvers strengthened the economic status of the middle-classes. Such moves augmented a revival of sorts in the country's cultural activities as modern art-forms such as popular music, fine arts and fashion thrived. Folk music too made a brief comeback as the regime tried to harness its moderate/liberal image by promoting Sufism among the growing urban middle and lower middle classes.

The regime also initiated a revolution in the country's electronic media, allowing a number of privately-owned news and entertainment TV channels to mushroom. However, the feel-good sentiment that the regime managed to inoculate in its first few years was achieved through political repression. Also, it was awkwardly paralleled by the rise of resistance to the regime by violent religious outfits that began to emerge after Musharraf agreed to join the United States' 'War on Terror.'

The euphoria lasted till about 2006. Both the PPP and PML-N remained sidelined and Musharraf seemed to have been enjoying a continuous stretch of popularity when the northern areas of the country (including the capital, Islamabad) were hit by a devastating earthquake. Thousands died in the catastrophe but the regime was quick to offer aid backed by an unprecedented charity drive undertaken by various civilian organizations and individuals.

Interestingly, the drive also seemed to have stirred some latent resentment against the regime, especially in the Punjab and Khyber Pakhtunkhwa (KP). When the economy (that seemed to have been bloated like a bubble), began to deflate, Musharraf started to face his first round of direct criticism that mostly came from opposition groups who were enthusiastically invited by the string of private TV channels that had emerged from 2002 onwards. Then, in late 2006, Musharraf casually dismissed a controversial and ambitious Supreme Court judge, Iftikhar Chaudhry. The TV channels gave a sensationalist twist to the episode and drummed-up a narrative which explained Chaudhry as deifying 'the illegitimate orders of a dictator.'

Lawyers poured out on the streets of Lahore and Islamabad and demanded that Chaudhry be restored. As the protests of the lawyers grew louder, they now also demanded that Musharraf resign and fresh elections held. Seeing the protests as an opening and with the way the agitation began to be covered by the electronic media, PPP and PML-N too jumped in, as did parties such as the JI and Pakistan Tehreek-i-Insaf (PTI).

Musharraf was clearly taken aback by the commotion which was then followed by another crisis when radical clerics and their supporters from Islamabad's Red Mosque began to abduct cops and women working at beauty parlors. They also attacked music shops. After negotiations between the government and the clerics failed, Musharraf ordered the army to storm the mosque where the armed clerics were holed up. The military used teargas, guns and missiles to clear out the mosque.

The event was freely covered by the new TV channels which, in an exhibition of some of the most anarchic coverage of a sensitive issue, further compounded the tense situation. Exaggerated figures of the civilians killed (especially women and children) were often quoted[6] and the clerics were given more airtime to sound out their views than the government officials. The confusion created by the media and the regime's own weakness to counter the narrative that was being built, eventually saw the emergence of an alliance of extremist militants who began to target public places supposedly to avenge 'Musharraf's Red Mosque massacre.'

It was at this point that the Lawyers' Movement that had been initially started by progressive groups of lawyers began its shift to the right. It was also believed (in some quarters) that the PML-N had begun to bankroll the movement. This has never been substantiated, though. The movement's greatest presence was felt in urban Punjab and the KP. It was almost non-existent in Sindh. This was the first major protest movement ever since 1968 and 1977 in which Punjab participated whole-heartedly. The province had largely remained quiet during the movements against Zia. Many of Musharraf's supporters in Sindh and in its Mohajir-majority capital, Karachi, suggested that Punjab only rises against non-Punjabi rulers. Some events may actually substantiate this, but the recent rise of Imran Khan in the Punjab against Nawaz Sharif (a Punjabi) largely negates this perception.

Unlike the movement against Ayub (which included the participation of the working classes and the peasants as well), the movement against Musharraf was more like the one against ZA Bhutto in 1977 in which the majority of participants had belonged to the urban middle and lower middle-classes. Opposition parties such as the PPP and PML-N managed to oust the 'King's Party' (PML-Q) in the 2008 election and the same year Musharraf was forced to resign. He left behind memories of

---

[6] Musharraf quoted in The News International (February 23, 2013).

a stable Pakistan which, however, by the end of his regime had become a place of deep political and ideological cleavages, a crumbling economy, a blood-soaked insurgency in Balochistan and in the tribal areas, and deadly sectarian conflicts.

****

The Reluctant Militant

Conflicting views and feelings become the order of the day whenever former military dictator, Gen Musharraf is put in the dock for his regime's action against militants holed up in Islamabad's Lal Masjid (Red Mosque). Though the action took place more now 9 years ago, it still generates (at least in the media) heated debates and extreme stances.

One Abdul Rashid Ghazi had become the centerpiece of the event; a radical cleric who was said to have been leading a group of armed militants from the mosque and its seminary. Ghazi today is remembered as a militant who had asked his followers to burn down CD shops and kidnap 'obscene women' in Islamabad because he wanted to force the government to impose *sharia* laws cross Pakistan. After refusing to give in to the orders of the government of Gen Musharraf, the mosque and its seminary were stormed by the army and Ghazi was shot dead.

If one monitors what has been said about Ghazi in the media, two distinct views come to the surface: The first one describes him as a terrorist who wanted to impose his version of the *sharia* by force, while the other hails him as a 'mujahid'[7] who stood up to the might of an 'infidel state.'

---

[7] Holy warrior

But often we picture our heroes and villains as caricatures drawn from conflicting perceptions that are wildly aired in the media. I've always wondered why isn't there any serious attempt to study them as we would any of our immediate contemporaries. In 2015, while on a visit to Islamabad, a journalist colleague of mine introduced me to a former college friend of Abdul Rashid Ghazi. Without any hesitation I got down to probe him about the less talked about (or even unknown) aspects of Ghazi's life. Who was he and what made him so desperately angry? I am sure he wasn't born this way. Ghazi's friend told me that he (Ghazi) was a militant for a very brief period of his life. Otherwise he was an extremely bright man with normal career ambitions.

'He could have been a diplomat in the foreign office or an educationist,' his friend told me. The friend added that Ghazi's greatest ambition was to become a diplomat at the United Nations. This is what Ghazi was planning to become when he joined college in 1982. Ghazi was born into in a religious family. His father was a cleric who had founded the Red Mosque in the late 1960s.[8] He enrolled his two sons into an Islamic seminary. But Ghazi rebelled and dropped out, demanding that he be put into a 'normal school'. This was in 1976 when he was about to enter his teens. His father reluctantly got him admitted into an all-boys school from where Ghazi did his matriculation in 1979.

Ghazi's friend fondly remembers him as an enthusiastic fan of music, films and political history. Ghazi had already begun dreaming of becoming a diplomat. Nevertheless, Ghazi once again got into an altercation with his father. According to his friend, his father wanted him to grow a beard and join the seminary that he was running. Not only did Ghazi refuse to grow a beard, he went on to join a co-ed college. Here he got involved

---

[8] A Dolnik; K. Iqbal: *Negotiating the Siege of the Lal Masjid* (Oxford University Press, 2016)

with various student groups opposed to the reactionary dictatorship of General Zia. All communication between his father and him had broken down. They were not on talking terms when in 1984 Ghazi joined the Quaid-i-Azam University in Islamabad that was then a hotbed of anti-Zia activities.

He enrolled as a student of International Relations. His friend remembers him as a bright student and an active member of a progressive student organization. This created a problem for his father, who was being facilitated by the Zia dictatorship to help produce fighters for the anti-Soviet Afghan insurgency that Pakistan was backing. 'He hardly ever went to a mosque, let alone visited his father's mosque,' his friend claimed. 'He was reading writings by Marx and Henry Kissinger. He was a lively fellow but always focused on becoming an international figure in international diplomacy,' the friend added.

But Ghazi's brother, who had followed his father into becoming a cleric, would never miss an opportunity to admonish Ghazi for going against family tradition and bringing a bad name to their father due to his 'westernized' ideas and lifestyle. According to Ghazi's friend, after getting his Master's degree in International Relations, he managed to bag a job at the Ministry of Education. The friend suggested that Ghazi was not happy with his job and was impatient to realize his dream of becoming a diplomat. Estranged from his family and not achieving his goal quickly enough, Ghazi became agitated. Then in 1998 his father died. He was assassinated by unknown gunmen. 'All that guilt that had been instilled into him by his brother came to the forefront,' his friend explained. 'His brother told him how he had hurt his father's feelings.'

Ghazi went into a depression and began attending gatherings of a variety of Islamic evangelical groups. Then, in 1999, he joined his brother at the Red Mosque where both became leaders. After Pakistan entered the 'War on Terror' as a US ally, the brothers are said to have established links with militant Islamist organizations. Ghazi was now a changed man. He'd grown a beard, renounced his 'secular' past and had become a vehement militant insisting that the state of Pakistan impose strict *sharia* laws. But, as his friend interestingly noted: 'He wasn't built to fight. He was too intelligent to become a militant. His philosophy might have become aggressive, but I don't think he was willing to die for it.'

This statement makes sense. During the military operation against the Red Mosque militants, some TV channels began to report that Ghazi was willing to surrender but was held hostage (through 'emotional blackmail') by some militants in his entourage until the military finally barged in and shot dead each one of them. Ironically, this man who had dreamt and studied to be an international diplomat died for ideas and cause he had actually rejected for most of his life.

****

The Last Sage

In 1965 a lengthy paper titled, 'Peasants and Revolution,' caused a considerable storm in the international academic circles associated with the left. The paper was authored by Pakistani social scientist and historian, Hamza Alavi. The paper was published during a period when China's communist set up was about to implode due Mao Tse-tung's 'Cultural Revolution;' and when Mao's thesis (through which he had constructed China's 1949 revolution), had begun to inspire peasant-based revolutionary movements in various developing countries.

Mao's thesis (aka 'Maoism') had attempted to include peasants as the main forces of a communist revolution in countries that did not meet the conditions set by classic Marxism.[9] The conditions required that countries must first have a developed bourgeoisie and an equally developed urban proletariat class. The economic conflict between the two was predicted by Marx to produce a revolution that would lead to a dynamic state of perpetual communism. Alavi, a Marxist intellectual as well as a vehement Pakistani nationalist, argued that in agricultural economies and developing countries (especially Pakistan and India), the 'middle peasantry' should be treated as the main militant element of a socialist movement.[10] He suggested that it was this section of the peasant class which was a natural ally of the urban working classes, as opposed to the poorer peasants.[11]

Mao, who had largely used poor peasants as his foot soldiers during the 1949 communist revolution in China, did not agree with Alavi. Mao critiqued Alavi's proposition by observing that the middle peasantry had a lot to lose from indulging in a make-or-break revolutionary movement, whereas the poor peasants did not because they were less burdened by economic interests and ties, and, thus, were freer to play a more assertive role in a revolution.

Alavi propagated the flip side. In his paper he suggested that just like men from urban working classes who can always find employment and were thus not afraid to lose a job due to their involvement in a revolutionary movement, this is the same

[9] Timothy Cheek: *A Critical Introduction to Mao* (Cambridge University Press, 2010) p.176

[10] Marshall M. Bouton: *Agrarian Radicalism in South Asia* (Princeton University Press, 2014) p.25

[11] Hamza Alavi: *Peasants and Revolution* (Radical Education Project, 1965)

aspect that makes the middle peasantry an important revolutionary player. This was because unlike the poor peasants, the middle peasants can survive the onslaught of opposing forces (because they were more resourceful), whereas the poor peasants for fear of losing whatever little they had, prefer to remain subdued during a movement.[12] Alavi's paper was widely debated by scholars and contemporary theorists of the left around the world. The paper propelled Alavi's status in the international arena of scholarly Marxism.

Alavi was born into a well-to-do business family in Karachi. He got an economics degree from a university in Puna (in pre-partition India)[13], before returning to Karachi after the creation of Pakistan in 1947. He was a passionate supporter of Pakistan's founder, Mohammad Ali Jinnah, and played a key role in helping the government set up the State Bank of Pakistan. He was still in his 20s when, instead of continuing his high profile career in the bank, he opted to accompany his wife to East Africa where both set up a farm.[14] It was here that Alavi began to study the political and economic dynamics of the peasants. In the late 1950s he moved to the UK to study at the London School of Economics.

Alavi returned to Pakistan in 1960 as editor of the left-leaning *Pakistan Times*. But he quit and flew back to the UK after the newspaper was taken over by the military regime of Ayub Khan. After establishing his scholarly credentials with his 1965 paper on the middle peasantry's role in a revolution, Alavi delivered his second most important thesis in 1972: 'The State in Post-Colonial Societies.'

---

[12] Evolving Political Structures According to Hamza Alavi: Haneen Rafi (DAWN, April 19, 2015).

[13] Maneesha Tikeka: *Across The Wagah* (Bibliophile South Asia, 2004) p.148

[14] Muslim India: Issues: 253-264 (University of Michigan, 2004) p.117

This paper too highlights his highly original thinking. In addressing the reasons behind the frequent occurrence of military coups in post-colonial countries in Asia, Africa and South America, Alavi suggested that most post-colonial countries (such as Pakistan) already had an 'overdeveloped military'[15] even at the time of their inception. According to Alavi, though at the time of their creation the new countries lacked economic resources and political institutions, they inherited established militaries from the receding colonial powers. Thus, when such countries struggled to develop civilian political institutions, their militaries were the only organized state entities to resolve issues triggered by political conflicts between underdeveloped civilian bodies. This politicized the military and retarted the process needed to make civilian institutions reach maturity.

Alavi settled in the UK, becoming a professor of sociology, first at Leeds University and then at the Manchester University. He wrote scathing critiques against the reactionary dictatorship of General Ziaul Haq in various academic journals. By then, along with Eqbal Ahmad, Alavi had become one of the most cited Pakistani scholars in the West. In 1987, two years after deadly ethnic riots erupted in Pakistan's largest city and economic hub, Karachi, Alavi emerged with his third most significant paper: Nationhood and Nationalities in Pakistan.

To get to the bottom of ethnic turmoil in Pakistan, Alavi observed that the movement to create Pakistan had a larger economic motive rather than a purely religious or ideological one. Alavi noted that bulk of the movement was driven by India's Muslim 'salaried classes'[16] who were competing for

---

[15] Aqil Shah: *The Army and Democracy* (Harvard University Press, 2014) p.290

[16] Ravi Kalia: *Pakistan: From the Rhetoric of Democracy to the Rise of Militancy* (Routledge, 2012) p.17

government jobs against their Hindu counterparts from the same class. He wrote that the salaried Muslims believed that this competition will be eliminated with the creation of Pakistan but this sense of severe competition was not resolved with the creation of the new Muslim-majority country. Instead it got carried over (into Pakistan) and took the shape of competition between the salaried classes belonging to different ethnic groups. This, according to Alavi, created ethnic tensions and turmoil in the country.

In 1997, Alavi turned his attention to the rise of religious extremism in Pakistan. In his fourth most significant thesis, 'The Contradictions of the Khilafat Movement', Alavi analyzed the Khilafat Movement in India (1919-1926) in depth. He suggested that it was the emergence of this movement that enhanced the political role of the Muslim clergy in South Asia. Alavi writes that despite the fact that the movement pretended to be an anti-imperialist entity, its main aim was to promote a communalist understanding of politics among Indian Muslims. He added: 'it was no small irony that the Khilafat Movement was supported by Gandhi and opposed by Jinnah ...'

Until his demise in 2003, Alavi continued to insist that Jinnah had envisaged a very different Pakistan from what it eventually became after his death. On being a Marxist, he once told renowned historian, Dr Mubarak Ali, that Marxism works best as a tool to analyze history, economics and politics, but does not hold quite so well as a political ideology.[17]

****

---

[17] Hamza Alavi: A Personal Tribute: Dr. Maubarek Ali (DAWN December 7, 2003).

The Fighting Scholar

When I dropped out of the Karachi University (due to 'political reasons') in 1990 and joined journalism, I found myself in an ideological limbo. Having styled myself as a 'Marxist' at college in the mid-1980s,[18] by the decade's end I wasn't quite so sure where I stood during a time when the Cold War was winding up and the Soviet Union had begun to collapse. This is when I stumbled upon the columns of Eqbal Ahmed. Almost immediately I found myself relating to his every word. Thanks to him, I believe, I finally discovered something that was always in me, but for which I didn't have the academic discipline and the intellectual tools to fully articulate and shape. For me, Eqbal became an intellectual guru. A guru I actually met only once. I bumped into him in 1993 in a hallway of the offices of the Dawn newspaper. I was too much in awe of him to say much, but was quietly thrilled to learn that he had heard of me, despite the fact that I was still in my early 20s and had been in journalism for a mere three years.

So what did I find in Eqbal that I couldn't in Marx and Mao (on the left) and in Abul Ala Maududi (on the right)?

My days as a rash student activist had seen me fervently trying to complement this recklessness with the writings and thoughts of classical and modern leftist and rightest ideologues. In hindsight I now believe I was always searching for some sort of a progressive middle ground. Eqbal Ahmed had been a well-known intellectual and writer ever since the early 1960s, but I somehow didn't pay a lot of attention to him till 1990. But I

---

[18] I was associated with two left-leaning student groups: The 'pro-Soviet' faction of the National Students Federation (NSF), and then with the Peoples Students Federation (PSF), the student-wing of the Pakistan People's Party.

believe that he is still a relatively lesser known intellectual entity in Pakistan compared to the country's other intellectual giants and political thinkers. Nevertheless, he remains to be perhaps the most relevant because whereas the thoughts of his many contemporaries are firmly rooted in the ebb and flow of Cold War politics and ideologies, Eqbal had the uncanny ability to transcend the tyranny of being stuck in the myopia of contemporary political trends and events.

He did this by understanding the present with the help of historical dialecticism (that he was a master of), and then actually predict what certain current events were warning about the future. Eqbal was able to derive uncanny insights from political and social events and then use them to make predictions.[19] This was mainly due to the fact that these insights were not only being shaped by Eqbal's immaculate grasp of political histories and philosophies, but also by his first-hand experiences as an activist. The latter clearly sets Eqbal apart.

Born into an aristocratic Muslim family in Bihar, Eqbal migrated to Pakistan with his elder brother in 1947. His parents were supporters of the Indian National Congress, but Eqbal became smitten by the future founder of Pakistan, Muhammad Ali Jinnah[20] who remained to hold a special place in Eqbal's thoughts. Eqbal, who was just 14 when Pakistan emerged as a separate South Asian country in 1947, made most of his journey to his new homeland on foot along with millions of other Muslim migrants. He often spoke about the violence that he witnessed during this mass migration. It reminded him of the brutal murder of his father by his opponents in Bihar. His father was stabbed to death in front of Eqbal when Eqbal was just 9.

---

[19] Stuart Schaar: *Eqbal Ahmad: Critical Outsider in a Turbulent Age* (Columbia University Press, 2015)
[20] Ibid.

In Pakistan, Eqbal lived with his elder brother and joined college. In 1948, he volunteered to join a battalion of Muslim League youth who had come to his college to recruit men to fight in Pakistan's first war against India in Kashmir. He was wounded in action.[21] In 1958, he won a scholarship to study at the prestigious Princeton University in the United States. Here he immersed himself in the study of Middle Eastern and African history and politics and also learned Arabic. He was already fluent in Urdu, English and Persian.

In 1961, he travelled to Paris where he learned French and came into contact with Algerian nationalists who were fighting a war of liberation against the French in Algeria. For his PhD thesis he travelled to Tunis and then entered Algeria in 1962 where he fought alongside Algerian nationalists [22] against the French till Algeria became an independent republic. By now Eqbal had also begun to study and master Islamic history. He was invited to join the first independent government in Algeria but he declined and returned to the US. He began to teach at a university in Massachusetts where he became an early opponent of America's involvement in Vietnam. In 1971, he was arrested for his anti-war activism, tried, but eventually released.[23]

He had already begun to describe himself as a progressive Muslim and vehemently opposed 'Soviet Communism' and 'American imperialism.'[24] He was also extremely critical of dictatorships in Third World countries and of Arab Sheikhdoms in the Middle East.[25] He became a passionate supporter of the

---

[21] Ibid.
[22] The Secular Sufi: Noam Chomsky (2000)
[23] David Barsamian: *Eqbal Ahmad, Confronting Empire: Interviews with David Barsamian* (South End Press, 2000) p.XXII
[24] Stuart Schaar: *Eqbal Ahmad: Critical Outsider in a Turbulent Age* (Columbia University Press, 2015)
[25] Ibid.

Palestinian cause. Eqbal took great pride in the cultural history of his faith. In his writings and lectures he often denounced Muslim rulers and the clergy who he believed were hell-bent on whitewashing this history to meet their myopic and avaricious desires. Now well armed with immaculate academic and experiential knowledge of Islam, the Middle East and Africa, Eqbal travelled to Paris in 1978 to interview Iranian spiritual leader, Ayatollah Khomeini, who had been living there in exile. Eqbal hailed the Iranian Revolution in 1979, but predicted that the Shah's pro-West autocracy in Iran will be replaced by the religious despotism of the clerics.[26] He was proven right.

In the early 1980s when the US openly began to arm Afghan insurgents against Soviet troops that had invaded Afghanistan, Eqbal predicted that 'this will come back to haunt the US.'[27] And it did, as it did the other parties in the conflict as well, such as Pakistan and Saudi Arabia. Eqbal also warned the US against attacking Saddam in Iraq in 1990. He predicted that Saddam's fall would usher in sectarian chaos in the region.[28] 14 years later, he was once again proven right when the US finally toppled Saddam in 2004 and the region went up in flames. Eqbal also anticipated tragic events such as 9/11.[29] He had interviewed Osama Bin Laden in Peshawar in 1986; and in the early 1990s, Eqbal suggested that the same ideology that had been drummed into men like Osama by the Americans and the Pakistanis in the 1980s, would spiral out of control and turn the indoctrinated into adversaries. Right again.

---

[26] The Iranian Hundred Years War: Eqbal Ahmad (Mother Jones Magazine, April, 1979) p.18.

[27] A Reporter at Large: Bloody Games: Eqbal Ahmad & Richard Barnet (The New Yorker, April 11, 1988).

[28] Stuart Schaar: *Eqbal Ahmad: Critical Outsider in a Turbulent Age* (Columbia University Press, 2015)

[29] Ibid.

Eqbal spend the last decade of his life in Pakistan writing a weekly column for Dawn. He continued to advocate social democracy in Muslim countries as an antidote to extremism, poverty and injustice. His greatest ambition was to establish a large social sciences university in Pakistan that could herald in a progressive and enlightened Muslim Renaissance. Unable to raise the $30 million that was required to build such a project, Eqbal succumbed to cancer in 1999. He was 65.

****

An Angry Old Man

In 2006, an obituary appeared on the pages of Pakistan's leading English daily, Dawn. It was of someone called A. Cowasjee. Many well-meaning fans and friends of famous columnist and social activist, Ardeshir Cowasjee, rushed to his home, only to find the man up and about, playing with his dogs and inspecting his garden. Yes, the obituary was of some other Cowasjee. Ardeshir couldn't help but exhibit his amusement in one of his columns. He was first bemused by seeing people appear at his gate, look at him as he walked around in his shorts, and then turn away, some without uttering a single word.

The bemusement turned into a dark comedy of sorts when he finally realized what was going on. An old colleague of his told me how he laughed at a bureaucrat who, like many others, appeared at his gate, stood on his toes, and silently peeked at Cowasjee. In the typical style that he spoke his Urdu, Cowasjee shouted out: '*Tum fikar na karo. Hum abhi tak zinda hai*!' (Don't you worry, I'm still alive).

Six years later, in November 2012, Dawn published another obituary for an A. Cowasjee. But this time it was of the

Cowasjee so many Pakistanis had come to love, loath or simply get perplexed by. For almost three decades, Ardeshir Cowasjee remained to be one of the most read and influential columnists in Pakistan. Though he wrote for an English daily (Dawn), his words reached and echoed in the most significant corners and corridors of power.

Cowasjee came from a well-off Zoroastrian (*Parsee*) family. Based in Karachi, he was still managing his family business when in 1972, Prime Minster Zulfikar Ali Bhutto appointed him as the Managing Director of the Pakistan Tourism Development Board (PTDB) - a body formed to accommodate and further attract Western tourists who had begun to come in droves to Pakistan from the late 1960s onward.

Despite the fact that Cowasjee turned out to be an asset for the board, three years later, in 1976, Bhutto suddenly got him arrested. Cowasjee spent days behind bars, where he continued writing letters to Bhutto asking him why he was put in jail.[30] Bhutto never answered. He finally ordered his release after 72 days.[31] Many believe that Cowasjee faced Bhutto's wrath because he had begun to criticize the Bhutto regime's growing authoritarianism.

After Bhutto was toppled by Zia in 1977, Cowasjee began writing letters to Dawn's influential 'Letters to the Editor' section castigating the fallen Bhutto regime. His well-written and evocatively worded letters became a frequent fixture in Dawn. He then ventured into commenting on other topics; topics which gradually began to attract the anger of the Zia dictatorship as well. During a time when the press was being gagged and harassed, Cowasjee was one of the first Pakistanis to invent and articulate a

---

[30] Syed Abdul Quddus: *Zulfikar Ali Bhutto: Politics of Charisma* (Progressive Publishers, 1994) p.96
[31] Ibid.

method of writing that has now become a common device used by liberals to critique religious conservatives in Pakistan.

After taking Bhutto to task, his letters turned their attention towards the draconian laws being introduced by the Zia dictatorship and its so-called 'Islamisation' project. Cowasjee did this by simply stating over and over again that the Jinnah (founder of Pakistan) he had met and followed as a young man did not conceptualize Pakistan the way the country's politicians and military generals were doing.

This argument of his struck a nerve with a number of Dawn readers and soon Cowasjee was invited by the newspaper's editor, Ahmed Ali Khan, to write a regular column for the daily. In his columns of the mid and late 1980s, he continued to bemoan how both Bhutto and Zia had shattered Jinnah's vision. After Zia's demise in 1988, Cowasjee became even more pointed against the civilian governments which followed Zia, accusing them of corruption and nepotism. Also, by the early 1990s, he had slowly been moving away from his old rhetorical style and towards putting on paper hard facts and stats as he went about his business of being a man on a one-way mission of putting powerful men to sword.

Also being a passionate Karachiite with a desire to see his beloved city return to being what it had been before the 1980s, Cowasjee directly confronted the influential 'building and land mafias,' using both his pen and the courts to halt the construction of a number of gaudy shopping arcades and parking lots – especially on lands which were originally allotted to support parks. This was also the period when Cowasjee began receiving serious death threats. But he soldiered on.

In his columns of the 1980s and 1990s Cowasjee had always spoken about his understanding of Jinnah being a progressive man, it was from the late 1990s onward that he openly began to suggest that Jinnah perceived Pakistan to be a secular Muslim country. This was Cowasjee reacting to what the second Nawaz Sharif government was planning to do: i.e. to introduce a constitutional bill that would have actually endorsed Sharif's jump from being a prime minster to becoming an '*Ameerul Momineen.*'[32]

So when General Pervez Musharraf overthrew the Nawaz regime in 1999, Cowasjee cynically mocked Sharif almost exactly the way he had done Bhutto, Zia and Benazir. His overall message remained to be that all these leaders were misfits in a Pakistan that Jinnah had conceived. To him, they were misfits because they were selfish, authoritarian and never far from using religion and other populist gimmicks to retain power. Cowasjee seemed supportive of Musharraf, but all the while advised him not to repeat the mistakes of other Pakistani military dictators such as Ayub Khan and Ziaul Haq. Cowasjee was warning him to stay away from the bunch of politicians who only become active when allowed into the corridors of power through the backdoor. As the Pakistani society under Musharraf and after the 9/11 episode began to fully reap what was sown in the name of faith by Zia, Cowasjee started to sound extremely bitter and cynical.

He became more critical of the religious lobbies and parties, so much so that many of them began to accuse him of being 'anti-Islam.' In 2003, banners went up in Karachi cursing Cowasjee of working against the so-called 'ideology of Pakistan' and Islam. The government had to post police guards outside his home in Karachi's Bath Island area.

This was also the period when Cowasjee began appearing on privately owned television news channels which had

---

[32] Arabic for Commander of the Faithful; a designation held by ancient Muslim rulers.

mushroomed after 2003. But on TV Cowasjee was nothing like he was in print. Instead of the articulate columnist with a great command over the English language, Cowasjee decided to almost entirely speak in Urdu. His Urdu was crude and unsophisticated but ironically perfect to express the more frustrated aspects of his personality that had been building up for decades as he saw his country rapidly slide into a quagmire of authoritarianism, corruption, intolerance and violence.

By now he had also become extremely cynical. First, about this country's leadership that kept producing one bad apple after another, and then about the Pakistani people, whom he began to describe as a lot without any ability to learn from past mistakes or correctly decide what was actually good for them. So on TV, no matter how hard an anchor would try to make Cowasjee sound like he did in his columns, Cowasjee would refuse and instead continue to use Urdu slang and words like '*khachar*' (donkey), '*chariya*' (demented), '*chor*' (thief), among others, to define politicians, military men and their followers.

For example, during one such TV show when asked what he thought about Pakistan's status of being a nuclear power, he smirked, pressed mischievously upon his walking stick, and said: '*Sala iss qaum sey gutter to bundh hota nahi, bum kya chalaye ga ...*' (how can this nation be a nuclear power when it doesn't even know how to stop the flow of an overflowing gutter).[33] Though he first appeared to be a man whose old age had given him the license to scold influential men in the crudest of Urdu, he ultimately became a caricature of himself; or rather was reduced to being one by an electronic media whose own cynicism was entirely amoral.

---

[33] PJ Mir Show (ARY News, 2004)

Alas, better sense prevailed and Cowasjee's TV appearances gradually came to a halt. But his columns kept coming and by the time he announced his retirement in 2011, he had gone back to once again remind his many readers that this was certainly not the Pakistan Jinnah had dreamt of. He lamented the fact that Jinnah had passed away too early and that it was left to old men like him to see this dream crumble, piece by piece, right in front of their eyes.

At the time of his death the police guards were still posted outside his house as threats from the building mafia and religious outfits never stopped. But these guards, though provided by the government, were largely financed and fed by Cowasjee himself. A Zoroastrian, he always explained himself to be a humanist. Cowasjee was also involved in a number of charities, where he liberally donated money for the education of needy students and the construction of parks.

In his columns, he usually came across as being an angry old man, in private life, however, he was a warm-hearted family man and someone who always cherished receiving all kinds of people at his home. In the area where he lived in Karachi (Bath Island), his beautiful old bungalow with old shady trees, a neatly manicured garden and low walls is a reminder of what Karachi was once like.

CHAPTER 10
POSSIBLE FUTURES:
BACK TO THE MODERN MUSLIM REPUBLIC?

During his 11-year rule, Zia furthered the project of the divergent strand of Pakistani nationalism and turned it into a dogma that explained Pakistan as a unique emergence in the Muslim world that was conceived to become a bastion of faith driven entirely by 'divine laws.' What made it a dogma (that was aggressively proliferated through school textbooks and propaganda), was that it refused to recognize the multi-ethnic and multi-sectarian make-up of the country, and, instead, offered a rather convoluted, rigid and artificial understanding of nationhood.

This ended up promoting an inelastic and entirely myopic strains of the faith, transporting them from the fringes of society into the mainstream, and, in the process, retarding the natural evolution of Pakistan's multicultural ethos and polity. It ended up offending various ethnic groups, Muslim sects and sub-sects and alienated the minority religious communities.

Zia's maneuvers in this context were a culmination of what actually began as an ambitious project in the 1970s. The project reached its limits during the Zia regime. The shape that it finally took was so inflexible that it could not adapt to and address the rapid political changes which followed after the end of the Cold War (in 1991) and during the emergence of the severe forms of religious extremism and terrorism which engulfed the country after 9/11.

It can thus be suggested that the project is now facing a serious crises. It cannot be stretched any further. It ate itself up after devouring everything else that could have halted the political and social retardation that it triggered over the decades. That is why, today, Pakistan's ruling and military establishments and a good part of the intelligentsia are trying to replace it with something that would directly challenge the doctrinal rigidity and the political and cultural isolation this divergent nationalist narrative ended up promoting and encouraging. Pakistan's existentialist status is in a dire need of a fresh new narrative — a narrative that should have begun where Jinnah's first speech to the Constituent Assembly had left.[1]

Musharraf was forced to resign in 2008 after the PPP and PMLN won the most seats in that year's election. Both became the top two parties in the National Assembly. But things got even worse. The PPP was swept out by the centre-right PML-N in the 2013 election and Prime Minister Nawaz Sharif's government inherited a disaster.

The economy was spiraling down, terrorism was at its peak, an extremist mindset seemed to have deeply penetrated every section of the polity and the state, and there was a new populist entity in the shape of Imran Khan's PTI, hell-bent on toppling the Nawaz regime on corruption charges.

For months the government seemed to be paralyzed and baffled by the magnitude of the problems facing it. Then, in

---

[1] Jinnah's August 11 1947 speech in which he clearly desired a Pakistan in which the state would have nothing to do with matters of the faith of its citizens.

December 2014, one of the worst incidents of extremist terror in Pakistan woke the state, government and society from its defeatist slumber. When terrorists killed at least 144 students at a school in Peshawar, the government instead of capitulating, finally grew some teeth. Backed by the new army chief, General Raheel Sharif, the regime began to initiate various unprecedented maneuvers that saw Pakistan shifting its political and ideological paradigm once again.

The state and government began to return to the narrative of 'modernist Islam' that had begun to erode in the 1970s and was replaced by an entirely reactive one from the 1980s onward. But the new narrative is more pragmatic than ideological. It is still very much a work-in-progress. It simply suggests that to make Pakistan an important economic player in the world, certain radical steps are necessary. These steps include the proliferation of free enterprise and foreign investment, which, in turn, requires Pakistan to change its security policies and crackdown on anything threatening the erosion of local and international economic confidence.

Optimists have already predicted that Pakistan is well on its way to pull itself out of the quicksand which it created and then fell into; whereas the skeptics have advised caution. They say it was just too early to predict anything conclusive because the mountain through which the country is now trying to drill a tunnel, has been piling upwards for over 30 years now.

Former chief of Pakistan's premier intelligence agency, the ISI, General Hamid Gul, who recently passed away, epitomized the way the Pakistan military began to see itself from the 1980s. Influenced by ideological and strategic dynamics of the right-wing insurgency that Pakistan facilitated (during the Zia dictatorship) against the Soviet-backed regime in Kabul, Gul remained to be a staunch advocate of the ideological mindset that was cultivated during that conflict.

This mindset, apart from being programmed into young insurgents, also proliferated across some influential sections of the Pakistan military. That is why even after Zia's demise in 1988 and Gul's ouster as intelligence chief in 1989, a number of top ranking officers continued to be identified with this ideology, despite the fact that General Parvez Musharraf (who took over power in 1999), attempted to somewhat reverse the trend.

General Raheel Sharif, who took over as the country's military chief during the third Nawaz Sharif government in 2013, clearly attempted to promote a more temperate outlook within the armed forces; or a point of view articulated to free the state's war against religious militancy from any confusion which can arise in a soldier's mind about an enemy that overtly uses religious symbolism and rhetoric.

General Raheel's command signaled a shift on multiple fronts, gradually steering the military's ideological narrative from the right to a more centrist disposition. It's still a volatile undertaking because it is attempting to phase out a narrative that emerged in the 1980s and was then allowed to compound for various 'strategic' and political reasons.

****

The Guilt Generation

In the early 1930s, three young German academics, Theodore Adorno, Max Horrkheimer and Herbet Marcuse, formed an intellectual clique that came to be known as the Frankfurt School. Based in the German city of Frankfurt, the three men developed a way of studying Marxism (in Europe) with the aid of Freudian psychology, and, in the process, came up with an intellectual and analytical tool called 'critical theory'.

With the rise of Nazism in Germany, the three men moved to the United States and set themselves up at New York's prestigious Columbia University. Here they applied critical theory to the emergence of fascism in Europe, and concluded that fascism was the outcome and by-product of 'advanced capitalism'. Some 30 years after the three men had first published their study of the rise of fascism in Europe, their thesis were enthusiastically picked up by sections of young middle-class Germans, many of whom were not even born when the Frankfurt School and critical theory were being formed. Suddenly, the idea that fascism was the outcome of advanced capitalism became all the rage among a large number of university and college students in West Berlin and Frankfurt.

But why did it take almost 30 years for German youth to embrace the idea? Journalist and author Hans Kundani in his excellent book, *Utopia or Auschwitz*, informs that many Germans who were born during Nazi rule in Germany (1933-45), entered their teens and 20s in the 1950s. By the late 1950s and early 1960s, university students associated with the left-wing German student outfit, the SDS, had begun to question the silence adopted (on Nazi rule) by their parents and the German state after the collapse of Nazism in 1945.

Articles began to emerge in radical youth magazines, and treatises authored by the intellectual wing of the SDS denounced their parents' generation for remaining quiet or even supporting the 'murderous rise' of Nazism in Germany. They coined the term the 'Auschwitz generation' for their parents and accused them of destroying Germany by facilitating the emergence of Nazism and then trying to repress the gruesome memory of it after its collapse.

By 1967, membership of the SDS and other progressive youth outfits witnessed a threefold rise and many of the young intellectuals and leaders associated with these organizations began to apply the theoretical conclusions of the Frankfurt School to the prevailing situation in Germany. According to the students, their parents had facilitated the rise of Nazism in the 1930s and had looked the other way when the Nazi regime was committing violent crimes against those Germans who had refused to submit to the dictates of the Nazi regime.

They added that even after the collapse of Nazism (in 1945), Germany had rebuilt itself with the help of advanced capitalism that was being facilitated by their parents' generation, and that by keeping the memory of Nazism repressed, it was now forming an authoritarian state run by former Nazis and their sympathizers. The rage associated with this sentiment finally exploded in 1967 and the student movement turned violent. The violence continued across the 1970s until the German state finally decided to confront the country's violent past, instead of suppressing it.

Now imagine what might happen when Pakistani children born in the early and mid-2000s, enter their late teens and 20s. Hopefully, by then Pakistan would be a largely extremism-free country, but will that be enough?

Today's young parents should indeed be prepared to be asked some awkward questions by their children when they grow up. Why you were quiet even after thousands of Pakistanis were slaughtered by extremists? What was the state waiting for before finally launching a military operation against the extremists? Were you looking the other way when schoolgirls were being shot in the face and then called agents? How did you react when students were being cut down at schools and universities? Why did you allow such a situation to exist? Why don't you talk about it? Are you ashamed of it, or did you actually defend what the extremists were doing?

Pakistani children today are living in extremely testing times. Their memory of such a time is bound to finally make them ask some pointed and difficult questions from their parents and the state of Pakistan when they grow up. So be ready, and more so, be honest.

****

How Green was his Valley?

Many years ago, when Pakistan's Swat region didn't have any bushy warlords, I knew a middle-aged man there who was also a tracking guide. His name was Atique Ali Khan and I remember every time I used to ask him about how his two children were doing at school, he was in the habit of constantly quoting a well-known hadith. 'Allah be praised', he used to say. 'They are doing well at school. As the Prophet used to say, go as far as China for knowledge.'

Well, I haven't been to Swat in a long time and I have no idea what became of Atique. But thanks to the rude mushrooming of the rowdy keepers of faith in that part of Pakistan in the early and mid-2000s) children in Swat could not even attend a neighborhood school, let alone visiting one in China. Of course, this is the same region where religious extremists shot Malala Yousafzai in the face.

Though the 2009 military operation in that area largely cleared the place of the mad men, in 2012 the shooting of the then 15-year-old Malala confirmed the apprehension that these men are still embedded in Swat among its otherwise peaceful populace. These men were an angry lot. Once upon a time, it is said, they used to let off steam by chopping down trees. That was bad enough, but I guess ever since trees have become somewhat scarce in Swat, they began ranting incoherent loud nothings on clandestine FM radio stations about how extremely angry they were about all the obscenity and injustice in the world and about matters related to the education of girls.

Well, the FM stations too didn't seem to satisfy their monstrous appetites for 'divinely inspired' action, so off they went blowing up CD shops and girls' schools. Blow them all, became their heartfelt mantra, as they became angrier, louder, and a lot bushier. Unfortunately, since supposedly their faith was much stronger than that of us 'bad Muslims,' it required more from them. So these angry men started blowing themselves up! What's more, for an impressive display and effect, they did this in public places. Off they went with a bang, taking along with them mutilated and severed bodies of dozens of men, women and children. And up they all went to paradise, or so they said, and so they believed. As for Atique Ali Khan, I wonder if he's still alive. One thing's for sure, though. His children won't have many schools left to go to.

****

Not that Pakhtun

Many Pakistani Pakhtuns find themselves in a spot of bother when some political commentators define right-wing extremist/militant organizations as extensions and expressions of Pakhtun nationalism. Ever since the beginning of the US/Pakistan/Saudi-backed insurgency against the Soviet forces in Afghanistan in the 1980s, Pakhtun identity (at least in popular imagination) has been gradually mutating to mean something that is akin to being entirely conservative, even fanatical.

At the end of the Afghan insurgency (that was followed by a civil war between various insurgent groups in Afghanistan), the rugged expanses of Khyber Pakhtunkhwa's tribal areas began teeming with anarchic extremist organizations. Many of them were mutations of the groups that had taken part in the anti-Soviet 'Afghan Jihad' in the 1980s from Pakistani soil.

In 2008, while on a trip to Islamabad, I met a 60-something Pakhtun who owned a chain of shoe stores in the city. He had a flowing grey beard and seemed to be a very religious man. But as we got talking, and after I told him that I was a journalist, he said he too once wanted to become a journalist: 'I was studying journalism at the Peshawar University more than 40 years ago when I was picked up by the police and jailed without a trial,' he said.

The man then sat me down and ordered some tea: 'I was a guerilla fighter too' He announced.

'During the Afghan jihad?' I asked.

'No, that came later. I was fighting in the mountains of NWFP (present-day KP), long before the jihad,' he explained.

Intrigued, I immediately requested him to order another round of tea. Though he claimed to have taken part in the anti-Soviet insurgency in Afghanistan in the 1980s with the 'mujahedeen' forces, he had once been a committed communist! He spoke about how long before KP's tribal areas became bastions of all kinds of extremist/militant outfits, they were the domain of Maoist fighters. I did have some superficial knowledge about this: a now largely forgotten piece of modern Pakhtun history about large patches of land in the KP that for decades have been the domain of extreme religious outfits, were once swarming with Pakhtuns quoting Marx and Mao.

In the 1960s, the Pakhtun and Baloch dominated National Awami Party (NAP) was the country's largest left-wing outfit.

Even after the rise of the populist PPP in 1967, NAP remained popular in KP and Balochistan. However, in the late 1960s NAP split into three factions. During its analysis of how to achieve a socialist revolution in Pakistan, the NAP leadership had failed to come to a mutual agreement. The pro-Soviet faction (led by Wali Khan), suggested working to put Pakistan on a democratic path and then achieve the party's goals of provincial autonomy and socialism. The pro-China faction led by the fiery Bengali leader, Maulana Bhashani, rejected democracy and labelled it as being 'a tool of the bourgeoisie'.[2] The pro-Soviet NAP became NAP-Wali while the pro-China one became NAP-Bhashani. In 1968 another faction emerged when a more radical group within NAP-Wali broke away and decided to adopt the Maoist strategy of achieving a socialist revolution through an armed struggle by organizing peasant militias[3] in the countryside. Thus was born the Mazdoor Kissan Party (Worker & Peasants Party) which held its first convention in Peshawar in 1968.

The MKP refused to take part in the 1970 election. Inspired by the beginnings of the Maoist 'Naxalite' guerrilla movement in India and Mao's 'Cultural Revolution' in China, MKP activists, led by former NAP leader and Pakhtun Maoist, Afzal Bangash, travelled to Hashtnagar in KP's Charsaada district and began to arm and organize the peasants against local landlords.

MKP's early maneuvers in this respect were highly successful as its activists joined the area's peasants and fought running gun battles with the mercenaries hired by the landlords and against the police.[4] As the area of influence of MKP's

---

[2] Asian Survay, Vol.13 (University of California, 1973) p.204

[3] Syed M. Ali: *Development, Poverty and Power in Pakistan* (Routledge, 2014) p.128

[4] IH Burney in Outlook, Vo.13, 1974. p.73

struggle grew, another communist, Retired Major Ishaq Mohammad joined MKP with his men. Both men, Bangash and Ishaq, led MKP to spread its influence across various rural and semi-rural areas of the KP and gained the support of the area's peasants. MKP's guerrilla activities continued to grow and gather support in Hashtnagar, and its fighters even managed to 'liberate' some plots of lands by ousting the landlords.[5]

By 1972, Z.A. Bhutto's PPP had become the country's new ruling party, whereas NAP-Wali formed coalition provincial governments in KP and Balochistan. The old shoe trader that I was talking to told me that he was in his early 20s when he joined MKP militants in the mountains: 'I came from a peasant background in a small town near Charsaada. I was in grade 10 (in 1968) when some MKP cadres came to our school and gave us translations of writings by Mao. Many of us were soon converted and vowed to bring a socialist revolution,' he added.

The man claimed that action against MKP guerrillas was mostly taken by the NAP-Wali government in KP: 'Bhutto and Wali did not get along and Bhutto as PM indirectly encouraged MKP to destabilize the KP government,' he said.

MKP militants drove out a number of landlords in KP's hilly Hashtnagar area and redistributed some land among the area's peasants. 'We fought waves of police and mercenaries hired by the landlords,' the man explained. 'But (in 1974) after Bhutto was successful in getting rid of the KP government, he used federal security forces against us and our movement was crushed.'

He claimed that Bhutto also did this because by 1973 the MKP had begun to make inroads into Punjab's rural areas as well. But how did this young Maoist Pakhtun then end up

---

[5] Link, Vol.27, Issue: 2, 1984. p.33

becoming an anti-communist insurgent in neighboring Afghanistan? According to him after he was released from jail in 1978 (one year after the fall of the Bhutto regime at the hands of Zia), he went back to the university to complete his studies.

He finally got a degree in journalism in 1980 and was in Peshawar looking for a job when he received a visit by three men: 'They just appeared at the bedsit I was living in. They told me they were from an intelligence agency. I thought they had come to arrest me again, even though I had quit politics. But they told me that I had fought a just war but with a flawed ideology. The Soviet Union had invaded Afghanistan (December 1979) and they said they were looking for trained men to fight the Soviets.'

He said some of the first trained fighters among the mujahedeen (from Pakistan) were mostly men who had been MKP guerrillas: 'We joined because we were also angry at how fellow socialists like NAP-Wali and the PPP had persecuted us.'

He fought in Afghanistan till 1985 (with the Gulbuddin Hekmatyar group), but then quit: 'One day I returned from the Afghan border and refused to go back. I asked myself, how was my fighting for Afghan insurgents helping the poor Pakhtuns of Pakistan? So much money had also begun to pour in (from the US and Saudi Arabia) and it began to corrupt a lot of Pakhtuns. This totally destroyed our (Pakhtun) society and values.'

He migrated to Karachi where he got married to a cousin and joined an apolitical evangelical Islamic outfit (the *Tableeghi Jamat*). He then moved to Islamabad where he started a shoe business with a friend: 'Yes, men like me once believed in Marxism and Maoism and all that, but we were always Muslim,' he explained. 'We were against corrupt landlords and the mullahs who did their bidding. But when I saw these same mullahs becoming rich and turned into heroes (during the anti-Soviet insurgency) I gave up the fight.'

I asked him what he thought about the new breed of religious militants that had emerged in KP.

He just shrugged his shoulders: 'Only Allah knows,' he smiled. But then quickly added: 'To me all are puppets, like I was. First in the hands of leftists and then in the hands of those who wanted to use religion to make political and monitory gains. I really don't care anymore. It's all a waste of emotion and youth. Our (Pakhtun) society has been ravaged.'

For decades various areas in North West Pakistan have gained infamy for being bastions of a number of extreme right-wing militant outfits. Most major operations of the Pakistan Military in the last decade or so have almost entirely concentrated on such groups stationed in the tribal areas near the Afghanistan-Pakistan border, and also in certain more well-settled parts of the region, such as Swat. The immediate rationale behind the emergence of extremist groups in these areas has to do with the permissive policies of the Zia dictatorship that allowed the proliferation of non-conventional religious groups across Pakistan during the war which erupted between Afghan insurgents and the Soviet-backed government in Kabul.

Pakistan played the role of a facilitator in the war, channeling the funds and arms received from the US and Saudi Arabia to various insurgent groups who increasingly saw their battle against the Kabul regime as a holy struggle. Pakistan also provided indoctrination facilities to these groups. The indoctrination was largely undertaken by radical clerics who till the late 1970s had been on the fringes of society.

It is correct to suggest that such schemes by the state of Pakistan were instrumental in turning large swaths of Pakistan's Khyber Pakhtunkhwa (KP) province into areas that became

increasingly infested by a number of religious militant outfits
(many of which eventually turned against the state of Pakistan).
But there are some political scientists who suggest that the anti-
Soviet insurgency in the 1980s was just one reason that triggered
the appearance of religious militancy and insurgencies in KP.

As we saw above, some of the earliest fighters (from
Pakistan) who joined the Afghan insurrection at the start of the
anti-Soviet insurgency in early 1980 were actually first
radicalized by certain militant leftist groups that had been active
in KP in the 1970s. In *Beyond Swat* (edited by Magnus
Marsden), anthropologist Charles Lindholm in his essay —
based on his on-field study in Swat in the 1970s — suggests that
young men in Swat coming from less well-to-do families were
first radicalized by the socialist message of former prime
minister and chairman of the PPP, Zulfikar Ali Bhutto. Lindholm
saw young Swatis vote in droves for the PPP in the 1977 election
(that were declared void by the Zia dictatorship after that year's
military coup).

These young Bhutto enthusiasts worked actively against
religious parties and non-religious conservative groups whom
they accused of being in league with the landed elite of Swat.
Interestingly, Lindholm then goes on to inform that in the 1980s,
when politics based on religious populism began to peak and was
welded with right-wing militant outfits that had begun to crop
up, young men from Swat's working and lower-middle-class
backgrounds who had been radicalized by Bhutto's populist and
leftist rhetoric, started to colour their angry stances with an
equally angry 'Islamist' point of view.

There is weight in this observation. Because ever since the
1980s incidents have come to light in which some early recruits
of religious militant outfits in Swat once had links with the
politics of the radical left or with the equally radical Pakhtun

nationalist tendencies. One of the most prominent examples in this respect is of the renegade leader of perhaps the most belligerent factions of the Pakistani Taliban, Mullah Fazalullah.

As a teen in Swat in 1990, Fazalullah is reported to have been attached to the student-wing of the Pakhtun nationalist party, the Awami National Party (ANP), whereas other reports claim that he was associated with the youth wing of the PPP. On the surface this may suggest an inherent extremist moving from one extreme to another.

But in his study, Lindholm treats the phenomenon (in Swat), as being about a generation that was made aware (by Bhutto) of certain overpowering economic and political discrepancies and it expressed its discontent through an idea that was at the time promising radical change (socialism). But sections of this generation then moved to another idea (militant faith) once the earlier idea withered away from popular imagination.

If so, then these discrepancies are still present. And recently with the kind of battering the second radical idea has suffered (after it turned against the state and eventually on itself with its anarchic violence), what shape has the shifting radical tendency that (according to Lindholm) has been present in Swat since the 1970s, taken now?

****

An Ambiguous Man

Haris, an old college buddy of mine back in the mid-1980s, came from a highly conservative middle-class family in Pakistan's chaotic, colossal metropolis, Karachi. Yet, he was an impassioned member of the left-wing student outfit that we were both once an integral part of. However, I was never really quite sure about the nature of his ideological disposition.

Let me explain. Even though Haris would usually agree with our student outfit's views on matters such as democracy, and he supported the organization's opposition to the reactionary dictatorship that was in power in Pakistan at the time; yet, he would refuse to participate in the many demonstrations that we held on the campus against those who were aiding Afghan, Arab and Pakistani militants fighting against the Soviet-backed communist regime in Kabul.

Today, I can effortlessly call the entry of Soviet troops in Afghanistan as an all-out invasion, but back then, in a world still in the grip of the Cold War, I would passionately try to prove that the invasion was part of some glorious socialist revolution unfolding in Kabul. All of us who were on the left sides of Cold War politics described the other side as being nothing more than a bunch of counter-revolutionaries. But none of us were able to fully gauge the true nature of the fall-out of the Afghan Civil War, especially in Pakistan.

Benazir Bhutto, during her first term as PM (1988-90), was the one who first began to exhibit concerns about how the winding down of the Afghan Civil War would witness the wholesale return of fighters who had been radicalized while fighting the Soviets. But personally, I became a lot more conscious about this predicament by what I was once told by a cousin of Haris. In December 1990, I began my career as a journalist and hadn't been in contact with Haris after both of us graduated from college in late 1987. Bumping into his cousin at the Karachi Press Club in early 1991, I only casually inquired about Haris.

His cousin told me that right after graduation, Haris had travelled to Afghanistan. I instinctively asked whether he had gone there to side with the Soviet-backed regime. I was baffled when I was told that Haris had actually jumped on the other bandwagon: the one that hundreds of young Pakistanis had jumped on to ride into Afghanistan to join the anti-Soviet mujahedeen. I was told that Haris had fought alongside the mujahedeen for almost a year and only returned to Pakistan in late 1989 when he was wounded in the fighting.

I finally met Haris two years later in 1994. At the time he was rearing to go and fight in Indian-held Kashmir. I asked him what had made him turn right from left, and he told me that he had joined the leftist student outfit at college only to bother his conservative father with whom he was not on very good terms. So, after college, instead of trying to bother his father, Haris decided to impress him. Not by joining a government institution or a private firm (as his father had wanted him to); or by growing a beard (which he eventually did in Afghanistan); but by actively declaring his enmity against those his father detested the most: The *surkhas* (communists). By travelling to Afghanistan, he wanted to put this into action.

So, was the father impressed? Far from it. He was mortified. All he wanted was a 'pious' son with a stable professional career. Well, by going to Afghanistan, Haris had ended up bothering his father again. And he wasn't able to go to Kashmir because his parents just refused to let him go. I had jokingly suggested to him that he became a leftist again because maybe this time his dad would be more appreciative.

But Haris did not react jovially to the joke. With a stony expression, he responded by saying: 'But there is no Soviet Union anymore. We defeated it.' And when I inquired that whether by 'we' he also meant the United States, he remained stone-faced. Haris never went to India-held Kashmir. Instead (as

I found out in 1999), he travelled to Madrid and then ended up settling in Seattle in the United States.

Two of his paternal uncles had settled in Seattle in the early 1990s, and by the early 2000s, Haris was living with one of them and working (as a partner) at the three grocery stores that they owned in that city. He called me in May 2004 and told me he was visiting his family in Karachi. We met in my office for lunch. He had gotten married and had two young sons. He had arrived at my office with the aforementioned cousin.

As I was jokingly teasing him about his flip-flopping ways, his cousin suddenly jumped in and sarcastically mentioned something about how Haris had now been busy trying to make Pakistanis living in the US, 'better Muslims'. Haris had by then joined a Muslim 'study group' based out of Seattle. So I asked him what he was doing living in a western country. His reply was: 'They (the Westerners) are very tolerant and understanding people. They let you live according to your culture.'

His cousin again jumped in: 'Great. Why don't you now invite a group of American Jews and Christians to Pakistan? Let's show them how tolerant we are as well.' Haris was not amused.

Haris' cousin was totally apolitical in college. I never knew him as well as I did Haris, but he told me that he was very close to Haris' father who he had blamed when Haris had run off to Afghanistan. Haris returned to Seattle. I didn't hear from him again. Ten years later in 2014, when on Facebook I shared a picture of mine taken in Dubai, I got an SMS from a number that I did not recognize. It was Haris' cousin. He said that if I was still in Dubai, I should go meet Haris who now lived and worked in Kuwait and was visiting Dubai the same time I was.

I asked the cousin what Haris was doing in Kuwait. 'He runs a business there. He moved from the US two years ago,' the cousin texted. I asked him why. And this is what he texted back (with a smiley): 'He thinks they (the Westerners) are very intolerant and biased people.'

'But didn't he say they were very tolerant?' I asked.

'Yes' the cousin texted back. 'But Haris isn't.'

****

The Permanent Revolutionary

In late 2015, I received a hand-written letter addressed to me and delivered at the offices of Dawn newspaper. It was from a man I had last met in 1993 but first came to know in 1985. His name is Sohail Rathore and he remains to be one of the most remarkable men I have ever had the honour of befriending. I immediately called him on the phone number that he had scribbled at the bottom of his letter. I invited him to come meet me. Today, Sohail is about 64 years old. He was 35 when I first met him in 1985 — in a police lock-up!

In April 1985, I, along with a dozen or so boys from the state-owned college in Karachi that I was a student of, were arrested by the police for agitating against the Zia dictatorship and locked up at the then notorious '555 police station' in the Saddar area.[6] After being punched, kicked, slapped and accused of being 'KGB/Soviet agents' by the cops, we were all thrown into one of the many dirty, damp and windowless cells of the station.

But we weren't the only ones in that malodorous little cell. Three men were already there. One was a pick-pocket, one was a car thief, and one was Sohail, a political activist who had been

---

[6] This was not the official name of the station. But it was known as 555 for no appent reason, as such.

rotting in that cell for over two weeks and was scheduled to be taken to Karachi's Central Jail. After spending almost a whole day in the cell, my fellow comrades and I were finally bailed out by the student organization that we belonged to.[7] But throughout our stay there, Sohail had kept us enthralled with a rather intriguing tale.

Sohail was in that cell after he had been arrested the moment the plane he was travelling on (belonging to the now defunct BOAC[8]) landed at the Karachi airport. Sohail had been facing charges of setting a police bus on fire and of attacking two policemen (with a knife) in Rawalpindi in October 1978. Sohail told us that all he was doing was taking part in a small but highly charged protest rally against the then one-year-old Zia dictatorship when he was picked up, tried by a military court and thrown in a jail in Rawalpindi.

He was still in jail when in March 1981 the left-wing urban guerrilla outfit, the Al-Zulfikar Organisation (AZO), hijacked a PIA plane and negotiated the release of over 50 political prisoners stuffed inside Zia's cramped jails. Sohail was one of them.

Sohail was born into a deprived family headed by a struggling fruit vendor in the rural outskirts of Faisalabad in the Punjab province. He first went to a madrasah and then to a run-down government school before he was taken to Lahore by one of his uncles who owned a minor rickshaw and motorcycle repair shop in that city. Sohail was 16 years old when he first came to Lahore in 1966. But by 1968 he had had a falling out with his uncle after he decided to quit working at the shop and try his luck at becoming a film actor.

---

[7] The Peoples Students Federation (PSF), student-wing of the Pakistan Peoples Party (PPP)

[8] Former British national carrier, now defunct.

One evening he was woken up by the sound of a passing procession. The procession was of supporters of the Pakistan People's Party (PPP). After befriending a few PPP supporters, he was smitten by Bhutto's populist and socialist rhetoric. He volunteered to work for one of the many PPP offices that were being set-up across Lahore by the party's two leading leftist ideologues, Dr Mubasher Hassan and S. Rasheed.

In 1968, the PPP was at the epicentre of the movement against the Ayub Khan dictatorship, and Sohail was often arrested by the police. He also became a prominent member of the 'Red Guards', an organization formed by the PPP to ward off attacks by thugs employed by the regime; and by the members of the right-wing Jamaat-i-Islami.[9] Sohail returned to work at his uncle's shop soon after Bhutto came to power in December 1971. But his love affair with the party evaporated when a group of PPP thugs patronized by the then Chief Minister of Punjab, Mustafa Khar, roughed up his uncle. Sohail never told us why his uncle was beaten up by the thugs.

Though after the episode he kept himself away from politics, his resentment against his once beloved PPP boiled over when an alliance of right-wing parties began a protest movement against the Bhutto regime in 1977. Sohail wholeheartedly participated in the movement and was even arrested and thrown in jail. He was released after the regime fell to a reactionary military coup in July 1977. However, within months after Bhutto's fall, Sohail fell out with his uncle again and began to participate in protest rallies against the new military regime. In 1978 he was arrested and booked for arson and sentenced by a military court. In 1981 he was one of the 50 or so political prisoners who were released on the demands of the notorious AZO.

---

[9] Philip E. Jones: *Pakistan People's Party: Rise to Power* (Oxford University Press, 2003)

Sohail was put on a plane along with other prisoners and flown to Syria. Some joined the AZO in the then Soviet-controlled Afghanistan, some stayed on in Syria or moved to Libya and some made their way as asylum-seekers in various European countries. Sohail hung around in the Syrian capital, Damascus, and then travelled to Libya where after working as a mechanic for a few months, he managed to make his way to London.

He did odd jobs in London and also joined the PPP's London chapter before deciding to fly back to Pakistan after he was told that his mother was seriously ill. On his return to Pakistan (in 1985) he was immediately arrested and only released in December 1988 when Benazir Bhutto formed her first government following Zia's demise. After his release, Sohail tried to set-up his own mechanic shop in Lahore and reconciled with his uncle. His mother had passed away in 1987.

I met him again in 1993 in Karachi. I had gone to late Bhutto's home in 70 Clifton to interview Benazir's estranged brother Murtaza Bhutto for a newspaper. There, Sohail told me he had now joined Murtaza's faction of the PPP[10]. This was the last time I met him until 23 years later, after I received his letter. He was still struggling to set-up his own shop but had worked hard to expand his uncle's set-up. I asked him what else he was up to after we had last met in 1993. He said he quit politics all together, got married and became very religious. So much so that for a while he decided to become political again and worked for the large alliance of religious parties, the MMA, in 2002, until he witnessed the aftermath of a suicide blast orchestrated by religious extremists at a tea stall in Peshawar in 2006.

---

[10] PPP-Shaheed Bhutto PPP-SB).

'It was terrible,' he told me. 'This was not politics. This was sheer murder!' he said. He was in his 60s now and I asked him if that was it for this once robust political animal?

He laughed: 'Why do you think I am in Karachi?'

'Why?' I asked.

'*Merey dost* (my friend), I am here for Khan Saab's rally!' He announced. Sohail was now following Imran Khan, the charismatic cricketer-turned-politician. He then tried to convince me that Khan was like Bhutto.

'But you ended up being disappointed by Bhutto,' I said.

He sighed: '*Ghalti ki thi* (I made a mistake).'

'You followed Bhutto, then his opponents, then his daughter, then his son, then the *maulanas* (clerics) in the MMA, and now Khan ...' I jokingly said.

His smiled back: 'I made a deal with myself many years ago. In whoever's *badhshahi* (regime) I am able to set-up my own mechanic shop, is going to be the leader I will follow for as long as I live.'

The truth is, Sohail could have (and still can) easily set-up his own shop. But this eccentric fellow would only do it once he believed Pakistan has finally found a reliable leader. This is when he will finally close his business of constant flip-flops and open his mechanic shop.

****

Playing for tomorrow

A friend recently made an interesting comment after watching the thousands of tweets which greeted Pakistan cricket captain, Misbahul Haq when he smashed a brilliant century in his very first Test in England. The friend said: 'Misbah began to be perceived a champion on a much larger scale from early 2014. This is when General Raheel Sharif cut the slack and persuaded everyone to launch an extensive operation against the terrorists. As the operation gained momentum, so did Misbah's status.'

Misbahul Haq was never in the league of those spontaneous Pakistani cricketing talents who burst onto the international scene at a very young age, exhibiting an early promise to become one of the game's best. He was not a Mushtaq Mohammad, a Javed Miandad, a Wasim Akram, a Waqar Younus, a Shahid Afridi, or a Mohammad Amir. Unlike these folks, Misbah was nowhere close to playing international cricket as a teenager. There was nothing 'natural' about his talent and skill when he finally broke into the Pakistan Test side in 2001 at the age of 27.

One can suggest that like former Pakistan cricket captain and all-rounder, Imran Khan, Misbah too painstakingly worked his way to that elusive level of being considered a great. However, Khan made his debut when he was just 18. Nevertheless, between 2010 and 2016, Misbah not only became one of the most proficient middle-order batsmen in the Pakistan side, but also Pakistan's most successful Test captain.

But there are so many factors (some rather unique) related to Misbah's gradual rise as batsman and captain, which make his story quite special. Misbah's story is not just about a quiet, reflective and empathetic man who through sheer hard work and a finely measured amount of diplomacy, unhurriedly rose to become a cricketing icon.

Nor is it only about how, over and over again, as he resolutely battled the sporting equivalent of 'old age,' and years of constant criticism by the verbose talking heads on local TV channels, he continued to score heavily and that too, when it mattered the most. Indeed all this contributed to his gradual and measured rise to become a Pakistan cricket icon, placed right there with greats such as Hanif Mohammad, Fazal Mahmood, Majid Khan, Asif Iqbal, Mushtaq Mohammad, Imran Khan, Javed Miandad and Inzamam-ul-Haq.

But the thing in his story which truly sets him apart — not only from his illustrious contemporaries in Pakistan, but also from the greats produced by other cricket-playing nations — is the fact that his (late) blooming as a batsman, and, more so, as a captain, all took place during a period when Pakistan cricket was in shambles; torn to shreds by spot-fixing scandals and vicious infighting. It was trying to overcome an unprecedented and awkward slice of reality in which (after 2009), no team was willing to tour Pakistan.

Even more striking is the fact that Misbah was captaining a side of a cricket-crazy country which was fighting a chaotic and lingering existentialist battle with itself; a mêlée riddled with frequent terrorist attacks and bomb blasts which — between 2004 and 2014 — left over 60,000 innocent civilians, soldiers, cops and politicians dead. The UAE — with a sizeable Pakistani expat population — thus became a kind of a 'home ground' for Pakistan cricket.

But this is what Misbah told me after I was done conducting a long interview with him in Dubai in January 2014:

Playing in the UAE is nothing like playing at home. We come here as tourists, and each one of us requires a visa. I have no control here over how a pitch is to be prepared. It's just like two foreign teams playing on a neutral ground. We have no homes here to go back to. We are constantly in hotels and our families are not always with us. We come here as a touring side, just like our opponents …

He also lamented the fact that he has never led Pakistan in a Test at home; or on grounds and in front of crowds that the players were more familiar with. Yet, he went on to become the country's most successful Test captain, winning all his games on foreign soil, a feat unmatched by even the game's greatest captains.

He simply smirks and slowly shakes his head when told that Pakistan have a 'home advantage' when they play in the UAE: 'Home is where the home is,' he had told me, still smiling. 'Not where there are only hotels to go to; half-empty stadiums, and pitches one is never quite sure of.'

So Misbah's remarkable and somewhat unique story is about a batsman who began playing his cricket late; was picked when he was already 27; dropped, and then not selected for another five long years. He was then suddenly inducted into the country's T20 squad (at age 33) during the format's first World Cup in 2007. He batted brilliantly and almost won the final for Pakistan and then went on to establish himself in the Test side; but got dropped again and almost forgotten about, until suddenly earning a recall and made captain in 2010, at age 36. Quite a roller coaster ride, this.

But this is when his story takes the kind of turns which makes it so unique. In 2014 (in Dubai), former Pakistan captain and wicketkeeper-batsman, Moin Khan (who was then the manager of the team), told me a rather interesting little story. He said Misbah was first rescued from obscurity and recalled back into the side by the volatile all-rounder, Shoaib Malik. In 2007, Malik was made captain, replacing Inzamam-ul-Haq, whose team had a rather disastrous World Cup in the West Indies. Inzamam retired and the young, talented, and somewhat confrontational Malik was elevated and made the team's new captain.

When the team was being selected for the first T20 World Cup in South Africa, Malik insisted on the inclusion of the then 33-year-old Misbah; and that too at the expense of the stylish veteran, Mohammad Yousuf. Yousuf's exclusion created a storm among fans and in the media. The selectors weren't quite sure why Malik would want to include Misbah, a batsman who had been discarded in 2002 and largely forgotten about — even though he had continued to play in domestic tournaments.

Moin told me that Malik had kept an eye on Misbah and was impressed by 'his innovative stroke play and tenacity.' This is true because when Shoaib Malik, who had been dropped from the Test side in late 2009, but began to perform well in the limited overs formats of the game, Misbah as captain recalled him to play in the 2015 Test series against England. When asked why he had done that, Misbah explained that apart from the fact that Malik was in great batting form (in limited overs cricket), he (Malik) was the one who had fought with the Pakistan cricket board and the critics to include him (Misbah) in that 2007 T20 team.

Moin informed me that Misbah never harbors a grudge, but, at the same time, never forgets an act of empathy: 'He simply withdraws into himself if he believes he has been slighted or unjustly criticized. But he would go out of his way to appreciate a generous or humane act...'

So exactly how did a quiet, private man, making his third comeback (in 2010), go on to mold a team of overbearing egos, in-fighting and scandals, into becoming a solid, settled Test side, who today is enjoying a place in the upper most reaches of world rankings?

Misbah has often mentioned another veteran and mainstay of the team, Younis Khan, as the kind of empathetic soul who helped Misbah grow back into the squad both as batsman, and, more so, as a captain. Khan has often praised Misbah as being an extremely hard-working and 'pleasant' man. But then so is Younis.

But unlike Misbah, Younis has often gotten into spats with the cricket board, media, and fellow players; and, in fact, when he was captain, he faced an acrimonious players' rebellion, allegedly led by Shahid Afridi. Misbah clearly depended a lot on Younis and seemed to have discovered an apt way of handling him and win his respect.

A media manager of the PCB, Nadeem Sarwar, who had facilitated my interview with Misbah in Dubai, told me that two reasons helped Misbah the most in surviving so well as a captain of a volatile team: 'His batting temperament and the way he stays on the crease, while everyone else was falling apart...this has gained a lot of respect for him from the players; especially the youngsters.'

He continued: 'Secondly, his man-management is excellent. He strives and makes an extra effort to understand the personality of each and every player and deals with them accordingly, man-to-man, person-to-person. He hears them out.'

Another interesting aspect of Misbah's captaincy according to Sarwar was that Misbah made it plain through his own example that the seniors will have to earn their respect from the juniors and could not take it for granted: 'Once upon a time, the seniors would act like *pharos*, keeping the younger players at an arm's length and expecting them to do petty chores for the seniors,' Sarwar explained. 'Misbah changed all that. He and Younis are so approachable and they treat the youngsters like their little brothers. Players like Azhar Ali, Asad Shafique, Shan Masood and all the other youngsters treat him (Misbah) like a father figure,' he had added.

A sober, reflective, resolute elder statesman is how Misbah comes across to most. Yet, as Moin told me, there is a side to him very few know. In fact, in the interview, Misbah did allow himself to let me record that side when he said that as a person he wasn't as serious as everybody thought he was. A young PCB official (his name, unfortunately has slipped my mind), who had sprinted out of the Pakistan dressing room during the second Test in Dubai in the Pakistan-Sri Lanka series (in 2014), to hand me my press pass, told me that the players loved Misbah's sense of humor.

'He is actually very witty,' he said. 'His humor is like that of Anwar Maqsood's[11] ... he quietly slips in a witty remark which is extremely funny and yet, never offensive.'

Coming back to Misbah's now well-known man-management skills, I have always wondered how volatile and eruptive players such as Shoaib Akhtar would have fared had they played under Misbah. Most experts of the game and even Akhtar himself believe that he (Akhtar) was badly handled by Inzimam who seemed have had no clue how to manage a character like him.

Pakistani captains, such as Mushtaq Muhammad and Imran Khan, are known to have successfully handled erratic and impulsive men in the most intelligent and effective manner. Eccentrics such as Sarfaraz Nawaz and Wasim Raja were empathetically handled by Mushtaq. He succeeded where others had completely failed. Imran too was effective in handling men such as Nawaz and the moody Abdul Qadir, though one can say not so much, Raja. Akhtar, in his biography, wished he had had been captained by Imran.

So how would Akhtar have fared in Misbah's team? Early last year I posed this question to a former medium-pace bowler who had played for Pakistan in the 1980s.[12] He said: I don't think Misbah would have tolerated a character like Shoaib, like

---

[11] Famous Pakistani wit, satirist and playwright.
[12] Name withheld on request.

Inzi did. But, who knows, with the way Misbah is, Shoaib would have been made to calm down...'

Akhtar has often been critical of Misbah, and so has Mohammad Yousuf. But whereas a man such as Afridi would strike back and lash out at critical ex-cricketers (sometimes quite justifiably), not even once has Misbah responded directly to the barbs aimed at him. As he told me in the interview, he let his performance do the talking but he does often fall into despair when some unjustified remarks against him depress his wife and mother.

To Misbah, his family is everything. He is married to a cousin of his, Uzma, who, compared to him, is a lot more expressive, extroverted and animated. She has also been extremely supportive of him. Often seen in the stands (with their young children) at the stadiums, she jumps with joy, claps as loudly as possible, and at times even lets out a whistle or two, every time her husband crosses a cricketing milestone.

Her joy runs deeper than merely expressing happiness at what is taking place in the middle at that very moment. Because she has seen him sulk for years after he was first dropped in 2002. She saw him return (in 2007), but once again discarded a few years later. Misbah had told me that though he rarely reads or hears what is being written or said about him, his wife and mother can't help ignoring it. He added he is less pained by unjustified and malicious criticism than he is by how it brings down the spirits of his wife and mother.

At the end of the third Test match during the 2014 Pakistan-Sri Lanka series in which Misbah and Azhar Ali helped the team chase down over 350 runs in less than 60 overs to square the series, a TV channel immediately interviewed Misbah's mother in his hometown in Mianwali. This is what she said: 'I knew that by the grace of Almighty, my son's hard work will pay off. He is a stubborn person. He was stubborn even as a child. He never gives up. Yet, he is a loving person who is a good human being.'

Then she could not help it and launched into his critics: 'I have never understood why some people are so critical of him. What do they have to say now?'

But why was a batsman, who has continued to score big constantly in the last six years, left out of the team for five years, when he was a lot younger?

Over the years, newspaper reports, articles and even some books authored by insiders have all alluded that due to the fact that Misbah was well-educated and someone who keeps his faith to be an extremely private matter, he was unacceptable to Inzamamul Haq, who encouraged the players to wear their faith on their sleeves. However, Misbah has always refused to believe this, some say purely due to his diplomatic nature. To me, he said that no captain would like to keep out a good player. And that teams are picked by captains on how they judge the skills of the players and not on the captain's personal likes or dislikes.

So he wasn't skillful enough between 2002 and 2007?

This he explained by suggesting that at the time the Pakistan middle-order was packed with some very good batsmen and this is what kept him out. Ironically, Inzimam today is the chief selector and he gave Misbah exactly the team he asked for (for Pakistan's 2016 England tour).

Two years after Misbah's mother lambasted his critics, Misbah became his country's most successful Test captain with a very healthy batting average and an iconic stature. Indeed, this stature which he has worked so hard to achieve after years of languishing in obscurity has a lot to do with him performing so consistently and succeeding in molding a formidable and united Test squad from the debris of discontent and turmoil which he was handed in 2010.

Yet, it is also about when he did all this - during a period in time when his country was facing perhaps its gravest existential crisis; there was unprecedented violence and bloodshed, and Pakistan had begun to be treated as a pariah state, or even a failed state. Heroes had vanished, or couldn't last beyond those figurative 15 minutes of fame. Misbah lasted and so will his fame. In a better future, history would recall his feats as those of a sportsman who became a symbol of hope and tenacity during a particularly testing period in his country's history.